ON WITH THE SHOW

ON WITH THE SHOW!

THE FIRST CENTURY OF SHOW BUSINESS IN AMERICA

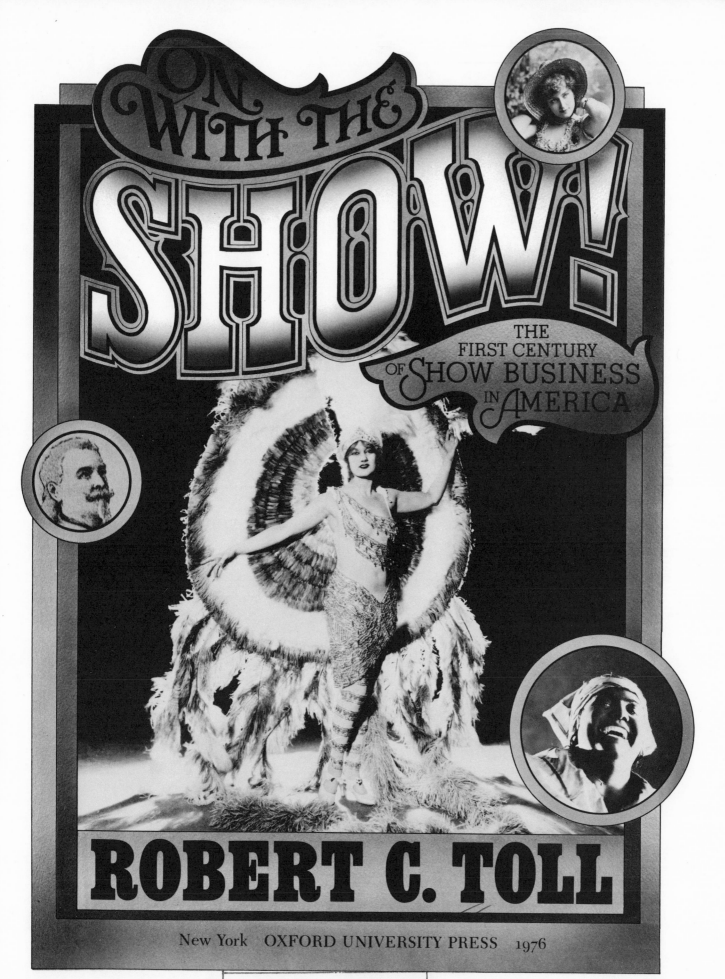

ROBERT C. TOLL

New York OXFORD UNIVERSITY PRESS 1976

Library of Congress Catalogue Card Number: 75-46355

Printed in the United States of America

FOR JUDY, MY PARTNER

CONTENTS

INTRODUCTION

It might be the dazzling splendor of a circus parade—lumbering elephants, garish wagons, and screaming calliopes. It might be an eye-catching blackface minstrel singing "Old Folks At Home" or "Dixie." It might be the snarling bloodhounds chasing Eliza across the ice in *Uncle Tom's Cabin.* It might be the wonder of a stupendous stage extravaganza like *Around the World in 80 Days,* or the thrill of Wild Bill Cody galloping at the head of his Wild West Show. It might be George M. Cohan prancing his way through *George Washington Jr.* or singing "Give My Regards To Broadway" or "You're A Grand Old Flag." It might be a titillating peep at Millie De Leon or her successors Ann Corio and Gypsy Rose Lee. It might be the fascination of watching Julian Eltinge transform himself into "the most beautiful woman on the American stage." It might be laughing until it hurt at Weber and Fields, Will Rogers, Lew Dockstader, Bert Lahr, or W. C. Fields. It might be the excitement of black dancers introducing the cakewalk, black bottom, or charleston, or of the flashing smile and feet of Bill "Bojangles" Robinson. It might be the moving comedy-pathos of Bert Williams or Fanny Brice. It might be the varied delights of a fast-paced vaudeville show at the Palace Theatre. It might be the dazzling beauty of the *Ziegfeld Follies.* Or, it might be the electric excitement of Eddie Cantor, Eva Tanguay, or Al Jolson. It might be a vivid memory, a vague recollection, a legend heard in childhood, or an entirely new subject. It might be any, or all, or none of these. Whatever it is to each individual, it was all of these and much, much more. It was the glamorous, exhilarating first century of American show business.

Today, most people get their entertainment from machines—radios, tape recorders, record players, television sets, and motion picture projectors. But before mass media pervaded the nation, average Americans crammed into theaters, auditoriums, halls, and tents to get their excitement, adventure, and escapism from live performers. Professional entertainment developed slowly in the American colonies, especially in Puritan New England. But once show business took root before the Civil War, it rapidly grew and matured, blossoming into a dazzling array of forms, features, and stars that provided the common people of America with shows that in scale, beauty, and artistry equalled anything available to the world's richest potentates. What had always been an aristocratic privilege had, in America, become a democratic right and reality.

This book seeks to recapture and explain the fascinating story of the development of American show business. Without losing sight of the sheer joy of the pursuit, it also takes seriously the classic barker's pitch that "the show is educational as well as entertaining." People, of course, went to performances to enjoy themselves. But show business was not just "meaningless fluff." Perhaps more than any other facet of American life, show business was created of, by, and for average Americans. Show business developed its forms, features, styles, and material out of its intimate relationship with its audiences. As it entertained, it reflected and spoke to its patrons' deepest concerns, desires, and needs. No one had to take the shows seriously, which meant they could deal with the most serious, most troubling subjects without threatening or irritating anyone. Whenever new public issues or problems surfaced, show business dealt with them, often with new entertainment forms centered on the new concerns.

The thesis of this book is that common people shaped show business in their own image. So, by looking at the most popular features, patterns, themes, and images of show business, by learning why everyday people booed, cheered, laughed, and cried, it is possible to get a much fuller understanding of the average Americans of the past. This book is a beginning. If its answers are not always satisfying, its questions hopefully will get more people thinking and writing about the social and cultural meanings of popular entertainment: Why did show business forms take the shapes they did, when they did? Why did they evolve the way they did? What made them so popular? What impacts did they have? What do these developments mean? What does all this reveal about America and Americans? Answers to such questions can begin to put common people, the people who built the country, into the history books where they belong.

To avoid the confusion of trying to discuss everything that took place at a particular time and to bring the many subjects it covers into sharper focus, the book is organized topically. Most chapters concern the evolution of individual entertainment forms—circuses, minstrel shows, popular plays, burlesque, musical comedies, and vaudeville. Others explore the origins of American show business and the careers of P. T. Barnum, black entertainers, sexual impersonators, and Florenz Ziegfeld. The book focuses on the people and events that *first* developed, popularized, or established important features of show business. The first prominent American lion-tamer, Isaac Van Amburgh, is included in the circus chapter, for example, while his successors, no matter how famous or how skilled, are not. While discussing the important new developments in their subjects, the chapters also focus on the lives and careers of important individuals, personalizing show business history for readers just as the shows did for patrons. In any far-ranging book of this sort, a great many significant developments, fine productions, and magnificent entertainers must be omitted or given only passing treatment. Obviously, another writer might justifiably concentrate on other material, people, or even subjects. There is an embarrassment of riches to choose from and a great many stories to be told. But no one book can tell them all.

This book does not pretend to be the last word on the many topics it covers. In some cases, it is in fact the first word. And in almost every case the detailed studies and comprehensive biographies on which such an interpretative survey should ideally be based are still to be written. There are, of course, a number of good books and articles, and they are acknowledged and discussed in the book's bibliographical essays. But show business history remains a sorely neglected field. Errors are likely in any book. But in a broadly based book in a new field, they are inevitable. Hopefully, the errors are minor and will not divert attention from the importance of show business history as a way to understand the American experience and the American people as well as a way to have fun.

So, ON WITH THE SHOW!

Oakland, Calif. R. C. T.
June 1976

ON WITH THE SHOW

CHAPTER ONE

THE ROOTS OF AMERICAN SHOW BUSINESS

Rowdies picked fights; mothers nursed babies; drunks staggered; immigrants partied; men spit tobacco juice; sailors leered; lovers held hands; old men took naps; blacks picnicked; prostitutes strutted; and socialites paraded their latest hair styles, fashions, and lovers. The odors of onions, cigar smoke, and whiskey and the sounds of masses of chattering, laughing people filled the air. It was a cross-section of America out to have a good time. Such outings took place almost every night in almost every nineteenth-century American city—but not in parks, as we might now expect. There were virtually no parks. All this activity and much, much more took place in theaters, which served as social clubs, picnic grounds, watering holes, and meeting places, as well as entertainment centers.

Theaters were nothing new in America. The upper classes had supported drama since the mid-eighteenth century. What *was* new was that masses of common people were flocking into theaters for the first time. After the War of 1812, American cities exploded in size and population, creating huge new concentrations of average people who needed something to take the place of the country amusements they had left behind. They found it in live stage entertainment, and they streamed into the nation's theaters in unheard of numbers. To accommodate this mass audience, new theaters

4

ON WITH THE SHOW

A typical nineteenth-century audience having a good time. The German Stadt Theatre. Harvard Theater Collection (HTC).

were built with much larger seating capacities and much lower ticket prices. The Park Theatre, which opened in New York City in the late eighteenth century, for example, charged $2.00, $1.50, and $1.00 for its 300 seats; its replacement, built in 1821, held 2500 people and charged 75¢, 50¢, and 37½¢. Five years later, the Bowery Theatre opened with a capacity of 4000 and a price range that made the Park seem expensive. The same sort of thing happened in every large American city.

The great influx of common people into theaters forced the popularization of drama—the first step in the development of show business in America. And ultimately it fragmented stage productions into separate popular and elitist forms. At first "high-brows" and "low-brows" coexisted peacefully in the same audiences. But over the years, common people reshaped stage performances to suit their own tastes. While this process produced actors and plays that average Americans un-

5

THE ROOTS OF AMERICAN SHOW BUSINESS

The John Street Theater—the one-story building with the two lamps—was the first permanent theater built in New York City (1767). HTC.

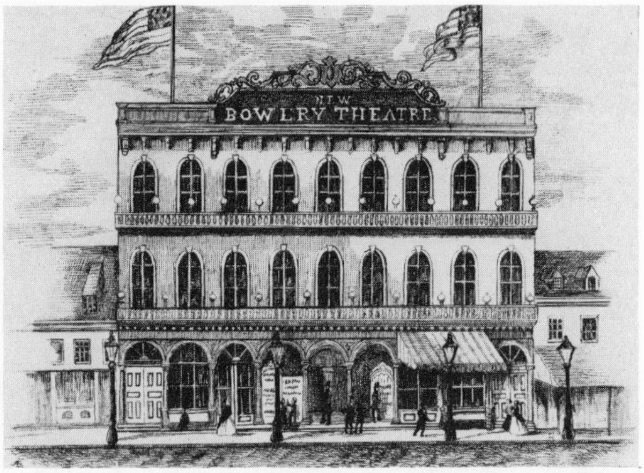

The Bowery Theatre, built in 1826, contrasts sharply in size and grandeur to its small eighteenth-century predecessors. HTC.

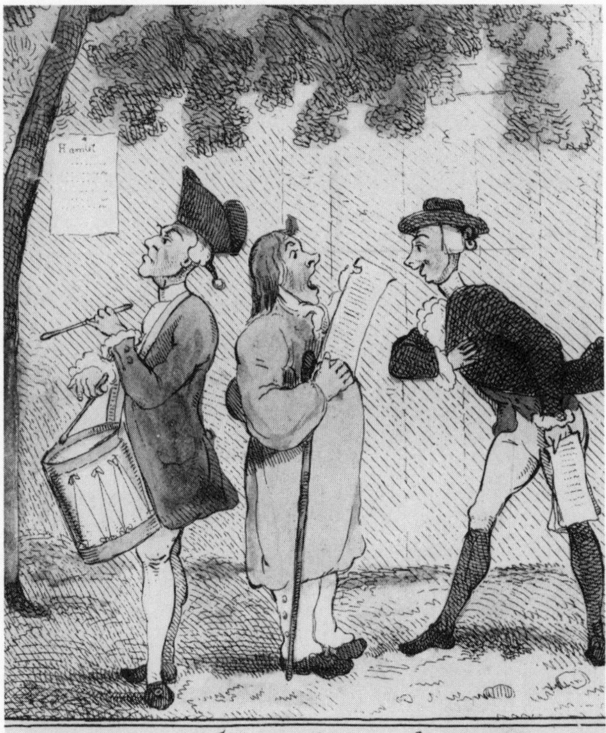

Delivering Play Bills in the Country.
My first Appearance, 'pon my honour,
Sir, in Hamlet the Great Prince of Denmark.

The personal appeal of an eighteenth-century actor, when audiences were small and elitist. HTC.

derstood, enjoyed, and identified with, it alienated the social and cultural elite. Critics warned against "the depraved taste of a corrupt multitude" and pleaded with theater managers and actors to satisfy "the judicious few" rather than the "noisy rabble that gapes at every puppet show and yells in every ale house." "The rapid increase in population in newly formed American cities," a visiting European actor complained, "produces a style of patrons whose habits and associations afford no opportunity for the cultivation of the arts." Some theater managers did try to create an American theater on an artistic par with Europe's best, but they usually found themselves facing financial bankruptcy even when they won critical accolades. There were simply not enough people willing to support that sort of drama. But there were a great many willing to support a common man's culture.

Theaters in the first half of the nineteenth century could house such disparate groups because each section of the audience—the boxes, the pit, and the gallery—attracted different social and economic classes. The most presti-

The lavish interior and large audience of a typical mid-nineteenth-century theater. Niblo's Garden, N.Y. HTC.

gious and expensive seats were the boxes, which offered privacy and the greatest measure of decorum. This was where the fashionable, "better people" went to be seen, to see each other, and perhaps even to see a play. One of the social butterflies even complained that there was too much light on the stage and not enough in the boxes, which made it difficult to "recognize a friend across the house." Physically and socially below the boxes, in front of the stage, was the pit, where the better "middling" classes who were serious about drama sat. In the pit there were also rowdies and undesirables who sometimes made it difficult for the serious playgoers to enjoy the plays. The gallery, the highest, most distant part of the theater, was occupied by Negroes (if they were allowed in at all), prostitutes, people who could afford only the cheapest seats in the house, and people who preferred the excellent throwing angle the gallery provided. It was from this part of the audience that barrages of objects of all sorts rained down during unpopular performances.

Audiences buzzed with activity, even during the show. In the boxes, the upper crust gossiped and flirted. In the gallery and pit, people stamped their feet in time with the music, sang along with familiar tunes, recited famous speeches along with the actors, and hollered out punch lines to old jokes. "The acting on stage was good," reported a St. Louis reviewer in 1844, but "the cavorting in the pit, boxes, and galleries was extremely interesting." Famous personalities in the audience commanded at least as much attention as the performers. Theater-owners, well aware of the drawing power of the celebrity, advertised in advance whenever people like George Washington, Martin Van Buren, or Henry Clay were going to attend, and Clay actually once got equal billing with a prominent British tragedian. Other curiosities in the audience were also great drawing cards, and theater owners advertised them extensively. Indians were especially popular, whether doing their dances on stage or giving what one New York City promoter billed as "their first performance in any boxes."

Despite all their own activity, the playgoers, especially in the pit and the gallery, did not ignore the performers and the performance. Common people did not just join audiences. They dominated them. Nineteenth-century audiences voiced their feelings about what they saw with a directness and a volume that would startle and outrage mid-twentieth-century theater-goers. Whenever those audiences liked a speech, song, or piece of acting, they cheered wildly and demanded encores, regardless of the nature of the performance or the script. This practice included interrupting *Hamlet* to have a speech repeated as often as demanding encores at variety shows. When displeased, audiences hissed, shouted insults, and threw things at the performers. Since many actors relied for their income on "benefit nights"—performances at the end of a run from which the actors got the proceeds—they gladly played to the vocal audiences. And since common people were a much larger and a much louder part of the audience than were the "better families," they had a much greater influence. Broad humor and comedy, ad libs with local allusions, exaggerated sentimentalism, flag-waving patriotism, flamboyant gestures, and overblown rhetoric all appealed to audience members "indifferent to [the] subtler dramatic beauties."

These same people preferred patriotic tunes and other popular songs to more refined "sonatas and other airs." So they shouted out their preferences, and the orchestra, being seated in direct firing line from the gallery, usually complied. The audience in the Bowery Theatre in New York City in 1833, for example, was displeased with the symphonic overture and insisted on hearing "Yankee Doodle," which was "more in unison with their patriotic ideas of propriety." When the orchestra changed its tune, the boisterous audience members "evinced their satisfaction by a gentle roar." Such incidents were quite common and were directed at performers on stage as well as at orchestras.

Far from being apologetic about their behavior, common people and their spokesmen in the popular press took great pride in the power they exercised in theaters. "We (the sovereigns) determine to have the worth of our money when we go to the theatre," a Boston writer boasted in 1846. "We made Blangy dance her best dances twice; we made Mrs. Seguin repeat 'Marble Halls,' . . . and to-night we are going to encore Mrs. Kean's 'I Don't Believe It' in *The Gamester*. . . . Perhaps we'll flatter Mr. [Edmund] Kean by making him take poison twice; the latter de-

Audiences left no doubt about their feelings. Bowery Theatre. HTC.

pends upon the furor of the moment." Such forceful intervention typified pre-Civil War audiences, as common people shaped stage shows to reflect popular tastes. "It is the American people who support the theatre," another champion of the mass audience blustered, "and this being the case, the people have an undoubted right to see and applaud who they please and we trust their right will never be relinquished. No Never!" These assertive common people certainly did not relinquish this "right." What, then, did they choose to see and applaud? What happened to drama as a result of its popularization?

A night at the theater in the early nineteenth century was much different from what it is today. The theatrical fare ranged from Shakespearean tragedies, through melodramas performed on horseback by troupes of equestrian circus performers, to productions like "the Original, Aboriginal, Erratic, Operatic, Semi-Civilized and Demi-Savage Extravaganza of Pocahontas." Since the number of people who would go to see any one show was still small, most plays in the 1830s and 1840s ran for no more than three or four performances, and bills changed frequently. In 1839, for example, a St. Louis theater gave no fewer than 157 different plays in one season. When Edwin Forrest, the foremost American tragedian, played Macbeth for twenty consecutive nights in New York City in 1853, it was considered a phenomenal run. The frequent change of bills meant a constant need for new productions, many of which were nothing more than popular scenes from familiar plays pieced together and given a new name. This constant change and flexibility also made it easier for the noisy patrons to shape the content of stage entertainment.

It may be surprising to many people to learn that Shakespeare was the most popular playwright in the United States before the Civil War. This was not because he was a revered artist who created dramatic masterpieces that had to be carefully analyzed and viewed with awe. Rather, it was because he wrote for the pit and gallery as well as for the boxes, because he wrote to amuse and entertain as well as to stimulate thought and reveal deep insights. American actors and theater managers freely altered his plays, often cutting scenes, consolidating characters, rewriting speeches, and removing "the vulgarity," "coarse allusions," and other "blemishes." The result was often little more than what might have been called Hamlet's or Macbeth's or Lear's Greatest Hits—a series of dramatic and comic highlights from the play being performed. No matter how serious the principal play and the production of it, theater patrons were entertained between acts by variety performers—jugglers, acrobats, song and dance acts, trained animals; "freaks" like giants, midgets, and "living skeletons"; and other peculiar specialties. With such features performed between acts of every play and with audiences that had very short attention spans, many actors did not concern themselves with continuity or plot development. Instead, they became more like variety performers who treated each scene, even each speech, as an emotional high point. After all, this was also the period of unrestrained rhetoric and overblown oratory. Americans who enjoyed the political performances of Henry Clay, Daniel Webster, and John C. Calhoun loved the fiery, dramatic styles of Edwin Forrest, Junius Booth, and Edmund Kean, the great actors of the time.

Besides Shakespeare and other standard drama, new plays emerged that reflected the new American audiences' values, needs, and desires. Many of these plays are insignificant

10

ON WITH THE SHOW

Act 5
Scene last
CONTRAST
Jon: Do you want to kill the Colonel?
I feel chock full of fight.

The American rustic, Yankee Jonathan, challenges British noblemen in *The Contrast* (1787), the play that first brought the rural American to the stage as a major character. HTC.

as dramatic literature, but they remain important as evidence of what nineteenth-century common people thought and felt. Each play had a message. Sentimentality, nationalism, democracy, traditional moral values, and the virtues of common people were the major themes of the popular new plays. *The Drunkard,* which warns of the corrupting evils of drink, focuses also on the villainous deeds of a scheming, big city lawyer, the epitome of the new urban immorality. After failing to seduce the innocent heroine, who married for love not money, the lawyer vengefully tries to destroy her marriage. Even though the hero is lured into becoming a drunkard, he is redeemed, the lawyer is thwarted, and the good, simple folks win out in the end. *The Fashion* portrays a rich, pretentious New York City woman who tries to learn French manners and fashion and wants her daughter to marry a French count, who is really a phony. Adam Trueman, a simple American farmer, exposes the French imposter and then dramatically denounces aristocracy and effete gentility: "We have honest men, warm-hearted and brave, and we have women, gentle, fair, and true, to whom no title could add nobility." The speech must have brought down the house. *The Lady of Lyons,* set in post-Revolutionary France argues the superiority of republican over aristocratic values. The hero, a gardener's son who has worked his way up in life, financially rescues the lovely daughter of a merchant facing bankruptcy just before she has to sacrifice herself to an immoral, corrupt businessman. Combining the simple virtues of melodrama with democratic, pro-common man rhetoric, the play proved a great success.

The most important new element to emerge in drama in the United States was the Yankee farm boy—a common-man character who symbolized the average American. During the Revolutionary War the British had sung "Yankee Doodle" to lampoon the American as an ignorant country bumpkin. But Americans quickly turned the mockery around and used it to ridicule the effete British. The first successful American play featuring this common-man character, *The Contrast* (1787), took Colonel Manly, a plain mannered, high-principled Revolutionary War hero, and Jonathan, his rustic Yankee servant, to New York

City, where they contrasted the emptiness of city life to the joys of the farm. The central contrast in the play was between the straightforward, honest American rustics and the foolish, empty-headed fops who tried to live aristocratic lives in the city. Although Jonathan at times was laughed at as a bumpkin who was dazzled by the city, as many farm boys must have been, he stood for the virtues of American democracy. When someone referred to Colonel Manly as his "master," Jonathan exploded: "Serving a man don't make him my master by a darned sight." Jonathan was a native-born American, and that meant he was his own master.

In the 1820s, when the new audiences demanding a common man's culture popularized drama, Brother Jonathan, as the Yankee was often known, appeared in a great many plays. Between 1826 and 1836, actor James Hackett became a star in these roles and established the Yankee as a comic fixture of the American stage. The stage Yankee provided common people with an entertaining, admirable symbol of the average American—rustic, proud, independent, morally strong, brave, and nationalistic. He came out of the American countryside, dressed oddly, and spoke a country dialect. He was honest, incorruptible, and piercing in his wit, a weapon he used to debunk the "high-falutin," the pretentious, and the corrupt. "It's odd," he once observed with a Will Rogers-like understatement, "but the most fashionable people borrow the most money." Cities also disturbed him. "No, I don't know where anybody lives in this big city, not I," another Yankee admitted, "I believe how they all lives in the street, there's such a monstrous sight of people a scrouging backards and forards." Many of the recent migrants in the urban audiences must have laughed in agreement with his observations.

After 1825, quick-witted Yankees delighted audiences with their attacks on the upper-crust. James Hackett, one of the first American comic acting stars, as Solomon Swap. HTC.

Though sometimes temporarily befuddled, he triumphed over city slickers who tried to dupe him and over would-be aristocrats who considered themselves his superiors because of their birth or breeding.

Hackett's success and the Yankee's popularity gave other talented American performers a chance to enter show business by specializing in this role, a role that Englishmen who had dominated the American stage found difficult because much of its success depended

12

ON WITH THE SHOW

George H. "Yankee" Hill, a native New Englander, became a star in Yankee roles, here as Hiram Dodge. HTC.

on its Yankee dialect. "You might as well try to back a heavy load up a hill as stop my thought coming right out in homely words," one Jonathan observed. And when they came out they had to sound like authentic Yankees' or at least like American country dialects. Even Hackett found that he could not compete with George Handell Hill, who was a native New Englander and a great performer. The Yankee had to be totally American and totally credible. He represented what many average Americans wanted to believe they were like. He was all that was naturally good, free from the decadence, pretention, and corruption of aristocratic, class-conscious European society and manners. Along with other folk heroes, he took the jibes at Americans for being uncivilized, unrefined rubes and turned them into a biting counterattack on those very standards of civilization and refinement. A blend of fact, fiction, and fantasy, the Yankee provided a symbol that ordinary Americans could identify with and believe in.

The backwoodsman—the boasting frontiersman who roared of his superhuman powers and deeds in so much of the popular literature of the period—rarely appeared in plays, probably because of the difficulties in staging his incredible, superhuman feats without making them look silly. When he did, he usually

James H. Hackett as Nimrod Wildfire, a role modeled on heroic backwoodsmen like Davy Crockett. HTC.

13

THE ROOTS OF AMERICAN SHOW BUSINESS

Mose the B'howery B'hoy, a New York City volunteer fireman, rescuing a baby from a burning building. HTC.

appeared with the Yankee, the two characters often merging into something of a composite figure in a new national mythology glorifying the rural American. As symbols of nationalism, democracy, and strength, they fed the identity-hungry egos of the many Americans who were undergoing the shocks of urbanization.

Urban characters began to join the frontiersman and the Yankee on the popular stage in the 1830s. By 1848, the trend culminated in Mose the B'howery B'hoy, a lengendary hard-working, hard-fighting New York City fireman, an unlikely combination of gutter bum, volunteer fireman, brawler, and heroic protector of the weak. Mose was a physical man who loved to fight both men and fires, especially men. "I'm bilein' over for a sousin' good fight with someone somewhere," he bellowed, "if I don't have a muss soon, I'll spile." Faced with burning buildings and especially with people trapped inside them, Mose became a fearless daredevil with a strong streak of sentimentality and chivalry. After saving a baby from death in a fire, Mose told how its mother "fell down on her knees and blessed me. (Wipes his eye with sleeve.) Ever since dat time I've had a great partiality for little babies. The fire-boys may be a little rough outside, but they're all right there. (Touches breast.)" Besides his heroic and sentimental

Frank Chanfrau became a star playing Mose. HTC.

rescues, which were played out on the stage with elaborate sets and props, Mose also protected the plain people of the Bowery from con-men and exploiters. He saved Linda the cigar girl from molesters, helped a rural migrant recover the goods city slickers had cheated him of, protected old men with money from muggers, and thwarted silver-tongued seducers. Mose was always on the side of common, unpretentious folks.

Played by Frank Chanfrau, who became a star in the role, Mose was an instant sensation in the 1850s, first in New York City and then in virtually every major theatrical city in the country. Plots took him to California, Britain, France, China, and Arabia. But he never lost the common touch. When he toured the British Museum, for example, he typically remarked that all that stuff "ain't good for nuttin'." Mose strutted across the American stage with puffed-out chest and puffed-up ego. Audiences throughout the country loved him. He was tough on the outside and sentimental and chivalrous, in his own rowdy way, within. Mose was a democratic man of action, a boisterous, violently anti-aristocratic figure glorifying the common man and ridiculing city slickers and effete, corrupt "gentlemen." No wonder urban audiences cheered for this common man who towered over the bewildering, menacing cities as completely as Davy Crockett and others had over the frontier.

During these same decades, mass audiences also cheered for a native-American actor who dominated his profession as totally as the fictional heroes dominated their domains. Edwin Forrest was a major figure in the transition from traditional, elitist drama to popular American plays. In a real sense, the story of his life and career is the story of the Americanization and popularization of drama, the first step in the evolution of American show business. Forrest actually lived the heroic life that dominated popular culture in the period: he rose from common American stock; he performed great deeds that took him to the top of his field, a field previously dominated by the British; and he was an American patriot who developed American drama for the American people.

Born in Philadelphia in 1806 to a working-class family, Edwin Forrest by age eleven was performing in public and knew that he wanted to become an actor. When in 1820 Edmund Kean, the great English tragedian, appeared in Philadelphia, Forrest sat enthralled at every performance, studying Kean's every gesture and intonation. Five years later, Forrest got a chance to serve a tutelage under Kean when Kean's American tour took him to Albany, where Forrest was part of the local acting company. Kean performed with an explosive, emotional display of feelings and passions. Through physical and vocal fireworks, he tried to move people emotionally, to make the audience *feel* what his characters felt. Forrest learned his lessons well. In 1826 when he finally got a chance to play a leading role, Othello, in New York City, Forrest was immediately propelled to stardom and to top billing in the new 4000-seat Bowery Theatre, where he was an instant sensation. Critics lauded him as the equal of Kean, and the Bowery's large, mass audience loved his muscular body, his booming voice, and his grand performance style, all of which made him seem the very essence of what a hero should be. He was the first and last tragedian to be America's most popular actor.

As a transitional figure between drama as art and drama as popular entertainment, Forrest pursued his trade with traditional dedication to perfecting his craft, while also building a mass following. He continually built his

Edwin Forrest as Lear. HTC.

body, experimented with phrasing and intonation, practiced his poses and gestures in front of mirrors, probed his texts for new meanings, and refined his roles. "He heightened here and mellowed there, rounded this and smoothed that," a critic applauded, "long after the average actor would have ceased to see that there was room for betterment." For his greatest Shakespearean role, Lear, he not only analyzed the script, he also read about insanity and visited mental institutions until he could claim with some validity that he knew more about insanity than doctors did. When praised for the way he played the part, he reportedly replied: "Play Lear! What do you mean, sir? . . . by God, sir, I *am* Lear." If, as critics charged, he could never quite

Edwin Forrest, the first famous American tragedian, in a traditional heroic stance as Coriolanus. HTC.

16

ON WITH THE SHOW

Pocahontas performed to a full house in the Bowery Theatre. HTC.

capture the inner complexities of Hamlet, Forrest was a master of the physical and emotional outbursts of Lear and Othello. And unlike others of his day, he insisted on fidelity to the texts. He was an uncompromising perfectionist who made himself a model for other American actors.

Forrest became a popular hero, not because he was the equal of Kean, but because he was an *American* Kean. Committed to nationalizing drama in the United States and flushed with financial success, Forrest was the first actor to subsidize American playwrights. In 1828 he announced a prize of $500 plus half the receipts from the third performance for "the best Tragedy, in five acts, of which the hero or principal character shall be an aboriginal of this country." In calling for an Indian tragedy, Forrest reflected both his own and the society's interest in native Americans. On one of his youthful Western tours, he had lived with and been greatly impressed by the Choctaws. After that, he played Indian roles whenever he got a chance.

By the 1820s, though Indians were still being cleared from rich cotton land in the Southwest, most white Americans viewed Indians more as symbols than as people, more as curiosities than as threats. Urban residents knew little about Indians except what they read in books, like *Last of the Mohicans,* heard in songs, like "The Noble Indian Warrior's Grave," or saw in productions of plays, like *Pocohontas.* Urban, white common people, who were nostalgic about their rural backgrounds, tended to glorify the Indian as a symbol of the innocent, natural man living in bliss outside of civilization. In this nationalistic period, white Americans thought of themselves as a great, noble people just because they lived in the United States. Popular opinion had long been that immigrants would inevitably be transformed by the American environment into white, Anglo-Saxon Protestants. Indians, the original Americans, the natural human fruit of the wonderworking continent, were regarded as a fiercely independent, noble people who would rather fight to the death than become anyone's subordinates, which was what whites wanted to believe about themselves as native Americans.

Edwin Forrest as the noble Indian chief, Metamora, a very popular role glorifying the American natural man. Theater Collection, New York Public Library at Lincoln Center, Astor, Lenox, and Tilden Foundations (NYLC). (All items are from the Theater Collection unless otherwise noted.)

In John Augustus Stone's *Metamora,* the prize winner for 1828, Forrest got just the sort of majestic, natural character he had hoped for when he announced his contest. Metamora was "the grandest model of a mighty man [who] sleeps amidst the roar of a mighty cataract." He loved his people, his land, and his family, and he heroically fought to the death to prevent them from being destroyed. Determined to have his prize play succeed, Forrest took three weeks off to work on the script and later took another ten days to rehearse the production, an unusually long time then. What the play lacked in structure, it made up for in raw power. It was crammed with exciting action scenes which gave Forrest the opportunity to show off his body and his athletic ability. The drama centers on Metamora's nobility, which heightens the tragedy of his destruction. He lectures whites that "the red man took you as a little child and opened the

ON WITH THE SHOW

door of his wigwam to you." But now "we are hunted back like the wounded elk . . . our hatchets broken, our bows unstrung and war whoop hushed." After futilely appealing to the teachings of brotherhood in the white man's "Great Book," Metamora finally reconciles himself to the inevitable: "Snatch your keen weapons and follow me!" he calls to his men. "Call on the happy spirit of the warriors dead and cry: 'Our Lands! Our nation's freedom! Or the Grave.'" In the emotional final scene, Metamora's warriors are scattered, his child dead, and his wife alone with him in the woods. As the white men approach, he nestles his wife in his arms one last time and then stabs her to death. "She felt no white man's bondage—free as the air she lived," he consoled himself, "pure as the snow she died." Surrounded by whites, like a stag held at bay by hounds, Metamora died cursing his oppressors with his last breath. "My curses on you, white men! . . . And may the wolf and the panther howl o'er your fleshless bones, fit banquet for destroyers."

Mustering all of his physical might, all of his oratorical power and volume, and all of his acting skill, Forrest stunned audiences and critics alike with his Metamora. "His voice surged and roared like the angry sea," one reviewer exclaimed, "as it reached its boiling seething climax, in which the serpent hiss of hate was heard, at intervals amidst its louder, deeper, hoarser tones, it was like the falls of Niagara, in its tremendous down-sweeping cadence; it was a whirlwind, a tornado, a cataract of illimitable rage." People flocked to the performances. But following his usual practice, Forrest kept the play in repertory—it was just one of his series of plays, even if the most acclaimed and most popular. Throughout the rest of his life, whenever he needed a boost to his box office or to his ego, he became Metamora.

The 1831 play contest produced Richard Montgomery Bird's *The Gladiator,* a play that rivalled *Metamora* in popularity. It told the story of Spartacus leading the slave rebellion against Roman tyranny, a theme with great appeal for democratic Americans who somehow avoided making what now seems the obvious connection between American and Roman slaves. (American slaves were blacks, which in nineteenth-century popular mythology meant natural inferiors who were happy with their "place" on the plantation.) In *The Gladiator* when Spartacus is thrown into the ring to fight his brother, Pharsarius, the two men embrace and Pharsarius shouts: "Freedom for gladiators!" Spartacus broadens the call to "freedom for bondsmen" as the gladiators victoriously turn on their Roman tutors. Spartacus cautions his brother not to imitate the enemy by plundering Roman cities, but when Spartacus finds his wife and child killed by Roman soldiers, he wildly attacks the Roman army, kills a general, and is fatally wounded. After a long heroic struggle and after torrents of democratic rhetoric extolling the inherent virtue of the plain barbarian over the cultivated aristocrat, Spartacus dies, falling melodramatically in the pose of the well-known sculpture The Dying Gladiator. As Spartacus, Forrest again had ample opportunity to display his strength, physique, acrobatics, and fighting skills, and to voice the anti-aristocratic sentiments average Americans loved to hear.

As the first famous American tragedian—one who looked every inch the manly hero—Forrest was a wildly popular star for nationalistic, democratic, and emotional reasons more than for his acting skills. Theater audiences loved Forrest's heroic portrayals of common men fighting for their freedom, their families, and their nation's honor. Early in 1834, Forrest announced plans to act in London, but he

Caricature of Forrest as Spartacus in *The Gladiator*. NYLC.

Edwin Forrest as Spartacus, before he
man slaves in their fight for freedom. HT

assured his fans that he planned the trip only to see whether the English received American actors as hospitably as Americans received the British. Forrest certainly did not want his nationalistic fans to think he had become a plaything of foreign aristocrats. Instead, he presented his quest for fame as an American counterattack against British cultural dominance.

On his English tour, Forrest won praise for his electrifying performances, especially of *Metamora,* and was favorably compared to Kean. He also developed a rivalry with William Macready, London's most prominent tragedian. The rivalry between the two actors who competed for both accolades and status in England and America was not surprising or especially significant in itself. But it took on great importance in the 1840s when Forrest

and his American supporters ex
actors' squabble into a nationalisti
conscious struggle that ultimat
"high-brow" and "low-brow" Ame
ter-goers into warring camps in a v
York City riot.

During a British tour in 184
hissed one of Macready's perform
then publicly defended his hissing
fectly legitimate response of a disp
tron. Forrest also argued that Mac
organized a conspiracy to ridicule h
drive him off the British stage. Wh
returned to the United States in 18
ceived a hero's welcome from large
the dock and at the theater. After l
the English, especially Macready,
anti-Americanism, he set off on a t
acting tour that took him to New O

Charles Macready, the British tragedian, became Edwin Forrest's adversary in a bitter rivalry. NYLC.

Louis, Cincinnati, Pittsburgh, Chicago, Detroit, Cleveland, and Buffalo—then the American heartland. He returned to the area he had toured as a boy, but now he came as a conquering hero who had defied a British aristocrat.

In 1848, Macready returned to the United States, and the conflict exploded into open warfare. Newspapers attacked Macready for trying to drive Forrest from England, and this agitated the nationalistic, class-conscious common people who idolized Forrest. Then Forrest moved into action, opening opposite Macready in Philadelphia. Macready responded to his noisy audience's mixed greeting of cheers, hisses, pennies, and rotten eggs by struggling through his opening performance and then by publicly professing his innocence in the London affair. Forrest responded by bitterly denouncing Macready in the press. Upset by the ruckus, Macready cut short his Philadelphia run and began his planned southern and western tour. There, he faced even rowdier, more nationalistic, more pro-Forrest audiences. In Cincinnati, "the bully butcher boys," a newspaper reported, "made life miserable for the English actor." "A ruffian from the left side of the gallery," an outraged Macready protested to his diary, "threw into the middle of the stage the half carcass of a sheep!"

Macready returned East to end his tour in New York at the Astor Place Opera House, a theater designed for the upper classes and for high culture. Forrest was also performing in New York, and the conflict came to a head, agitated by inflammatory copy churned out by popular newspapers. When Macready finally opened, he and his cast were bombarded with rotten eggs and vegetables, and there was a din that forced the company to give a "dumb show," that is, to pantomime the performance. Finally, when the rowdy Forrest supporters started throwing chairs, Macready stopped the production to avoid serious injuries and resolved to return to England immediately. Then the struggle took on a much more serious, more menacing significance. A group of prominent, upper-crust New Yorkers, which included Washington Irving and Herman Melville, confronted Macready with a "law and order" argument that such rowdy behavior could not be allowed to succeed and persuaded him to finish his booking. The long-smoldering antagonism between anti-aristocratic groups and America's upper class burst out into the open in 1849, when the "better families" who had been losing control of the nation's stage entertainment to the common

man's culture, chose literally to fight rather than to accept a final symbolic defeat at the Astor Place Opera House.

Posters plastered around the city issued the call to arms to repulse Macready in nationalistic terms that linked upper-class Americans to the despised British. "WORKINGMEN," one of these posters trumpeted, "SHALL AMERICANS OR ENGLISH RULE IN THIS CITY? The crew of the English steamer has threatened all Americans who shall dare to express their opinion this night at the English Aristocratic Opera House!! . . . WORKINGMEN! FREEMEN! Stand by your lawful rights!" Newspapers on both sides added fuel to the fire while each side mobilized its forces. On the night of Macready's next performance, 325 policemen and 4 troops of soldiers were stationed in and around the theater to preserve order. Meanwhile huge, noisy crowds milled around outside despite repeated announcements that all of the 1800 seats had long been sold.

The audience in the theater received the first two scenes rather calmly, cheering an American actor in the cast but otherwise showing few signs of what was to come. Then, Macready made his entrance. The people in the audience who supported him and/or law and order rose to give him a fifteen minute standing ovation. At the urging of the management they finally returned to their seats. Then Macready's opponents took over and, from that point on, no one in the audience could hear anything that took place on stage. When the leaders of the anti-Macready demonstration in the pit were arrested, the gallery picked up the struggle, and the crowd outside began bombarding the theater with bricks and stones. The crowd attempted to storm the door; the police tried to stop the mob, and a full scale riot broke out in the streets of Astor Place. The soldiers moved into action and ultimately opened fire on the rock throwing mob. Thirty-one rioters and spectators were killed and 150 police, soldiers, and civilians injured. Macready left for England. But the damage had been done—to the victims, to the theater, and to the uneasy truce between the conflicting groups of theater-goers.

The Astor Place Riot forced people in and out of the entertainment business to acknowledge and to come to grips with what long had been taking place in American society. "There is now in our country, in New York City," the *Philadelphia Ledger* reluctantly admitted, "what every good patriot has hitherto considered it his duty to deny—a high class and a low class." "The B'hoys of New York and the 'Upper Ten' are as divided as the white and red roses of York and Lancaster," another newspaper ominously observed with this reference to the English civil war. "Let but the more passive aristocratic party select a favorite, and let there be but a symptom of a handle for the B'hoys to express dissent, and the undercurrent breaks forth like an uncapped hydrant."

In the context of aggressively anti-aristocratic popular culture heroes, the violent reaction to Macready seems almost predictable. Macready seemed the epitome of aristocracy, and just as their favorite stage characters, like Mose the B'howery B'hoy might have done, the rowdies in the audience drove Macready from the stage and from the country. To do it, they even confronted armed soldiers. "Take the life of a free-born American for a bloody British actor! Do it," dared a "burly ruffian" baring his chest through his red flannel shirt much as Mose might have done, "Ay, you daren't." The struggle between the upper classes and the "middling" groups for control over the content and direction of American entertainment was a battle over the nation's cul-

The mob outside assaults the Astor Place Opera House in the 1849 riot that brought the Forrest-Macready conflict to a violent climax. HTC.

Troops open fire on the mob, as "high-brows" and "low-brows" fight for control of drama. HTC.

ture and its values, and it was fought in the arenas of popular entertainment.

The Astor Place Riot played an important part in accelerating the development of show business. Before 1850, most theaters in America tried to offer entertainment packages with something for everyone. More and more conflicting patrons and acts were crammed into the same theaters. Like a balloon, stage entertainment stretched and stretched. Finally it exploded. The Astor Place Riot was the pinprick that did it. It symbolized the irreconcilable conflicts between the desires, values, and needs of middle- and upper-class Americans. Both groups had legitimate needs, but the disparity between them made it impossible to satisfy both in the same place at the same time with the same thing. And as cities grew and transportation improved, expanding potential audiences, there was no longer any need to try. American entertainment fragmented into many separate pieces.

In Edwin Forrest's time, stage entertainment had undergone far-reaching changes. Drama had been transformed from an elitist art form featuring European plays performed by English actors into democratic entertainment featuring American themes, plays, actors, and characters. There were also signs of the development of new show business forms that did not pretend to do anything but amuse the masses of entertainment-starved common people. From its origins in itinerant acrobatic, equestrian, and wild animal shows, the modern circus began to emerge. From the variety segments between the acts of plays, white song and dance men wearing burnt-cork makeup and using what they claimed were Negro dialects began to evolve the routines that were to culminate in the minstrel show, the most popular entertainment form of the mid-nineteenth century. And perhaps most significantly of all, Phineas Taylor Barnum was developing and perfecting the promotional and publicity techniques that made him the premiere American showman of his day and made show business a permanent part of American life.

CHAPTER TWO

P. T. BARNUM

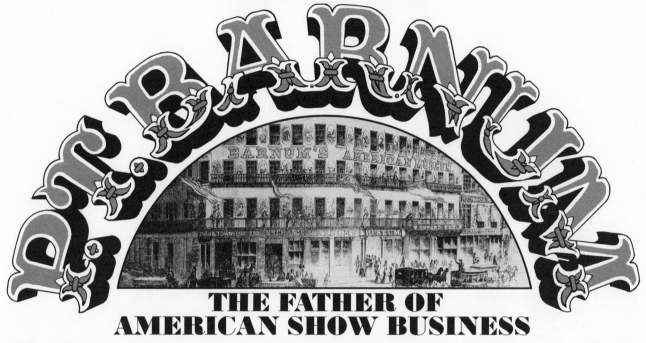

THE FATHER OF AMERICAN SHOW BUSINESS

He lured customers into his New York City museum with promises of an embalmed "Feejee Mermaid" that turned out to be a half-monkey, half-fish fabrication, with "The Great Model of Niagara Falls" that was actually only eighteen inches high, and with an almost unending string of similar hoaxes and deceptions. He staged crowd-drawing, controversial publicity stunts like having his war-dancing Indians threaten to scalp people and planting anonymous letters in the press charging that his exhibits were fakes. And when he drew so many people that his museum was literally full and there were still crowds outside waiting to get in, he had his staff put up a tantalizing sign reading, "To The Egress." The curious customers who thronged down the stairs expecting to see a new exhibit found themselves outside in the back alley instead. How did aggressive common people respond to these tricks, to these "humbugs"? Did they raise a public outcry against this charlatan? Did they drive him out of business as they drove Macready off the stage?

Average Americans not only did not denounce P. T. Barnum and refuse to go to his shows, they adored him and flocked to his museum time and time again to see his shows and to see him. His stunts themselves even became attractions. "First he humbugs them," a Barnum ticket-seller admiringly observed, "and then they pay to

Caricature of P. T. Barnum as a "hum-bug" the word used for his hoaxes and publicity stunts. HTC.

hear him tell how he did it." They laughed at his tricks because they knew that, however he got them in, he always gave them a good show. For twenty-five cents, they got the some 600,000 items in the museum plus live, popular entertainment in the "lecture room."

In the decades after 1820 when the country was young and unsophisticated and when a common man's culture was taking shape, Barnum was an entertainment pioneer, blazing a trail that many others would follow. He was in many ways the father of American show business. He not only demonstrated the profits that could be made by providing inexpensive entertainment for common people, but he also pioneered, and in some cases perfected, publicity and promotional techniques that even twentieth-century public relations men could envy. Long before advertising and psychology even existed as professions or fields of study, Barnum mastered both. Perhaps better than anyone else of his day, he understood average Americans' feelings, desires, tastes, and needs.

Through his own image-building efforts, Barnum made himself a national celebrity. To his contemporaries—especially to common people—he seemed a giant. Yet one of the reasons that he understood average Americans so well was that he was one of them. Barnum, observed Heywood Broun, an astute twentieth-century theater critic, "was made up of characteristics common to many Americans. He stood out because in his case they were vastly heightened." Barnum's story, then, is more than the story of the foundation of American show business, more than the story of an advertising and promotional genius. It is, in a real sense, the story of the mid-nineteenth-century American.

Born in a small, rural Connecticut town in 1810, Phineas Taylor Barnum had a fairly ordinary American boyhood, one that permanently shaped his character. His Yankee father worked hard at a number of jobs—tailor, farmer, tavern-keeper, livery-stable operator, and country-store merchant—but, like many others of his day, he was never economically successful. Perhaps for this reason, his son became obsessed with money at an early age. "Before I was five years of age," P. T. Barnum recalled, "I began to accumulate pennies." By the time he was six, he had a silver dollar, which, he remembered, made him "feel far richer and more independent than I have ever felt since." For the rest of his life, he continually drove himself to acquire money and recognition, trying to recapture the feelings he had gotten from that first dollar. By the time he was twelve, P. T. had begun to learn merchandising by tending his father's and others' general stores. There he quickly realized that "sharp trades, tricks, dishonesty, and deception are by no means confined to the city." He learned to live by his cunning and wits. The country stores were his schools; Yankee business ethics were his lessons. "It was dog eat dog—tit for tat," he recalled. "The customers cheated us in their fabrics; we cheated the customers with our goods. Each party expected to be cheated." To illustrate the business ethics that he and many other boys learned, Barnum later told the story of the New England grocer and deacon, who asked his clerk: " 'John, have you watered the rum?' 'Yes, Sir.' 'And sanded the sugar?' 'Yes, Sir.' 'And dusted the pepper?' 'Yes, Sir.' 'Then come up to prayers.' "

In his youth, Barnum also learned the art of practical joking, which, combined with his morality and calculated deception, allowed him to produce great promotional campaigns, publicity stunts, and contrived attractions. The man who most influenced his development, his maternal grandfather Phineas Taylor, "would go farther, wait longer, work harder, and contrive deeper," P. T. reminisced, "to carry out a practical joke, than for anything else under heaven." Barnum loved the stories about his grandfather's legendary pranks. But he was also sometimes the butt of these jokes. For a christening present, Phineas Taylor gave his namesake a piece of land, Ivy Island. Over the years, he regaled the young boy with glowing stories of it as the most valuable farmland in Connecticut. When twelve-year-old P. T., bursting with pride and expectation, finally got to visit his "landed estate," he found only a hornet- and snake-infested bog where nothing but ivy grew. With such cruel pranks considered normal family affairs, it was natural for Barnum to feel as he matured that strangers were fair game for almost any deception.

When Barnum was fifteen, his father died in bankruptcy, and the young man set out to make something of himself. Like many other ambitious country boys, he headed for New York, but he soon returned to rural Connecticut and went into the grocery business. When he became a Jacksonian Democrat in conservative Connecticut, his business suffered, and in 1834 the recently married young man returned to New York City, again going into the grocery business. Up to this point Barnum had had a relatively conventional career for an ambitious young Yankee, one that offered little promise of anything grander than moderate middle-class success. But then, in July 1835, Coley Bartram stopped by Barnum's grocery store, and all that quickly changed.

In the course of chatting, Bartram told Barnum that he had just sold his share in an old black woman who claimed to be 161 years old and to have nursed George Washington when he was an infant. Exhibiting oddities and "freaks" was already a well-established practice, and Barnum, ever the speculator, became excited at what seemed to him a potentially great drawing card and a great business opportunity. By the mid-1830s, George Washington had already been mythologized into the Father of His Country. Information, myths, anecdotes, and stories about him were in great demand. So Barnum felt that Joice Heth, who claimed to have been baby George's nurse, offered an irresistible combination of exoticism (an ancient Negro slave) and nationalistic hero worship (the inside stories about "dear little George").

When he saw her on exhibit in Philadelphia, he was absolutely certain. With skin like ancient parchment and paralyzed, bony legs, she lay curled up with her left arm clenched across her chest, her left hand with fingernails at least four inches long. The blind, toothless, bushy-haired forty-nine-pound woman, whose sunken eyes were nearly invisible in their sockets, "might almost as well have been called a thousand years old as any other age," Barnum observed when he first saw her. A 1727 bill of sale for a Joice Heth signed by George Washington's father, her claim that she had lived in obscurity as a slave until discovered only five years before, and the prospect of great profits convinced Barnum that her story was plausible. Even this early in his life, he knew a great attraction when he saw one. He borrowed money, sold his interest in the grocery store, and purchased her for $1000. Barnum had begun his life as a showman.

Unlike others at the time, Barnum realized that publicity was the key to success in "the show business." "At the outset of my career I saw that everything depended upon getting people to think, and talk, and become curious and excited about the 'rare spectacle.'" He poured out a torrent of posters, handbills, and newspaper promotions. And the New York public poured in to see and listen to Joice sing hymns, tell stories about the Revolutionary War and about "dear little George," and appear to have lived every one of her claimed 161 years. "Her appearance," one New York newspaper observed, "is much like an Egyptian mummy [then also a rage] just escaped from its sarcophagus." With his promotion, Barnum made Joice a sensation.

After she drew $1500 a week in New York City for several weeks, he took her on a tour of New England. When attendance decreased in Boston, Barnum adapted his Yankee business training to "the show business" by planting an anonymous newspaper item claiming that Barnum was a ventriloquist and that Joice was made of india rubber, whalebone, and hidden springs. Attendance shot up as curious people who had already seen her returned to decide whether they had been duped, and others flocked to examine the controversial exhibit. From that time on, Barnum realized full well that controversy, albeit falsely created, was great advertising that stimulated public interest and attendance. His profits from exhibiting Joice exceeded his expectations, and he felt that he had found a suitable career. "I had at last found my true vocation," he concluded. But he had not yet found his formula for success. He still had to learn his new trade.

While touring with Joice, he saw Signor Antonio, a performer who walked on stilts, spun plates, and balanced crockery, guns, and bayonets on his nose. Barnum left Joice to an agent, Levi Lyman, signed Antonio to a one-year contract, and began to lay plans for promoting his new attraction. First displaying what became one of his regular patterns, Barnum played up his attraction's exoticism. He had Antonio adopt the more dashing name, "Signor Vivalla," stressed his Italian origin, and refused to allow him to speak English in public. With these embellishments and with inflated claims about Vivalla's act, Barnum turned a nice initial profit when he got bookings for Vivalla at $50 and $150 per week. But Vivalla had a poor act; word spread; and attendance, bookings, and fees decreased.

In early 1835 Joice Heth died, and with Vivalla still under contract but unable to draw, Barnum took a job as ticket-seller, secretary, and treasurer with Aaron Turner's Traveling Circus for enough money to pay Vivalla and 20 per cent of the profits from this typical early traveling show, which consisted of the two Turner boys as equestrians, a clown,

Vivalla, and a band. Barnum was able to stimulate business with his promotional techniques and within a few months had earned $1200 and set off with his own traveling show—musicians, horses and wagons, a blackface singer and dancer, and, of course, Vivalla. By May 1837, he had to disband the troupe due to poor business. But he soon had another small show on a southern tour, during which he bought a steamboat at Vicksburg, Mississippi, and toured on it down the river to New Orleans. There, he traded the boat for molasses and sugar, which he sold at a greater profit than he made from his show business tours. He was still a better Yankee trader than a showman.

Returning to New York with $2500, Barnum felt deeply disillusioned with his profession. "The itinerant amusement business is at the bottom of the [entertainment] ladder," he observed. "I had begun there, but I had no wish to stay there; in fact, I was thoroughly disgusted with the trade of traveling showman." Longing for "some permanent respectable business," he invested in a manufacturing firm that he knew nothing about and was quickly cheated of his money. Searching for a way to support his family, he staged variety shows in New York City in 1840 and, despite his resolves to the contrary, took another show on the road. Neither succeeded. Again back in New York, he reverted to selling, becoming sole agent for *Sear's Pictorial Illustrations of the Bible.* With good promotion, he and his sub-agents sold thousands, but again Barnum was swindled. Desperate for income, he took a job writing advertisements for the Bowery Theatre at $4 a week. At the age of thirty-one with a wife and two children, a time when most men were well established, Barnum was a failure, still floating from venture to venture, still grasping for a career. Sixteen years of determined hard work had gotten him nothing but experience. He had shown great flair for promotion but, except for Joice Heth, a ready-made attraction that had fallen into his lap, he had not yet learned to select his attractions as well as he promoted them.

Barnum's success began with a fortuitous accident, as had his first involvement in show business. While still broke, he learned in 1841 that Scudder's American Museum, a typical collection of curiosities, displays, and exhibits, was for sale for $15,000. Seeing great potential in it, located as it was on Broadway across from St. Paul's Church in New York City's burgeoning population center, he resolved to purchase it, even though he was earning only $4 per week. "What do you intend buying it with?" a friend asked. "Brass," Barnum replied, "for silver and gold have I none." Through fast-talking, conniving, and lots of "brass," he managed to lease the museum. Although theaters were then catering to urban common people's need for entertainment, there was no zoo, no aquarium, no museum of natural history, and little else to provide rural migrants with understandable, enjoyable information about the mysteries and wonders of the wider world they were beginning to discover. Furthermore, many people still considered theaters and plays immoral works of the devil. Realizing that a museum, although filled with sensational freaks and show business features, was still regarded as an educational, therefore perfectly moral, institution, Barnum felt that "it was only necessary to properly present the museum's merits to the public, to make it the most attractive and popular place of resort and entertainment in the United States." He was right. The museum's combination of information, amusement, self-improvement, titillation, and respectability perfectly suited the 1840s.

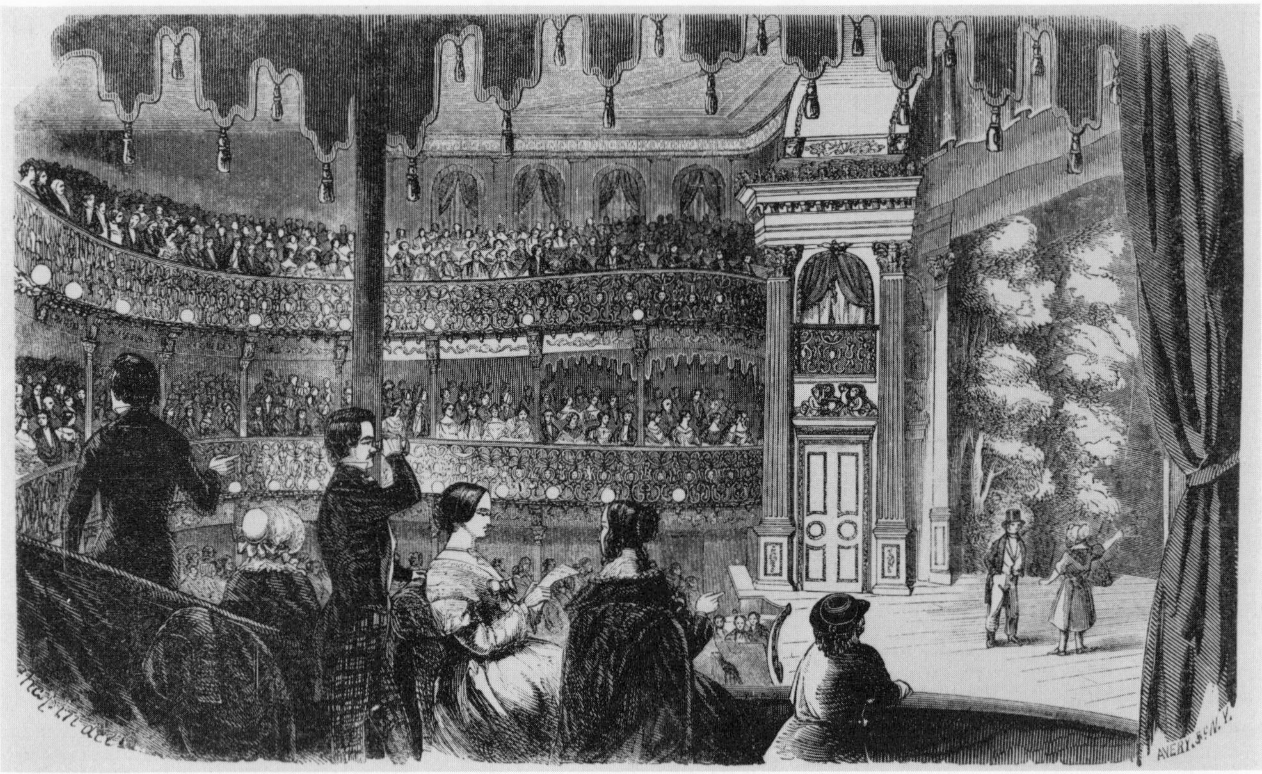

The 3000-seat lecture room at Barnum's museum. Is the caption, "the exhibition saloon," a humbug on temperance advocate Barnum? HTC.

Museums had begun in America as experiments in public education through displays of the wonders of natural history. Peale's Museum in Philadelphia, established in 1784, for example, was first housed in the American Philosophical Society building. Prominent Founding Fathers, including Benjamin Franklin, Thomas Jefferson, Alexander Hamilton, and James Madison, contributed both exhibits and funds, sanctioning it as an institution to enlighten the public. But by Barnum's time, the staid, heavily scientific displays, which were presented as the Great School of Nature did not satisfy the urban population's desire for amusement and entertainment. In response, museums, even Peale's, increasingly added more curiosities and substituted popular entertainment for scientific lectures, as Jacksonian Democracy replaced Jeffersonian rationalism. But museums retained their respectable reputations.

Barnum shrewdly made great use of this fact to attract the broadest possible range of patrons. When he expanded the American Museum's narrow, uncomfortable lecture room into a modern theater holding 3000 people, he changed everything but its name. Although Barnum featured popular plays and variety acts in his lecture room, he billed them as "chaste scenic entertainments" properly presented for "all those who disapprove of the dissipation, debaucheries, profanity, vulgarity, and other abominations, which characterize our modern theatres." He took great pleasure in retelling the story of the spinster who proudly announced to him that she never had set foot in a theater or place of amusement—and never intended to—but she had come to see Barnum's educational exhibit. On her way into the lecture room to see "The Pathetic Story of Charlotte Temple," an adaptation of a popular sentimental novel, she asked Barnum: "Are the services about to commence?" "Yes," he sanctimoniously declared, "the congregation is now going up."

He used the same sense of moral propriety and respectability for the entire museum, of which the lecture room was only one of the hundreds of thousands of items. Assured that it was an uplifting experience, the public flocked to be "educated" by Barnum's vast array of wonders, curiosities, and "freaks"—natural and unnatural, genuine and manufactured. Patrons could see giants and midgets, elephants and trained fleas, a mermaid and a bearded lady, statues of scriptural characters, waxwork displays of the horrors of intemperance, live Indians doing war dances, a working model of Niagara Falls, an English Punch and Judy, and a knitting machine run by a dog. Barnum had solved his earlier problem of selecting what his customers would like by completely overwhelming them with "such a variety, quantity and quality of amusement, blended with instruction, all for twenty-five cents, children half price, that my attractions would be irresistible and my fortune certain."

From Vivalla and his other failures he had learned the hard way that promotion alone was not enough and that to be successful he had to provide a good show. Bringing his past experience to bear, Barnum conceived of popular entertainment as a business, which he called "the show business," and he talked of amusements as "merchandise" that were subject to the same laws of trade as any other goods. He knew the museum, with all its features, was good merchandise that would delight its patrons, but first he had to attract their attention and get them in. He carefully "studied ways to arrest public attention; to startle; to make people talk and wonder; in short to let the world know that I had a museum." If it took a little deception, a "humbug," which to Barnum amounted to a practical joke on the public, he had no compunction about using it. Modifying the Yankee business ethics that he had been raised on, Barnum defined fraud as taking people's money and giving them nothing of value for it. As long as he made certain that people enjoyed themselves, he never felt he was cheating them, so he pulled out all the stops in his attention-getting publicity. "I thoroughly understood the art of advertising, not merely by means of printer's ink, which I have always used freely," he recalled of his early years, "but by turning every possible circumstance to my account. It was my monomania to make the Museum the town wonder and talk."

He began to demonstrate these publicity techniques as soon as he opened the museum. Barnum even used the building itself for eye-catching advertising, first draping it with bright banners, then lighting it up at night, which was unheard of in New York, and finally painting huge figures of exotic creatures on the outside. After they went up, business jumped $100 per day. Unlike other promoters and businessmen at the time, Barnum realized that newspapers needed material that would interest and entertain their increasingly mass audiences. And he never missed a chance to feed them copy or to stage publicity stunts for their benefit—the first media events. Besides his Siamese twins, fat boys, and bearded ladies, he held baby shows in which customers' babies won prizes for being prettiest, fat-

Scenes in the lives of Cheng and Eng, Barnum's genuine Siamese twins, each of whom somehow managed to marry and have children. HTC.

33

P. T. BARNUM

Barnum's American Museum in its prime in the early 1850s. Author's collection.

test, tallest, or anything else-est. They proved so popular and got such extensive press coverage that he followed them with flower, dog, bird, and poultry contests. When his two giants got in a fist fight, Barnum was furious, not because they might hurt each other but because they did it in private. "It must be duly advertised and must take place on the stage of the lecture room," the publicity-conscious Barnum scolded. "No performance of yours would be a greater attraction." Barnum admitted hiring acts and buying exhibits whose only value was that "they would incite a newspaper paragraph which would float through the columns of the American press." He also provided his patrons with colorful handbills and posters to use as house decorations and, of course, to spread the fame of the museum. Early in his career, recognition for the museum and for himself became his major goal. "As for the cry of humbug, it never harmed me. I was in the position of the actor

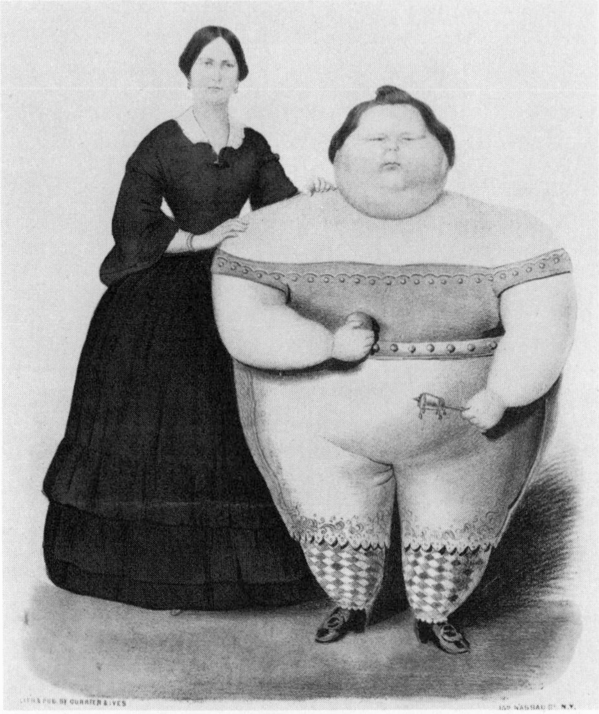

Barnum featured any oddity he could find, the more grotesque the better. HTC.

who had much rather be roundly abused than not to be noticed at all."

By mid-1842, Phineas Taylor Barnum, the grocery clerk, lottery operator, and itinerant showman had become P. T. Barnum, the premiere American showman. During his first year as proprietor of the American Museum, it earned $28,000, compared to the previous year's $11,000. Besides that, Barnum had made his museum and himself virtually household words and had conquered and purchased his New York competitors. The museum had become the major popular entertainment attraction in the largest city in the country. Barnum boasted—probably legitimately—that his private museum attracted more people than the free British Museum. With this solid basis, Barnum went on to perfect the promotional techniques of American show business. He also lived a highly visible life, one to which many American common people, many Yankee tinkerers' sons, would have aspired.

Near the end of his first year as *the* P. T. Barnum, while traveling on business, he stopped to see his brother in Bridgeport, Connecticut. There Barnum learned about Charles S. Stratton, an uncommonly small five-year-old boy. Impressed with Stratton's good looks, bearing, intelligence, and tiny size, Barnum hired the boy, who was 25 inches tall and weighed fifteen pounds. If Barnum's career had consisted of nothing more than what he did with this bright, precocious child, he would have become famous. His transformation of Charles S. Stratton into General Tom Thumb reveals another of Barnum's "modern" talents—image-maker. Midgets, like giants, were well-known curiosities in both England and America. But Barnum fashioned this one into something unique. While paying his salary, Barnum trained him to be a confident young gentleman, proficient at singing, dancing, telling jokes, and doing impersonations of famous men like Napoleon. Barnum also created a brilliant stage name for the boy. "General Tom Thumb" cleverly juxtaposed the incongruous images of great stature and dignity with tiny size in a humorous way. It also linked him to the legendary Tom Thumbe, a midget who, as one of King Arthur's knights of the round table, undertook great romantic adventures finally dying in mortal combat with a bumble bee. Only when Barnum thought his Tom Thumb was fully ready did he have the General perform for New York City newspaper editors. On one of these publicity appearances, Thumb leapt onto an editor's dinner table, dancing in between goblets and plates and jumping over the roast. Such antics, of course, produced a great deal of free publicity for Thumb, whom Barnum billed as

Barnum's baby shows gained him customers and publicity, including this 1855 sheet music cover. HTC.

"a dwarf eleven years of age, just arrived from England." Barnum selected the older age because he feared that five was so young that people might think he was just a slow grower. He invented the English origin so Thumb would seem more exotic and be further linked to the Arthurian legends. Thumb's good looks, wit, composure, and talent combined with Barnum's promotion fascinated the public. Barnum had molded Charles S. Stratton into a talented entertainer who was a curiosity but not just another freak. Tom Thumb was a *bona fide* star and in every way a P. T. Barnum production.

In early 1844, Barnum and Thumb left New York for an English tour. Like many other mid-nineteenth-century Americans, Barnum looked to Englishmen and Europeans as the final arbiters of respectability and stature. And although Barnum wrote that he did not foresee "close contact with kings, queens, lords, and illustrious commoners," he did admit that he "saw some such future, . . . dreamily, dimly, and with half-opened eyes."

General Tom Thumb (Charles S. Stratton) standing on a table, an example of Barnum's promotions. HTC.

37

P. T. BARNUM

Consciously or not, Barnum, after his American financial success, went to England seeking stature as well as money. At first the prospects in England for achieving them seemed dismally poor. Shortly after Barnum and Thumb arrived, the proprietor of a small waxworks called on Barnum and offered to exhibit Thumb for $10 a week when Barnum was paying him $50 and expenses. Shortly thereafter, when Barnum and Thumb went to a play, a woman told Barnum that he should exhibit Thumb for about two pence, which her husband felt was too much since the English were accustomed to paying half that for ordinary dwarfs and giants.

Ambitious and daring as always, Barnum had planned to go directly to London and to Buckingham Palace, relying for access on a letter of recommendation to the American ambassador from Horace Greeley, the editor of the *New York Tribune*. But he quickly realized that he had to lay a firm foundation first. Carefully controlling exposure, Barnum successfully exhibited Thumb for three nights in a first-rate London theater but declined to continue the engagement. Instead he rented a mansion, lavishly outfitted Thumb and himself, hired liveried servants, and sent out invitations to nobility, and, of course, newspaper editors, to call on his "ward" General Tom Thumb. No one was admitted without an invitation. By using contrived scarcity, Barnum made his attraction a sensation with the English upper classes. Sensitive to the workings of public opinion, he realized that in England, with its strong aristocratic heritage and the deep devotion of common people to the crown, the way to popular success lay through acceptance by the upper classes and royalty. In contrast, in democratic America the man in the street resented and rejected elite groups and their preferences.

When Baroness Rothschild sent a carriage for Barnum and Thumb, Barnum knew he had succeeded. Other such "audiences" followed, each of which Barnum made sure was well publicized in the press. Then, he finally decided it was time to put Thumb on public display. Soon thereafter, Barnum and Thumb got their command performance. Both of them broke protocol by talking directly to the Queen, but Thumb charmed and delighted her, imitating Napoleon and dashingly fighting off her poodle with his cane. Barnum made certain that the public knew how much the Queen had enjoyed General Tom Thumb. Soon, a Tom Thumb craze swept England. His picture was everywhere; songs and poets praised him; plays featured him; and *Punch* caricatured him. At an English country fair Barnum overheard an unwitting compliment to his promotional skill: "Tom Thumb has got the name," a disgruntled English showman complained, "and you all know the name's everything. Tom Thumb couldn't never shine, . . . 'long side a dozen dwarfs I knows, if this Yankee hadn't bamboozled our Queen—Gawd bless her—by getting him afore her a half dozen times." For years Barnum and Thumb triumphantly toured Europe bamboozling royal families and common people alike with Barnum's magic—building the image, generating publicity, creating demands, and masterfully timing performances.

Barnum and Tom Thumb returned to the United States in 1847 to acclaim from the White House and from upper-class Americans who had formerly snubbed Barnum. He delighted in this praise. Yet at the same time he remained a common man, unwilling to deny his background and somewhat resentful of his new "friends." "I could hardly credit my senses," he wrote in a newspaper article, "when I discovered so many wealthy men ex-

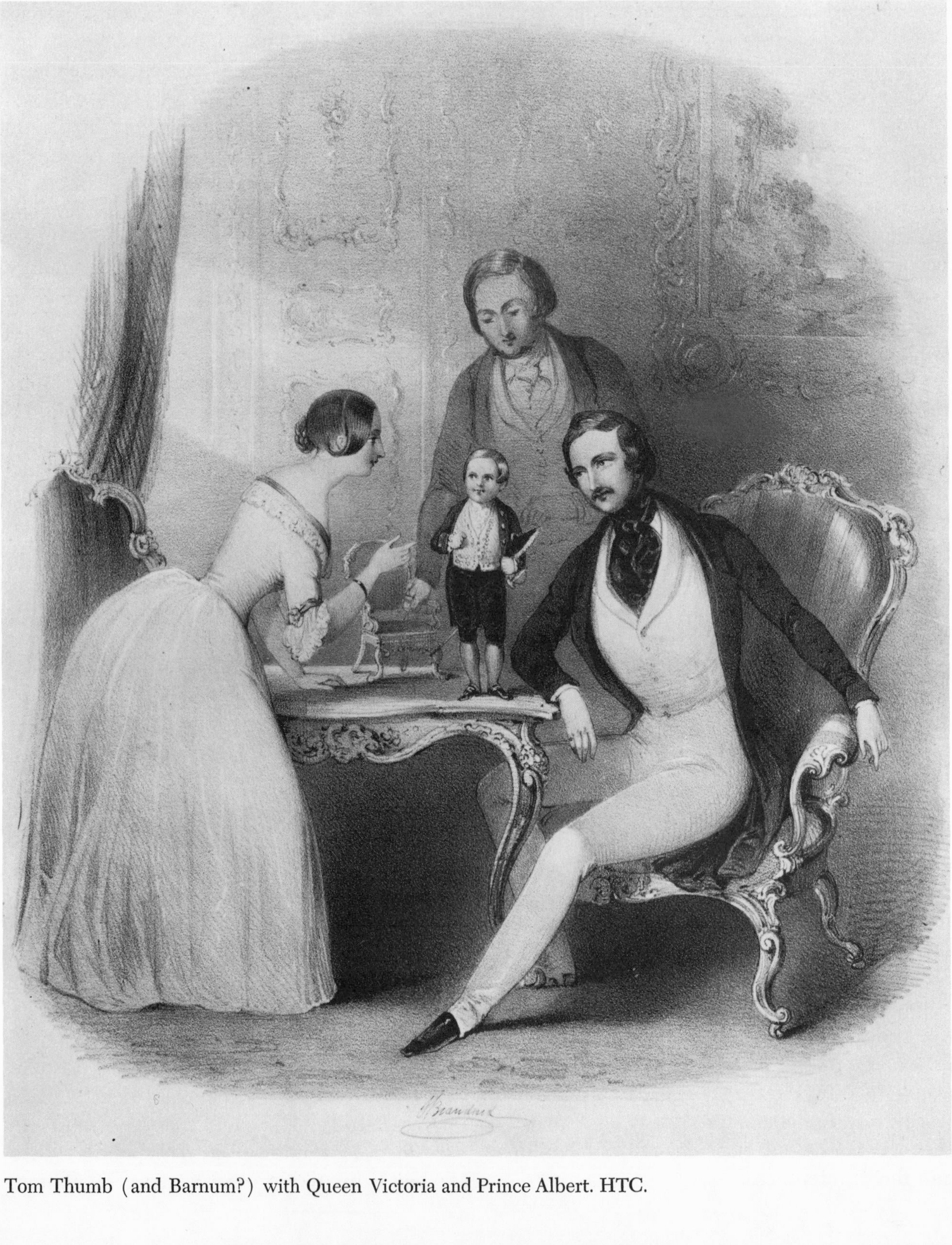

Tom Thumb (and Barnum?) with Queen Victoria and Prince Albert. HTC.

Barnum built palatial Iranistan, a copy of the Brighton Pavilion in England, as his personal residence in 1848. Here it adorns an 1850 sheet music cover. HTC.

tending their hands to me and expressing their delight at seeing me again, who before I left New York would have looked down on me with disdain had I presumed to speak to them." They deferred to their European superiors, and if Barnum was good enough for royalty, he was good enough for them. But even though he relished the accolades of European aristocrats, he was uncomfortable with the acceptance of American elite groups. "I wish *them,*" he wrote to both his new and old American friends, "and all the world to know that my father was a *tailor,* and that I am a *showman* by profession, and all the *gilding* shall make nothing else of me."

In the late 1840s when Barnum decided to build a fitting home for his family, the contradictions in his character clearly surfaced. Wanting a location near New York City and on a commercially promising site, he bought seventeen acres at a railroad crossing in Bridgeport, Connecticut, on Long Island Sound and made plans for a new home. "I cared little for style," he wrote of his plans, "and my wife cared still less; but as we meant to have a good house, it might as well, at the same time, be unique. In this, I confess, I had 'an eye for business' . . . as an advertisement of my museum." This self-made man of the people who rejected upper-class patronage,

P. T. Barnum served as mayor of Bridgeport, Conn., in 1875, a symbol of his continual quest for respectability and stature. NYLC.

"gilding," and privilege built nothing less than the San Simeon of his day. It was to be a replica of the only oriental palace in England, King George IV's pavilion at Brighton. Combining Byzantine, Moorish, and Turkish elements, Barnum's "Iranistan," the Eastern Country Place, rose in sight of the railroad tracks to three stories, its minarets and domes stretching even higher. The grounds were transformed from open fields to sculptured gardens dotted with fountains and grazed by herds of reindeer and elk. Inside, much less visible to the public, Barnum, who "cared little for style," surrounded himself with the sort of opulence he must have seen and admired at the Rothschilds' and at royal palaces. The drawing-room wall panels featured murals representing the four seasons and a white and gold ceiling; the oriental library contained Chinese landscapes, furniture, and tortoise shell tables; Barnum's study was done in rich orange satin brocade.

No train rider who passed by could ignore the splendiferous, almost fairy-tale-like sight of Iranistan rising out of the Connecticut countryside, and no doubt it did spread the fame of Barnum and of his museum. But his claim that Iranistan was principally "an advertisement" has a hollow ring. Barnum was already rich and famous when he built it; his museum and other ventures had proved lucrative successes; and he had demonstrated time and time again that he could get all the publicity he wanted without large expenditures. It was no accident that Iranistan was patterned on an English royal showplace and outfitted in regal splendor. Barnum did what many self-made Americans before and since have done. He used conspicuous consumption to testify to his success and also to his personal worth. After a boyhood spent near bankruptcy, after sixteen years of failure, after being snubbed by the social elite, he had made it. Costing some $150,000, Iranistan was proof that Barnum was no fly-by-night charlatan, no huckster that had struck it rich. He literally lived like a king. By surrounding himself with the trappings of sophistication, glamour, and culture, he sought to appropriate these qualities. Iranistan was no humbug and by implication neither was he. Implying that he was more cultivated than he usually let on, he once claimed that his museum did not reflect his idea of culture. "I myself relished a higher grade of amusement, and I was a frequent attendant at the opera, first-class concerts, lectures, and the like." Befitting an aspiring country gentleman, he in 1848 became president of both the Fairfield County Agriculture Society and the Pequennock Bank. Yet, because of the public image he built for himself, he could do all this and still retain the admiration, respect, and affection of common Americans.

While spending most of 1848 and 1849 at Iranistan with his family, he remained active in show business, directing the expansion of the museum business to Philadelphia and contemplating his next grand production. He considered a "Congress of Nations," an exhibition of a man and a woman "from every accessible people, civilized and barbarous, on the face of the globe." But this seemed too costly and too risky, even for Barnum. Then he heard of Jenny Lind, the "Swedish Nightingale," who was electrifying Europe with her operatic singing. With visions of profits and of elevating himself to still greater respectability and stature, he decided to bring her to America. Despite a rival promoter warning her that Barnum was a "mere showman" who might put her "in a box" and exhibit her for twenty-five cents, Barnum's highly placed London friends assured her that he was a true gentleman. Besides that, he made her an unheard of offer: $1000 a concert for 150 concerts, plus expenses for herself and two servants, the money to be deposited in a London bank before she even set sail for America. She accepted. In early 1850, Barnum deposited $187,000, a huge sum and a great risk at that time. Then he set about planning his great promotional campaign.

From the outset, he realized that the success of the venture depended on "the manner in which she should be brought before the public." This was a time when raucous, folk-based entertainment and blackface minstrel songs in Afro-American dialect—not opera—were the vogue in America. Anti-aristocratic feelings ran high. Only a year before, the Astor Place Riot had rocked New York City. And Jenny Lind, even more than Charles Macready, was a "Pet of Princes" who sang in "Aristocratic Opera Houses." But unlike Macready, Lind had Barnum to promote her, was not competing with an American performer for accolades, and was not yet associated with upper-class Americans. In fact, outside of elitist circles, she was not widely known in America. When Barnum asked a railroad conductor to identify Lind, he guessed that she was a dancer, probably because Fanny Ellsler, a prominent European ballet dancer, had successfully toured in America a few years before. Whether Barnum realized it or not, her lack of fame worked to his advantage, because it allowed him to create her public image himself.

Reversing the approach he used with Tom Thumb in England, he did not emphasize her high standing with European aristocracy or even her operatic virtuosity. Instead, he focused on her character, which he claimed was "charity, simplicity, and goodness personified," on her generous contributions to charity, and on her purported desire to visit America and see its great democratic institutions at work. When her ship docked in New York, Barnum assembled a huge crowd, well populated with b'hoys as well as with the upper classes, to greet her. On the wharf stood a bower of green trees decorated with flags and two triumphal arches, one crowned with a glistening American eagle, about which Barnum later conceded: "I do not know that I can reasonably find fault with those who suspected I had a hand in their erection." At midnight of her first night in New York, two hundred members of the New York Musical Fund Society, carefully balanced by three hundred torch-bearing, red-shirted firemen, serenaded

Barnum's reception for Jenny Lind carefully mixed common people with the elite to avoid the class conflict that exploded in the Astor Place Riot. NYLC (Music Collection).

Romanticized sheet music cover for Jenny Lind's song, "Greeting To America." HTC.

her. Barnum was extremely careful not to let her become the "Pet of Princes." "It was with some difficulty that I prevented the 'fashionables' from monopolizing her altogether," he recalled, "and thus, as I believed, sadly marring my interests by cutting her off from the warm sympathies she had awakened among the masses."

By planting Jenny Lind stories and anecdotes in newspapers and staging "media events" like the midnight serenade, which were, as always, calculated to get extensive press coverage, Barnum made her a sensation. Song writers dedicated melodies to her, poets sang of her virtues, and enterprising businessmen offered for sale Jenny Lind gloves, Jenny Lind riding hats, Jenny Lind shawls, mantillas, robes, chairs, sofas, and pianos. As both a publicity and a financial enterprise, Barnum auctioned off the tickets to her first concert, getting $225 for the first one sold and taking in $10,141 on the first day of sales. In a grand gesture that did nothing to alienate the public, she donated her entire first night's earnings to charity.

Carefully nurtured by Barnum, her fame mushroomed as she set out on a national tour. Barnum left nothing to chance. As in a na-

Jenny Lind on stage with her classical musicians and formally attired opening night audience. NYLC (Music Collection).

tional presidential election campaign today, he sent advance men ahead of the entourage to publicize the tour, to create huge welcoming crowds, and to sell tickets. Playing on local pride, he challenged each locality to surpass the previous in its turnout and enthusiasm. None of Barnum's contemporaries even approximated this magnificently planned, meticulously executed national publicity campaign and performance tour. It was far from a mere promotional exercise. Barnum made over half a million dollars from it.

Barnum's ballyhoo and Lind's charity and grace accounted much more accurately for her unprecedented success than her music did. "It is a mistake to say the fame of Jenny Lind rests solely upon her ability to sing," Barnum admitted. "She was a woman who would have been adored if she had had the voice of a crow." When Daniel Webster went to see her, he twisted impatiently through her arias and finally whispered to a friend, "Why doesn't she give us one of the simple mountain melodies of her native land?" As successful as she was under Barnum's management, she hated crowds, promotion, and publicity. Finally, the combination of other financial proposals and Barnum's excessive commercialism caused her to terminate the contract with him after her ninety-third concert. Although she continued to perform in America, she did not draw nearly as well as she had under Barnum's direction. Even her last American concert before returning to Europe in 1852, an event Barnum would undoubtedly have made into a dazzling gala, drew only moderately well. Her great popularity in America was a P. T. Barnum production. And the scope and scale of his national campaign remained unmatched for decades and decades, probably until the huge circuses and Wild West shows late in the century.

A new chapter in P. T. Barnum's life began in 1865 when the American Museum burned to the ground. He put together a new museum collection, but it did not prove as popular as his old one, so he joined with Isaac Van Amburgh, a well-known lion-tamer, to form the Barnum and Van Amburgh Museum and Menagerie Company, a show that would travel in summer and spend winters at the new museum. Although Barnum owned 40 per cent of the show and listed himself as general manager, he did not play an active part in running it. This was the beginning of the end of Barnum's power but not his influence, of his innovations but not his fame. The entertainment business was undergoing fundamental changes, changes Barnum could not master. Twenty-five years earlier, Barnum had put together an amusement package that captivated people who were caught up in the first stages of urbanization and first learning of the wonders of the world. For these basically naïve and ignorant people, Barnum's presentation of freaks, curiosities, wonders, humbugs, and stage shows in the form of an educational institution proved an irresistible attraction. But by the 1860s, conditions had radically changed. The moral bias against entertainment had virtually disappeared as a practical consideration, and urban audiences, especially in New York, had become much more sophisticated. Furthermore, after Barnum demonstrated the potential of show business, many new popular entertainment forms, including minstrel shows, variety, popular plays, and musicals, provided northeastern audiences with a wide range of show business choices. With this increased entertainment competition and the improved transportation system, traveling shows became much more practical than they had been. These shows could reach large new audiences that still had

This cartoon reflects the enduring appeal of Barnum's museum. NYLC.

the naïveté, curiosity, and sense of wonder that had characterized northeastern urban audiences before the Civil War. Traveling shows were, of course, not new. Barnum himself had traveled widely with several in the 1830s. But the nature and scale of these shows, especially the circuses, certainly were.

The new companies brought not only an unprecedented array of animals, curiosities, and performers to the backlands, but they also brought some of the qualities of modern life in their rapid-fire pace and highly organized structure and technology. Before the Civil War rural people took the country into the city and demanded amusements that would help make sense of their lives while also appealing to their rustic heritage. After the Civil War, when urbanization and industrialization modernized America, popular entertainment carried the city into the country. Barnum's promotional techniques easily made the transition, but he could not master the new technology. He had toured extensively even nationally with Jenny Lind, but never with a large entourage requiring extensive logistics and split-second scheduling. He never mastered the

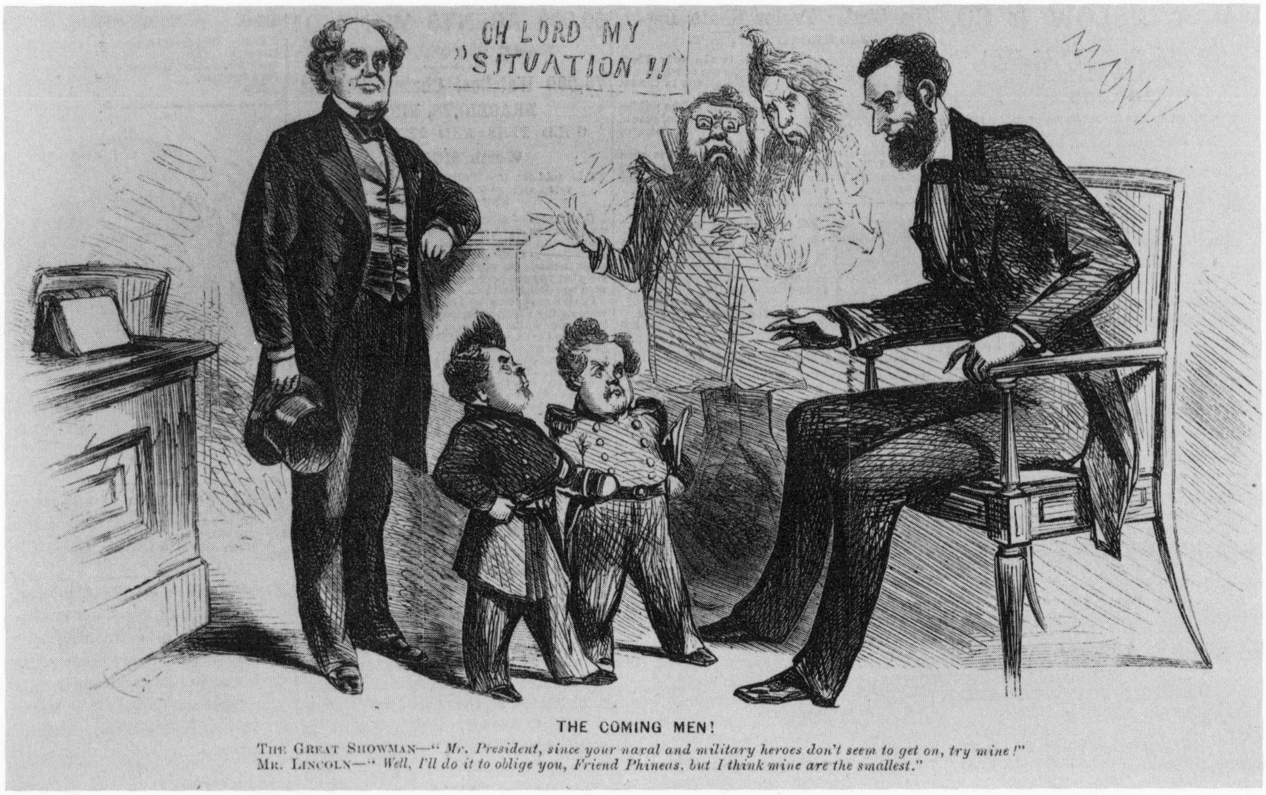

In 1862, General Tom Thumb and Commodore Nutt were received at the White House, and Barnum made sure the press covered the event.

railroad schedule, let alone the complexity of the traveling cities that modern circuses had become.

OH LORD MY
"SITUATION !!
THE COMING MEN!
THE GREAT SHOWMAN—"*Mr. President, since your naval and military heroes don't seem to get on, try mine!*"
MR. LINCOLN—"*Well, I'll do it to oblige you, Friend Phineas, but I think mine are the smallest.*"

After his new museum burned down in 1868, Barnum temporarily retired. But he quickly grew restless. Since his boyhood, his business enterprises had provided him with his identity. Stemming from his joke-swapping salesman background, popularity seemed to him the measure of success and happiness. He needed continual public acclaim to reaffirm his personal worth. So, when W. C. Coup and Dan Costello proposed an unprecedentedly large traveling show to him in 1870, he leapt at the chance. But Barnum lent little more to the huge new circus than his name and his presence as a parade-leading, crowd-drawing celebrity. Coup planned, organized, and managed the precedent-setting show, which opened in 1871 in Brooklyn, boasting more tent canvas, more men, more horses, more animals, more features, and more attractions than any previous circus. As with Barnum's museum, the circus was by design overwhelming. The old circus format of a small number of highly skilled people each performing his specialties, as in a variety show, began to be replaced by opulent spectacles and extravaganzas with "casts of thousands" performing in several rings at once, literally presenting more features than any viewer could absorb. Coup, in a real sense, created the modern American circus, but he never got public credit for it. The title of these circuses changed frequently, but it always had Barnum's name in it; Barnum rode at the head of the parade; and Barnum in his autobiography claimed the credit for all of Coup's innovations when in fact he initially opposed many of them and did not contribute significantly to any of them. Yet, after his many great innovations in the past, it was easy for the public to believe that Barnum had created the show that bore his name.

By 1873 Coup and Costello had sold their interests in the circus to Barnum, and he, with others actually running the shows, continued to travel at the head of the large circus, delighting in the great public adulation he got. But his circus faced increasing competition, especially from James A. Bailey's rival show. In the late 1870s the two circuses kept up a running battle of words, posters, and features, until in 1880 Barnum and Bailey agreed to combine their shows. They were an excellent partnership. Bailey was content to organize, produce, and run the circuses from behind the scenes. Barnum, until a year before his death in 1891, lived out his old age in fitting style—riding like an emperor among pomp and splendor before huge crowds of adoring Americans at the head of the Greatest Show on Earth.

While leading circuses, Barnum also continued to give his name to museums, for a percentage of the gross. HTC.

At last it was July 17, the day the circus was opening at the county seat only seventeen miles away. Since the bright, magical posters had gone up on barns and fences all around town, the farm boy and his friends could think and talk and dream of nothing but the circus. After getting his mother's permission, doing extra chores to earn the money to go, and waiting and waiting, seemingly forever, for the circus to come to the area, he was finally on his way. He could hardly believe it. Jumping off the train before it fully stopped, he ran all the way to the site. And there it was, the smell of the sawdust, the roar of the lions, the appetizing odors from the cook's tent, the singing men driving the tent stakes for the big top. He even got a chance to earn a free admission by carrying water for the elephants, which meant he could use his fifty cents for peanuts, lemonade, popcorn, and a balloon to take home to his little sister. Then, in what seemed no time at all, the parade began. Even his wildest fantasies proved inadequate beside the dazzling sights and sounds: the screaming calliope, the strange curiosities and "freaks," the lion-tamer in the den, the beautiful, spangled equestrians, the ornate coaches, the lumbering elephants, the breathtaking array of performers in exotic native costume in the pageant of nations, and P. T. Barnum, riding in a shining white chariot drawn by white horses, a smile on his face and a twinkle

Ricketts's Circus,

LOWER END OF GREENE-STREET.

On Friday, Auguſt the 4th, 1797,

A GREAT VARIETY OF

EQUESTRIAN EXERCISES,

By Mr. RICKETTS and his COMPANY.

Mr. RICKETTS will exhibit a GRAND PERFORMANCE with the

Broad Sword,

Going through the Guards of different Nations, Offenſive and Defenſive, as in real action, upon the

Celebrated Horſe, Cornplanter,

Who is thoroughly trained for the purpoſe. The ſagacity of this Horſe is truly wonderful.

CLOWN to the HORSEMANSHIP---By Mr. DURANG.

Still Vaulting, or a Trial of Skill, over a ſingle Horſe—By Mr. Ricketts and Mr. Durang.

Mr. Ricketts will ride with Maſter Hutchins on his ſhoulders, in the attitude of

A FLYING MERCURY.

A variety of other exerciſes, both Novel and Pleaſing.

THE WHOLE TO CONCLUDE WITH

The Taylor's Diſaſter;

Or, Johnny Gilpin's Journey to Brentford---By Mr. Durang.

Doors to be opened in future at five o'clock, and the Performance to begin preciſely at ſix.

Days of Performance---Mondays, Wedneſdays & Fridays.

☞ Tickets may be had at the City-Tavern, at the Circus, and at Barber & Southwick's Book-ſtore.

BOX 8ſ.—PITT 4ſ.

in his eye as he waved to the crowd. That farm boy and thousands upon thousands like him never forgot their first circus.

The circus has existed in America almost as long as there has been an America. Over the years, it has certainly changed, reflecting many of the general show business developments—especially the emphasis on size, spectacle, and opulence. But the core of the circus remained essentially the same. Its enduring appeal was, of course, partially the result of its being a "good show," but other "good shows" of the early decades of American show business have either disappeared or changed so totally that their original form is unrecognizable. The circus survived because it touched something central in its audience, something that spanned generations. Beneath all its razzle-dazzle, the circus was rooted in nature and in physical action. Its central features—animals, sideshows, lion-tamers, death-defying daredevils, equestrians, trapeze artists, clowns, even its "instant" appearance and disappearance—are intimately related to the precarious position of human beings in the elemental world of nature. When Americans were still struggling to understand and master nature, the circus provided information about the wonders and oddities of the world in its menageries and its sideshows; the circus presented models of control and order in its masterful equestrians and in its creation of perfectly ordered "instant" canvas cities; the circus offered reassuring symbolic rituals of man dominating nature's most ferocious animals in its lion-tamers, wish fulfillments of man transcending natural laws in its "fliers," and emotional outlets in the antics of its clowns. When other show business forms concentrated in cities, the circus toured widely, reaching into the backlands. It developed its format and rituals in the course of becoming rural Americans' major entertainment form. As decades passed, the circus evolved, but its basic format and features survived. In the long run, it became largely a relic, a nostalgic re-creation of the nature-based rituals of an earlier day, recalling the warm feelings of happy childhood for adults. It continued to delight young children with its timeless entertainment wonders, but in its heyday it was a show for people of all ages, not just for "children of all ages."

After virtually disappearing during the Middle Ages, the circus literally rode back into existence in the 1760s when Philip Astley organized equestrian exhibitions at his London "riding school." The skillful riders proved popular, so he broadened his shows to include tumblers and clowns, performers who had entertained individually at fairs and as itinerants but not as parts of organized shows. Astley's performances proved so successful and fashionable that he ultimately expanded into London's 3000-seat Royal Amphitheatre. Equestrian entertainments quickly caught on in Europe, and competition among performers and troupes intensified. Predictably, it was not long before an aspiring young equestrian, looking for a place to get a start, brought the riding-variety show to America.

In the early 1790s, John Bill Ricketts, a pupil of one of Astley's major British rivals, staged exhibitions in a Philadelphia "riding school"—a title carefully chosen to get around the bias against theaters. With a boy on his shoulders, Ricketts rode grandly around the ring. He did a popular dance on the saddle of his galloping horse and jumped "from one horse through a hoop suspended in the air

Playbill for John Bill Ricketts' equestrian circus (1797). HTC.

The building with the neoclassical façade and the conical roof is Ricketts' Philadelphia circus. HTC.

twelve feet" onto the back of another. His typical early equestrian circus also offered acrobats, "rope dancing," and "comic feats on horseback." President George Washington numbered among his pleased patrons, a fact that Ricketts prominently advertised when he took the show, supplemented with fireworks, to New York City where it was so popular that one writer complained, "Sheridan and 'The School For Scandal' gave way for Ricketts and Clown." Ricketts successfully toured Philadelphia, Albany, New York, Baltimore, and Boston, continually expanding his show and eventually investing in a theater. After one of his special effects in 1799 sparked a disastrous fire that burned down his $20,000 amphitheater—a curse of many other nineteenth-century theaters—Ricketts sailed for London. His ship was lost in a storm, but the equestrian-based variety show, the show that would provide the basis for the circus, was fully established as part of America's evolving show business.

In an age when the major means of transportation was the horse, equestrian performers took an ordinary, everyday experience and raised it to the level of an art. Audiences then fully realized just how difficult it was for the riders to control their horses and their own bodies so completely and effortlessly that the two figures merged into a single graceful form. In the ring, more fully than in real life, man was total master of the horse and of himself, so much so that he could nonchalantly perform incredible stunts while riding grandly and glamorously on a galloping horse. The performers were artists—not just trick riders. "As a bareback rider," old-time circus man Frank Melville in 1904 recalled of his early days, "I was required to take all sorts of dancing lessons. I had to walk just so, to hold my hands gracefully. Every motion was studied."

"The theatre has been deserted while the Circus has been full," an 1808 critic lamented as people flocked to see the new entertainment form. In 1810, a typical early circus opened in Boston with a young man doing stunts on horseback, including standing "erect on his Horse, with his Toe in his Mouth." Next, an acrobat went through his gyrations, climaxing with a "Dance on a Man's Head with his Feet extended in the Air." Then, an equestrian, while riding at full speed, picked handkerchiefs and a watch off the ground. The acrobat returned with "many extraordinary and surprising Feats of address and agility." After an equestrian leapt over four horses and a clown went through his antics, the show closed with a comedy farce, as did theatrical productions. These shows had many of the components of a modern circus: the riding ring, the exciting equestrians, the incredible acrobats, and the funny clowns. But several things were still missing.

Exotic animals—bears, monkeys, camels, and lions—had been commercially exhibited in America since the colonial period. But the elephant, the animal that now symbolizes the circus, did not appear in America until 1796, about the same time that Ricketts popularized the equestrian show. Owners of the first elephant apparently exhibited it as a single attraction until about 1811. The first giant strides toward making the elephant part of a show, not just another individual curiosity, were taken by the elephant Old Bet, which arrived in America in 1815. Purchased at a London auction for $20, the elephant brought $1000 in New York from Hackaliah Bailey (no relation to James A. Bailey, who became P. T. Barnum's famous circus partner). Bailey, an enterprising Yankee, imported other animals to join Old Bet in the first of many highly profitable touring menageries. To minimize the number of people who could see his collection free, Bailey moved his animal wagons at night whenever possible. But even then he occasionally found the road brightly lighted by torch-bearing freeloaders. By day, the growing menagerie was exhibited in barns or other large buildings.

John Bill Ricketts jumping over a pony. HTC.

Success bred imitation, and a number of such animal exhibits sprang up. In 1816, Salem, Massachusetts, residents, for example, could see a tiger, a buffalo, and dancing dogs. In 1828, people in Pennsylvania were offered a bear, a wolf, a camel, and a monkey. But the elephant was the biggest attraction. In 1825, a newspaper advertisement proudly announced that a "GRAND CARAVAN OF LIVING ANIMALS, being the largest that ever travelled in the United States," would appear in Portland, Maine. Top billing went to the elephant, which the ad explained "is not only the largest and most sagacious animal in the world, but from the peculiar manner in which he takes his food and drink of every kind with its trunk, is acknowledged to be one of the greatest natural curiosities ever offered to the public." The menagerie also advertised an African lion, an Arabian camel, a South American tiger, a leopard, a young American panther, a jackal, a wild cat, a black wolf, an African baboon, a Brazilian "weazle," and a monkey who walked a tight rope and did "unexampled feats of horse-monkey-ship on his small Shetland Poney." Band music provided accompaniment. Such menageries proved so popular and became so numerous that a group of promoters formed a co-operative association to control the field, and, of course, to maximize their profits. Soon, the "Zoological Institute," as the organization called itself, sent out "scientific and educational exhibits,"

TRONC.

INTERIOR VIEW OF THE HIPPOTHEATRON, FOURTEENTH STREET.

Interior of the Hippotheatron, an early-nineteenth-century circus. HTC.

bringing—usually to rented barns—the natural wonders of the animal kingdom to curious; entertainment-starved farmers, just as museums did for the nation's urban dwellers. By the 1830s some thirty such traveling exhibitions, claiming to be educational institutions, toured the country, many of them combined menageries and acrobatics companies into one show. It was only a matter of time until equestrians, menageries, and acrobats joined together into circuses.

But these enlarged shows outgrew barns and other rural buildings, forcing their managers to invent "portable barns" mobile enough to transport economically, large enough to hold the shows and their paying public, and private enough to shut out people who did not pay to see the shows. At first, troupes enclosed their shows in circular canvas walls as much as ten feet high. Unless patrons brought their own chairs or taverns supplied some, they had to stand to watch the performances. Soon, round tents provided shelter from the weather as well as from freeloading onlookers. By the mid-nineteenth century, blackface minstrels, street parades, and gleaming red and gold circus wagons were added, and menageries and equestrian troupes began to merge in one-ring circuses. Because of road and turnpike improvements the big caravans reached many more people than ever before.

The lion-tamer, one of the most enduring circus features, emerged as a star in the 1820s, when Isaac Van Amburgh, reportedly inspired by the biblical story of Daniel and the lion's den but more likely inspired by a vision of financial profit, entered lion cages with great fanfare and "tamed" the big cats with his flamboyant, though brutal, techniques. Van Amburgh did everything he could to create a feeling that he was in mortal danger, reportedly not feeding his cats until after the performance so they would be restless, noisy, and snarling in the ring. Before he entered, he also had the cages rattled, making the lions roar and mill about. Then, with his whip cracking and lashing out at the animals that he had worked up into a rage, the well-built, young man dramatically flung himself into the arena that was charged with an atmosphere of excitement, turbulence, and danger. Van Amburgh's showmanship made him a star.

Van Amburgh was certainly not the first lion-tamer in America. But earlier acts had focused on the lion, not on the tamer. In 1801, for example, a Boston newspaper advertisement addressed "To The Curious" announced

The equestrian acrobatics of Welch, Delevan and Nathan's National Circus. HTC.

Isaac Van Amburgh used stunts like pulling a lion's tongue to make himself the first famous American lion-tamer. HTC.

that "A beautiful African lion would be on display for a week." After detailing the animal's size, the exhibitor assured the public that "great attention has been paid in providing a strong substantial Cage, and to have the Lion under very good command. The person who has the care of him," the advertisement continued, almost as an afterthought, "can comb his mane, make him lie down and get up at any time." The charming woodcut illustrating the advertisement featured only the lion. In 1801, a lion, the solitary animal, was still enough of a curiosity that people would pay to see it. The trainer was portrayed as little more than protection for the patrons from the exotic beast. Yet, even then, there was some appeal in the idea that a man could tame, control, and command "the king of the jungle," one of the fiercest symbols of wild, untamed nature. This idea—the symbolic conquest of nature, the enthroning of man as the king of beasts—was one of the circus's major underlying appeals, one that was probably universal but had special meaning to nineteenth-century Americans who were fighting hard to tame the wilderness, to settle the frontier, and to reassure themselves that the struggle made them more noble, not more barbaric. Like Davy Crockett and the other mythic frontier supermen, the dashing lion-tamer stood as heroic testimony to the strength and power of American manhood.

But Crockett and the other folk heroes also provided belly laughs at the expense of the refined upper classes, laughter that glorified common Americans in the age of democratization. There was no room for laughs in the lion-tamer's performance. He acted out the life and death confrontation of man against savage beast—the stuff of which nightmares—and heroes—are made. But the circus certainly did not neglect laughter. One of the circus's greatest strengths, in fact, was its diversity. It is virtually impossible to think of a circus and not to think of clowns. Ever since the early equestrian shows, American circuses have featured clowns. But in the early one-ring circuses, they were not the white-masked, ruffle-suited gangs of pantomime clowns so familiar to fans of the modern, three-ring circus. Instead, a distinctively American clown emerged early in the nineteenth century, one that evolved into the universal clown only after significant changes took place in circuses and in other forms of show business.

Clowning is, of course, an ancient art, tracing its ancestry back through the comedia dell'arte at least to Greek and Roman buffoons. But clowning was not a well-developed, starring role until the mid-eighteenth century, though the quick-witted, sharp-tongued Fool and other comic roles were common in drama. About the same time that Astley made equestrianism into an entertainment form, Joseph Grimaldi, who as a young boy performed with his Italian ballet-master father in English pantomimes, developed the modern clown character. He took the stock commedia dell'arte Clown, who had traditionally played only minor parts as a clumsy oaf who got in other people's ways, and made it into *the* major comic role in pantomimes. Lavishly praised as the "Michael Angelo of buffoonery" and "the Jupiter of Joke," Grimaldi in the early 1800s became a major star in Great Britain, popularizing his comic songs as well as his clown pantomimes. He never performed in a circus, but the clowns at Astley's and other equestrian shows took their styles and material from him. Acknowledging their debt to Joseph Grimaldi, clowns ever since have been nicknamed "Joeys." In subsequent years, most English clowns remained pantomimists, one major branch developing the acrobatic-equestrian clown, whose trick stunts took great skill and drew great laughs (stunts that still survive in modern rodeos). A second school of British clowns, the Augusts, donned ill-fitting, formal wear and got laughs from their clumsiness, which mocked either the refinements of gentlemen or the pretensions of upstarts, depending on the patron's point of view. Other clowns developed in the tradition of cultivated court jesters.

In America, clowns, like many other people, could not keep quiet. They delighted audiences with their comic songs and convulsed them with their barbed jokes, as well as with their physical gags. It is difficult for people who have known only modern three-ring extravaganzas to realize that in the one-ring circus only one act performed at a time with the audience's full, undivided attention. It is also difficult to realize that individual clowns were among the circus's greatest stars. They were the nation's first stand-up comedians, a role they ultimately lost because of changes in the circus. The sheer size of the circus tents, which continually expanded to hold the ever-growing shows and audiences, made subtlety and individual performers ineffective. Magicians, for example, never became major features of big-top shows. When they traveled with circuses, it was in the small sideshows. As they matured, circuses increasingly devoted themselves to dazzling audiences with lavish spectacles and with a great many acts performed simultaneously, a type of show that was much more conducive to the splashy sight gags of swarms of frolicking clowns than to individual, verbal comedy. As a result, many potential talking clowns became comedians in other show business forms, forms that concentrated on comedy. Tony Pastor, for example, "the father of American vaudeville," first gained fame before the Civil War as a circus clown noted for his snappy jokes and his topical songs. But when the circus changed to extravaganzas leaving no featured role for his talents, Pastor took his act into rowdy variety houses, which he ultimately transformed into respectable, family-oriented vaudeville shows. Similarly, many famous minstrel comedians began their careers with circuses before shifting to the new comedy-based form.

Dan Rice, America's first famous clown, worked his way up from lower-class, frontier American origins. By the age of ten, Rice was a professional jockey, touring the Kentucky-Ohio racing circuit in the 1830s. But he grew too heavy to race, took to the fast life of riverboats, and was an ex-cardsharp as well as an ex-jockey by the age of seventeen. He then bought part interest in a Pittsburgh livery stable that was next door to a circus, where Rice learned the tricks of a new trade. Joining the circus, he danced, sang, and performed a strongman act as "Young Hercules." He also tamed lions, trained an elephant to walk a tightrope, reportedly never lost a fist fight, and owned half-interest in Lord Byron, an educated pig. By the mid-1840s he had become a famous clown, traveling the Mississippi river route with leading circuses. Well aware of the tastes and feelings of the common people he had lived with and performed for since he was a boy, Rice played to the gallery with a combination of wisecracks, songs parodying popular topics, and jibes at the educated. "People used to go to a circus to laugh," he recalled. "I discovered that fact early in my career, and made money out of it."

Before Rice, American talking clowns were cultured men of wit, in the British court jester tradition. William R. Wallett, renowned as the Queen's Jester, the leading clown in England and America, was a well-educated man with the "polish of society" who "recited Shakespeare inimitably in the ring . . . interpreting truly the language of the author. Now I had a different idea of the character," Rice recalled of his rise to stardom, "and early won the title of Shakespearian Jester by my little paraphrases of the Bard of Avon." Shakespeare was then the most popular playwright in America, so audiences were familiar with many of the famous speeches in his plays. Rice, like schoolchildren ever since, made up silly words parodying the serious speeches. Heading his own circus by 1848, he scored a major *coup* by hiring Wallett away from a rival. The two proved a great team.

The sharp contrast between the two clowns, with the raucous mid-American roustabout jibing at the cultured English gentleman, delighted American audiences who loved to see common people make fun of the pompous and cultivated. Wallett, using the thundering, grandiloquent rhetorical style of an Edwin Forrest, passionately delivered a famous Shakespearean speech, and then Rice followed with a ludicrous paraphrase delivered in his American twang. Wallett, as the tormented Macbeth, for example, agonized through the speech:

Is this a dagger which I see before me
The handle toward my hand?
Come, let me clutch thee! I have thee not,
And yet I see thee still . . .
I see thee yet, in form as palpable
As this which now I draw.

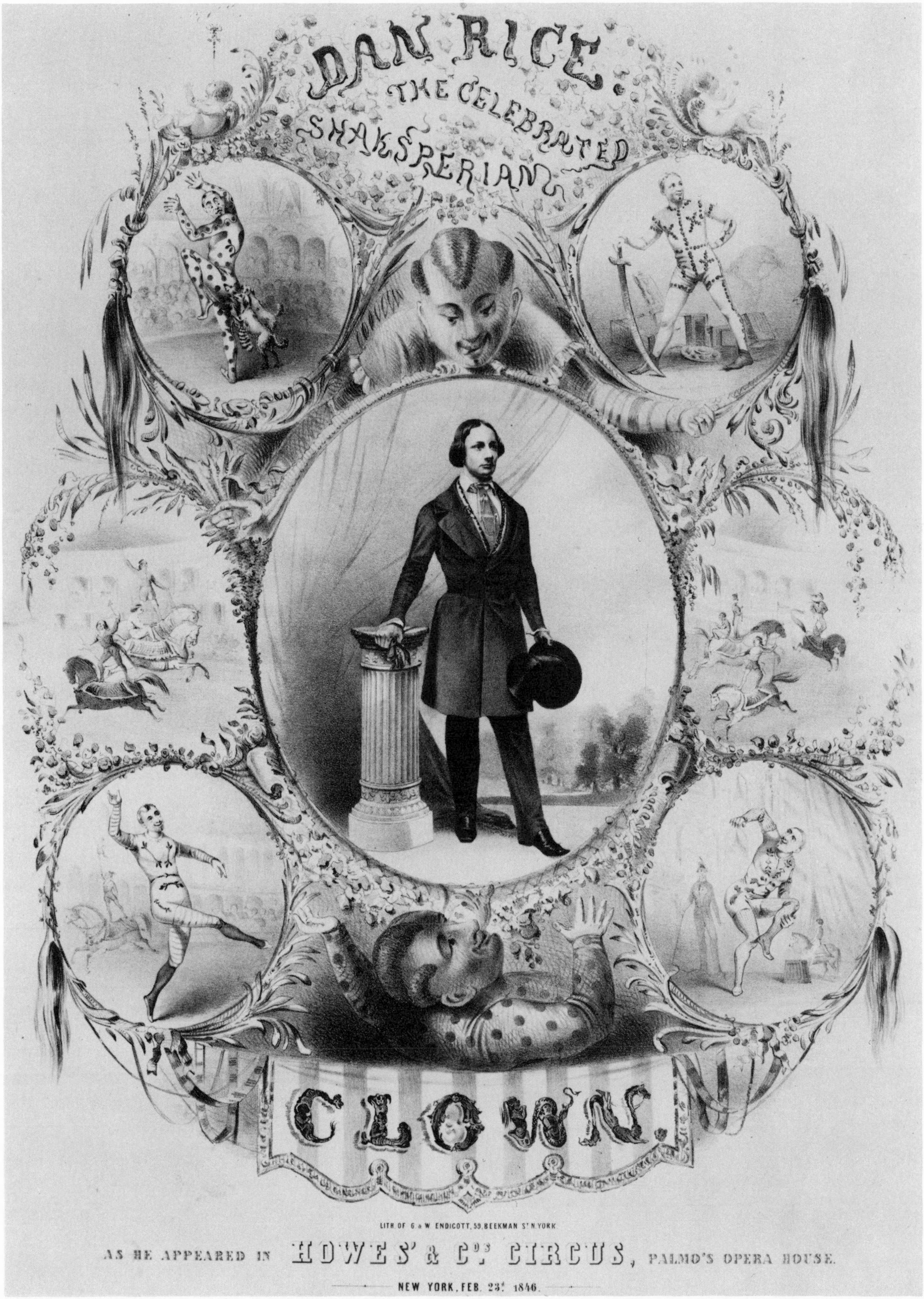

Dan Rice, "The Celebrated Shakespearean Clown," is shown in his stunts on this 1846 sheet music cover. HTC.

Dan Rice, the premiere American clown, in his "Uncle Sam" suit. HTC.

Then Rice took over with:

> *Is that a beefsteak I see before me*
> *With the burnt side toward my hand?*
> *Let me clutch thee! I have thee not,*
> *And yet I see thee! I have thee not,*
> *And yet I see thee still in form as palpable*
> *As that I ate for breakfast this morning.*

In the late 1840s, material like that made audiences roll in the aisles. Malaprop-laden, mumble-jumble language in pretentious form proved as effective for Rice as it did for stump speakers in the minstrel show.

And that was only part of Rice's act. "I had added to my comicalities," he recollected, "by dancing, tumbling, leaping, and riding." But most importantly of all, he and Wallett developed a distinctive anti-intellectual, anti-elitist ritual out of the give and take between the pompous ringmaster, with his formal language and continual efforts to maintain "law and order," and the sniping, anarchic clown who disrupted the ringmaster's plans and interrupted the ringmaster's speeches, poking fun at and mocking his dignified "better," as the endmen in the minstrel show did to the interlocutor. Rice fully understood the dynamics of the exchange, observing that the clown "to the ringmaster, is a stupid fool, a buffoon; to the audience a wise man whose every remark is impregnated with philosophy as well as humor." Rice's clown was a debunking common American in the manner of the stage Yankee or Mose the B'howery B'hoy. Rice's appearance also reinforced the idea that he represented the true blue b'hoy. He did not wear the anonymous clown-white mask—only his Uncle Sam beard adorned his face—and he did not wear the ruffled, flounced clown suit; instead, he wore regular clothing and sometimes dressed in a striped Uncle Sam suit.

Like Barnum, Rice realized the importance of publicity, even notoriety, in building public curiosity about a performer or a show. "I found no advertising more profitable," he recalled, "than that obtained by one of my circuses being attacked from the pulpit." He also courted and publicized his run-ins with the law, either for slandering competitors in the cutthroat advertising that was common in circus promotion, or for the vagrancy charges that some communities used to keep traveling entertainers out. "In fact," Rice admitted, "I enjoyed the arrests, which were the cheapest and most effective advertising my shows could get." With this flair for publicity added to his great appeal as a clown, Rice became a famous, highly paid star, who consistently earned $1000 a week, an absolutely unprecedented salary in the mid-nineteenth century. But Rice was plagued by the hard drinking he had begun in his early life on the road—an indulgence that became a serious problem as he grew older and was inclined to disappear at times regardless of bookings or contracts. Several of his own shows went bankrupt. Yet, he remained such a great drawing card that he could successfully start over from scratch with his own shows or could continually—despite his lack of reliability—get new bookings at $1000 a week from the biggest circuses. But when in the 1870s Adam Forepaugh, a major competitor of the Barnum circuses, offered Rice whatever salary he requested for a season if he would guarantee to remain sober, or when he got a similar offer for only four weeks in New York City, he flatly refused. Eventually, Rice disappeared from the scene, a loss which was as much the result of major changes in the circus itself as of deterioration in his physical condition.

Like the rest of the nation and the other branches of show business, the circus expanded tremendously after the Civil War. As a traveling entertainment form, the circus was the first part of show business to feel the impact and to take advantage of the westward population shift and the development of a truly national railroad network. In the late nineteenth century, the circus reached out into the American heartland, the railroads making feasible both the long distance travel and the huge multi-ringed circus extravaganzas that would otherwise have been impossible to move quickly and cheaply. Ironically, the innovative genius who first developed the modern circus, W. C. Coup, never got the public credit he deserved. Coup masterminded the huge Barnum circus of 1870, the largest traveling show up to that time, one that supplemented the usual circus features with Barnum's freaks and museum exhibits housed in separate tents as sideshows. Most of all, Coup's administration and planning, especially his organization and travel scheduling, made the huge circus a success. Every previous circus had confined its advertising to the town in which it performed and its immediate vicinity. But Coup ordered his advance men to paper all the territory within 50-75 miles of the performance site with his large, colorful posters. Instead of trying to take the huge show to every community, Coup, as Barnum had done in New York City, got people to travel to his show, by organizing excursion trains to the circus location. As a result, his circus usually drew two to three times the population of the towns it set up in. Coup also purchased and outfitted the first circus trains, and by 1872 his entire company traveled by rail, skipping more small towns, cutting costs, promoting travel to the shows, and increasing attendance and profits. Coup perfected the smoothly functioning operation that could set up and take down its canvas city so quickly that it seemed like a colossal magician's trick. In 1873, Coup for the first time made his show a two-ring circus, literally offering more entertainment at once than anyone could possibly absorb. But Barnum got the initial credit for Coup's innovations, and other enterprising showmen adopted them so quickly and fully that they became synonymous with the word "circus."

Like many other circus-struck youngsters, James A. McGinness sought his fortune in the circus. Unlike most others, he made a fortune at it. In 1859 at age twelve, James began working with a small circus run by Fred Bailey, a man claiming to be a descendant of Hackaliah Bailey, the owner of the elephant Old Bet. The McGinness boy appropriated both the circus promoter's name and his knowledge, emerging in the late-1860s as James A. Bailey, an ambitious, young circus man who worked his way up from billposter to general manager of small-time concert companies and circuses. By 1876, the twenty-nine year old was half owner of Cooper and Bailey's circus, a show that he loaded—lock, stock, barrel, rhinos, and elephants—aboard a steamer and took to Australia, New Zealand, Peru, Chile, Argentina, and Brazil. Two years, 76,000 miles, and substantial profits later, Bailey returned to New York with enough money to purchase another circus, merge it with his own, and make it a serious competitor to Barnum's. The two shows engaged in a vicious and expensive rivalry trying to outdo each other with new attractions, overblown advertising, and head-to-head bookings, a rivalry that hurt both shows financially. Then, one of Bailey's elephants gave birth to the first American-born elephant, and Barnum made the mistake of telegraphing an offer of $100,000 for it. Bailey quickly made the telegram into a poster boasting that: "This is what Barnum thinks of Cooper and Bailey's baby Elephant."

Unable to compete with the cleverly named new attraction, "Young America," Barnum in 1880 offered to merge the two shows. Buying out Cooper, the two men formed Barnum and Bailey's Circus, which they legitimately advertised as "The Greatest Show on Earth." With Barnum fronting the show and Bailey running it, their new circus premiered in Madison Square Garden with great fanfare, and with so much entertainment in and around their three rings that no one could absorb it all. "The only drawback to the performance," a New York critic gasped in 1881 after the opening, "was that the spectator was compelled to receive more than his money's worth; in other words, that while his head was turned in one direction he felt he was losing something good in another." Barnum's principle of satisfaction through saturation had been extended from exhibitions and museums to live performances, from New York City, ultimately, to the nation. Perhaps nothing is more typical of America—the richest nation on earth—than that the principle of overabundance, of planned waste, characterized even its amusements.

As indicated by "Young America" forcing the merger of Barnum and Bailey, elephants, the largest land animals on earth, became the status symbols of the huge, new circuses, as they had earlier been of the small menageries. As a result of the intense competition of the 1880s, the size of circuses and of their herds of pachyderms became elephantine. In the 1870s, big circuses boasted five elephants. The first gigantic Barnum and Bailey show in 1881 claimed twenty! By 1887, when the Barnum and Bailey and the Forepaugh circuses held a joint exhibition in Madison Square Garden, they paraded *sixty* elephants. The American public, which often equates biggest with best,

The many wonders of the combined multi-ringed circuses of P. T. Barnum and Adam Forepaugh (1887). HTC.

delighted in the escalation. But there were physical limits to the numbers of elephants (which ate 150 pounds of food a day) that circuses could economically maintain, so their numbers peaked in the 1880s. But the public was no less fascinated by size. It was the American way.

At the 1876 Centennial celebration, Americans took great nationalistic pride in the enormity of American machinery and in the largest building in the world. Similarly, when Barnum and Bailey, combining Barnum's genius for promotion with Bailey's circus sense, bought from the London Zoo the largest elephant in captivity, the public was curious to see it, especially after the rash of publicity about it. Whether at Barnum's instigation or not, there was a flood of British protests that losing Jumbo was a national disgrace and that separating him from his "wife" Alice was a national sin, protests that Barnum and Bailey made sure got good coverage in the American press. An English lawsuit challenging the sale failed, and Jumbo was scheduled to leave for

Ringling Bros. Barnum and Bailey poster, indicating the great appeal of elephants. NYLC.

America. But when he saw his traveling cage, he, as if on cue, lay down and refused to budge. When Barnum was telegraphed for instructions, he quickly cabled back: "Let him lie there a week if he wants to. It is the best advertisement in the world." When Jumbo finally reached the United States in 1882, he proved an even greater drawing card than his owners anticipated, but they continued to promote him in every way possible, outfitting a special "palace" car for the monarch of monarchs and trumpeting his supposed friendship for a baby elephant that they named Tom Thumb. When Jumbo was killed in an 1885 railroad crash, Barnum and Bailey circulated the story that he had given his life to save Tom Thumb. The partners then purchased Jumbo's "widow" Alice, whom they exhibited along with Jumbo's preserved carcass until Alice died in an 1887 fire. In the 1890s, circuses, having exploited elephants for about all they were worth, shifted their emphasis to other exciting attractions.

"He floats through the air with the greatest of ease," sang Dan Rice and many others in the most celebrated of all clown songs. "The

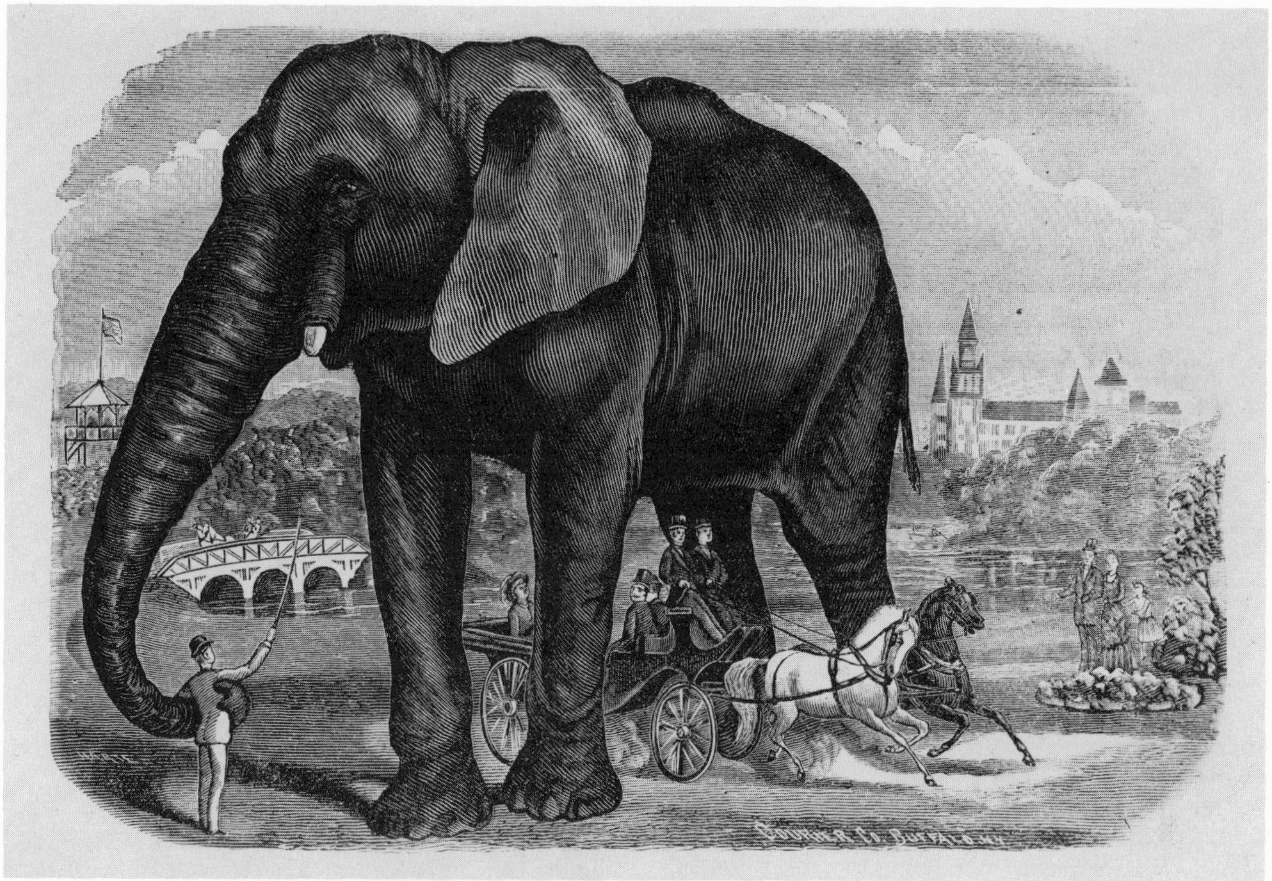

Promotion exaggerating Jumbo's height. HTC.

daring young man on the flying trapeze." Until the late nineteenth century, this song introduced "leapers," not "fliers"—gymnastic acrobats who sprinted down a ramp, catapulted off a springboard into the air, and somersaulted over horses, camels, and elephants, hopefully landing safely in a soft mattress. Acrobats, tightrope walkers, and "leapers" had long circus histories, having performed in European circuses, in American colonial tavern shows, and in John Bill Rickett's early equestrian circuses. But in the late nineteenth century, leaping acts became much more sensational, exciting, and dangerous, swelling their popularity and improving their billing until they were replaced by even more daring acts, acts that literally defied gravity and seemed—if only for a few seconds—to be living out man's age-old dream of being able to fly like a bird.

When leapers became famous celebrities, stars with their own followings, a lively debate developed about who was the greatest of these daredevils. The debate finally centered on whether anyone could ever complete three full somersaults in the air after the leap, a feat

MUTUAL ADMIRATION.

BARNUM TO JUMBO. "You are a *humbug* after my own heart. You have even beat me in advertising."

Even the caustic wit of Thomas Nast warmed to P. T. Barnum's promotion of Jumbo. Author's collection.

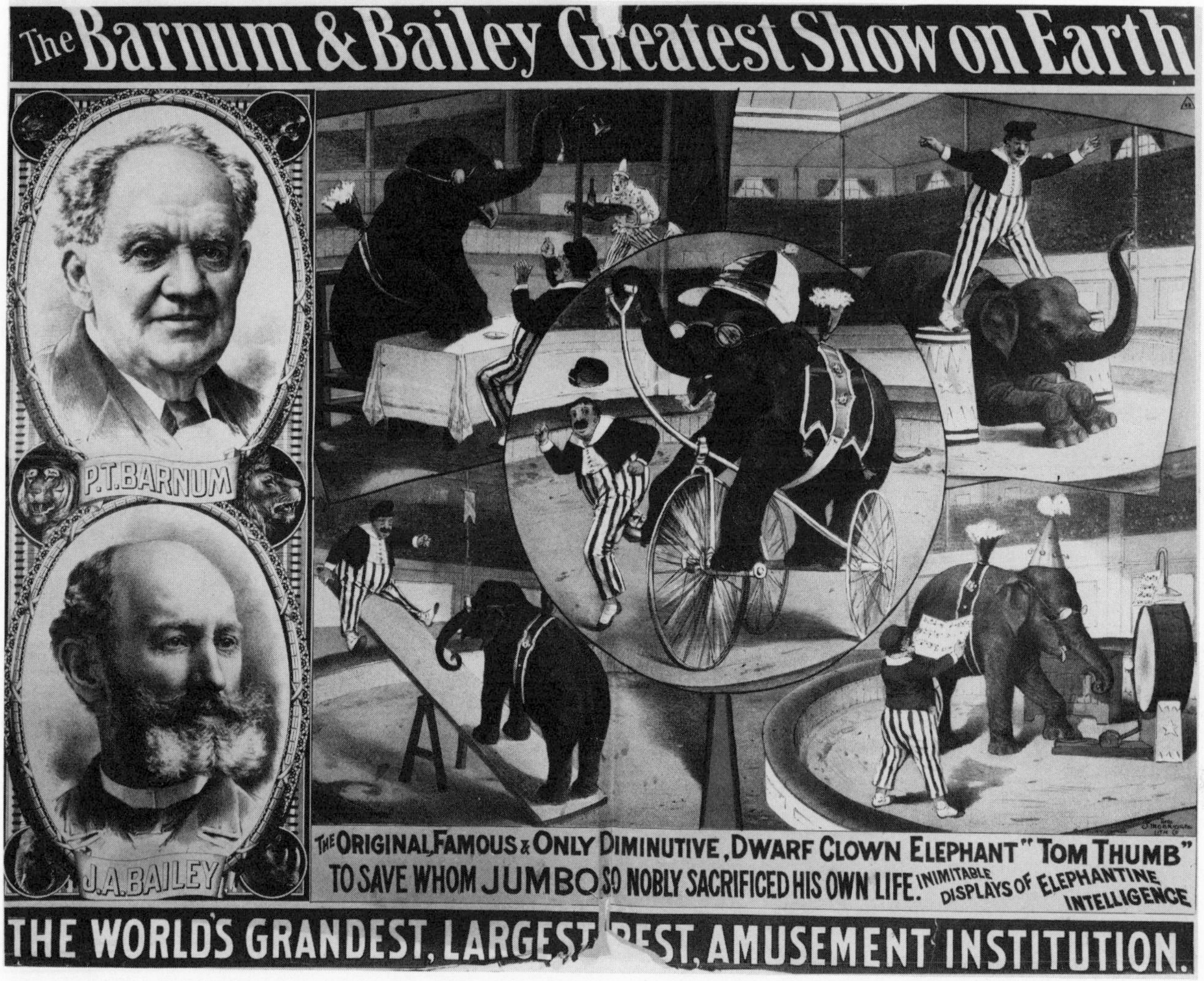

Tom Thumb, the comic elephant, succeeded Jumbo as Barnum and Bailey's major attraction. NYLC.

that seemed as unattainable as the four-minute mile, the seven-foot high-jump, the sixty-foot put, or the sixteen-foot pole vault seemed in the early twentieth century. Several leapers tried the "full three" and paid the price in twisted limbs, paralyzed bodies, broken necks, and even death, catastrophes which only stimulated public interest in the event. Finally, in 1874, John Worland succeeded in one of his three attempts at the triple somersault. Two years later, he was goaded into proving he could still do it, but he failed at the dangerous stunt. After five years and many charges from rival leapers and rival circus managers that he had never really made the three, he in 1881 tried again and succeeded twice, collecting affidavits from many of the witnesses. Yet, he still faced charges that he was just lucky. With great hoopla he announced that he would do the triple at the Forepaugh circus opening in New Haven. As the time approached, everything else in the

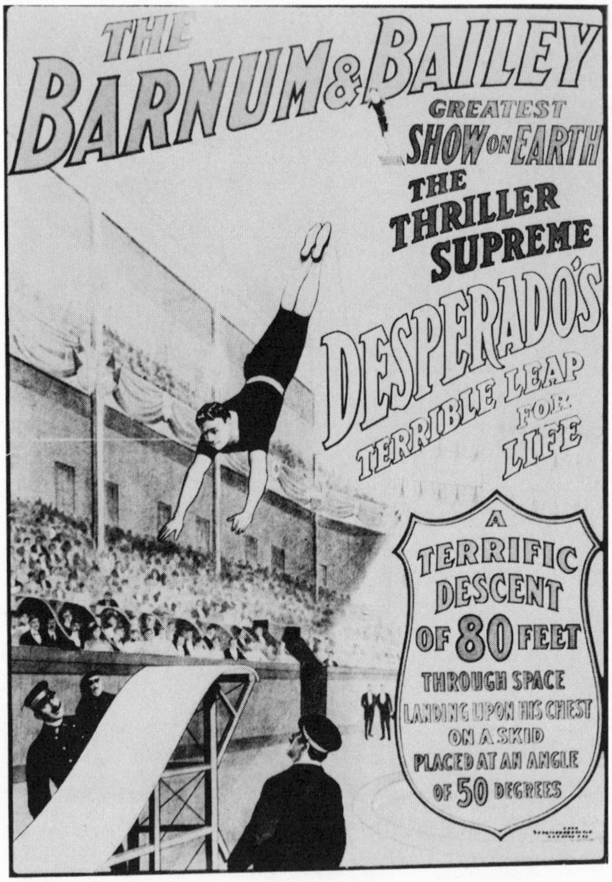

Leapers excited audiences with their daredevil stunts. NYLC.

huge tent stopped; preliminary leapers did singles and doubles. Then, after a great fanfare and a dramatic build-up from the master of ceremonies, the huge crowd hushed, holding its breath while Worland composed himself, exploded down the ramp, took off into the air, completed the triple, and landed safely. After that, there was no other mark for leapers to jump at, no more suspense.

As circuses grew more committed to spectacular shows and to continual entertainment and as "leapers" reached the extent of their repertoires, they were replaced as stars by the more spectacular, seemingly more dangerous (but actually safer) trapeze acts that filled the big-top with flying bodies. Trapeze artists have remained staples of circuses to this day. Their appeal transcends time or place. Without any mechanical device, they defy gravity, emulating birds, as even their name "fliers" testifies. But besides soaring through the air with grace and beauty, fliers and leapers took their lives in their hands every time they performed. A great many people, though they rarely admit it, are fascinated and excited by death-defying acts, a fascination that circuses have long catered to and exploited.

"The evolution of the thriller or death-defying act of the circus is really the evolution of the show," argued long-time circus public relations man Tody Hamilton in what was only a minor overstatement. When bareback riders first stood up on their horses and did somersaults, it seemed, Hamilton recalled in 1907, "a greater thriller than the 'dip of death,' " an extremely risky turn of the twentieth-century stunt. Lion-taming acts, of course, belonged in the same category, as did the leapers and their flying successors. Seeing each of these, the audience could thrill to the prospect of danger, waiting for the occasional catastrophe. A tightrope or trapeze act performed only a few feet off a soft mat, or a lion-taming act done with toothless, clawless, domesticated cats would have had little appeal, because there was no chance of serious injury—not because there was less artistry involved.

In the late nineteenth century, this dangerous, spine-tingling circus fare was supplemented by mechanical devices that added new thrills in the machine age. In 1879, Ella Richter, as Mlle. Zazel, was shot sixty feet out of a cannon as the "Human Cannon Ball." Actually, springs, not gunpowder, "blasted" her into flight, but the audience did not know

Aerialists followed leapers as "flying" circus attractions. NYLC.

that. The act proved so popular that many Zazels and many human cannon balls followed. "Human flies" wearing suction plates on their feet walked upside down on platforms suspended high above the ground. Audiences liked the act, but the suction cups did not always work, so the dangerous act, along with several human flies, disappeared. A spring-propelled catapult flung Lulu, the Human Meteor, about a hundred feet through the air, long enough to allow her to make two full somersaults before she hit the catching net. In the Human Arrow variation, a woman was shot from a fifteen-foot crossbow through a paper bull's-eye target and into the hands of a trapeze "catcher" hanging upside down on his swinging bar.

The fad for bicycles was quickly incorporated into these crowd-pleasing stunts much as the horseback antics had been for an earlier age. Riding a bicycle across a tightrope quickly proved too ordinary and tame. But then performers found risky and exciting new stunts. Diavolo showed the way when he "looped the loop," a trick that involved riding at top speed on a track that rose sharply in a full backwards loop, the rider being completely upside down at the top of the loop, and then, having gone full circle, riding off in the original direction. Larger and larger loops

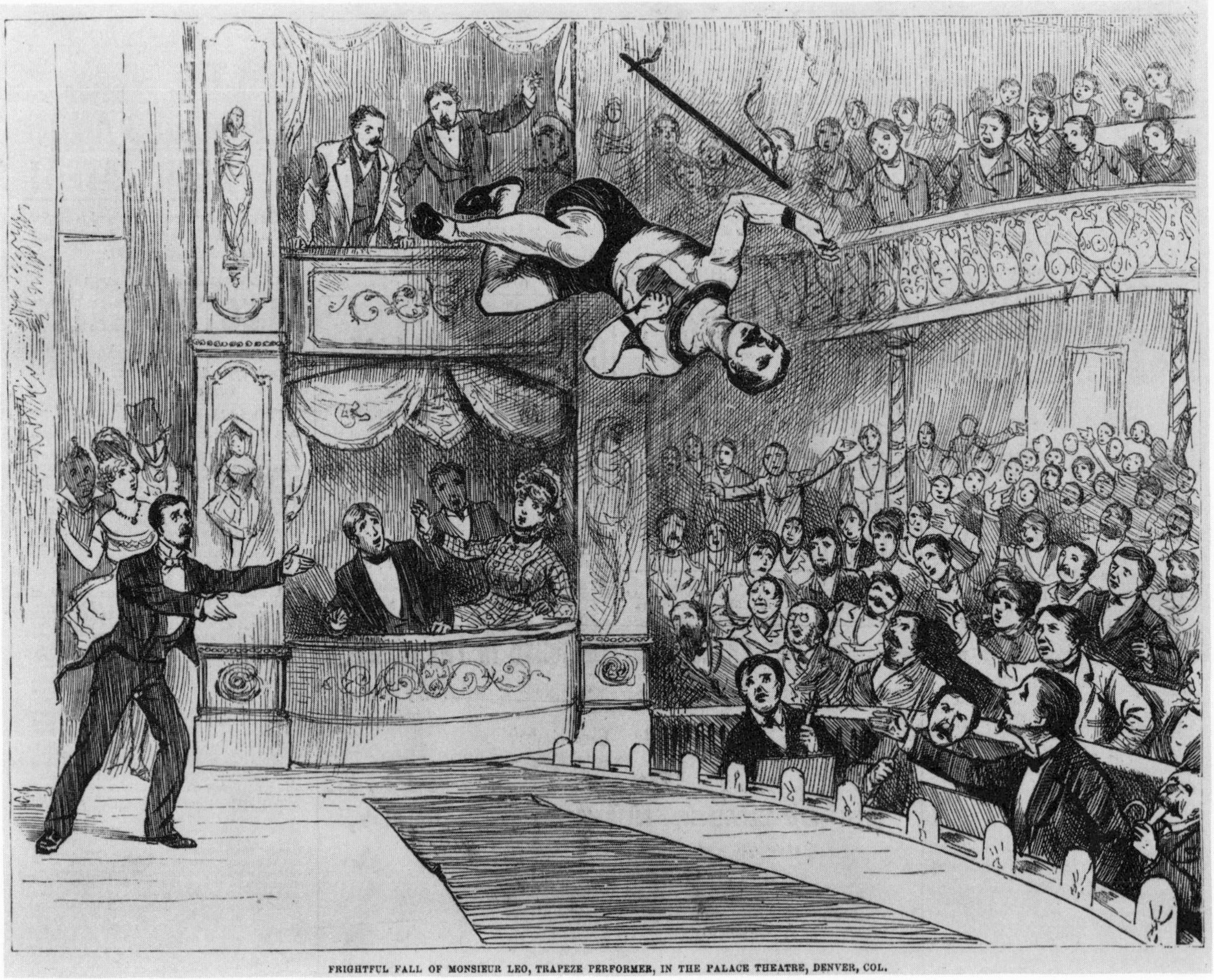
FRIGHTFUL FALL OF MONSIEUR LEO, TRAPEZE PERFORMER, IN THE PALACE THEATRE, DENVER, COL.

The prospect of such accidents enticed audiences in vaudeville as well as in circuses. HTC.

were used and the stunt became *passé*. So a performer removed a piece of track at the top of the loop and "looped the gap." The Kinetic Demon rode around the inside walls of a large barrel with spaces between the slats so that the audience could see him. Volo the Volitant pedaled down a long ramp that curved sharply up at the end, throwing bicycle and rider off into space. The Double Paradox—two bicyclists riding down opposite long inclines with one looping the gap and the other flying over a chasm and the two supposedly striking the ground at the same time—caused so many accidents and problems with timing that it was abandoned. In the early twentieth century, automobiles replaced bicycles in stunts, culminating in "The Limit," in which a car roared down a long ramp, shot off the upturned end, flipped over in a full somersault, and drove off—if it could.

The thrill of watching performers risk life and limb in "impossible" stunts and the pros-

Richard Sands, "a human fly," defied gravity with his suction-cup shoes. HTC.

Death-defying automobile acrobatics grew out of the search for ever more exciting acts. HTC.

pect of seeing performers beat the odds or be beaten by them had proved irresistible for thousands of years, which probably reflects human beings' fascination with and fear of death as well as their hope of transcending it. A great many people have also enjoyed gawking at and making fun of unfortunate "freaks" of nature, perhaps because doing this makes patrons feel superior to or at least thankfully better off than the deformed. Whatever the explanation, freakish people and animals and dangerous acts, that ranged from graceful artistry to graceless lunacy, have provided the circus with two of its basic attractions.

But the circus was certainly not just a collection of crazy daredevils and accidents of nature. The clowns produced happy laughter, whether talking and singing in the early shows or silently running through their timeless sight gags and slapstick stunts, like the tiny car that disgorged seemingly endless numbers of them, or the water pail that doused the shrieking crowd with confetti. The pageants and spectacles presented the fairy-tale-like visions of which dreams are made. The acrobats, fliers, and equestrians displayed the artistic beauty of the perfectly developed and controlled human body. And the huge tent shows that emerged full grown in one night and then disappeared just as quickly, were themselves sources of wonder.

Few people, even devoted circus fans, saw the circus go up and come down, but the process fascinated the public, as evidenced by the great many turn-of-the-twentieth-century newspaper and magazine articles that described it in great detail. Americans, as a people, are tinkerers. They love to know how a thing works, how it is put together, and how it comes apart. Virtually every day somewhere in the country, a gigantic canvas city covering six to twelve acres and housing perhaps a thousand people and hundreds of animals sprang into existence for a day. It seemed, quite literally, a work of magic. In fact, as the detailed descriptions of the process revealed, it was the result of meticulous planning and highly specialized division of labor, almost like a huge, mobile, outdoor factory—the farthest thing from magic wands and incantations. Besides the inherent fascination of the complex operation that one writer called "The

An aerial view of the huge tent cities that circuses assembled and dismantled every day. HTC.

Moving of a Modern Caravan," the story had special meaning at the turn of the twentieth century when American life was becoming increasingly standardized and routinized, when many communities felt threatened with destruction by the forces of modernization. The circus provided an encouraging example of the great potential of blending the efficient and thorough planning and specialization of the factory with the co-ordinated efforts of different people working together for a common goal. It was "a human machine." "The great circus, like all the other great complex enterprises of modern civilization," a writer for *Harper's Weekly* observed with praise in 1895, "is a perfectly ordered machine that goes as by clock-work." The working of that machine offers a fuller understanding of how complex and elaborate the management and operation of big entertainment businesses had become by the turn of the twentieth century.

While the circus equipment and animals rested in their winter quarters and the performers scattered to their homes, the managers of the show set about the critically important job of planning next season's route. Specialists analyzed the previous year's receipts and reports of weather, crops, production, strikes, and disasters to determine the economic desirability of potential stops. They also studied railroad lines, schedules, and rates, and tried to anticipate what their rivals would do and to temper their analysis with the teachings of experience. No matter what the data said, they had learned over the years that some unlikely spots were good circus towns. Maryville, Missouri, population 4000, for example, produced larger circus crowds, drawing as it did from a large rural population, than did the city of St. Louis. Using all this information, analysis, experience, and intuition, the planners charted the next year's itinerary, which to a great extent determined the show's success or failure. "Any boob can *run* a circus," one oldtimer snorted, "but it's the wise showman who knows where to *put* it."

Months before the season began in the spring, waves of circus advance men set out on the route to prepare the way for the show. Three months before the show was to visit any given town, the Railway Contractor arrived to arrange transportation for the show and to book the excursion trains that would bring people to the site. Six weeks in advance, the Contracting Agent spent only one day, ordering provisions from local farmers and merchants, room and board for the advertising men, space for posting ads, and licenses for the show. Then, he sent all the contracts to Advertising Car No. 2, which traveled the route thirty days ahead of the circus. When Car No. 2 arrived in the town, its billposters traveled prearranged routes, pasting up posters. (Circuses regularly "pasted over" rivals' advertising.) Fourteen days ahead of the show, Car No. 3 arrived with lithographs that its crews placed in storekeepers' windows and pasted over or beside the show's posters. A week in advance, Car No. 4 arrived and its men covered the same advertising routes again and confirmed the excursion schedules. Three days ahead of the circus traveled two Outriders, who checked to see that the previous crews had done their jobs and that shopkeepers had earned their free passes by displaying the lithographs. Car No. 1, the "skirmishing car," had no regular route. It carried trouble-shooters who might check out reports of floods, fires, strikes, or other unexpected events, sometimes making last-minute arrangements to reroute the show. Other times, they might learn that another circus was scheduled into a town just before theirs, and

Besides stressing the show's size, this poster includes the excursion trains that carried people to the circus site. NYLC.

they would race in and put up posters belittling the other show and urging people to wait for their truly great circus. A day before the circus reached town, two Layers Out arrived to make final arrangements and to confirm that the grain and hay contracts were fulfilled. The boss-canvas man also arrived, but he went directly to the circus site. With the precision of a surveyor and the quick decisiveness of an experienced circus man, he marked the some fifteen tent locations with colored iron stakes, leaving a watchman to guard the layout while he moved on to the next town.

On the appointed day, the first train to pull into town carried the tents, which were carefully loaded onto wagons that rented horses pulled to the site. Beginning by 5:00 A.M., the crew of nearly one hundred canvasmen smoothly, quickly, and efficiently pounded, pulled, lifted, and hoisted the circus tents into place. By the time the menagerie train arrived, the cages could be immediately moved into their proper places. The ornate circus wagons were made ready, and when the performers arrived, they dressed in their pageant costumes, and the parade began. After the colorful, noisy trip through town, which was really the last step in the advertising campaign, the circus people had an eleven-thirty lunch. The first show began at 2:00 P.M., and the canvas crews rested until the night performance, when they swung back into action, taking down and packing the tents and equipment not in use, handling everything precisely as they had the previous day and would the following day. As each act concluded for the night, its props, animals, and costumes were carefully put in their places. An hour after the finale, the entire caravan was ready to roll, leaving the town with only quickly fading handbills to remind its citizens of this magical vision—the circus—that might not reappear for another year. In 1895, between March 15 and November 15, Barnum and Bailey's Greatest Show on Earth played 190 towns, all but eight of them one-night stands. What writers called "the kingdom on wheels," the "city that folds itself up like an umbrella" appeared and disappeared 182 times in eight months.

Curiously enough, considering this constant moving, circus performers developed deeper roots than most other show business performers. Their roots were not sunk into a place, but into a process, an institution, a closed community. Their nomadic life created this sense of belonging. Because of the standardization that made it possible to set up the show efficiently after each move, everything, *every thing,* was put in precisely the same place every day. Performers, for example, could walk through cramped dressing quarters in the dark without bumping into anything. They always knew exactly where everything was. For the performers, it was as if their town had been picked up in one piece and put down somewhere else, or like different scenery had been set up around their grounds. "To the Circus people themselves, each day so precisely reproducing another in their immediate work and surroundings," a writer who traveled with the show in 1895 reported with great surprise, "the constant movement in which they live ceases to exist. They lose all sense of distance and of locality; all places, all crowds, are alike to them."

The circus was literally a world apart. For eight months a year, circus performers lived like gypsies, and like gypsies they compensated for not belonging to the society around them by thinking of themselves as superior people. Circus people, for example, had their own distinctive jargon, calling the non-circus people "towners," "gawks," or "rubes," and themselves "tent-squirrels" or "sawdust-eaters." The circus was their home and the other performers were their families. "The outside world, in fact, becomes a dream to them," a startled journalist observed of their tight-knit way of life, "and outside people a kind of vague unreality. . . . The great crowds in the tent are not people at all, but only a colored background of no more importance than the dingy wall of the tent itself." Circus people and "towners" had little contact outside of the shows. They did not even eat, sleep, or drink in the same places, and there was no time to form even passing relationships, not positive ones at any rate.

Until James A. Bailey and the Ringling Brothers absolutely forbade it, the common practice was for circus owners to sell the "grift" concession—the right to pick pockets, swindle, cheat, and defraud the "rubes," just as they sold the food, candy, and drink concessions. This practice not only meant that circuses got bad reputations, it also meant that circus people got in a number of fights and brawls. When "clems" (serious fights) broke out between "towners" and "sawdust-eaters," all circus people, regardless of the cause of the conflict, rallied to the S.O.S. cry of "Hey Rube!" They beat off the attackers, like a family pulling together against outsiders. Animal trainer George Conklin even taught one of his elephants to swing a twelve-foot tentpole. In serious scrapes, Conklin sent the pole-wielding bull "in so fast that the bunch would be piled up in heaps." Another show turned loose one of its tame lions when it felt under siege. The occasional fights did not interfere with the show's ability to work its magic for its patrons. But they did reinforce circus people's feeling of separateness, which grew out of their being part of a huge, traveling city, a city bringing the wonders of the world to the American people.

"The circus," one writer correctly observed in 1910, "has become a highly organized business machine that sells amusement and instruction upon a big scale." Nothing demonstrated that scale better than the circus parade, in many ways the epitome of the modern circus. In the nineteenth century, after circuses stopped trying to outdo each other in the size of their elephant herds, they spent fortunes mounting incredibly lavish and expensive street parades. Golden chariots, ornate calliopes, and elaborately carved, brightly painted wagons and carriages carried garishly outfitted performers, exotic animals, and misshapen freaks through the streets of cities and towns across the nation. The splendor and spectacles of these parades left an indelible impression on thousands upon thousands of Americans, especially in the rural areas where there were few shows of any sort, let alone these truly extraordinary displays. The lavish bandwagon became the elephant of parade vehicles, the biggest, most eye-catching, part of the caravan. The Jumbo of these bandwagons, fittingly, was Barnum and Bailey's Two Hemispheres, built in 1896 at a cost of $40,000. Each side of the mammoth wagon bore a hemisphere with the continents carved in low relief. Flanking that were lions and bears four times life size. Golden eagles on the same scale held the driver, and gold-leafed figures wove around the two life-sized elephants on the rear of the wagon. A team of forty horses pulled the stupendous vehicle through the streets. Other incredible wagons and floats depicting scenes from ancient Egypt to modern America, from mythology to Mother Goose, joined in this ever-escalating battle of parades, some of which stretched as long as three miles.

As with elephants, the parade competition between circuses forced an unsustainable escalation that sapped shows of their profits. In 1905, Barnum and Bailey's Greatest Show on Earth gave up the free parades, in part because of their incredible costs and in part because Bailey felt that parades had become such good shows in themselves that they decreased, rather than stimulated, box-office business. By the end of World War I, the other major shows followed his example, and this long circus tradition disappeared, the victim of escalating costs, a jaded public, and technological developments.

Besides his other problems, Bailey also had difficulty keeping up with the newest and last major circus dynasty to emerge in America—the Ringling brothers, who were born between 1854 and 1868 to German immigrant parents. When the oldest boy, Al, was sixteen, he saw his first circus, one of Dan Rice's shows, and, like countless other boys, he decided to make the circus his career. He taught

Opulent street parades were major circus attractions. NYLC.

himself to ride bareback, to do acrobatics, to juggle, and to walk a tightrope, which he did well enough to walk a rope stretched across a street to attract customers to his father's harness shop. He also got his brothers interested in the circus, and they began to entertain locally. In 1882 five of them staged the Ringling Brothers Classic and Comic Concert Company, an amateurish variety show. By 1884, they had graduated to a circus with two old horses, a couple of wagons, and a home-made tent. By spring, they had fourteen horses and a menagerie, which consisted of one solitary hyena, which they billed, with typical circus ballyhoo: "HIDEOUS HYENA STRIATA GIGANTIUM! The Mammoth Midnight Marauding Man-Eating Monstrosity, The Prowling Grave Robbing Demon."

Traveling with their small wagon show in rural Minnesota and Wisconsin, the Ringlings had a great deal of difficulty with poor weather and bad roads. Still, they gave good, enthusiastic shows and grew more prosperous. By 1888, they bought their first two elephants, important symbols of their success. A year later they traveled by railroad as Ringling

Brothers and Van Amburgh's Circus (the name having outlived the lion-tamer). Their dreams were coming true. They soon had a well-established two-ring circus touring in the Midwest. By 1890, each of the brothers had found a specialty in the management of the show, roles that enabled them to function smoothly as a team with a minimum of conflict and inefficiency as they moved into the big time.

In 1896, James A. Bailey took The Greatest Show on Earth on what turned out to be a six-year European tour, leaving the combined Forepaugh-Sells circus that he owned to hold the lucrative Eastern market and the Barnum and Bailey national circuit against the expanding Ringling show and the other competition. But the ambitious Ringlings moved quickly into the East, prospering even in the "Barnum towns" of Hartford, New Haven, and Bridgeport, Barnum's "capitol city." In 1902, Bailey returned to find that the upstart Ringlings had become major rivals, proprietors of a modernized, highly mobile circus that could exploit changes in market conditions better than Bailey's slower, somewhat outmoded show. By 1904, the two managements agreed to stop competing with each other and to divide the territory. Bailey sealed the bargain, which was a great victory for the Ringlings, by selling the Forepaugh-Sells circus to the brothers. Bailey died in 1906, and a year later his legacy belonged to the Ringlings.

The two circuses continued to travel separately in their own territories until World War I when they were merged into the Ringling Brothers and Barnum and Bailey Combined Shows. Over the years the huge show took on more and more qualities of big business, including consolidation, corporation structures, and union difficulties. In 1956, the Ringling Brothers, Barnum and Bailey Circus performed for the last time under the canvas big top, abandoning one of the circus's most distinctive characteristics. But for all the changes, the central core of the show remained basically the same as it had been for a century, as the Ringling Brothers, Barnum and Bailey Circus carried the traditions of The Greatest Show on Earth into the atomic age.

Chapter Four

SHOW·BIZ·IN·BLACKFACE
THE MINSTREL SHOW

"Our best poets and authors contribute to the progress of this our only original American institution," a performer in 1863 proudly boasted about his profession. "Its songs are sung by Fifth Avenue belles and are hummed by modest serving-girls. Brass bands march through streets playing songs the newsboys will soon be whistling." To some mid-nineteenth-century Americans, it was "the only true American drama" or the "American National Opera." But to most people, it was simply the minstrel show, the best show in town, any town. Performed by white men in blackface make-up using what they claimed were Negro dialects, songs, dances, and jokes, minstrel shows literally swept the nation in the 1840s, from the White House to the California gold fields, from New Orleans to New England, from riverboats and saloons to 2500-seat theaters. The minstrel show was the first uniquely American show business form. As the most popular entertainment form in the nation for a half-century, it had a great impact on vaudeville, burlesque, and its other show business successors. But the minstrel show also created and perpetuated negative stereotypes of Negroes that endured in American popular thought long after the minstrel show had disappeared.

"Ethiopian delineators," as the blackfaced white entertainers called themselves, claimed that they authentically portrayed American Negroes. By the late 1820s,

Thomas D. Rice in his rag-tag "Jim-Crow" outfit. HTC.

when the stories and characters of American folklore—especially the Yankee and the Frontiersman—played such an important role in the emergence of the common man's culture, Ethiopian delineators added the Negro to the cast of folk characters in American popular culture. With their unusual material and their striking appearance, the blackface performers grew steadily in popularity, touring the nation performing with circuses, between the acts of plays, and at Barnum's Museum. But their lively performances were in no way accurate reflections of the life and culture of black people—just as Brother Jonathan did not represent real Yankees, Davy Crockett did not represent real Frontiersmen, and Mose the B'howery B'hoy did not represent real urban firemen. Blackface entertainers were entertainers—not anthropologists. All they wanted was to amuse their audiences. They cared nothing about accuracy for its own sake and about being fair to Negroes. But on their travels they saw enough blacks and "borrowed" enough material from them to create routines that were different from anything else on the American stage.

By the late 1820s, Ethiopian delineators had become regular features of popular stage shows. Then, around 1828, Thomas D. Rice saw a crippled Negro stableman do a catchy little song and dance as he worked. Always on the lookout for new material for his blackface act, Rice instantly recognized the makings for a striking new number. He bought the black stableman's shabby clothing, learned the song and dance, added a number of topical verses, quickened the tune, and went on stage singing:

Weel about, and turn about
And do jis so;
Eb'ry time I weel about,
I jump Jim Crow.

The routine, especially the quaint new Afro-American dance, was an immediate sensation, winning Rice (now known as "Jim Crow Rice") great acclaim in New York and London in the mid-1830s. Jim Crow songs and dances swept Americans off their feet, or at least up onto their feet to try the shuffling dance with the little twisting hop. T. D. Rice made a career out of the Jim Crow routine that he learned from the black stableman, performing it into the 1850s. He never progressed beyond it. But ironically the phrase "Jim Crow," a phrase made famous by a blackface white performer who got rich on a Negro's

T. D. Rice dancing Jim Crow to a rowdy, overflow audience at the Bowery Theatre in 1833. HTC.

creation, ultimately became the slang word for the white-created system of racial segregation that was aimed at eliminating contact between blacks and whites.

After Rice created such a sensation with "Jump Jim Crow," Ethiopian delineators became much more popular and much more diligent in searching out distinctive new material from blacks. Billy Whitlock, later a member of the first minstrel troupe, spent a great deal of time in the 1830s touring the South with circuses. When he was not performing, he claimed that he would "steal off to some negro hut to hear the darkies sing and see them dance, taking a jug of whisky to make things merrier." And he was certainly not the only one to do this field work. Ben Cotton, another minstrel who specialized in portrayals of Southern Negroes, also claimed that he closely studied blacks when he worked on Mississippi riverboats. "I used to sit with them in front of their cabins," he reminisced, "and we would start the banjo twanging, and their voices would ring out in the quiet night air in their weird melodies. . . . I was the first white man they had seen who sang as they did." Those "weird melodies" and exotic dances provided white entertainers with foot-tapping, eye-catching, "new" material that captivated white audiences who had never before seen or heard anything like it.

In 1842, four experienced Ethiopian delineators found themselves out of work in New York City. Hoping to make some money to get through their difficulties, they decided to unite and to stage the first whole show of nothing but blackface entertainment. Their performance and the audience response changed the course of American show business. The four men billed themselves as the Virginia Minstrels, using the name of the most famous Southern state to make their claims of authenticity in their "delineations" of Southern Negroes seem more credible. They called themselves "minstrels" to cash in on the recent popularity of the Tyrolese Minstrel Family, a group of touring European singers. The accidental performance and the opportunistic choice of names both had lasting impacts because the Virginia Minstrels were not just another success. They were an absolute rage, a rage that people could not get enough of, a rage that almost immediately produced a flood of competitors as other Ethiopian delineators joined together to form minstrel troupes all over the country. Virtually overnight, the minstrel show became a national entertainment form. Its greatest strongholds before the Civil War were the cities of the Northeast, where massive audiences craved popular entertainment. For the next fifty years, the minstrel show dominated American show business.

It was no accident that blackface entertainment dominated American show business in the middle decades of the nineteenth century when slavery, the plantation system, and the proper place of the Negro in America were the most important public issues, issues that challenged both the nation's democratic creed and its continued existence as one country. The sectional conflict over slavery surfaced around 1820, and was temporarily "settled" by the Missouri Compromise. But in the 1830s slavery again emerged as an explosive issue. Led by Nat Turner, Virginia slaves revolted, killing a number of whites before they were brutally repressed. White Southerners could never forget this and other less successful slave revolts because they seemed a portent of the nightmare that haunted slave-owners everywhere. Southern defenders of slavery began to argue that their "peculiar institution" was a blessing for America—not a curse—because it allowed Negroes to achieve all their limited potential while it freed whites from menial labor. At the same time, Northern opponents of slavery, black and white, castigated slavery as an un-American sin and campaigned for full equality of Negroes as citizens. These highly emotional arguments soon made the conflict more a shrill, name-calling, shouting match than a debate, one that grew more menacing each year.

The minstrel show, in which white entertainers blackened their faces and literally acted out images of Negroes that satisfied their patrons, provided its primarily Northern white audiences with a non-threatening way to work out their feelings about race and slavery. No one had to take the shows or the performers seriously. No one even had to admit that the shows addressed important issues, which is why minstrel shows and other forms of show business could so effectively and fully address the public's deepest concerns and anxieties. But the minstrel show did not dominate show business because it was effective popular sociology, an outlet for anxiety and tension, or a kind of mass social therapy. The minstrel show dominated show business because it was a damned good show!

Even if it had not portrayed Afro-American life and culture, the minstrel show would have been a dazzling entertainment package that was right for the times. As the first new show business form to emerge out of the turbulent 1830s and 1840s, the minstrel

This early minstrel sheetmusic cover showing the performers in and out of makeup made clear to naïve audiences that the minstrels were white men. HTC.

show avoided many of the problems that plagued drama. Unequivocally committed to pleasing the new common man audiences, the minstrel show was housed in its own show places which gave no hint of being "aristocratic opera houses"; it was performed by middling Americans, focused on humble, folk characters, and featured earthy, robust song, dance, and humor. Every part of the minstrel show, from its format to its content, grew out of minstrels' attempts to please their audiences. "I've got only one method," explained J. H. Haverly, the greatest minstrel promoter, in a classic statement of the popular entertainer's creed, "and that is to find out what the people want and then give them that thing. . . . There's no use trying to force the public into a theater." Minstrels certainly did not have to force anyone into their theaters. Their only problem in this regard was to accommodate everyone that wanted to see their exciting shows.

Besides being responsive to its audiences, the show was very much like them. It was immediate, unpretentious, and devoted to fun. It was not concerned with developing characterization, unraveling a plot, playing a complex, unified musical score, or building slowly to climactic moments. In fact, it had no script at all. Each act—each song, dance, joke, and skit—was a self-contained routine that attempted to be a highlight of the performance, one that would make the audience "stop the show" and demand encores from the performer. In other words, the minstrel show tried to be a continual series of hit numbers. With no fixed script, minstrels could also adjust their choice of material to suit their specific audience, a flexibility that added greatly to their success.

The Virginia Minstrels and their successors were something new, unusual, and captivating on the American stage. To begin with, they had a powerful visual impact that riveted the audience's attention to the performers. Their coal-black, burnt-cork makeup created a striking mask with a great theatrical impact. The choice of colors was hardly realistic: Negroes are not black, any more than Caucasians are white. In fact, clown-white, like minstrel-black, are both theatrical masks, conventions of the stage. If they had wanted to be authentic in their portrayals of Negroes, minstrels could have used shades of brown. But they chose black, a choice that drew the greatest possible contrast between Negroes and Caucasians, the contrast between black and white, between evil and goodness. Besides their choice of color, minstrels made themselves up to exaggerate Negroes' supposed physical peculiarities, putting on "woolly" wigs and painting huge eyes and gaping mouths on their faces. Every facet of minstrels' appearance emphasized the differences between blacks and whites.

The early minstrels' visual impact only began with their bizarre black masks. They wore baggy, mismatched patchwork clothes and huge shoes, adding the stereotype of big feet to their facial stereotypes of Negroes. Once on stage, the Virginia Minstrels erupted into continual motion, contorting their bodies, cocking their heads, rolling their eyes, and twisting their legs. Even before the entertainment began, they could not sit still. When the music started, they exploded in a non-stop, rapid-fire flurry of frenetic motion, wild hollering, bursts of laughter, catchy songs, salty jokes, and stomping dances that did not stop until the curtain fell. Their performance seemed more a wild, uninhibited party than a professional show, which projected Negroes as impulsive and uncontrolled, even as it recaptured the feelings of the country hoedowns that many newly urban residents must have sorely missed. Minstrels not only seemed to be having a great time, they also got their audience to join in the fun until the entire minstrel house shook with foot-stomping, hand-clapping, whistling, shouting, laughing, singing, dancing people. Early minstrels encouraged just the sort of audience involvement that so disturbed actors and dramatic theater managers. The minstrel show was the emotional outlet that its urban patrons so desperately needed.

Another appealing feature of the early minstrel show was its use of frontier folk stories and heroes, especially the rowdy, flamboyant riverboatsmen, like Mike Fink, and the cocky supermen of the American forest, like Davy Crockett, the characters who dominated popular literature with their extravagant boasts and their tall tales of incredible feats of strength, bravery, and power. These swaggering, two-fisted giants, who rarely appeared in plays, proved better suited to the minstrel show's upbeat, raucous style than did the understated, low-keyed Yankee. Even though they always wore their blackface make-up, early minstrels made frontier lore part of their shows and part of show business. As blackface "Western Roarers," they laughed at aristocratic "panty-waists," challenged Europeans to fight or to leave the United States alone, and dreamed of American expansion to Texas, Oregon, Canada, and Cuba. They captured the sights, sounds, and songs of the West that were to become lasting parts of American popular culture. "De boatmen dance, de boatmen sing, de boatmen up to ebery ting," sang Dan Emmett, an original Virginia Minstrel in one of his early dialect songs, a song that schoolchildren still sing over a century after it was written. "Den dance de boatmen dance, O dance de boatmen dance, O dance all night till broad daylight, go home wid de gals in de morning." Blackface minstrel riverboatsmen sang about dancing, courting, and fighting their ways up and down rivers from the Susquehanna to the Mississippi.

Blackface minstrels also bragged about their own power and their fantastic exploits on the frontier. "Half fire, half smoke, a little touch of thunder," one minstrel character boasted about himself; "I'm what dey call de eighth wonder." Others, including "Jim Crow," claimed that they whipped their weight in wildcats, panthers, or crocodiles. Still others claimed they fearlessly sailed down the Mississippi River on the backs of alligators that had teeth like broad swords or on logs that turned into sea serpents, monsters that the blackface supermen casually steered by the tail. When one of these characters found his entrance to a river blocked by a giant catfish, he simply rammed his boat into its mouth, turned it inside out, and sailed out the other side—as simple a feat as when Davy Crockett greased the earth's axle to keep it turning. Minstrel audiences in the 1840s loved this kind of material, which glorified the power of common people as it entertained them. But such familiar material was common in the popular press and popular literature of the period, and the minstrel show seemed unique. It *was* unique. The frontier lore was only one of many minstrel features, a feature that took on less importance as the minstrel show evolved its own distinctive entertainment attractions.

The minstrel show started as a temporary coalition of blackface entertainers accustomed to performing as singles. But as the minstrel show grew into a well-established show business form with several resident companies in every major city and many others on tour, and as the shows grew larger and more ambitious, the performers inevitably had to organ-

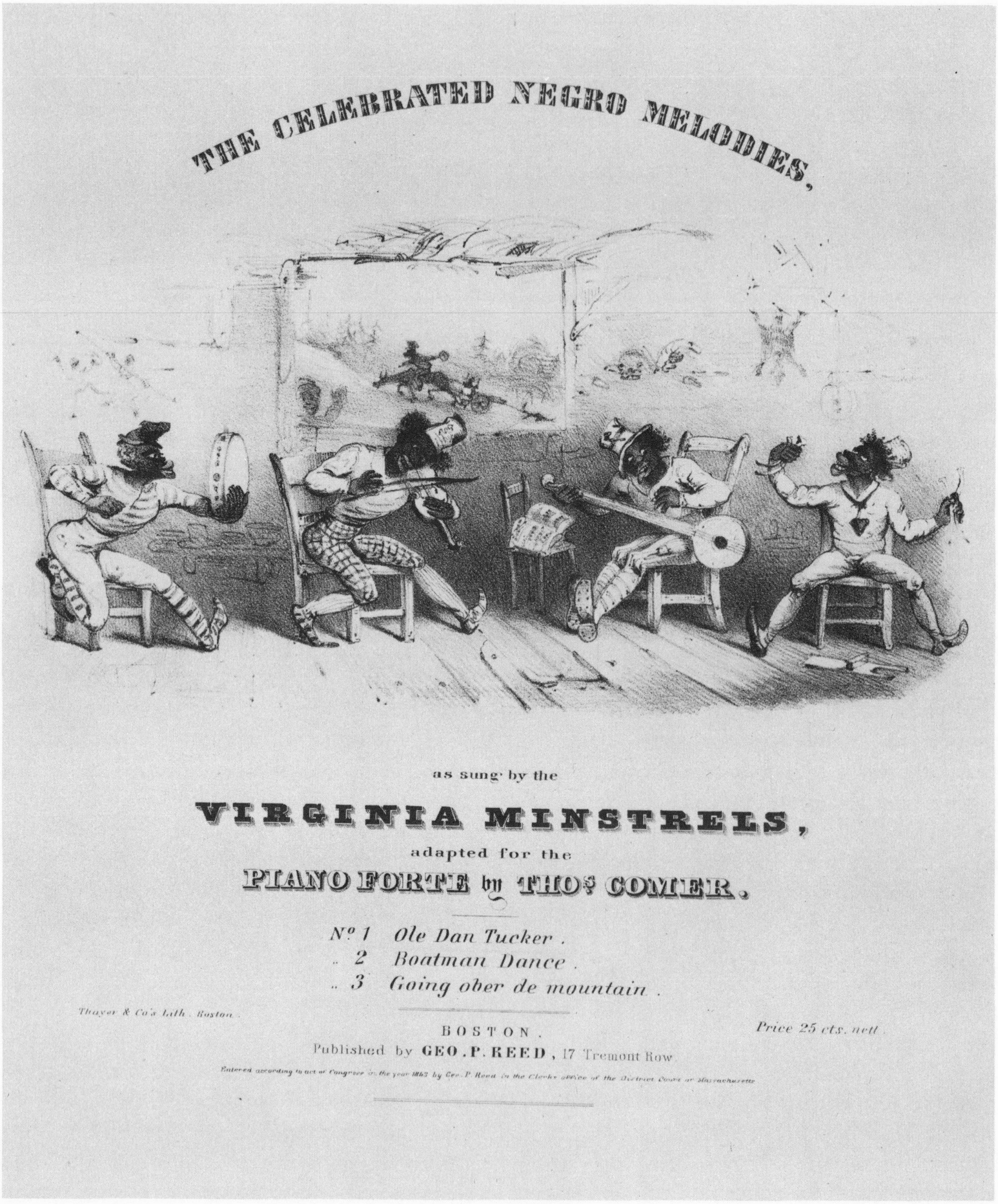

This sheetmusic cover shows the Virginia Minstrel's contorted gestures and grotesque racial caricatures. HTC.

ize and structure the shows to ensure a well-mixed, rapidly paced, varied performance. After a great deal of diversity and experimentation, the minstrel show had evolved its standard format by the early 1850s. To open the three-part show, all the performers entered singing an upbeat song, took their places in a semi-circle, and waited for the command: "Gentlemen Be Seated!" The order came from the interlocutor, the master of ceremonies and onstage director—the ringmaster of the minstrel show—who sat in the center of the semi-circle. On the ends sat the company's leading comedians, Brudder Tambo and Brudder Bones, who were named for their instruments, the tambourine and the rhythm clacker bones. Besides comic repartee between endmen and interlocutor, the first part of the show offered individual and group songs and dances, ranging from sentimental tearjerkers to foolish nonsense songs, from ballroom dances to high-stepping Irish jigs. The first part closed with an upbeat, group musical number. After an intermission, the second part, the variety section, or olio, offered a wide range of individual acts including song and dance teams, acrobats, comedians, and novelties like people playing combs, porcupine quills, or water glasses. This part of the program, which ultimately evolved into the variety show, took place in front of a drop curtain with only the performing act on stage, so the stage crew could set up the scenery for the one-act skit that concluded the evening's performance. In early minstrel shows these finales were almost invariably set on plantations. But by the mid-1850s many minstrel troups closed with takeoffs on current events or popular fads.

While the entire minstrel show had great audience appeal, the show's music and comedy had the greatest appeal and the greatest long-range impact on American show business. Early minstrels caught the public's imagination with their catchy songs, which were easy to sing and to play, songs that captured the feeling of the American folk and became permanent parts of American musical tradition, including "Buffalo Gals (Won't You Come Out Tonight?)," "The Old Grey Goose," "Turkey in the Straw," "Old Dan Tucker," "Blue Tail Fly," and "Jim Along Josey." But one man produced far more of these lasting early minstrel songs than any other composer.

Stephen Collins Foster, often hailed as "America's Troubadour," was born in 1826 near Pittsburgh and grew up in a cultured middle-class family that enjoyed only "genteel" music fit for the proper parlor. But the Fosters lived in the culturally underdeveloped West, in a relatively small town, so they were not as thoroughly "Europeanized" or as musically limited as they might have been if they had lived in Philadelphia, Boston, or New York City. As a result, Stephen in his youth was exposed to the full range of American music. From his older sisters, he heard the refined, sentimental music of the day; from the family's Negro servant he heard Afro-American spirituals; and from Ethiopian delineators he heard minstrel songs. Like a great many other people of all ages, young Foster was captivated by the minstrels' infectious, new popular music. When about nine years old, Stephen starred in a "thespian company," singing popular Negro dialect songs of the mid-1830s including, of course, "Jim Crow." In the next ten years, he began to write music and reportedly tried unsuccessfully to sell some minstrel songs to T. D. "Jim Crow" Rice. By 1847, Foster already had several romantic ballads published and began to produce the songs that made him immortal—but not wealthy. In 1848, he sold a new song outright for $100. The song, "Oh! Susanna," which remains one

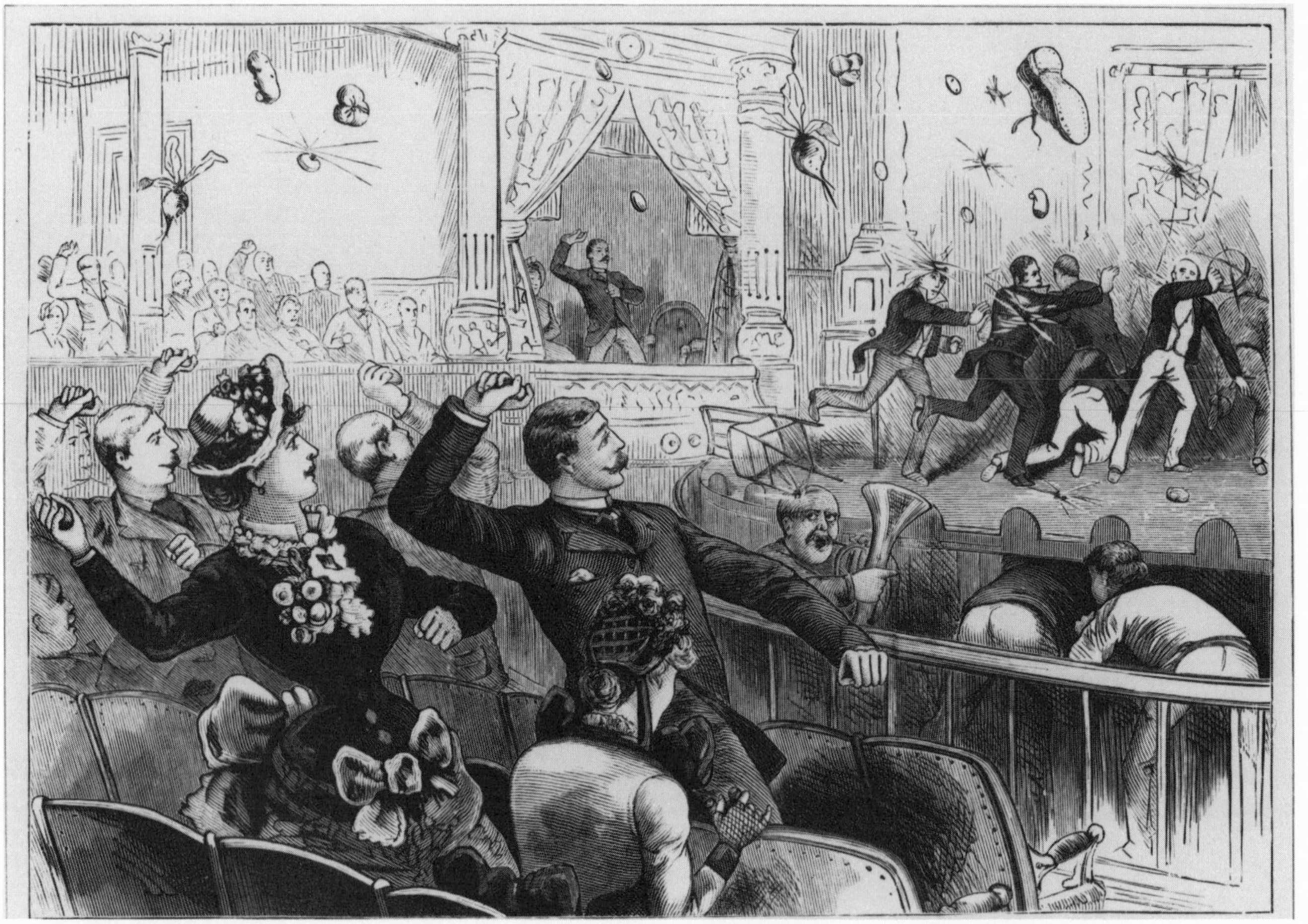

Minstrels faced patrons at least as vocal as actors did. HTC.

of America's best known songs, and one of Foster's early plantation songs, "Old Uncle Ned," were featured by practically every minstrel troupe, but Foster profited very little from the success.

Foster's own cultural values partially explain why he failed to reap the financial harvest produced by his crop of minstrel songs. Raised with genteel values that condemned minstrel songs as disreputable saloon music that was totally unfit for ladies and proper society, Foster felt that he should be writing songs for the parlor, not for the minstrel stage. He liked minstrel songs, and he was a master of them, but he felt guilty and unworthy about his taste and his association with this disreputable entertainment form. Perhaps to avoid the charge that he was prostituting his talents by writing these songs for money and perhaps because he only gradually realized just how valuable these songs really were, Foster virtually, and sometimes literally, gave away his "worthless" minstrel songs. In 1849, he quit his job as bookkeeper and decided to try to earn a living as a songwriter. Still torn between popular and genteel values, he in the next few years wrote a great many songs, about half of them intended for the minstrel stage. Most, like most of any composer's songs, were quickly, easily, and properly forgotten.

But by 1850, he had added "Camptown Races" to his legacy and had offered his songs to E. P. Christy, leader of the Christy Minstrels, the most celebrated blackface group in the country.

In summer 1851, Foster produced perhaps his most famous song, "Old Folks at Home." For fifteen dollars, E. P. Christy bought the right to introduce the song and to list himself as the composer. The song was a sensational hit and was widely acclaimed, even by serious music critics, who grudgingly admitted its merits while decrying its success over more traditional music. Elated by this success and acceptance, Foster soon tried to claim the credit for composing the bestseller. "I find," he wrote to Christy in 1852, "that by my efforts I have done a great deal to build up a taste for the Ethiopian songs among refined people" and "have concluded . . . to pursue the Ethiopian business without fear or shame." In other words, he felt that the minstrel show had become respectable and that he wanted the credit for the song that was sweeping the nation. But Christy retained his name on the song while paying Foster all the royalties he deserved.

In the early 1850s, Foster continued to write successful songs, including "Massa's in de Cold Ground" (1852), "My Old Kentucky Home" (1853), and "Jeannie with the Light Brown Hair" (1854). He earned royalties of between $1500 and $2000 a year, but he and his wife sank deeper into debt every year. Finally, in 1857, Foster sold the future royalties to all his published songs for about $2000. After that, his private and professional lives deteriorated. Foster sank into depression and alcoholism, churning out hundreds of songs to support his habit. Unable to help him or to watch his disintegration, his wife left him in 1861. Of his last hundreds of songs, the only memorable ones were "Old Black Joe" (1860) and "Beautiful Dreamer, Wake Unto Me" (1863). But his wish for beautiful dreams was met only with more nightmares. In 1864, he died a destitute drunk in a New York City flea-bag hotel.

Before radio and television brought professional entertainment into homes, people customarily gathered in the parlor to play and sing popular music. Foster's songs were great favorites partially because he used ordinary harmonies, kept his notes within the range of the normal voice, employed a firm, regular beat, and wrote simple lyrics, often using monosyllablic words. His melodies flowed smoothly along and his lyrics were easy to remember and to sing. Some of Foster's songs, like "Oh! Susanna" and "Camptown Races," represent the upbeat, raucous folk-based tunes of the early minstrel show. Others, like "Wilt Thou Be Gone, Love?" or "I Will Be True To Thee," reflect the romanticized, sentimental ballads of the salon. But most of his greatest hits draw elements from both of these traditions, blending together sentimentalism with simple catchy tunes, lyricism with rhythm, respectability with folksiness. In three of his greatest plantation hits—"Old Folks At Home," "My Old Kentucky Home," and "Old Black Joe"— he did not use the minstrel show's exaggerated Negro dialect which many people, for cultural if not social or humane reasons, found offensive even then. Such blending of popular and refined musical traditions ultimately found expression in the American musical comedy. But in Foster's day, the only musical comedies were minstrel shows.

Foster was a romanticist, writing to move his audience's tender emotions and sentiments. His songs offered escapes from the frustrations and anxieties of living through the shocks of urbanization and industrialism, escapes from

FOSTER'S MELODIES
Nº 21
OLD DOG TRAY
Nº 24
MY OLD KENTUCKY HOME
ELLEN BAYNE
Nº 23
Nº 22
SUNG BY
EDWIN P. CHRISTY.
WRITTEN & COMPOSED BY
STEPHEN C. FOSTER
LITTLE ELLA.
OLD MEMORIES.
New York,
Published by FIRTH, POND & Co. 1 Franklin Sq.

materialism and progress, and escapes from the sense that traditional values had been "lost in the shuffle." On the Southern plantation, Foster and other minstrel composers found the happy, carefree world of the "darky"—a world of innocent childhood pleasures that must have seemed especially appealing to rural migrants facing the perplexing problems of adulthood. Foster also found the leisurely pace of the country and the strong, loving family ties that seemed lacking in the hustle-bustle world of Northern cities. Loyalty and love—not fear and violence—made Foster's plantations run. The "darkies" (he, like most other minstrel song writers, rarely used the ugly word "slave") *wanted* to live with their masters, just as children wanted to live with good parents.

Foster often used tearful death scenes to underscore the strength of these relationships. In "Old Uncle Ned," when Ned, an aging Negro, fell ill, his master dutifully cared for the old man throughout a long illness. But Ned finally died and his master wept openly and unashamedly for the loss of his beloved "servant," an expression of tender feelings and emotions that many Northern men considered unmanly. Similarly, in another Foster classic, Negroes mourned because "Massa's in de Cold Ground." These songs also revealed another appealing quality of the plantation myth—that, unlike industrial, urban society which heartlessly cast off the weak and aged, the agrarian plantation society cared for them. Whether or not Foster and the other songwriters realized and intended it, they made the strongest possible cases for slavery because they linked the plantation myth to Northern whites' deepest emotional needs and desires. And they did it with intensely moving songs that struck deep into the public's consciousness.

Foster also offered an escape from materialism, with his plantation songs and with his songs of love and death that placed human values above monetary values. His songs often had a sad, even maudlin, quality of mourning for something or someone precious that had been lost forever. Even many of his romantic songs had this sense of loss or melancholy. His tender love songs were often addressed to aging or dead mothers or to fragile, weak, or dying sweethearts who were soon to "sleep forever," which ensured that his love songs would not be "tarnished" by sexuality. Foster's use of the specter of death to threaten romance perhaps reflected his own personal unhappiness, depression, and despair. But on a broader scale, combining death and romance maximized the impact of Foster's songs by tapping the deep reservoirs of emotion and sentiment.

In many ways, Foster's songs were typical minstrel songs. His themes were the minstrel show's themes—the happy plantation, nostalgia for the rural past, the joys of family life, loyalty to and love for the aged, the beauty of romantic love, and the maudlin sentimentality associated with death. In short, minstrel songs exalted emotions, feelings, and traditional values over thought, materialism, and progress. Other popular minstrel songs also had catchy, playable tunes and learnable lyrics like Foster's. His blending of Afro-American music, Euro-American folk song, and genteel melodies was much less common but not totally unprecedented. Foster's songs were not unique. But no other pre-Tin Pan Alley composer put all these appealing elements together as well as Foster did—nor as often.

This sheetmusic cover portrays Stephen Foster's romantic sentimentalism. NYLC (Music Collection).

Charles Wilson, a comic banjo player. HTC.

The minstrel show's great popularity depended at least as much on its comedy as on its music. Comedians, in fact, were the greatest minstrel stars, stars who developed many of the comic devices that became standard techniques of American stage humor. Each part of the minstrel show had its own structure, format, and comedy style. In the first part of the show the endmen hollered back and forth to each other and especially to the pompous interlocutor whose precise, pompous English made Tambo and Bones' heavy Negro dialects and malaprops seem even funnier. Besides being the master of ceremonies, the interlocutor was critically important to the success of the endmen's comedy. When the endmen mocked his pomposity, audiences could indulge their anti-intellectualism and anti-elitism by laughing at him as they did at the ringmaster in the circus. But when he patiently corrected the ignorant comedians, audiences could feel superior to the stupid endmen, who wore exaggerated make-up and continually contorted their bodies and twisted their words. The endmen's seemingly endless store of puns, malaprops, riddles, and jokes kept audiences laughing.

Billy Emerson, a leading song and dance man. HTC.

"Mr. Interlocutor, why is the letter 'T' like an island?" a typical endman asked. "I don't know, Mr. Bones, why is the letter 'T' like an island?" the interlocutor replied slowly, repeating the line so that the audiences could understand the question and think about the answer. "Because it is in the middle of 'water,'" Bones shot back. A man who fell overboard, took out a bar of soap and washed himself a shore; firemen wore red suspenders to hold up their pants; chickens crossed the road to get to the other side; and audiences howled.

This was a new verbal humor that in effect educated patrons about the subleties of the language and the foolishness of taking words literally. In the rapid-fire exchanges between interlocutor and endmen lay the origin of modern urban humor, the humor of vaudeville and radio, the humor that depended on playing with the use and misuse of words, and on cold, impersonal relationships between people. In modern American cities, people usually had only brief, meaningless encounters, often with strangers, and had no time and no inclination to do anything but exchange a few inanities. The new humor that began to emerge in minstrel shows taught the public about communicating with strangers who had no interest in them and about the fast pace and problems of city life. Minstrel comics, especially in New York, often complained about high rents and the poor quality of housing, problems everyone had to face, problems that have furnished material for stand-up comedians ever since. Endman Charlie Fox, for example, complained that when he was looking for a place to live, a cigar-smoking landlord asked him whether smoke bothered him. Fox said it did not, paid his money, and only then learned that the fireplace (the only source of heat) was clogged up. "My new place," he boasted, "does not have a single bug. All of them are married and have large families."

Dan Bryant, a famous comic, wearing the typical endman's three-pointed wig. HTC.

Such punchy, compressed gags, which became standard features of American comedy, were initially popularized in the first part of the minstrel show. In fact, the endmen who furnished local "wits" with a continual supply of new jokes were the greatest minstrel attractions. In the 1880s, for example, the advance

Billy Rice, a blustering stump speaker. HTC.

agent for a serious concert orchestra visited the newspaper editor in a small Michigan town and inquired about the prospects for his first-rate musical aggregation. "If you have two durned good endmen you'll do well," the editor growled to the advance man's chagrin. "But if you ain't got good endmen our people won't patronize the show." But even in the first part of the minstrel show, with its emphasis on rapid-fire verbal exchanges, endmen did not ignore tried and true physical comedy. "He stands upon his chair in excitement frantically rattling the bones," actress, critic, and writer Olive Logan observed of a typical endman's comic song. "He dances to the tune, he throws open the lapel of his coat, and in a final spasm of delight . . . he stands upon his head on the chair seat and for a thrilling and evanescent instant extends his nether extremities in the air."

The major comedy feature of the olio, the variety section, was the stump speech, the minstrel version of the traditional story-telling monologue. Here minstrels concentrated on misuse of the language, making the stump speech more an exercise in the infinite possibilities for malaprops and non-sequiturs than a commentary on the subject of the "lecture." The typical stump speech, a leading minstrel comedian observed, was "just such an oration as a pompous darkey, better stocked with words than Judgement" might give:

> *Transcendentalism is dat spiritual cognoscence ob psychological irrefragibility, connected wid conscientient ademption ob incolumbient spirituality and etherialized connection—which is deribed from a profound contemplation ob de irregability ob dose incessimable divisions ob de more minute portions ob subdivided particles ob invisible atoms dat become anatom-cati-cally tattalable in de circumambulatin commotion ob ambiloquous voluminiousness.*

Besides showing how foolish blacks could sound when they presumed to deal with complex matters, this overblown, nonsensical verbosity appealed to common people's anti-intellectualism. Many politicians, doctors, and lawyers who used big words and vague abstractions to "explain" their work, must have sounded like stump speakers to everyday people. While many stump speakers babbled only about frivolous nonsense, others voiced serious social criticism. One of the leading stump speakers, for example, regularly "lectured" on education, temperance, and women's rights (opposing all of them). But whatever their topics, stump speakers always played for laughs, mixing physical stunts with their verbal humor. After discoursing with "mock dignity and absurd seriousness," a typical stump speaker concluded by "diving under the table and standing rigidly upon his head with heels in the air, sending the audience into screams of laughter." (Without the dialect, the stump speech is still practiced, most notably by "Professor" Irwin Corey.)

Minstrels also made heavy use of slapstick, particularly in their concluding farces. By the early 1850s, the plantation production numbers that had closed most early minstrel shows had to share the final slot on the bill with non-plantation farces like the "new serio-comico-tragico-melodramatical negro version of *Macbeth.*" Whether these farces took popular plays, fads, or current events for their subjects, they were basically slapstick skits, dominated by stupid Negro low-comedy types who murdered the language with their heavy dialects and mental confusion. These farces almost always ended with frantic chases, flurries of slapsticks, bombardments of cream pies, or explosions of fireworks that literally closed the shows with a bang. The heyday of these skits came after the Civil War. Their greatest practitioners, the greatest comedians of their day, were Charley Backus and Billy Birch, stars of the San Francisco Minstrels, a troupe that began in its namesake city but played in New York City for nineteen consecutive years beginning in 1865, a longer run in one place than any other minstrel troupe achieved. Birch and Backus raised the slapstick romp to the level of art, playing to the b'hoys with rollicking, earthy, slightly off-color humor and lampooning virtually every well-known event or celebrity.

The San Francisco Minstrels were considered unrivaled masters of the free-wheeling ad lib and of improvisation, so it is extremely difficult to recapture their performances from the scripts, which served them as little more than points of departure. But anyone familiar with the crazy antics of the Marx Brothers can imagine what a wacky Birch-Backus skit must have been like. In 1880, these zany, unpredictable comedians performed one of their funniest farces, "Pleasant Companions." Set in an asylum for sleepwalkers, the skit had a cast that was hilarious in itself. Roaming the stage in their sleep are: Tobias Elect, a politician who incessantly throws firecrackers and spouts flag-waving Fourth of July rhetoric; Romeo Bazan, a compulsive lover who constantly gushes drippingly romantic speeches; Abigail, a kleptomaniac who tries to steal everything in sight, including the other characters' clothing; and Reuben Canine, a "Canine Hydrophobia patient," who imagines he has been bitten by a mad dog. Played by the hulking Charley Backus, Reuben prowls the stage, barking, snarling, and even biting the other patients. Into this incredible array of nuts creeps Zeb Doolittle, a burglar played by Billy Birch. As a thief among sleepwalkers, the nearly rotund Zeb tries to commit his robbery and dodge his way out without awakening the inmates, all of whom roam the stage compulsively acting out their individual obsessions. Deluged with Tobias' patriotic rhetoric and dodging his firecrackers, Zeb is wooed and

An advertisement revealing the San Francisco Minstrels' heavy reliance on comedy. HTC.

kissed by Romeo while Abigail steals his booty and his clothes. Finally, the growling, snarling Backus pounces on him, biting and howling like a giant, rabid dog in human form. The skit closes with all the characters wildly chasing each other around the stage and with the audience rolling on the floor with laughter, and hollering for more.

Despite all its great general entertainment appeal, the minstrel show was, after all, blackface entertainment. It was based on race, on portrayals of Negroes, in the decades when race and slavery threatened to destroy the Union itself. Before the minstrel show was born in 1843, Ethiopian delineators tended to focus their portrayals on western characters—the Jim Crows as well as the blackface boatsmen and frontiersmen—or on urban dandies. The dandies remained a minstrel staple, but the western characters did not. It was slavery and the South that made Negroes a source of great public concern and curiosity. From the beginning, minstrels concentrated their infectious music, captivating dance, and rollicking humor on what the Virginia Minstrels called the "sports and pastimes of the Virginia Colored Race, through medium of Songs, Refrains and ditties as sung by Southern slaves."

The Northern white public did not know what Negroes were like, but it did not welcome images of blacks as equals. As blackface versions of western folk heroes, minstrel blacks differed little from whites, something that must have disturbed many insecure, identity-hungry white common people. But as slaves, happy slaves, Negroes seemed very different from and inferior to white Americans, who, any b'hoy could testify, would never have tolerated being slaves or acknowledging anyone as master. Whites wanted this great distinction between blacks and whites clearly drawn, so minstrels consistently emphasized the "oddities, peculiarities, eccentricities, and comicalities of that Sable Genus of Humanity." Everything about minstrel caricatures of Negroes—their grotesque looks, their silly dialects, their strange behavior, their incredible stupidity, and their unusual music and dance—made blacks something to feel superior to and to laugh at. The minstrel show offered no heroic white characters as popular plays and books did, but its stereotyped blacks provided even more certain assurances of white common people's status and identity.

The San Francisco Minstrels parodied everything, including the "girlie" show. HTC.

Minstrels always portrayed Northern Negroes as incompetent fools who were "out of their places." Some of these Northern blacks were ignorant, bumbling buffoons, totally unable to care for themselves or to cope with city life. They got tricked out of money by con men, run down by trolleys, shocked by electric batteries, and jailed for breaking laws they did not understand. No one in the audience could be as stupid or incompetent as these foolish malaprop-speaking dummies. As audiences laughed down at these black fools, they also learned about city life, at least by learning what *not* to do and how *not* to act. The other Northern Negro minstrel type, the dandy, illustrated just how ridiculous and ludicrous Negroes could be when they tried to live like white "gemmen." These dandies thought only of flashy clothes, flirtatious courting, new dances, and their good looks, characteristics which proved hilariously funny when voiced by big-lipped, pop-eyed, woolly haired minstrel caricatures. In laughing at these pretentious black fops, white common people also ridiculed aristocratic whites who aped European manners and cultivation, a ridicule made even funnier and more biting by linking white dandies with these totally laughable black upstarts.

Throughout its long history, the minstrel show continually acted out these negative caricatures of Northern Negroes—the lazy, ignorant, incompetent fool and the pretentious, empty-headed, worthless dandy, often contrasting them in the farces. The minstrel show created no positive portrayals of Northern Negroes living constructive, wholesome lives—not even as servants or laborers. The Northern white public that minstrels represented and served had no "place" for Negroes. With its

George Washington Dixon as Zip Coon, the prototype of the foppish minstrel dandy. HTC.

caricatures, the minstrel show demonstrated that Negroes were totally unsuited for life in the North. Like overgrown children who needed constant supervision and discipline, minstrel blacks could not handle freedom. These stereotypes allowed Northern whites to feel superior to Negroes, to justify treating them as inferiors (if they had to treat them at all), and to embrace the myths of the happy plantation, myths that described an undemocratic but benevolent society that kept Negroes in their places as inferiors, not only because it was good for them, allowing them to live happy, fulfilled lives, but also because blacks wanted it that way.

From its inception, the minstrel show focused on the plantation and the Southern "darky." The minstrel plantation, as opposed to the real plantation, was an overwhelmingly happy place, a model of a secure, loving family home and of an innocent, carefree rural life. The Virginia Minstrels and their early successors made the slave party the central feature of their shows, which made for good entertainment, lent an air of authenticity to the minstrel frolics, and embedded the image of Southern Negroes as little more than carefree children who "tink ob nothin but to play." For these minstrel "dancing darkies," daytime was just the time between parties. Minstrels tended to ignore work just as they did the word "slave," which freed them from having to confront the tyrannical and materialistic bases of the plantation. When minstrels did refer to work, they treated it as if it were nothing more strenuous than playing with hoes. With these images, minstrels portrayed plantation Negroes as singing, dancing, banjo-playing, feasting, happy-go-lucky children who were protected and cared for by loving masters and mistresses who acted like doting parents. "He loved us as few masters do," a typical minstrel "darky" boasted about his master. Time after time after time, minstrel blacks described how well their kind masters took care of them, generously giving the "darkies" all they wanted to eat, indulgently letting them play and frolic, encouraging them to court and marry, and proudly helping them set up their own homes on the plantation, like a model extended family.

Minstrels created their most moving and enduring symbols of this idealized plantation family in the aging Negro couple—the Uncle and the Auntie, character types that capital-

This sheetmusic cover typifies minstrel caricatures of frolicking, partying black folks. HTC.

ized on the intense sentimentalism associated with old people about to die, with lifelong friendships, and with loving family ties. The Old Uncle possessed what nineteenth-century romanticism considered the highest virtues—the "womanly," sentimental qualities of the "heart" without the balancing "masculine," rational qualities of the mind. He represented feelings and emotions in their pure form, the traits so often felt lacking in Northern white men. No matter how aged these Old Uncles grew, they always remained basically dependent children. Masters mourned for their deceased Old Uncles, as in Foster's "Old Uncle Ned," but there was never any doubt that the masters had the strength to go on. When Old Uncles mourned for deceased masters, though, the old men often saw no reason for living without their masters. Many of these bereaved old minstrel characters wanted only to join their masters in death. The other half of the familiar plantation matching set, the Mammy or Old Auntie, represented an American counterpart to the European peasant Earth Mother, a matriarch who was as tough as necessary and as tender as possible. Together the Old Uncle and Auntie represented openness, warmth, devotion, family, and love. The romanticized plantation served as a mythic sanctuary where these traditional values had a chance to thrive immune from the destructive forces of progress.

To underscore the point that blacks were happy only on the plantation, minstrels created the repentant runaway, a character who had experienced both Southern and Northern life and invariably longed to return to the old folks at home. Even when freed by benevolent masters, some minstrel "darkies" refused to leave the plantation: "We'd best stay here, whar we are near, wid old massa an' de rest." When Negroes did leave the plantation, they quickly regretted it. "Dis being free," one typical repentant runaway lamented, "is worser den being a slave." To avoid reformers' charges that Negroes were severely discriminated against in the North, charges that minstrels and their audiences neither wanted to hear nor to act on, minstrels paid little attention to ex-slaves' problems in the North. Instead they focused on the runaways' glowing recollections of the joys of plantation life, weaving an appealing web of nostalgia for the families, parties, food, masters, and youth they had left behind. Some of the most moving and enduring minstrel songs were written to express the feelings of the repentant runaway, including Stephen Foster's "Old Folks At Home" and "My Old Kentucky Home."

In the late 1850s as the conflict between North and South intensified and a horrendous Civil War drew near, minstrels increased their portrayals of the happy plantation myth. It was as if minstrels were trying to end the sectional crisis by showing Northerners that slaves were happy in the South under the care and protection of whites who understood them best, and that Negroes were unhappy in the North on their own. It was as if minstrels wanted to convince themselves and their audiences that there was no need to fight a war over slavery, no need to accept Negroes as equals, and no need to feel guilty about the contradictions between human slavery and the American democratic creed. Minstrels repeatedly drummed out their racial message: blacks would lead happy, fulfilled lives only on the plantation where whites did their thinking for them. Blacks not only needed but *wanted* to be subordinates. They were not like whites who longed for freedom. For blacks, slavery was a blessing, and they knew it. For them, the fundamental American equation had to be altered. If blacks were to enjoy their

A typical minstrel Old Uncle, the most moving symbol of the loving plantation. HTC.

rights to Life and to the Pursuit of Happiness, they could not have their Liberty.

Out of the flurry of minstrel pro-plantation material that intensified along with the sectional crisis came one of America's most famous songs. Written by Dan Emmett, one of the original Virginia Minstrels, for a typical plantation skit closing a leading New York City minstrel show, the song told of a typical runaway's compulsion to return to his happy plantation home. "I wish I was in de land ob cotton," the famous song began. "Old times dar am not forgotten." Dan Emmett's song, first published as "I Wish I Was In Dixie's Land," was premiered in April 1859 in New York City. It proved an immediate success throughout the North where the minstrel show was concentrated before the Civil War. Calling it "one of the most popular compositions ever produced," the New York *Clipper*, the *Variety* of its day, claimed in 1861 that "Dixie" had "been sung, whistled, and played in every quarter of the globe." Even after the Civil War erupted, the song remained "an irrepressible institution in this section of the country," as a New York writer noted. At least until 1862, the Union Army played and sang "Dixie," along with other minstrel songs, and Emmett's publisher issued war editions: "Dixie for the Union" and "Dixie Unionized." But the song, of course, soon became the Confederacy's property. Played at Jefferson Davis' inauguration as president of the Confederate States of America in 1861, the song with new war verses became a Confederate army marching song and what one Southern writer called "the musical symbol of a new nationality." At the war's end, Abraham Lincoln ac-

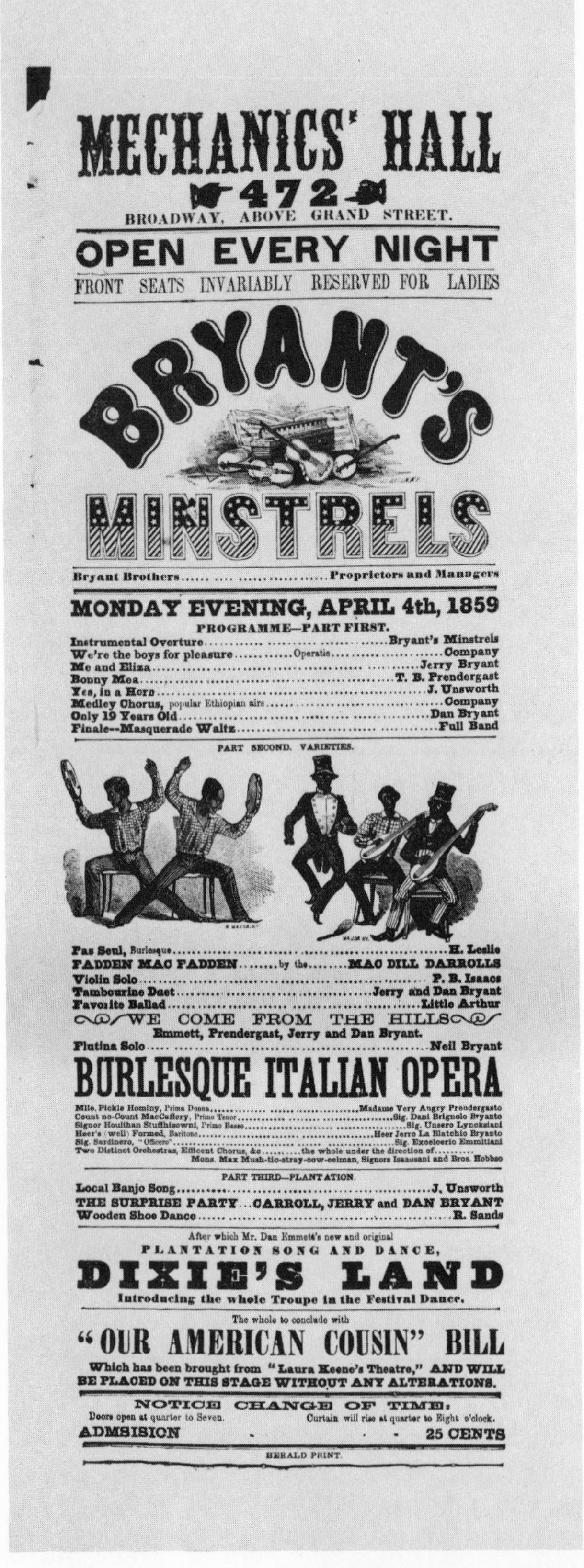

MECHANICS' HALL
472
BROADWAY, ABOVE GRAND STREET.
OPEN EVERY NIGHT
FRONT SEATS INVARIABLY RESERVED FOR LADIES
BRYANT'S
MINSTRELS
Bryant Brothers............Proprietors and Managers
MONDAY EVENING, APRIL 4th, 1859
PROGRAMME—PART FIRST.
Instrumental Overture............Bryant's Minstrels
We're the boys for pleasure............Operatic............Company
Me and Eliza............Jerry Bryant
Bonny Mea............T. B. Prendergast
Yes, in a Horn............J. Unsworth
Medley Chorus, popular Ethiopian airs............Company
Only 19 Years Old............Dan Bryant
Finale--Masquerade Waltz............Full Band
PART SECOND. VARIETIES.
Pas Seul, Burlesque............H. Leslie
FADDEN MAC FADDEN............by the............MAC DILL DARROLLS
Violin Solo............P. B. Isaacs
Tambourine Duet............Jerry and Dan Bryant
Favorite Ballad............Little Arthur
WE COME FROM THE HILLS
Emmett, Prendergast, Jerry and Dan Bryant.
Flutina Solo............Neil Bryant
BURLESQUE ITALIAN OPERA
Mlle. Pickle Hominy, Prima Donna............Madame Very Angry Prendergasto
Count no-Count MacCaffery, Primo Tenor............Sig. Dani Brignolo Bryanto
Signor Houlihan Stuffhisowni, Primo Basso............Sig. Unsero Lyncksiani
Heer's (well) Formed, Baritone............Heer Jerro La Blatchio Bryanto
Sig. Sardinero, "Officero"............Sig. Excelcerio Emmitiani
Two Distinct Orchestras, Efficent Chorus, &c............the whole under the direction of............
Mons. Max Mush-tic-stray-cow-ceiman, Signors Isaacsani and Bros. Hobbso
PART THIRD—PLANTATION.
Local Banjo Song............J. Unsworth
THE SURPRISE PARTY...CARROLL, JERRY and DAN BRYANT
Wooden Shoe Dance............R. Sands
After which Mr. Dan Emmett's new and original
PLANTATION SONG AND DANCE,
DIXIE'S LAND
Introducing the whole Troupe in the Festival Dance.
The whole to conclude with
"OUR AMERICAN COUSIN" BILL
Which has been brought from "Laura Keene's Theatre," AND WILL BE PLACED ON THIS STAGE WITHOUT ANY ALTERATIONS.
NOTICE CHANGE OF TIME:
Doors open at quarter to Seven. Curtain will rise at quarter to Eight o'clock.
ADMSISION - - - 25 CENTS
HERALD PRINT.

Playbill announcing the first performance of "Dixie" at Dan Bryant's New York theater. HTC.

knowledged the significance of the minstrel song that had become a national symbol. The day after Robert E. Lee's surrender, Lincoln asked a Union Army band to play "Dixie," "one of the best tunes I ever heard. . . . I had heard that our adversaries . . . had attempted to appropriate it," he quipped; "I insisted yesterday that we had fairly captured it."

After the Civil War the minstrel show underwent fundamental changes. Like other institutions, it felt the impact of the new developments that profoundly changed the quality of American life: the completion of a national transportation system, the westward population shift, the influx of immigrants, the rapid expansion of industry, and the accelerated growth of the size and influence of cities. These factors alone would have forced changes in the minstrel show because they changed the lives of the people the shows served. But, more immediately, the minstrel show changed because, for the first time, it faced serious show business competition. After 1865, popular entertainment greatly expanded in diversity and scope, offering more people than ever before, more amusements than ever before, amusements that included plays geared to common people's tastes, lavish extravaganzas, "girlie" shows, musical comedies, and variety shows. Minstrels even faced competition as portrayers of Negroes from the large numbers of black people who first entered show business as minstrels.

Responding to these forces and challenges, minstrels made major changes in both their format and their repertoires, changes that prolonged the minstrel show's life but ultimately destroyed its identity. To broaden their audience, to reach new markets, and to avoid the entertainment competition in the cities of the Northeast, major troupes, which had in the past permanently resided in the big cities of the Eastern seaboard, began to travel widely. To enhance their appeals and to respond to the new entertainment competition, minstrels increased the size of their troupes, expanded their olios, added new specialties, and staged much more lavish production numbers. Reflecting the general public's post War shift in concern from the South and Negroes to the problems of white Americans in the North, white minstrels shifted their emphasis away from "Southern Negro Subjects," a shift that also freed them from directly competing with black minstrels. White minstrels still performed the old stereotypes of Negroes that the public loved, but these stereotypes were no longer the focal points of the shows. Instead, they concentrated on urban problems and on "explaining" the new immigrants—Asians, Germans, and the Irish—to their audiences.

The strange-looking, strange-sounding immigrants delighted minstrels, who were always on the lookout for unusual material. As they did with Negroes, minstrels focused on each group's peculiarities to create their simplified, easily understood caricatures. Minstrel Asians, though rarely portrayed, had odd-sounding languages, ate weird food, and wore pigtails; Germans spoke "Dutch," drank lager beer, and ate sauerkraut and sausages; and Irishmen had brogues, drank whisky, partied, and fought. The Germans got the most favorable treatment as amusing but hard-working, practical people who closely resembled native-born Americans. At first, minstrels portrayed heavily negative images of the Irish as lazy, belligerent drunks. But over the years these images softened and became much warmer and much more human, in part as a result of the growing number of Irish in minstrelsy, as patrons and as performers, in part as a result of the integration of the Irish into American life, and in part as a result of the phenomenal impact of Edward Harrigan, a show business star of the late 1870s who presented the complexity and humanity of Irish life. In their treatments of immigrants, minstrels created vivid, eye-catching ethnic caricatures with great popular appeal, ethnic caricatures that vaudeville and burlesque comedians later exploited and expanded. But minstrels' blackface make-up limited their effectiveness when they moved away from portrayals of Negroes, and this contributed to the end of the minstrel show as a separate entertainment form.

In the 1870s, J. H. Haverly, the P. T. Barnum of minstrelsy, emerged as the dominant force in the minstrel show. Like Barnum, Haverly had an uncanny ability to sense shifts in public tastes and desires and to appeal to them with flamboyant advertising and exciting productions. Haverly realized that the American public had become caught up in an expansive spirit of unbounded growth, a development that found its symbols in the colossal scale of its new buildings, bridges, and factories. At the Centennial celebration in 1876, for example, Americans gloried in the display of the country's massive machinery and in the largest building in the world, the central attractions of the exposition. Haverly realized that the huge herds of gigantic circus elephants fascinated the public and that the other show business forms had "increased and enlarged their dimensions until their proportions and attractive qualities have appeared unlimited." To bring the minstrel show up to date, Haverly resolved to create a minstrel troupe "that for extraordinary excellence, merit, and magnitude will astonish and satisfy the most exacting amusement seeker in the world." His productions permanently changed the minstrel show.

"FORTY—40—COUNT 'EM—40—FORTY," trumpeted the posters, playbills, and huge newspaper advertisements for "HAVERLY'S UNITED MASTODON MINSTRELS." Haverly combined four minstrel troupes into one large company, complete with four sets of endmen, and he promoted his "Mastodons" with a flair that rivaled Barnum. "Forty is a magical and historical number," one ad explained. "In the time of Noah it rained forty days and nights. The Children of Israel wandered forty years in the wilderness. Haverly's famous forty are just as important." They at least looked important. Led by a brass band, dressed grandly in shining silk hats, frock coats, and lavender trousers, Haverly's Mastodons paraded two abreast strung out in as long a line as possible through every town they entered, bringing an aura of success, grandeur, and glamour to dazzle common people throughout the nation, as the company continually toured the American heartland. Haverly was a master of staging as well as promotion, a talent he also used to impress his audiences with the magnitude of his productions. In 1879, for example, the curtain went up for a Chicago performance of the Mastodons, and the audience saw nineteen men seated in front of a curtain decorated with a female figure of Dance; then it rose to reveal more men in front of a curtain portraying Music; when that went up, there were even more men in front of a curtain with Art on it; it too rose to reveal still more men against a backdrop depicting Haverly's New York and Chicago theaters. By using this series of dramatic openings, each incrementally building and enhancing the impression of huge numbers of performers on stage, Haverly ingeniously made his large troupe seem even larger.

Combining his sense for the visually dramatic with his willingness to spend money, Haverly created dazzling productions. "The attention of the public is respectfully called to the magnificent scene representing a Turkish Barbaric Palace in Silver and Gold," an

THE CROWNING CLIMAX
AND
REALIZATION OF TWENTY YEARS' ACTIVE AMBITION!
A Genuine Minstrel Novelty, Original in Conception and Stupendous in Magnitude, rejecting the Old-fashioned, Old Fogy Ideas, and presenting the Choicest Repertoire of Select Minstrel Specialties in quadruple form.

Advertisement stressing the size of Haverly's United Mastodon Minstrels. HTC.

1880 program boasted of the *first part* finale. The skit opened with uniformed Turkish soldiers passing in review, and then the setting shifted into the palace for a dance contest and for scenes of "Base-ball," "The Strong Defending the Weak," "United We Stand," and "The Dying Athlete." Consistency was irrelevant. The public liked the grandeur of a Turkish palace, exotic costumes, nationalism, and baseball, so Haverly simply combined them in one glittering production number. After an extensive olio with a wide range of variety specialties, the show closed with "PEA-TEA-BAR-NONE'S KOLLOSAL CIRKUSS, MUSEUM, MENAGERIE AND KAYNE'S KICKADROME KAVALKADE." This lavish parody of Barnum's circus opened with an "Equestrian Kavalkade and Karaven—Glittering Pageant—Magnificent Costumes—Gorgeous Effects" and included bareback riders, clowns, tumblers, tightrope walkers, and men in elephant costumes. With his lavish

The final refinements of Primrose and West removed the minstrel show far from its folk origins. HTC.

productions, Haverly made conspicuous consumption available to ordinary citizens, just as builders of vaudeville palaces and producers of opulent extravaganzas and musical spectaculars later did. Haverly's minstrel shows proved tremendously popular, but they barely resembled early minstrel shows.

After Haverly showed the way, it was not long before other minstrel troupes increased their personnel, expanded the scale and elegance of their productions, and became permanent national traveling companies. These large touring troupes, which played one-night stands or limited runs in small towns on the ways to big cities, virtually blanketed the nation with their lavish shows, which meant that small minstrel troupes found it hard to survive. Also, as these big troupes reached out into the American countryside, they had to homogenize their shows so that they would please Iowa farmers as well as New York b'hoys. The safest way to do this was to emphasize innocuous material and glittering productions, which came to be known as "refined" minstrelsy, removing the late-nineteenth-century minstrel shows even further from its folk roots.

The minstrel troupes headed by George Primrose and Billy West took the last step in the evolution of the show. Stressing the "refinement and genuine artistic excellence" of their shows, Primrose and West richly costumed their company, virtually eliminated the Negro material, dropped the Negro dialect, and performed without blackface, which left almost nothing identifiable as minstrelsy except the troupe name. One of their typical shows, for example, opened with the cast, wearing no blackface make-up, and dressed in the "court dress of the fops and beaux of the early nineteenth century." The singers and musicians wore white wigs, blue satin coats, cream-colored satin vests, and blue satin knee breeches with matching silk stockings. The stars wore "Louis XI court dress"—white satin, lace, and diamonds. This was not a parody or satire! The Primrose and West troupes concentrated on inoffensive material, light songs and dances, and lavish productions. Their performances more closely resembled light musical comedy skits than minstrel shows. Such productions made Primrose and West the "Millionaires of Minstrelsy," but they brought the minstrel show to the point where it was indistinguishable from other entertainment forms. It was only a matter of time until vaudeville and musical comedy absorbed what was left of minstrel shows—the blackface act.

'They have refined all the fun out of it," lamented Lew Dockstader, a minstrel comedian who kept alive the Birch-Backus tradition. "Minstrelsy in silk stockings, set in square cuts and bag wigs," he quipped, "is about as palatable as an amusement as a salad of pine shavings and sawdust with a little salmon, lobster, or chicken . . . What is really good is killed by the surroundings." Almost singlehandedly Dockstader kept the spirit of minstrelsy alive in the early twentieth century. In the first decade of the century, he signed a talented young singer to perform with Lew Dockstader's Minstrels. The young man, who had been a blackface singer in vaudeville, learned how to entertain audiences from Dockstader. But after serving this tutelage under the old minstrel, Al Jolson went out on his own, quickly rising to stardom with his minstrel techniques, his blackface make-up, and his songs about the Swanee River and his Mammy. The minstrel show died, but its influence did not. Like the Cheshire Cat in the topsy-turvy world through the looking glass, the minstrel show, long after it disappeared, left its central image—the grinning black mask—lingering on, deeply embedded in American consciousness.

Chapter Five

A Place to BE Somebody?

Negroes in Show Business

In the 1840s when the minstrel show was still in its infancy, a young dancer William Henry Lane quickly catapulted to the top of his new profession. Like other minstrel dancers, Lane based his act primarily on the Irish folk dance, the jig, but unlike others he had a "wonderful and unique execution" that made him something special. Lane, known professionally as Juba, began with the normal Irish jig, but he added Afro-American rhythms to create an exciting new dance, one that set the standard for his many minstrel imitators. By 1845, Juba was widely acclaimed as "beyond question the very greatest of all dancers." In head-to-head competition, he outdanced every rival, and he headlined with a top-notch minstrel troupe in America and in England. Critics, including Charles Dickens, groped for the words to capture Lane's special qualities. "How could he tie his legs into such knots, and fling them about so recklessly, or make his feet twinkle until you lose sight of them altogether in his energy?" a British reviewer asked. Another writer simply declared: "the manner in which he beats time with his feet, and the extraordinary command he possesses over them can be believed only by those who have been present at his exhibition." Juba was one of a kind. His uniqueness as a dancer was his rhythm, "the manner in which he beats time with his feet." His uniqueness as an early minstrel was that he was the only

William Henry "Juba" Lane dancing the jig. HTC.

black man in a white man's profession.

In the opinion of dance historian Marian Hannah Winters, Juba was the "most influential single performer of nineteenth century American dance." But rarely is he given the credit he deserves as virtually the father of American tap-dancing. He did have a very short career. He performed in the United States for less than ten years in the 1840s. After his success with the Ethiopian Serenaders in England in 1848, Lane chose to remain there until his premature death in 1852 at age twenty-seven. But his importance derives less from his performing career than from his great impact on subsequent dancers. "The repertoire of any current tap-dancer," Winters wrote in 1947, "contains elements which were established theatrically by him." Gliding effortlessly through a wide variety of steps, beautifully timing his every graceful gesture and movement, using his feet as a musical instrument to beat out complex rhythms, Lane established tap dancing as a show business feature. He was the first of many black performers to make important contributions to American popular culture. Unfortunately, he was far from the last to be denied the full status, recognition, and financial rewards that he deserved.

The minstrel show made Negro life—its version of Negro life—a major feature of American show business. But Juba, who performed before the minstrel show became a fully respectable entertainment institution, was the only black performer in minstrelsy until after the Civil War, when large numbers of Negroes first entered show business as minstrels. The nineteenth-century black entertainment pioneers who struggled against great odds to make show business careers for themselves and to modify or break free of stage stereotypes and restrictions were among America's most creative and gifted entertainers, and they established enduring patterns for Negroes in show business. The story of Negroes in show business, like the more general story of Negroes in America, is a bittersweet blend of triumph and tragedy, of joy and tears.

Contrary to racial stereotypes of Negroes as inherently musical, black people are certainly not natural entertainers. No people as a whole have genetic talents. But once they got a chance, a great many Negroes excelled in show business, primarily because Afro-American traditions and experiences prepared them well for it. Virtually all the political, economic, and civil rights and privileges of citizenship were denied to nineteenth-century Negroes, whether they were slaves or not. But in their religion and in their music, stories, and dances, black people found outlets for their otherwise pent-up energies, talents, and emotions. Over the years, they created new blends of European and African arts that matured into a distinctive Afro-American culture—spirituals, folklore, blues, jazz, and dance—probably America's most innovative and creative cultural tradition, one that proved a major source of material and vitality for American popular culture. Negroes excelled in show business, then, because of their own rich cultural heritage and because it was one of the very few opportunities for advancement open to blacks—once it did open to them.

Since early in the colonial period (the first blacks landed on the eastern seaboard before both the Pilgrims and the Puritans), Negroes entertained each other and white folks. But with only a few exceptions, like Juba, the black people who furnished white minstrels with their inspiration and much of their early material got neither credit nor money. The Jim Crow dance, for example, provided a successful and lucrative stage career for T. D. Rice, not for the black stablehand who originated it. The minstrel show remained a white man's charade until after the Civil War.

When large numbers of Negroes finally broke into minstrelsy, it was with segregated companies. All-black minstrel troupes began to appear sporadically throughout the North in the late 1850s and early 1860s, usually disappearing as quickly as they surfaced. But during the Civil War, Northern white curiosity about slaves increased and so did the number of black minstrel shows. In 1865-66, Brooker and Clayton's Georgia Minstrels, who billed themselves as "the Only Simon Pure Negro Troupe in the World," successfully toured the Northeast, reportedly outdrawing all other minstrel troupes and establishing black minstrels' first toehold in American show business. But black entertainers still had to work hard to establish themselves as minstrels. Realizing that the content and form of minstrelsy was already well established and deeply engrained and that pleasing curious white audiences was the only road to success, black minstrels stressed their authenticity as "real" Negroes and claimed close ties to slaves, which they said made them better than whites at acting out minstrel images of Negroes and plantations. To further distinguish themselves from whites, most early black minstrels did not wear burnt cork, although the endmen used blackface as a comic mask. White audiences and reviewers, who were accustomed to seeing uniformly blackface whites, were fascinated by black minstrels' varied skin colors. One typical critic marveled that a black minstrel troupe was of "all hues and complexions from light cream tint down to the darkness visible at Sanford's House [a white minstrel theater]." For at least ten years, white reviewers regularly made such comments, as they testified that black minstrels were "genuine," "bona-fide," "authentic" Negroes with "unbleachable complexions."

Because minstrel shows had firmly planted the notion that Negroes were inher-

A black minstrel troupe in a typical slapstick farce laughing at Negroes as soldiers. HTC.

ently musical into America's racial mythology and because the performers repeatedly stressed that they were untutored plantation Negroes, the white public thought of black minstrels as natural, spontaneous people on exhibit, rather than as skilled, professional entertainers, an image of black performers that endured long after the minstrel show was gone. "Being genuine Negroes," one critic succinctly put it, "they indulge in reality." Again and again, promoters and reviewers declared that black minstrelsy was less a performance than a display of "the music of nature untrammeled by art or any degree of affectation," an intuitive outburst by black people who "unquestionably have the air of doing it for love rather than money." Because whites believed black minstrel shows were exhibitions of Negroes doing what came naturally, black minstrels' performances reinforced and added credibility to white minstrels' caricatures. But they also established Negroes as minstrels. Some white critics even began to attack the white minstrel as "at best a base imitator," while "there is nothing like the natural thing." These pioneer Negro entertainers' identification with minstrel caricatures of Negroes severely limited the credit they got as performers and the range and depth of their repertoires. White audiences still wanted the old racial stereotypes. "The success of this [black minstrel] troupe," a reviewer applauded, "goes to disprove the saying that a negro cannot act the nigger." "Acting the nigger" is exactly what white audiences expected Negroes to do.

By the mid-1870s, black minstrels had become highly popular, well-traveled performers. Besides playing in virtually every part of the United States, black minstrel troupes, in the decades after 1865, entertained in Canada, England, Ireland, Scotland, Germany, Australia, New Zealand, and Java. They traveled in small, rag-tag groups and in well-outfitted companies of over one-hundred, touring in their own railroad cars; they played the smallest frontier towns and the biggest cities; they performed in barns, saloons, and tents, as well as in the largest, grandest theaters; they entertained blacks and whites, rich and poor, back-country farmers and European royalty; they owned and operated their own black minstrel troupes and became major stars.

James Bland, composer of "Carry Me Back To Old Virginny," "In The Evening By The Moonlight," "Dem Golden Slippers," and hundreds of other songs, was the most prolific, famous, and influential black minstrel composer. While unquestionably demonstrating Negroes' skill at songwriting, Bland's music embraced minstrelsy's caricatures of Negroes, which only added to his popularity with the white public. Bland, praised as "the Negro Stephen Foster," wrote of old Negroes living only for their white folks, of flashily dressed, self-indulgent church-goers, and of strutting, foolish Northern Negroes with huge feet and gaping mouths. Bland's caricature-laden work symbolizes the price blacks had to pay to succeed in minstrelsy and in other forms of show business. But for a quarter-century, the minstrel show was virtually the only steady entertainment opportunity for black performers. "All the best [Negro] talent of that generation came down the same drain," recalled W. C. Handy, "Father of the Blues," who began his own career as a black minstrel. "The composers, the singers, the musicians, the speakers, the stage performers—the minstrel show got them all."

The struggles of Sam Lucas, an extraordinarily talented, proudly independent black performer who was determined to break out of the restrictions on Negro entertainers, clearly reveals the frustrating limits imposed on these black show business pioneers. The son of Ohio free Negroes, Lucas began his minstrel career at the age of nineteen in 1869. Within four years, he had become a top-notch minstrel star as a singer, composer, and character actor specializing in the pathos of old men. In 1875, he broke with minstrelsy, costarring with black singers Anna and Emma Hyer in their serious operatic and dramatic production *Out of Bondage,* which traced the development of the Negro from slavery to his "attainment of education and refinement." This show, one of the few black exceptions to minstrelsy, was in many ways a forerunner of Negro musicals. It featured a continuous story, consistent characters, and serious music. But it lacked sufficient audience support. After it closed, Lucas had to return to minstrel shows. Later, he rejoined the Hyer sisters for their productions of *The Underground Railroad* and *Princess Orelia of Madagascar*. But Lucas again had to return to minstrelsy to support himself. Even the operatically trained Hyer Sisters found themselves performing in minstrel shows, which proved much more in keeping with popular tastes than did the

This sheetmusic cover advertised James Bland's songs in a favorable, though still stereotyped, way. HTC.

Hyers' Coloured Operatic and Dramatic Company.

But Lucas had only begun to chart new courses for blacks. In 1878, he became the first black man to play the title role in a serious dramatic production of *Uncle Tom's Cabin,* a role long considered too difficult for a Negro to learn and perform. The opportunity arose when managers of a faltering comedy troupe decided to increase business by staging the tried and true *Uncle Tom's Cabin* with the added attraction of a black man as Tom. When they sent for Lucas, the promoters told him to be sure and bring his diamond jewelry, which they knew could serve the troupe as traveling collateral. With a poor cast, including a Little Eva who was so fat that she "almost prostrated" her father when she sat on his lap, the troupe predictably found itself stranded on tour, and Lucas had to pawn his jewels to get them back to the nearest city.

Again, Lucas reluctantly returned to minstrelsy. Since his interests lay elsewhere, Lucas never tried to run his own black minstrel troupe as many other black stars did. But he played in all the best companies and published a number of minstrel songs. Some, like "Grandfather's Clock," endured, but most were soon forgotten. Unlike Bland, Lucas worked to modify stereotypes of Negroes. His old Negroes loved freedom, not their "master and missus." "I nebber shall forget, no nebber," one of Lucas' characters sang, "De day I was sot free." Another of his songs praised emancipation day as the "happiest day de colored man e'er knew."

Fittingly, in the 1890s, Lucas had the chance to participate in the shows that brought Negroes into the mainstream of American show business. When blacks got a chance to perform in "white" vaudeville, Lucas and his wife toured on the prominent Loew circuit. He played in the path-breaking Negro musicals that broke free of minstrel structures. And in 1915, he was the first black man to star in a motion picture, a version of *Uncle Tom's Cabin.* After completing the film in 1916, Lucas died. His career fully earned him the title "The Grand Old Man of the Negro Stage" that black poet, songwriter, historian, and civil rights leader James Weldon Johnson bestowed upon him. Lucas was a truly extraordinary man with extraordinary talents. Few black minstrels had the ability, determination, or strength to follow his example. And because of his independent, stereotype-fighting activities, Lucas never gained the fame or wealth that other less talented, less assertive black minstrels were accorded.

Besides being compelled to act out caricatures of Negroes, black minstrels had to suffer the painful wounds of racial discrimination in virtually every aspect of their lives, incidents that ranged from "hate stares" to lynchings. But despite these difficulties, literally thousands of blacks leapt at the chance to become minstrels. Minstrelsy, after all, was one of the few chances black people had in the nineteenth century to be somebody. And when most blacks were moving from slavery to serfdom, a chance to be somebody must have seemed worth some extra risks.

Black minstrels must have been proud of the praise they won from white critics and performers, but their greatest gratification probably came from their black fans. It was not only black children who worshipped the well-dressed, swaggering performers. When Tom Fletcher entered minstrelsy, for example, his father told him that he would never be good enough to win a place in a show with Sam Lucas, who was his father's idol. From the beginning, black minstrels drew a great many black people into their audiences. At times theater-owners even broke their normal segregation patterns to accommodate all the Negroes who wanted to buy tickets. But it was only in the black communities among their black fans that black minstrels could fully enjoy all the advantages of being somebody. There, they found places to stay, starstruck, pretty young women, and admiring people to talk with. At least among black people, these performers were important people, who could act like *people,* not caricatures. Sadly, the minstrel show rarely allowed them to project that humanity on stage.

By the turn of the twentieth century, though minstrel troupes and heavily minstrelized musicals like *In Old Kentucky* and *The South Before the War* still toured, a major change was taking place in the entertainment forms featuring black performers. In the 1890s, public interest in the plantation—the minstrel show's major theme—began to wane. But the more general minstrel images of Negroes as happy frolicking children proved as popular as ever. The scene simply shifted from the rural South to the urban North; the dances shifted from country hoedowns to city struts; and the music shifted from banjo-based folk tunes to piano-based, jazzy ragtime. Blending black American rhythms with white American melodies, ragtime was a lively, infectious music with a driving, pulsating beat that almost forced listeners to tap their feet or nod their heads in time with the tune. In the late 1890s this light, upbeat music, which later became the "voice" of silent motion pictures, proved just the right tonic for the weary public that had suffered through a severe economic depression. Ragtime rhythms, accenting the weak rather than the strong beat, had been present in some of the early minstrel tunes, so strictly speaking ragtime was not a turn-of-the century innovation. But the new songs' concentration on the buoyant beat, which prompted W. C. Handy to describe ragtime as "rhythm without much melody," was new to the general public, and the catchy, happy music rapidly swept the nation, from red-light districts to society balls. In the exhilarating, optimistic decades between the Spanish-American War and World War I, America danced to a syncopated beat.

Many of the new popular songs of the nineties combined ragtime rhythms with lyrics that ridiculed Negroes with a new vehemence. Besides continuing minstrel stereotypes of blacks as watermelon- and chicken-eating mindless fools, these new "coon songs" emphasized grotesque physical caricatures of big-lipped, pop-eyed black people and added the menacing image of razor-toting, violent black men. These lyrics almost made the romanticized plantation stereotypes seem good. In the turn-of-the-century craze for the new Negro material, "coon songs," containing what are now highly objectionable titles and lyrics, were a sensation, songs like "He's Just a Little Nigger, But He's Mine, All Mine," "Coon, Coon, Coon, How I Wish My Color Would Change," "Every Race Has a Flag, But The Coon," and "You May Be a Hawaiian On Old Broadway, But You're Just Another Nigger To Me." In describing what a "coon flag" might look like "Every Race Has a Flag, But The Coon" suggested a red cloth decorated with a possum, a pork chop, a ham bone, a banjo, a numbers' gambling slip, and a chicken with poker dice for eyes and razors in each hand. As with the minstrel show, black performers and writers who wanted show business careers had no choice but to work within this heavily caricatured climate, struggling to make places for themselves in musical comedy and vaudeville as their predecessors had done in minstrelsy. The result of their efforts was

Sam Lucas, the dignified Negro entertainment pioneer, continually fought to remove restrictions on blacks. HTC.

A scene from *In Old Kentucky*, one of the shows perpetuating plantation stereotypes. The boys are boxing, cock-fighting, and shooting dice. The Old Uncle—probably a white in blackface—provides banjo accompaniment. HTC.

the extremely popular Negro musical, a blend of minstrel shows, ragtime, Afro-American dances, vaudeville, and musical comedy. The Negro musical did not allow blacks to break free of stereotypes, but it broadened and diversified the roles blacks played, and it ultimately brought them to new heights of fame and glory as Broadway stars of the highest magnitude.

In 1890, burlesque producer Sam T. Jack's *The Creole Show* began the transition to non-minstrel Negro musicals. *The Creole Show* retained the three-part minstrel structure (complete with its semi-circle) and starred Sam Lucas, but it also featured a typical musical comedy chorus line of sixteen beautiful Negro women and focused on the women's shapely bodies and on popular songs and topical jokes—not on plantation material. *The Creole Show* proved immensely popular, touring for years in the 1890s and prompting a number of Negro shows that combined minstrel format and material with the appeal of feminine figures, a greater emphasis on variety features, and heavy doses of the new musical sensation ragtime. In 1898, Bob Cole, a college-educated Negro composer and performer, made a major breakthrough for blacks in show business when he wrote, produced, and directed *A Trip to Coontown,* a musical with continuity of characters and plot that represented a total break from the disjointed, plotless minstrel show. Featuring Sam Lucas and other first-rate black entertainers, it was the first full-length musical written, produced, directed, and performed by Negroes. As its title suggests, it was far from free of stereotypes, but it was still a major step forward. Also in 1898, Will Marion Cook, a classically trained Negro musician who had studied in Berlin, at Oberlin Conservatory, and at the National Conservatory of Music in New York, wrote a musical sketch, *Clorindy,* that also set precedents for blacks. Utilizing ragtime rhythms, a big, booming chorale, flashy dancers, and stars like Ernest Hogan—a leading ragtime composer and performer—*Clorindy* had all the elements that should have made it a hit.

But even after Cook had thoroughly rehearsed his talented black cast, he tried in vain to get an audition with Edward E. Rice, the white manager of the Casino Theatre roof garden. Cook wanted to open on, actually above, Broadway. Every day for a month Cook went to Rice's office, waiting, planning, and dreaming. But every day Rice turned him away. Finally, the determined Cook took his cast uninvited to a Monday audition. As soon as Rice entered the room, Cook signalled his twenty-six performers to begin their opening, "Darktown Is Out Tonight," a "mighty anthem in rhythm" that stunned Rice with its swinging power. The show was booked. And its rousing, rollicking songs and dances made it a success. "Negroes were at last on Broadway, and there to stay," Cook over-optimistically crowed. "Gone was the uff-dah of the minstrel! Gone the Massa Linkum stuff! We were artists and we were going a long, long way." Blacks were artists; they were going to go a long way; and they had come a long way. But they were still restricted by stereotypes and discrimination.

Neither Bob Cole nor Will Marion Cook, both classically trained musicians, could freely express their talents. To earn livings, they had to write caricatured sketches and "coon songs" that perpetuated negative images of Negroes. After all, *Clorindy* for all its artistry was only a rooftop sketch featuring strutting dances that typified virtually every black show and stereotype-laden songs like "Who Dat Say Chicken in Dis Crowd," "Darktown Is Out Tonight," and "Hottest Coon in Dixie." When *Clorindy* closed its New York summer run and its star Ernest Hogan left to join another show, the rising Negro vaudeville team of Bert Williams and George Walker headlined the show's tour of Boston, Philadelphia, Cincinnati, and Washington, D.C. Even though the "Senegambian Carnival" did not draw well and the company was soon dissolved, Williams and Walker continued to rise in popularity.

The careers of Williams and Walker personified the story of Negroes in show business at the turn of the twentieth century—the opportunities and the limitations, the achievements and the failures, the glory and the despair. Bert Williams, who became the most famous, beloved, and highly paid black entertainer in America, lived out a tragedy that revealed the torment of being a talented, sensitive black performer in white America.

Born in Antigua in the West Indies in 1874, Bert Williams moved in 1885 with his family to Riverside, California, where his father worked as a railroad conductor. After graduating from high school, Williams went north to Stanford University. But after only a semester or so there, he decided to try to support himself as an entertainer, working in Barbary Coast saloons, studying the piano, performing with a Hawaiian song and dance group, and leaping at the chance to tour northern California lumber camps with a small black minstrel troupe. The applause that he and the other minstrels received showed Williams that "acting the nigger" was the road to success for a Negro entertainer in 1893. After a futile attempt to succeed as a serious singer, he reconciled himself to learning the exaggerated "stage Negro" dialect that was to his ear "as much a foreign dialect as that of Italian." With his newly acquired minstrel dialect, he was working with a small minstrel troupe for $7 a week in San Francisco when he met George Walker. Although Walker at twenty was only one year older than Williams, the Kansan already had years of experience touring in minstrel and medicine shows. While working together in the minstrel troupe, the two young men discovered that their natural contrasts—Walker was shorter, darker, cockier, and more at ease on stage—made them a good two-man team, and they formed a partnership that lasted sixteen years.

Between 1893 and 1895, Williams and Walker performed in shoddy San Francisco variety houses and were unable to get better bookings. They even took a job wearing animal skins to imitate "real savages from Africa" at an "African Dahomean Village" exhibit in Golden Gate Park. With nothing to lose but their animal skins and their sleazy surroundings, Williams and Walker decided to go to Chicago where they had heard that *The Octoroons,* one of the successors of *The Creole Show,* was playing to large audiences and hiring a great many black entertainers. But being penniless, they had to work their way across the country, and the only job they could find was with a medicine show headed for Texas. Like many other itinerant entertainers, black and white, before and since, Williams and Walker sang and danced on a small stage at the back of a huckster's wagon to draw crowds. In a small town near El Paso, a crowd of rowdy whites, the sort of people that intimidated black minstrels and other "uppity niggers" who got "out of their places," decided that Williams and Walker were too well dressed for Negroes and forced them to take off all their clothes and to put on burlap sacks. When the white "medicine doctors" laughed at the insult, Williams and Walker quit the show in disgust and resolved never to set foot in the South again. Such discrimination deeply and permanently scarred Bert Williams, a sensitive integrationist who wanted to be accepted by whites as well as by blacks. In contrast, Walker fumed at such outrages, but he was primarily concerned with the black community and did not allow white insults to wound him.

The team finally reached Chicago and got a tryout with *The Otoroons* but was fired at the end of the first week. Williams and Walker had nothing more than an ordinary vaudeville song, dance, and comedy act. Having failed at their first chance to break into the "big time," they realized that they had to improve their act, which they did by falling back on proven minstrel caricatures. Billing themselves "The Two Real Coons," they toured the Midwest with a small variety troupe, increasingly differentiating their roles—Walker as a flashily dressed, wisecracking dandy, and Williams donning mismatched clothes, shuffling across the stage, and stumbling over his words like an ignorant

George Walker (left) and Bert Williams in their youth. Even then, Williams had a sad, pained look on his face. NYLC.

buffoon. To complete the minstrel images, the light-skinned Williams added the final touch—blackface.

Blackface—a comic mask that minstrel endmen wore even when the rest of the companies shunned it—liberated Bert Williams the comedian, as it had many others, both black and white. "Then I began to find myself," he recalled of the first time he blacked up. "It was not until I was able to see myself as another person that my sense of humor developed." As "clown white" did for some performers, the black mask allowed Williams to act differently than he otherwise could have. But Williams was not just another clown. He was a black man wearing a black mask, a mask that had come to symbolize the stereotyped, simple-minded black fool, a symbol of racial inferiority in race-conscious America. The mask liberated Williams as an entertainer, but it stifled him as a man.

Adopting the minstrel stereotypes of the "darky" and the "dandy" brought Williams and Walker immediate success. By 1896 they

Famous Negro cakewalkers, Charles E. Johnson and Dora Dean. HTC.

found themselves in New York, the nation's show business capital, at the height of the rage for "coon songs" and caricatures. In this extremely offensive context, "The Two Real Coons" got a trial booking at Koster and Bial's Music Hall, a major New York variety house. "The dude member of the team does various funny walks," the reviewer for the influential *New York Dramatic Mirror* applauded. In what then passed for praise, he noted that "the common every-day Nigger has only to open his mouth to bring laughs." With Williams blooming as a comedian behind his blackface mask, the team quickly became "celebrated delineators of darky characters," hits at the nation's top variety houses including Tony Pastor's Music Hall, Oscar Hammerstein's Olympia Roof Garden, and B. F. Keith's in Boston. On their manager's advice, they set out to build a national reputation by touring with a first-rate, otherwise white vaudeville troupe that included McIntyre and Heath, experienced masters of blackface comedy who must have given Williams and Walker many useful lessons. In 1898, Williams and Walker returned to New York and cakewalked and clowned their ways around the music hall circuit.

The high-kicking, strutting cakewalk that Williams and Walker did with two "coffee-colored ladies" was a great hit, but it was certainly not a new dance. Minstrel troupes often did it in the 1870s, and it became a popular sensation in the 1890s largely as a result of *The Creole Show,* which prominently featured the cakewalk done by two Negroes in formal wear, Charlie Johnson and Dora Dean, a dance team that became so popular that the *Dramatic Mirror* for the first time featured photographs of "Popular Colored Artists." All the Negro shows of the 1890s highlighted the cakewalk—basically a strut with a high-kicking step, a dance that supposedly originated on plantations when slaves dressed in their owners' discarded clothes and held dance competitions to win a cake that the master and mistress offered as a prize. Although the dance probably began as a black lampoon of refined whites, by the 1890s the cakewalk became the newest rage in high society circles. When prominent New Yorkers were featured in the newspapers doing the dance, Williams and Walker cleverly attracted a great deal of publicity by challenging William K. Vanderbilt to a cakewalking contest for the title of world champion and for a fifty-dollar prize. Besides such publicity stunts, Williams and Walker gained fame for their version of the cakewalk because of their unique combination of George's dancing skills and Bert's comical ineptitude. George provided a model of the dance at its best, while Bert offered laughs and relief to all the poor, clumsy people who were not dancing acrobats.

Williams and Walker emerged from vaudeville in 1899 to head their own show, *A Lucky Coon,* "a hodge-podge of nearly everything in the coon line," that enjoyed great success touring the nation's second-rate theaters, a success that made the team the equal of black stars like Ernest Hogan and Bob Cole. When George married Ada Overton, a beautiful, talented dancer, the team added a lovely woman to its array of major attractions. They followed *A Lucky Coon* with another success, *The Policy Players,* a variety show organized around a gambling farce. After two tours with another hit, *Sons of Ham,* Williams and Walker in 1902 took time off to plan the biggest Negro musical ever. Walker wanted to concentrate on the African elements in Afro-American culture, but, since neither of them knew anything about Africa, *In Dahomey* actually had little to do with Africa. The plot involved conniving Boston businessmen planning to colonize Negroes to Africa. The Boston group sends Rareback Pinkerton (Walker) to Florida to convince a rich, senile Negro to finance the scheme. Shylock Homestead (Williams), a happy simpleton who beats a drum in the Salvation Army, is duped by Rareback into going to Florida to present the scheme. Shylock turns out to be the old man's heir, and Rareback finagles himself into a large share of the inheritance until Shylock finally denounces Rareback as a fraud and signs all the money over to the Dahomey colony. Besides abundant opportunities for Williams and Walker to go through their usual antics, the plot's major value was the excellent opportunities it provided for rousing production numbers: the salvation army, society balls in Florida, and the Dahomean Village.

After great success on the road, the show, *their* show, opened on Broadway. At last they had made it. "I used to be tempted to beg for a fifteen-dollar job in a chorus just for one week," a jubilant Williams told an interviewer, "so as to say I'd been on Broadway once." He not only was *on* Broadway, he was on it as a widely acclaimed star, "a vastly funnier man," raved *Theatre Magazine* in 1903, "than any white comedian now on the stage." Williams's portrayal of the unlucky, victimized dupe was summed up in his new hit song, "Jonah Man":

> *My luck started when I was born*
> *Leas' so the old folks say.*
> *Dat same hard luck's been my bes' frien'*
> *To dis very day.*

After its New York run, *In Dahomey* began an English tour that included a command performance at Buckingham Palace. Williams thrived on the British Isles' relative lack of racial discrimination, chatting with admirers with unaccustomed ease and joining an integrated Masonic Lodge, a level of acceptance in the general society that he was denied at home. In the United States, he would have been able to join only a segregated, all-black Masonic Lodge. In the next four years, the team continued to frolic through a series of successful musical comedies cast from their foolproof formula: an exotic, colorful location; a well-trained, booming chorus; an exciting dance troupe; a choice role for Ada Overton Walker; a clowning, hard-luck simpleton part for Williams; and a strutting, wise-cracking role for Walker.

George Walker (left), the dandy, tried to take Bert Williams' money in a scene from *In Dahomey,* which showed their contrasting roles. NYLC.

Unlike Williams, Walker fully enjoyed his fame, even in racially restrictive America. "There was as much difference between Bert and George," observed a black songwriter who knew them both, "as between the Atlantic and Pacific Oceans." Unlike Williams, Walker was basically the same on and off stage—an outgoing, boisterous dandy. Dressed in the latest fashions meticulously tailored to hug his trim body, Walker sauntered around the theater districts, basking in the adulation of his black fans and keeping on the look-out for pretty, friendly young women. He also made sure that reporters got good copy from him, especially the Negro newspapers that ballyhooed Williams and Walker as "the pride of the race." To them, Walker boasted that the team's shows unquestionably proved that "it was possible for the black performer to do better . . . [than] beating the tamborine and rattling the bones." Although Williams and Walker had not really shaken

A dance scene from *In Dahomey.* Ada Overton Walker was between Williams and Walker. NYLC.

free from minstrel stereotypes, they had personally risen above minstrelsy to the pinnacle of American show business. And Walker, the troupe manager, had certainly demonstrated the ability of blacks to run their own large, first-rate companies. But in 1909, Walker fell seriously ill and left for a sanitorium in Kansas, never returning to show business. He died two years later in 1911.

Williams was without a partner for the first time in sixteen years. He fulfilled the team's advance bookings, with Ada Overton Walker performing her husband's hit dance as a tribute to him. But within a month, Williams closed the show despite lavish praise that he was "a show in himself." Williams could take up the slack on stage but lacked the talents and temperment to fill Walker's off-stage role as manager of the large company, so Williams returned to vaudeville, where he played in the best houses. But even though he was the most acclaimed comedian in America, he never

Caricature of George Walker, NYLC.

headlined a bill. He must have begun to realize that his race would keep him from ever getting the sort of recognition he needed and deserved. But he continued to cling to his belief that, without pushing himself or publicly protesting discrimination, his talents as a performer and his dignity off stage would gain him full acceptance as an entertainer and as a man.

For the first decade of the twentieth century, all-Negro musicals had played on Broadway and in other prestigious theater districts. But for a decade after 1910, Negroes virtually disappeared from the center of big-time show business, an exclusion that reflected the worsening position of blacks in the country. In the South, laws separated the races in every facet of their lives (even forbidding interracial checker games); using various forms of pressure including violence, whites took the vote away from Negroes; and lynching was in its heyday. Under Southerner Woodrow Wilson, the federal government was segregated. Race riots, in which white mobs victimized blacks, erupted throughout the country spreading terror and death among Negroes. An outburst of vicious anti-Negro literature pictured blacks as stupid, menacing beasts and romanticized the Ku Klux Klan. Pushed by conditions in the South and pulled by the prospects of jobs in Northern industry, large numbers of black people swelled the Negro population in Northern cities, a migration that disturbed and threatened Northern white men, who feared that their jobs and their women would be lost to the black "intruders." This old racial nightmare was further inflamed by the towering figure of Jack Johnson, the black boxer who became heavyweight champion in 1908, a proud black man who beat up white men for a living and lived with white mistresses for fun.

In New York, as Harlem changed from a suburb planned and built for well-to-do whites into a black ghetto, Negro entertainers were pushed off Broadway and confined to Harlem's Lincoln and Lafayette theaters. Although the *Darktown Follies'* finale at the Lafayette was good enough that Florenz Ziegfeld bought it for his *Follies,* for example, the black cast did not go with it. As early as 1898, white critics railed against "the all pervading negro" dominating show business. It was not just their presence as entertainers that bothered critics, it was that blacks were breaking away from stereotypes. "If they were content to be 'darkies' with an exhibition of the rhythmic charm which made the 'darky' fascinating, one might endure them," a critic explained. But, spurred on by applause, they "do white sketch acts." In other words, as stereotyped as many of these early twentieth-century shows now seem, they then seemed threatening. Negroes seemed to be stepping "out of their places." A Washington, D.C., theater manager, for example, swore he would never again book Williams and Walker, even though they filled his theater every night, because the black people who flocked to see them demanded to sit with whites. Where would it end? In the bedroom and the nursery, of course. The worst part of the Negro's prominence in show business, an 1898 critic thought, was "the growing commonness of the intermingling of the races, which cannot but end in results that will be extensively discussed in medical publications." Such bias, which was centuries old in America, re-emerged in the North when the black population in Northern cities strikingly increased, and when Negro stars emerged, stars who seemed to represent the first evidence that black people would no longer remain content with inferior positions.

In 1900, a violent race riot exploded in

Caricature of Bert Williams, NYLC.

New York after a black criminal killed a white policeman. White mobs, with the apparent approval and even encouragement of the police, ravaged the black community, the mobs reportedly singling out Negro entertainers by calling out: "get Ernest Hogan, and Williams and Walker and Cole and Johnson." As in the Astor Place Riot of 1849, show business seemed important enough to fight over, but now the b'hoys struck at "uppity niggers" instead of upper-class white aristocrats. In the riot, Ernest Hogan was so badly beaten that he had to leave his show. George Walker escaped injury only by hiding all night in a dark cellar.

When *In Dahomey* opened on Broadway in 1903, some people feared a "race war." But it did not erupt. Violence did not drive Negroes off Broadway, nor did the b'hoys. Bias, insidious invisible bias and middle-class financiers and producers did. Although the exclusion was not a single, sudden event, 1910 can be pinpointed as the critical date. By that time illness had claimed Bob Cole, Ernest Hogan, and George Walker, all of whom were also businessmen and troupe managers with influence and successful "track records" that probably could have commanded bookings and financing. Also in 1910, Bert Williams signed as the first Negro to perform in the *Ziegfeld Follies*. The last black star with the reputation to carry a whole show was gone, and with him went producers' most compelling reason to keep presenting Negro musicals—money. In the absence of these major figures and in the North's mounting racial tension, show business, like the city, became ghettoized.

But for Bert Williams personally the years after 1910 were years of professional triumph. The *Follies* proved an excellent vehicle for him. Released from Walker's emphasis on the exotic and the African and on the contrast between stereotyped black "dandies and darkies," Williams was freer to do material with a universal appeal, material that at times transcended blackface stereotypes, as did his down-and-out lodger who complained about his landlady's clever and persistent efforts to collect the rent he could not pay. More often, he played conventional "Negro" roles that fell within traditional caricatures—porters, cab-drivers, crap-shooters, and poker-players—but the humanity of his characterizations and the artistry of his comic techniques came through better in the *Follies* than anywhere else. They probably gained impact because he was in an otherwise all-white cast, and was on stage for only short times amid beautiful production numbers, which made his understatement and economy of movement all the more effective. In any case, Bert Williams was great for the *Follies,* and the *Follies* was great for Bert Williams. One critic began his rave review of the 1914 *Follies* by itemizing the seven major attractions. The first six were shapely women. The seventh was Bert Williams. "He is a real artist. Every year his work improves," the critic raved. "He is no accident or racial freak. He is, of course, gifted to a rare degree with the comic spirit." Williams was finally receiving his long-overdue recognition as a performing genius. "Bert Williams is the Mark Twain of his color," wrote prominent Chicago critic Ashton Stevens after he saw Williams in the *Follies of 1910*. "His was kindly, infectious humor, humor that made humans of us all."

"The sight of other people in trouble is nearly always funny," Williams philosophized about the appeal of his humor in an article "The Comic Side of Trouble." "Nearly all of my successful songs have been based on the idea that I am getting the worst of it. I am 'The Jonah Man,' the man who, even if it rained soup, would be found with a fork in his hand and no spoon in sight." The key to getting people to laugh at troubles, he felt, was not just to pile woes on a victim but to have the victim tell the story so the audience could see that he was unharmed while picturing him "fielding flatirons with his head, carrying large bulldogs by the seat of his pants, and picking the bare bones of the chicken while his wife's relations eat the breasts, and so forth." Williams based his routines on his race, as great artists often base their material on their own experience and of those of their intimate friends and relations. But like other true artists he aimed for the universal.

The tragedy of Bert Williams was not that his use of blackface and his slow-witted, sad-sack "darky" character perpetuated minstrel stereotypes. Hundreds, if not thousands, of others did that. The tragedy was that his black mask and his black characters kept him from achieving his true greatness. All great entertainers have an intangible, indescribable quality that raises them far above others. Williams had it. He was a great comedian. "Whatever sense of timing I have," Eddie Cantor wrote in tribute to his partner in the *Ziegfeld Follies,* "I learned from him." At times his talent shone through the blackface and the caricatures. But because he depicted black characters who many whites thought were naturally clowns, much of his audience must have laughed at him, not with him, giving him credit for neither his artistry nor his humanity.

"Bert Williams is the funniest man I ever saw," observed W. C. Fields, another of his compatriots in the *Follies,* "and the saddest man I ever knew." Even when he was acclaimed as a great artist, Williams never felt accepted as a man, never felt he had a "place," a respectable, honorable place, in America. As a West Indian, he did not feel part of black America as George Walker did. (He reportedly preferred the company of his West Indian chauffeur to all other blacks except his beloved wife.) And, except for a very few whites, he felt unwanted and rejected by the general society. He was very sensitive to and deeply hurt by the discrimination and prejudice that he encountered even after he had proved himself as a performer and as a person. On one occasion when he was a *Follies* star, for example, he was allowed to live in a New York luxury hotel only if he promised to use nothing but the back elevator. One New Year's Eve when most of the cast headed for parties, he and Eddie Cantor went back to the hotel. As Cantor left to pick up food from a restaurant and Williams headed for the back door, the two men—Cantor, who had risen from an impoverished Jewish ghetto, and Williams, who was condemned to live in a black one—exchanged silent looks, acknowledging the pain. Finally Williams spoke: "It wouldn't be so bad, Eddie, if I didn't still hear the applause ringing in my ears."

Having achieved great success with the *Ziegfeld Follies* and still being restricted to back doors, Williams must have realized, even if only subconsciously, that his talent on stage would never win him acceptance off stage, that the applause for him would ring only in the theater, that in America he would always be a "nigger." Subject to chronic depression and heavy drinking in his private life and perhaps still clinging to his belief that his talent could gain him acceptance, Williams drove himself compulsively, performing at every chance he got. It was as if, being denied the personal acceptance he so desperately needed, he took refuge in "the other person" he discovered when he first blacked up, a person that in racially prejudiced America gained him acceptance, made the applause ring. All this sensitive human being found off stage were

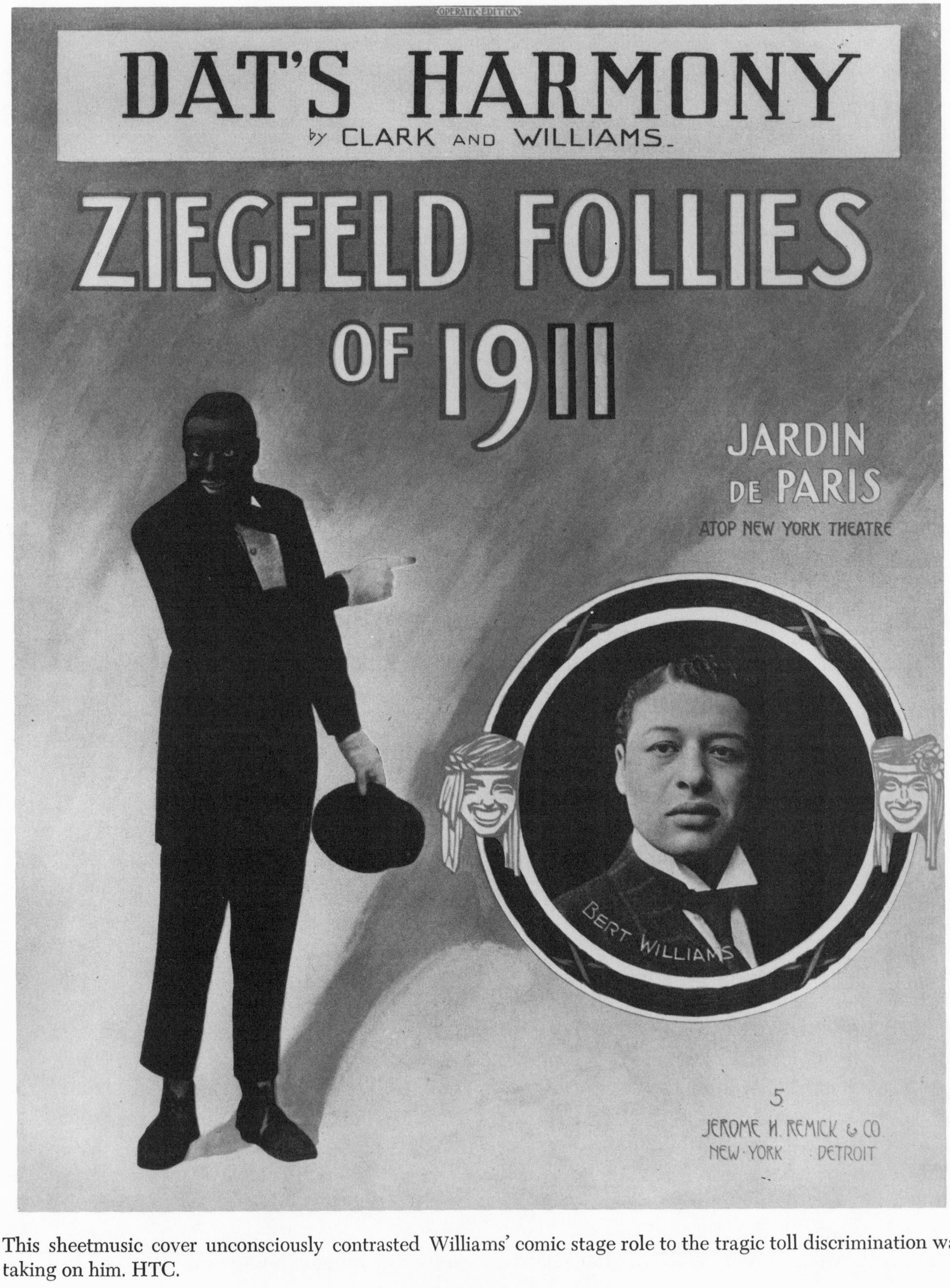

This sheetmusic cover unconsciously contrasted Williams' comic stage role to the tragic toll discrimination was taking on him. HTC.

"for whites only" signs—if not on public facilities then in the public's eyes.

Williams worked himself to death, trying to humanize "the other person" and the people who laughed at him. Even though he was ill in 1918, he performed in both Ziegfeld's *Midnight Frolics* and at the Palace Theatre. He had to take a week off at a sanitorium, but early the next year he was starring in vaudeville and playing in the *Frolics,* doing two shows a day and one at midnight. Again, he ended up in a sanitorium. But he was soon back at work, demanding and getting more stage time in the *Follies of 1919*. Still unsatisfied, he financed his own revue, *Broadway Brevities.* By late 1921, Williams grew weaker but drove himself harder. In early 1922, he began rehearsal for a starring role in a new comedy, *Under The Bamboo Tree,* in which he was the only Negro. Even after he contracted pneumonia, he insisted on continuing with the show. On February 25, 1922, after struggling through a matinee, Williams collapsed halfway through an evening performance. In a week he was dead. Lying in state, he prominently wore his Masonic medallion, his one symbol of interracial acceptance—the fruit of a short trip to England almost twenty years before.

"Bert Williams found prosperity and success in the theatre, but his high talents were largely wasted," wrote journalist Heywood Broun in a thoughtful, sensitive obituary. "His death merely masked the end of the tragedy." Broun felt that Williams' greatest gift was as a storyteller but that prejudice dictated that "since he was a Negro he must be funny." He had to do racial humor. He could not have used the clown-white mask. And unlike Cantor, Jolson, and others, who could shed their blackface, Williams could not shed his. "The burnt cork," Broun movingly concluded, "weighed him down. It smothered what may have been genius." And it killed what definitely was a sensitive human being. His own greatest hit, "Nobody," provides perhaps his best epitaph:

When life seems full of clouds and rain,
And I am full of nothin' but pain,
Who soothes my thumpin', bumpin' brain?
Nobody!

In the 1920s—the Jazz Age—many upper-class, society whites went "slumming" to Harlem nightclubs to hear black musicians play "watered-down," popularized jazz and to see black dancers perform the new Afro-American dance crazes—the Charleston, Truckin', the Shimmy, the Black Bottom, and the Lindy Hop. But for each of these privileged "slummers," thousands of common people saw and heard much the same things in a new wave of Negro musicals that introduced the general public to the black music and dances that now symbolize the twenties. In 1920, Noble Sissle and Eubie Blake, a singing and piano playing duo, and Flourney E. Miller and Aubrey Lyles, a comedy-dancing act, combined to write a new Negro musical comedy, *Shuffle Along*, the show that ultimately brought large numbers of black entertainers back to Broadway. Both teams, having toured successfully on "white" vaudeville circuits, understood how to adapt Afro-American culture to white tastes, as the popularity of their show and its numerous black successors demonstrated.

Even though Miller, Lyles, Sissle, and Blake were established vaudeville artists, they had to fight long and hard to get their own musical financed and booked. They got the money to begin from Al Mayer, a white booking agent they knew and trusted. But after putting the show together, they lacked the

Flourney E. Miller (left) and Aubrey Lyles in a slapstick scene from *Shuffle Along*. NYLC.

money to get to their first booking, and Mayer had to sell half of his share in the show for ticket money. Even after the show drew well in black areas, white promoters were still unwilling to book it into "white" houses, so the troupe began a tour of one-night stands in New Jersey and Pennsylvania trying to prove that it could attract white audiences. Lacking the money for effective advance agents, the troupe drew good reviews but poor crowds because local people did not hear about the show until after it had left town. But *Shuffle Along* survived, returning to New York to open in a broken-down musical hall on 63rd Street—a step downtown from Harlem but still far short of the Broadway theater district.

Once *Shuffle Along* opened, it no longer shuffled along. It galloped! The show's flimsy, unimportant plot centers on a three-man race for mayor of Jimtown. Two of the candidates, Miller and Lyles, are crooked partners in a grocery business, each promising to appoint the other chief of police if he wins. The two shifty men win and begin exploiting their positions, but the reform candidate soon unseats them, and goodness triumphs. The humor relies on the minstrel show's caricatured dialect, rollicking slapstick, and empty-headed, convoluted misuse of words, a humor made familiar to modern audiences by the *Amos n' Andy* show, for which Flourney E. Miller wrote in the 1930s. But what made *Shuffle Along* so successful was not its ordinary plot, nor its familiar, though popular, stereotyped humor. It was the show's new attractions that dazzled audiences. Eubie Blake, a ragtime master and a fine composer, produced a jazzy score that included "I'm Just Wild About Harry," "Love Will Find a Way," "Shuffle Along," "Gipsy Blues," and "If You Haven't Been Vamped By A Brown Skin, You Haven't Been Vamped At All." Even more sensational than the music were the dances, a virtual sampler of the dances that had long been featured on the black vaudeville circuit but were still new to most whites: time-steps, buck and wings, soft shoes, rapid-fire tapping, flips, somersaults, twisting shimmies—dances that were performed with a vitality that left audiences breathless. "The dancing, both by chorus and individuals," a typical critic applauded, "goes with tremendous speed and precision and the shuffling, buck-and-wing and acrobatic numbers left their participants exhausted at the finish." After *Shuffle Along*, "all stage dancing," a New York critic observed, "under-

Noble Sissle, Eubie Blake, Flourney E. Miller, and Aubrey Lyles (l-r), creators and stars of *Shuffle Along*. NYLC.

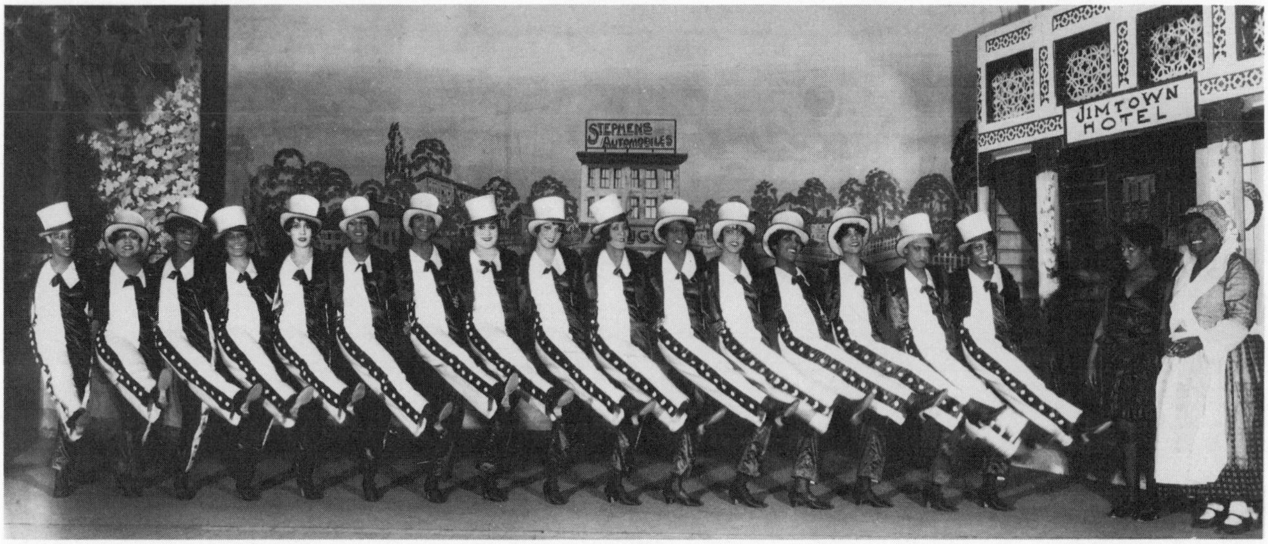

Chorus line from *Shuffle Along* with a smiling "mammy" enjoying the scene. Josephine Baker, later a great star in Europe, was sixth from the right in the chorus. NYLC.

went a change—steps became more intricate, daring, perilous." With its foot-tapping music, its wacky comedy, and its dazzling dances, the show literally burst with explosive energy. *Shuffle Along* revitalized musical comedy in the twenties much as George M. Cohan had done in the first decade of the twentieth century when he brought the vitality of vaudeville to the musical stage. Word quickly spread about the exciting new show, and such throngs of people choked its 63rd Street Theatre that the New York City traffic commissioner had to make 63rd Street a one-way street to keep traffic moving.

Despite its great critical and financial success in New York, the show still had difficulty getting bookings for a tour in 1922. Producers considered New York and the show to be freaks and felt that the black show would not draw well on the road. Finally, the show got booked into a Boston theater for the last two weeks in August, when, Sissle recalled, "nobody else wanted it because of the stifling heat and no business." Even in the pre-air-conditioning summer heat, the show drew full crowds, stretching the two weeks into four months. Yet, to book another theater—and a rundown burlesque house at that—they had to go all the way to Chicago. Again, *Shuffle Along* defied white producers' skepticism, drawing full houses in Chicago and then triumphantly touring to Milwaukee, St. Louis, Indianapolis, Cincinnati, Pittsburgh, Philadelphia, and Atlantic City. In 1923, Miller and Lyles left to work on a new show of their own, but Sissle and Blake, after a little rest, continued to tour with the show. Two other road companies performed *Shuffle Along* until 1924, making it the first Negro musical to play first-rate theaters from coast to coast, something even Williams and Walker never achieved. Its great success made many producers and financiers, for whom dollars overcame discrimination, eager to mount Negro musicals.

Between 1921 and 1924, while *Shuffle Along* delighted the nation's audiences, at least eight Negro musicals opened *downtown* in New York, hoping to cash in on the public's interest in upbeat, quick-stepping, jazzy black performances. In 1923, Miller and Lyles came out with their own show, *Runnin' Wild,* which first made "The Charleston," the song and the dance, popular with the white public. It also featured the complex rhythms generated by the chorus clapping its hands and tapping its feet on different beats while the band played the jazz arrangement. The following year, the show *Dinah* gave the public the second most popular dance rage of the decade, the Black Bottom. When an all-white show, *Go Go,* tried in 1923 to exploit the rage for jazz music and Afro-American dances, critics panned it as "a white edition of *Shuffle Along,*" much as reviewers in the 1870s ridiculed white minstrels for being inferior to black minstrels at doing Negro material. When Sissle and Blake decided in 1924 to do a new show, *Chocolate Dandies,* they had none of their earlier problems with financing or bookings. "We played deluxe houses," Blake recalled, "and were booked by William Morris—the fight we had to get *Shuffle Along* on the road seemed like a bad dream."

In the 1920s, Negroes also made some significant gains in serious drama. After Charles Gilpin, who had suffered years of frustration trying to support himself as a serious actor, starred in Eugene O'Neill's tragedy *Emperor Jones,* other black actors, like Paul Robeson, Jules Bledsoe, and Richard B. Harrison, landed starring roles in major dramatic productions. But for every black entertainer who made it into the mainstream of show business, even at the height of the 1920s fad for Negro performers, many other languished in the poor-paying, low-status black theater and vaudeville circuits that emerged in the black ghettoes in the early twentieth century. At the top of black

A scene from the integrated musical *Lula Belle,* portraying white "slummers" in a black night club. HTC.

Bill "Bojangles" Robinson in action. HTC.

show business stood the Theatre Owners Bookers Association, T.O.B.A., which black performers called "Tough on Black Artists," or in Dewey "Pigmeat" Markham's words: "Tough On Black Asses." It brought order as well as exploitation to this growing business, booking shows to tour the circuit of member theaters, as the Frohmans, Klaw and Erlanger's Syndicate did with popular "white" plays and the Scribner and other "wheels" did with burlesque shows. Virtually every great black entertainer spent some time on the brutally competitive T.O.B.A. circuit where only the best acts survived. Some excellent performers, like Pigmeat Markham and Moms Mabley, spent virtually their entire careers on what later became known as "the chitlin' circuit." Others moved from an internship there to the center of show business. For Negroes as a group, show business made very little impact, but for individuals even the narrowly limited opportunities meant a chance at fame and wealth.

In the late 1920s when white audiences were fascinated with black singing and dancing, a talented black dancer rose from T.O.B.A. to the high pay and high status of Broadway and then Hollywood. Bill "Bojangles" Robinson may not have been the best dancer in the black entertainment world. (Many people who saw all of them considered Robinson inferior to King Rastus.) But once white audiences got a good look at Robinson, they were enthralled. He not only knew how to dance, he also knew how to entertain, lessons he had learned in a long, difficult struggle to stardom. Born in Richmond, Virginia, in 1878, Robinson began performing as a young boy, dancing for fifty cents a night as a "pick" (short for picaninny). (It was common at the turn of the century for white performers to hire talented black children to sing and dance in "pick" choruses, lively cute groups that ensured the act dynamic openings, strong finishes, and hearty applause—another example of the blatant way blacks were exploited in show business.) At age twelve Robinson toured in *The South Before the War,* a typical late-nineteenth-century minstrelized plantation musical. He slowly worked his way up in black show business and finally became one of the few blacks who performed solo on the prominent Keith vaudeville circuit. While he was still an "unknown," Robinson perfected the routines that later made him famous, including his stair dance, in which he tapped his way up and down a staircase. He "didn't change his style for sixty years," one of his old friends boasted of him. "He didn't need to." Yet, he became famous only after his fiftieth birthday, only after black performers had become a popular fad.

In the late 1920s, white critics and audiences finally discovered Robinson, when he performed in a number of typical Negro musicals, *Blackbirds of 1928, Keep Shufflin', Deep Harlem, Hot Rhythm,* and *Brown Buddies.* "He croons with his feet and laughs with them," a critic marveled at his performance in *Brown Buddies.* Skilled in playing to audiences after years on the cutthroat black circuit, Robinson focused audiences' attention on his dances by talking to his feet as he moved, "coaxing them to do the impossible," a reviewer observed. "When they obey him, as they always do, he beams with delight." In effect, he gave white critics, audiences, and performers lessons in the artistry of tap-dancing, as William Henry "Juba" Lane had done almost a century before. Robinson's fluid movement, his grace, and his total control of every movement finally brought him success. But the show business limitations on black performers kept him from fully expressing his talent and from taking his rightful place as one of the few truly great dancers in American show business history. While Fred Astaire continually developed his dancing and his cultured, debonair image, Bill Robinson's career culminated with his stereotyped film roles as the servile foil to Shirley Temple. Robinson's great skill, his long wait for a chance, and his stereotyped roles, all typified the history of Negroes in show business.

Theresa Gardella as Aunt Jemima in *Scandals of 1919.* The mammy was an enduring image of blacks in American popular culture. HTC.

Black performers had come a long, long way from the days when they were narrowly restricted to minstrel caricatures. Individuals had become famous stars, had broadened stage images of Negroes, and had made remarkable contributions to American show business. But for all the gains, all the progress, all the achievements, the stereotypes and restrictions persisted. Long after the minstrel show was gone as an entertainment form, it strongly influenced Negro performers just as it did American popular culture. As the decade of the 1920s, the golden age for black performers, ended, the Negro roles that carried over to the massive movie audiences of the 1930s and 1940s were still primarily the minstrel-originated caricatures—the slow-moving, slow-witted, pop-eyed buffoon, the warm, loving mammy and uncle, and the "dancing darky"—Uncle Remus in tap shoes.

PLAYS *for the* PEOPLE

CHAPTER • SIX

Beaver Dam, Wisconsin's Concert Hall, was typical of the hundreds, perhaps thousands, of similar theaters that dignified small towns across the nation in the late nineteenth century. Even for strangers, the Concert Hall was easy to find. Like so many others of its type, it proudly stood as part of the only three story building in town. When you entered the building, you walked past the two stores on the first floor, climbed a flight of stairs, walked past Tommy Hughes' Beaver Dam *Citizen* office, past the Revera Club tavern, past the lawyer's office, to the ticket window/cloakroom. Then, up a long flight of stairs, and there it was. Empty, it did not look like too much more than a ninety-foot-long, flat-floored room with a raised stage at one end, the only glamour being the grand proscenium arch that towered twelve feet over the stage. Empty, that was all the room was. After all, it also served as the town's lecture hall, athletic arena, ballroom, city council chamber, political headquarters, skating rink, and National Guard drill room. But when the folding chairs were lined up in neat rows and filled with people, when the curtain with its beautiful painting of the Bay of Naples dropped, when the kerosene footlights cast their warm glow, when the anticipation of the crowd electrified the room, it became a *real* theater, as good—well, almost as good—as any other.

The Academy of Music in Minneapolis, Minn., a typical middle-American office building with a theater on the third floor. HTC.

Admittedly, the Concert Hall did not have a lot of scenery—two curtains with matching side flats, one with a simple wooden kitchen on one side and a forest on the other, the second with an elaborate parlor on the front and a dingy prison on the back. But these were usually enough to suit all needs. The hero of a typical play began in his own plain kitchen, was unjustly cast into prison, escaped into the woods, and finally burst into the heroine's fancy parlor, exposing the villain's dastardly plan, righting all wrongs, and winning the heroine's heart and hand. What else could anybody want? Besides, a good performance could make the sets seem to be whatever the play called for—the Capulet's ballroom, the Count of Monte Cristo's dungeon, or Uncle Tom's cabin. For drama, the most important developments in the late nineteenth century took place, not in New York

City but in the Beaver Dams of America, not in grand, well-equipped theaters but in the small-town Concert Halls.

In Beaver Dam it was called the Concert Hall; in other similar towns, it might have been the Town Hall or the Opera House. Few were called theaters. In the late nineteenth century, the word "theater" with its traditional taint of immorality still disturbed many people, especially in rural areas. But if it was not quite proper to go to a theater, it was perfectly respectable to go to a concert hall, a town hall, or an opera house. And in small towns all around the nation people gathered to have traveling performers make them laugh, cry, shriek with fear, gasp with incredulity, and sigh with longing. They went to have fun, and they had it. As popular theaters had done for decades, the Concert Hall asked its patrons to refrain at least during the performance from stamping their feet, eating peanuts, whistling, shouting, standing on chairs, and spitting on

An audience in Cheyenne, Wyoming. HTC.

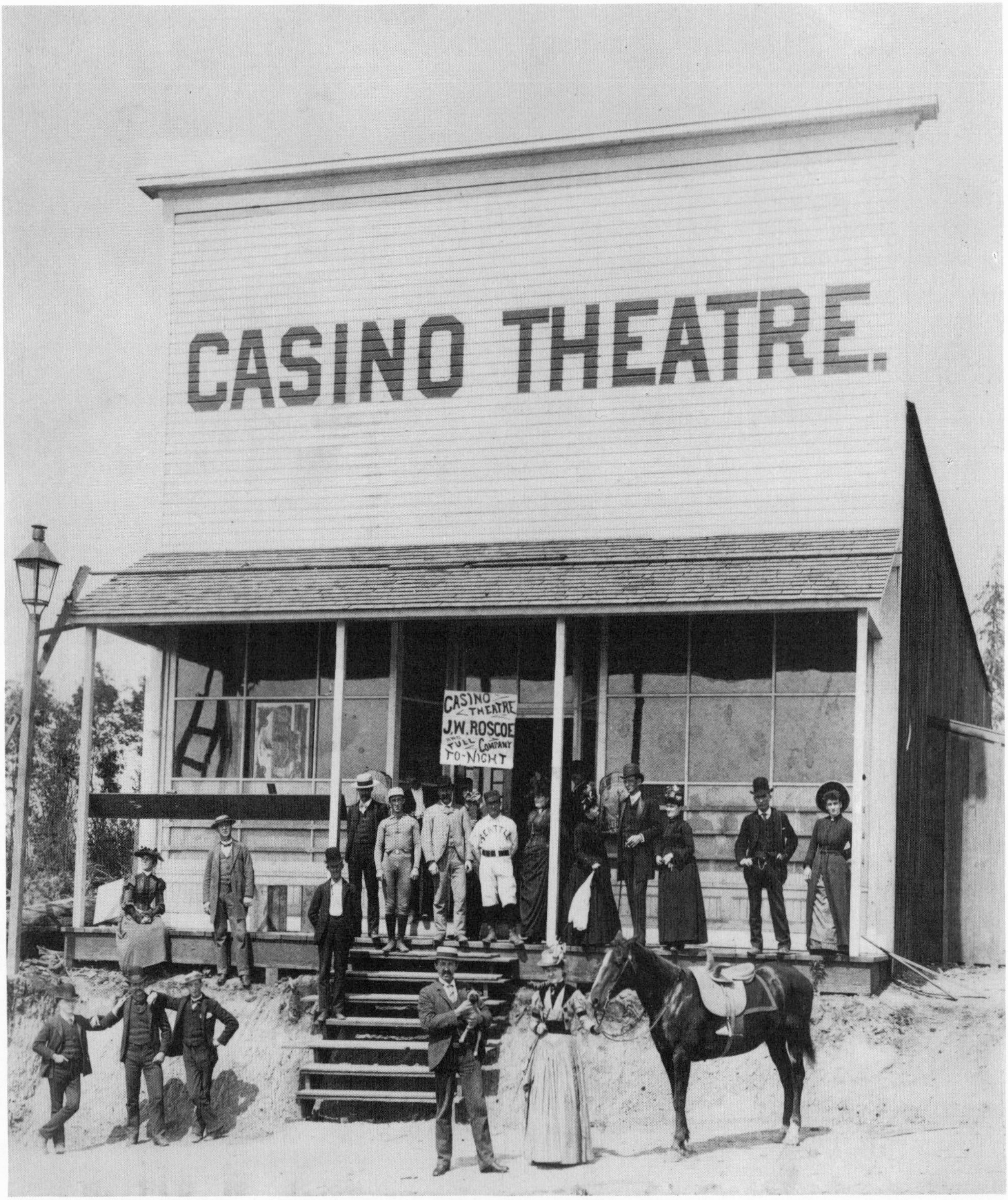

Drama reached virtually every part of the nation in the late nineteenth century, including this Portland, Oregon, theater. HTC.

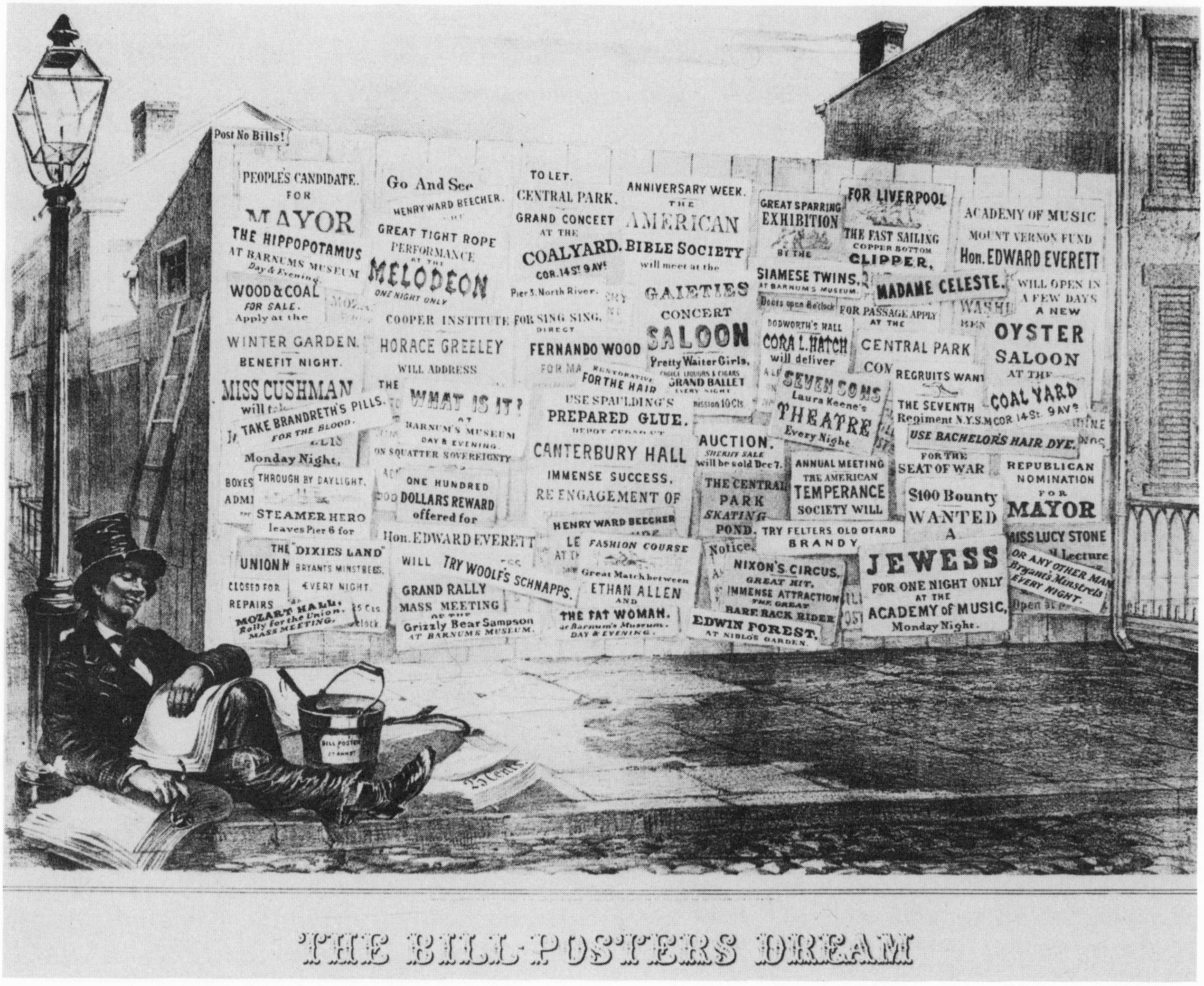

Bill posters regularly "pasted over" other playbills. This is also a parody if read down each column. NYLC.

the floor. But the injunctions succeeded no more often in the Beaver Dams than they did in the big cities. Nineteenth-century audiences left no doubt about how they felt about performers and performances. They were also determined to enjoy themselves even if they had to entertain each other. But despite all the audiences' socializing and rowdyism, the play was the thing, the play and all the other attractions: P. T. Barnum lecturing on temperance and exhibiting General and Mrs. Tom Thumb, Mark Twain drawling out his sarcastic barbs, the blackface minstrels frolicking, dancing, and wise-cracking, the Wild West shows, the singers, dancers, musicians, freaks, magicians, variety artists, and actors.

Before railroads made traveling companies financially feasible, stage entertainment did not reach much beyond the large towns and cities that could support resident companies. True, the great stars—the Edwin Forrests, Charlotte Cushmans, and Edwin Booths—traveled to play with some local companies, and some dramatic troupes did tour. But it was only after the Civil War that performers honeycombed the nation, bringing virtually every type of popular entertainment to virtually every settlement in the country. Long before the movies began to reach out into the American backlands, long before radio and then television brought a dazzling array of entertainment into people's homes, live stage performances provided Americans with virtually all their entertainment—their adventure and escapism, their romance and "soap operas." Many of the best performers and productions did not reach Beaver Dam. Traveling Broadway shows came only as close as Milwaukee, a distant sixty miles away. But some versions of all the most popular plays, the standard late-nineteenth-century repertoire, reached all the Beaver Dams. In fact, small town audiences saw many of the same popular plays year after year, sometimes several times in the same season.

The period roughly between 1850 and 1920 was the heyday of popular theater in America. Before 1850, drama had a principally urban, heavily elitist audience; after 1920, movies and radio supplied the popular drama, and theater returned to its elitist base. But for the seventy years in between, live drama was everywhere in the nation. This period is usually ignored or at best skimmed over in theater histories because it produced few plays that critics judge to be important. But in that period more than any other, drama belonged to the people, the common people. It reflected their desires, needs, and tastes. While trying to plot successful careers for themselves, actors and promoters playing to the average American unconsciously discovered basic formulas that virtually guaranteed success, formulas that continually re-emerged in American popular culture.

To people living at the time, the period's popular plays would have seemed a patternless hodge-podge. But underlying the dazzling variety of productions there was a common thread, more a mood than a theme. In the late nineteenth century, common people all over the nation were jolted by the "culture shock" that before the Civil War was largely confined to city dwellers. The same railroads that brought the popular entertainers to the Beaver Dams also brought the forces of modernization. All over the heartland of America, average citizens felt the bewilderment, the loss of control, the anxiety, and the frustration that accompanied the basic changes in the nature and quality of their lives. Their most cherished traditions, their values, and their morality all seemed to be threatened by the new industrial order. In response, small-town Americans found a political voice in the Populist party, later transferred to William Jennings Bryan's crusading campaigns as a Democratic party presidential candidate. In their concert halls, they found emotional outlets if not practical programs, solace if not solutions.

The popular stage reaffirmed traditional values in its innumerable melodramas centered on the conflict between virtuous plain people and immoral, conniving businessmen. It provided vicarious escape into the sometimes carefree, sometimes tragic emotional world of stage Negroes in its widely diverse versions of *Uncle Tom's Cabin*. It offered sentimental nostalgia for a romanticized rural and frontier past in plays like *Rip Van Winkle* and *Davy Crockett*, preached the unity of Northerners and Southerners in its Civil War love stories, and staged exciting, reassuring myths of pre-industrial national greatness and strength in its Wild West shows. In these and the other perennial favorites that touring actors brought to the Beaver Dams of the nation lies at least part of the story of how average Americans reacted to and coped with the unsettling shocks of modernization.

Melodrama has proved perhaps the most enduring formula in American popular culture, one that has survived for centuries, from eighteenth-century gothic novels to modern sex sagas, from the relatively primitive pre-Civil War stage to the highly complex television soap operas. In various forms, melodrama dominated the popular stage during its heyday. Since its principal appeals and distinguishing traits were its formulas and its central values, melodrama could accommodate any setting, time, or character; it could end either happily or tragically. But whatever its particulars, at its heart stood Virtue, epitomized by the heroine, the miracle of love and delicacy, the paragon of excellence, the earthly angel. Her vulnerability, especially to the scheming blackguard of a villain, which placed her virtue under siege, supplied the dramatic tension. While minor characters provided some comic relief, the major characters suffered through an incredible series of predicaments. Being tied to railroad tracks in front of an oncoming locomotive, trapped in a burning building, fed to a buzzsaw, or threatened with the loss of the heroine's "honor" were all in a night's work for the hero and heroine. After as many setbacks and near disasters as time would allow (there seemed to be no limit to the audiences' appetite for them), the action came to a morally edifying conclusion in which Right, Justice, and Goodness triumphed. Even when major characters had to accept earthly death rather than tarnish their virtue, they were assured of the higher rewards and glories of the Almighty. To make its moralisms clear and simple, melodrama employed only simplistic characters who were entirely good, entirely bad, or entirely silly. It also blamed the existence of evil on the villain's personal character defects, not on more complex, more uncontrollable social or environmental problems. The answer to the villain's evil schemes was also personal, a matter of faith and strength not a matter of social change or group organization. Plain, pure, old-fashioned American righteousness, personified by simple farmers or urban working-class people, was the universal and certain cure-all for any problem.

Melodrama conveyed a fantasy or fairy-tale-like mood, its unrealistic characters and its consistent use of archaic language—its "thous," "whithers," and "yons"—being signals of make-believe as clearly as was "once upon a time." Yet because melodrama exalted the traditional values to which people desperately clung in the face of fundamental change, audiences credited melodrama with being more real than reality, a higher truth that transcended everyday experience. An ideal statement of the way life ought to be, melodrama made evil and corruption easy to identify and solutions easy to find; it made heroes of common, simple people; and it made virtue and the virtuous triumph; it testified that, no matter how unfair life seemed, justice was not dead. Besides the welcome simplicity, reassurance, and hope that it offered in a complex, uncertain, and disillusioning world, it offered vicarious thrills in the titillation provided by the villain's immoral intentions toward the heroine. At the same time, the hero's and heroine's faith and composure also served as models for and challenges to viewers undergoing perplexing trials and tribulations of their own. Melodrama served perhaps an even more important, certainly more concrete and immedi-

Hazel Kirke was one of the most popular melodramas. NYLC.

ate function for audience members by providing an outlet for their feelings and emotions—a chance to scream, to laugh, to gasp, and to cry. It was at once a celebration of the traditional American way of life and an elegy for it.

Although melodrama took a wide range of forms, one of its classic patterns forced the heroine to choose between her feelings and her sense of duty, often between her love for a poor but worthy farmboy and her responsibility to redeem the family mortgage by marrying the corrupt villain. Worked and reworked with innumerable variations and complications, this basic dilemma provided sentimental and emotional quandries for thousands upon thousands of theater-goers, especially women, to worry about, fret over, and sob through. In *Hazel Kirke,* "always a favorite with the ladies who sympathize with Hazel's troubles," as a San Francisco critic observed in 1888, Hazel refuses to clear her father's debts by marrying the mortgage-holder, instead wedding the man she truly loves, even though this means that her father disowns her. Her husband, too, marries for love, not family obligation. Having cut themselves off from their parents, a serious social sin, the couple inevitably suffers. Among other calamities, Hazel's father goes blind, his mill is repossessed, and Hazel attempts suicide. But ultimately, after all the potential tears have been wrung out of the audience, all the characters are reunited and live happily ever after.

Since melodrama like other show business forms evolved to suit its audiences, it, too, reflected changes in its public's concerns and anxieties, especially those that involved the family, the core of the melodrama. In particular, the emergence of the "liberated" woman seemed to many people to challenge the very bases of society—marriage, home, and family. Thus, it is no surprise that a melodrama that addressed this issue, *East Lynne,* a dramaticization of an English novel published and adapted for the stage in 1861, proved to be one of America's most popular plays for at least half a century. In it, Lady Isabel's philandering husband unjustly accuses her of infidelity. Uncertain of his fidelity and unable to accept his jealous restrictions, she falls in love with another man. After much fretting and soul-searching, she finally runs away with her lover, abandoning her marriage, her husband, *and,* sin of all female sins, her infant son, Willie. When she should be totally willing to sacrifice personal happiness for her family, she turns her back on her domestic "duty," woman's highest calling. So she pays. Her lover predictably turns out to be a ne'er-do-well who deserts her. Alone and pulled by the maternal ties that even a liberated woman in a melodrama cannot cut, she returns home in disguise to visit baby Willie, just in time to find him on his death bed, to reveal her true identity and deep love for him, and to hear him use his last breath to gasp out, "Mama, Mama." A broken woman, Isabel falls ill, a victim of the sentimental swoon that plagued so many nineteenth-century heroines. On her death bed, her husband, never even thinking to apologize for his past behavior, magnanimously forgives her, to the delight and sobs of all. Although audiences apparently felt Isabel had to suffer, they also wanted to see her forgiven after she had paid for her sins. When Edwin Forrest changed the ending, having her husband castigate the dying Isabel for her transgressions, audiences booed and hissed so vehemently that Forrest quickly returned to the traditional ending. Although they did not realize it, common Americans, at least the women that dominated audiences for these plays, were becoming more tolerant of some of the ideas voiced by "new women" like Isabel, even as they outwardly clung to their old values.

Although melodramatic villains most often were urban businessmen, melodrama did not portray city life or commercialism as the *cause* of problems. Instead, melodrama personified evil in the warped psyches of its villains. Consequently, it dealt directly with few broad social issues or problems. But there were two glaring exceptions, two of the most performed plays in American history: *Ten Nights in a Barroom* and *Uncle Tom's Cabin.* Making the cases for temperance and against slavery, two major moral crusades, these plays got support and patronage from people who otherwise considered drama to be immoral. But the plays became perennials not because they pleased a few people who otherwise disliked the theater but because they pleased so many people who loved it. The plays' emotionally moving, melodramatic scenes, not their moral messages, made them two of American drama's greatest hits.

Ten Nights in a Barroom, first adapted for the stage from T. S. Arthur's temperance novel in the 1850s, detailed the destruction of Joe Morgan and his family by demon rum. Beginning with "harmless" drinks at the local tavern, Joe becomes a helplessly addicted drunkard, throwing away his every cent trying to quench his insatiable thirst. When he has money to buy booze, everyone in the tavern loves him, but when he is broke, his "friends" want nothing to do with him. Yet he cannot stay away from them or from the tavern, which becomes virtually his only home. One of the high points, or perhaps it should be

THE GREAT EMOTIONAL DRAMA
EAST LYNNE
"LOOK AT ME, I AM YOUR MOTHER!"

low points, of the play comes when Joe's lovely, little daughter, Mary, pursues him into the saloon—a young innocent girl in a saloon!—urging him in song:

Father, dear father, come home with me now!
The clock in the steeple strikes one.
You said you were coming right home from the shop,
As soon as your day's work was done.
Our fire has gone out, our house's all dark,
And mother's been watching since tea
With poor brother Benny so sick in her arms,
And none to help her but me.
Come home, come home, come home!
Please, father, dear father, come home!

Joe chooses to stay in the bar and try to mooch one for the road. Instead, he gets a whisky glass thrown at him. It sails over Joe's head and smashes into Mary's forehead, mortally wounding her as she pathetically pleads with her father to go home to his family. After a properly long and tearful death scene in which Mary extracts a vow from her father never again to enter a tavern, she expires. Seeking solace and strength from the only source he knows, Joe takes refuge in drink, not in the tavern but in a bottle of whisky he has stashed at home in case of just such a medicinal emergency. This backsliding leads to the biggest scene of the play, a writhing, screaming, fear-crazed onslaught of delirum tremens, that would either scare the hell out of drinkers or drive men to drink. After the red-eyed, hissing serpents stop crawling all over him and disappear back into the wallpaper where they have come from, Joe, remembering his pledge to his martyred Mary, dries himself out and is "restored once more to happiness." Combining temperance, emotionally charged family images, the tragic death of the morally precocious child, the delirum scene, which made it impossible even for nineteenth-century actors to overact, and the happy ending, the play ran well into the twentieth century.

The other perennial favorite that dealt directly with a controversial social issue, slavery, was also based on a sensational novel, *Uncle Tom's Cabin,* a landmark bestseller in American popular literature. In it, Harriet Beecher Stowe uses every sentimental and romantic device of the period to portray slaves as human beings who feel the same pain and anguish as whites when they suffer indignities and oppression. The novel opens on the Shelby's idyllic Kentucky plantation, a model of a happy inter-racial family, with the slaves, regardless of age, as the children. But then a crass slave-trader forces Shelby to sell some slaves to pay his debts. When Eliza Harris learns that her young son is to be sold, she takes him and runs away to the North. Ultimately, after outracing her pursuers over the frozen Ohio River to freedom, she rejoins her husband George, who fights off slave-catchers and takes his family to sanctuary in Canada. Loyal, devoutly Christian Uncle Tom learns that he, too, is to be sold but refuses to flee with Eliza because he feels it is his Christian duty to submit to his superiors. On the way to be sold in the deep South, Tom meets Evangeline St. Clair, Little Eva, a saintly young white girl who, like Mary in *Ten Nights,* possesses the innate purity and wisdom that nineteenth-century romantics attributed to children. Eva persuades her father to buy Tom and to take

Repentant Lady Isabel is reunited with her dying son in this *East Lynne* poster. HTC.

Little Mary is struck down by demon rum in *Ten Nights in a Bar-room*. HTC.

him home to the benevolent St. Clair plantation, where Eva radiates her Christian love for all God's children, black and white. But slavery weighs heavily on Eva's pure heart, and she dies a slow, sentimental death, the angel of goodness destroyed by the sins of slavery. At a vile slave auction, Tom is sold to Simon Legree, a brutal, immoral slave-driver who has turned his plantation into an inhuman agrarian factory. After refusing to whip other slaves, Tom dies a Christ-like martyr's death at Legree's hands.

The novel's emotionally moving, melodramatic scenes were a natural for adaptation to the mid-nineteenth-century stage. Almost immediately, many competing dramatizations emerged, differing in tone, emphasis, characters, and even message. Over its roughly eighty-year life as a major show business fixture, "Uncle Tom's Cabin" became more a catch phrase for a wide range of shows than the name of a specific play with a specific script, more an institution that evolved to suit its audiences than even a relatively fixed production. The variations in the stage versions of the novel provide a fascinating example of how changes in audiences' interests and tastes shaped popular drama.

The first successful dramatic production of *Uncle Tom's Cabin* enjoyed an unprecedented run of 325 consecutive performances in New York City during 1853-54. Written by George L. Aiken for George C. Howard's family-based repertory company, the play featured four-year-old Cordelia Howard as Little Eva. The production climaxed, not with Tom's death, but with Little Eva soaring up to heaven on the back of a white dove, her arms extended in a benediction as the orchestra played "Nearer My God To Thee." Using a pattern for popular drama that dated back at least to Shakespeare, Aiken ensured the entertainment value of his sentimental melodrama by adding heavy doses of music and comedy. But he also retained many of the novel's emotionally moving antislavery scenes, scenes that provoked increasing controversy and divisiveness in the 1850s as the sectional conflict over slavery intensified.

Ever the barometer of public opinion, P. T. Barnum in 1853 offered in the American Museum's lecture room a "just and sensible dramatic version of Mrs. Stowe's book" that toned down the anti-slavery, pro-Negro sentiments of the original. Barnum boasted that his play, while presenting a "true picture of negro life in the South," did not "foolishly and unjustly elevate the negro above the white man in intellect or morals . . . and instead of turning away the audience in tears the author has wisely consulted dramatic taste by having Virtue triumphant at last." As always, Barnum geared his production to offend none and dazzle all. He featured a beautiful panoramic view of a Mississippi River sunrise and a riverboat that smoked grandly as it moved across the stage. He also had brutal scenes like the slave auction deleted or played lightly and ended the production happily—George Shelby racing just in the nick of time to rescue Uncle Tom from manaical Simon Legree. Productions like Barnum's and the minstrel parodies

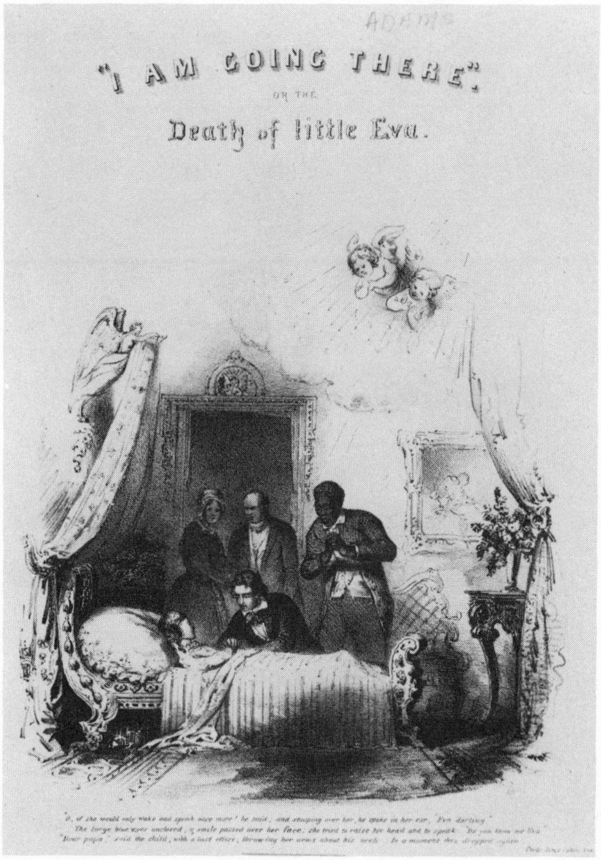

Romanticized 1852 sheetmusic cover of "The Death of Little Eva." HTC.

of *Uncle Tom's Cabin* that transformed it into *Happy Uncle Tom* and portrayed none of the cruelty and inhumanity of slavery proved far more popular in the strife-torn late-1850s than did serious stage versions of the novel.

After the Civil War, productions of *Uncle Tom's Cabin* proliferated, making it probably America's most performed play. It proved so popular that many actors and companies, called "Tommers" and "Tom Shows," toured the nation presenting nothing but *Uncle Tom's Cabin* and an occasional *Ten Nights in a Barroom*. The Tommers, who knew all the lines and all the scenes in all the versions, varied

A realistic portrayal of Eliza fleeing from slave-chasers with dogs in a serious 1901 production. HTC.

the blend to suit their personnel and their audiences. Once slavery was abolished, many Tom troupes restored previously censored anti-slavery speeches and scenes because they provided such powerful melodrama. Tommers also drew material from other show business forms, especially minstrel shows. The result was a dazzling variety of productions with the same name. One *Uncle Tom's Cabin* fan who had seen the show at least twenty-five times claimed that he had never seen the same version twice.

Beginning with the play's comic and melodramatic basics, Tommers added their own special features and novelties, which often proved greater attractions than the classic scenes. In the 1870s, a promoter realized that Eliza's flight to freedom would be much more exciting if she were hounded by live, snarling dogs. The "bloodhounds"—actually mastiffs or Great Danes—were such great hits that they became necessities for Tom Shows, just as good endmen were for minstrel troupes. From minstrels, Tommers drew other novelty features: plantation material, heavy dialects, ludicrous caricatures of Negroes, and the practice of making up forty-year-old Uncle Tom to look like an old uncle. Tom Shows also reflected the great impact black entertainers made on show business. In the 1870s, the Northern public "discovered" and became fascinated with slaves' religious music, the spirituals. It was not long until traveling Tom Shows added jubilee songs and singers to their companies. In 1877, for example, the Howards, still at it after twenty-five years, played *Uncle Tom's Cabin* with one hundred Negroes from Slavin's Original Georgia Jubilee Singers. By the late-1870s most Tom Shows included black specialty acts and what one company boasted was a "stage packed with Colored people." Ironically, these Tom troupes were the only racially integrated shows in the country.

For many Tom troupes the jubilee choruses and black specialty performers became the major attractions. Abbey's Double Mammoth Uncle Tom's Cabin Company, for example, gave such a poor show, one critic complained, that "not till the jubilee singers appeared was the audience pleased." By the end of the century, when Negro musicals and stars like Williams and Walker created public sensations, many so-called Tom Shows were in reality little more than vehicles for Negroes to perform the plantation caricatures and other "Negro specialties" that white audiences loved. One 1879 Tom Show bore such "little resemblance to the original," a critic sniped, that it should be called, "The Cake Walk, with Spasmodic Glimpses of Uncle Tom and His Newly Painted Cabin." The show contained, the critic protested, "an intolerable deal of cake walking, plantation singing, buck [tap] dancing, voudoo [sic] festivalizing and various other irrelevant things." Yet even this critic had to admit that "without all these specialties the play and the acting would induce a combined attack of hypochondria and insomnia."

Uncle Tom's Cabin became a show business institution, "America's Greatest Hit," because of its emotional melodramatic content and its flexible incorporation of novelties, minstrel features, and black performers. On deeper, less conscious levels, it offered a myth of a loving, rural American home life—the romanticized plantation—destroyed by slave-traders' and Legree's crass commercialism; it provided a full range of sentimental family images, from loving security to tragic destruction; it allowed insecure, frustrated whites to escape vicariously into the carefree world of stereotyped stage Negroes while at the same time feeling superior to the irresponsible, childish blacks. Most of all, *Uncle Tom's Cabin* was a smashing good show, one that gave average white Americans a chance to feel good about themselves and a chance to let out their pent-up feelings.

Nostalgia for the American past, or rather the creation of myths of an idyllic American past—a simpler, nobler, more carefree, more humane time—ran throughout late-nineteenth-century popular drama. As people around the nation felt themselves caught up in modernization, they grasped for escapist amusement, for a sense of stability, for some reassurance about the worth, dignity, and power of common Americans. In this atmosphere, plays centered on positive images of rural and frontier America proved tremendously popular and provided actors specializing in such roles with long prosperous careers, many of them playing only one character, a longevity possible only because national touring to the heartland meant constantly changing audiences.

In 1876, Denman Thompson began his twenty-four year stint as Uncle Joshua in *The Old Homestead.* This stage fixture opens in a beautiful New Hampshire farm, the stage realistically set with a barn, haystacks, and live oxen. While Uncle Josh, a simple old farmer, goes about his chores happily singing to himself, he learns that his son Reuben has been accused of robbing a bank. Josh immediately sets out to find and redeem his son, a journey that exposes him to cities and commercialism, both of which make him thankful for his life on the farm. First, he visits an ex-boyhood friend, who has grown rich but still longs for the rural simplicity of their youth, an experience Josh would still be enjoying if city life

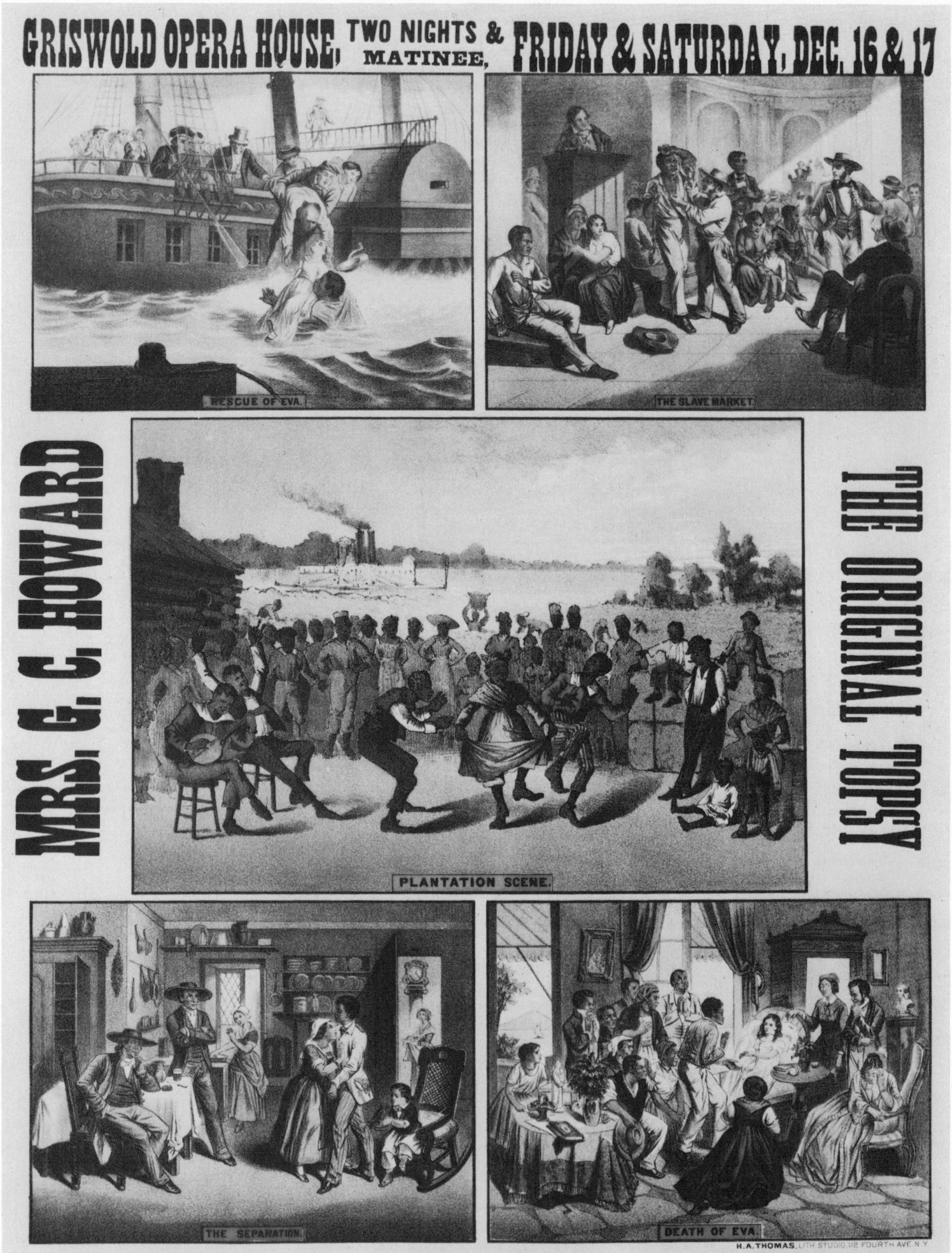

Poster for a lavish late-nineteenth-century production featuring Mrs. Howard and plantation scenes. HTC.

had not tempted and corrupted his son. Josh's quest for Reuben ultimately takes him to New York City, the epitome of urban life, Sodom and Gomorrah itself. This journey gives rural audiences a good glimpse of life in the big city, contrasting the beauty of Grace Cathedral, complete with its dazzling stained-glass windows, to the general urban degradation and corruption. When Josh finally finds Reuben, he is lying in a gutter, an impoverished drunk. Josh takes him home to the farm, where the healthy, curative country atmosphere restores Reuben, and he and his father live happily ever after. With pieces borrowed from other melodramas, innumerable Uncle Shows based on *The Old Homestead* toured the country, carrying the message that the traditional rural values were far superior to the new urban ways.

But the type of rural images that pervaded the popular stage were in fact undergoing major changes themselves along with the fundamental changes in the lives of the audiences they entertained and served. The Yankee and the frontiersman who before the Civil War embodied the coarse, earthy vitality of the backland folk, who lambasted and ridiculed civilization, and who stood for change and a "new order" were transformed for playgoers after the Civil War into objects of sentimentalism, quaint, colorful relics, just the sorts of characters they themselves had once ridiculed as effete weaklings. Superficial folksy charm replaced hardy folk realities.

"Well, here's your good health, and your families' good health, and may they all live long and prosper!" For nearly half a century, roughly 1865 to 1904, Joseph Jefferson III as Rip Van Winkle delivered this toast to his drinking companions on stage and to the thousands upon thousands of people from every part of the nation who sat in his audiences.

Denman Thompson as Uncle Joshua, a late-nineteenth-century nostalgic version of the Yankee. NYLC.

Before Jefferson began to play Rip, this third-generation American actor had only a moderately successful acting career, never recapturing the acclaim he received when as a four-year-old boy with a blackened face he danced as "Jim Crow Jr." with T. D. Rice. Jefferson and others had staged versions of Washington Irving's story of the New York Dutchman who slept away twenty years of his life after drinking a toast of elves' brew with the ghost of Henry Hudson. But they were not successful until Dion Boucicault, a British playwright who became an American as well

The rustic warmth of *The Old Homestead.* HTC.

as an English favorite, rewrote the play so that it began with Rip, Boucicault explained, "as a young scamp, thoughtless gay, just a curly-headed, good-humored fellow such as all the village girls would love and the children and dogs run after." Opening with Rip as a prancing, frolicking boy in a grown-up's body gave Rip his warm human appeal and provided a dramatic background for his aging and rejection.

Early in the play, Rip innocently cavorts in the tavern like a boy with his playmates, drinking too much but always in a gay, harmless way until a villain hoodwinks him into signing away a fortune in land. His wife, like a mother with an overgrown boy, scolds him, and in a fit of rage orders him to leave home forever. Even after she catches herself and urges him to stay, his wounded pride still forces him to go, to go to his rendezvous with the elves and dwarfs, to his meeting with Henry Hudson's ghost, and to his twenty year "nap." When he emerges from his long sleep, digging his way out from beneath a blanket of leaves, his hair and beard bleached white, he returns to town only to find, like so many people in the audience, that time has passed him by, that everything he knew and loved has changed, that he has been "forgotten so soon." In nineteenth-century America, each generation felt that it had to undergo more fundamental and pervasive change than any others, that its youth had been a simpler, less hectic time. And each generation was right. America developed at a lightning pace, physical changes far outracing psychological evolution. Like Rip, many Americans might well have felt that they woke up one morning to find that twenty years had somehow flown by and taken the world they knew with them. Rip embodied and played to this sense of "future shock."

Rip provided a fantasy, an escape, but also a parable that could teach modern, urban people valuable lessons. "Come with your shiftless, lazy ways," an 1896 reviewer wrote of and to Rip, "and teach the work-ridden citizens of a working city to sympathize, if not in fact, at least in fancy, with your magnificent exemption from the primal curse which bears too heavily in these later days . . . the avarice that drains men's blood of human kindliness and the ambition that tramples down the national affections." Mourning with Rip for the carefree, jolly days of their youth allowed audiences to endorse the humane sensitivities and values that so many people found lacking in American civilization, while at the same time castigating urbanization, industrialism, and commercialism as the villains, not the American people. Rip was a wish-fulfillment of what Americans wanted to believe they were or had been like and also a momentary escape into a world free of responsibility and anxiety, as stage Negroes were.

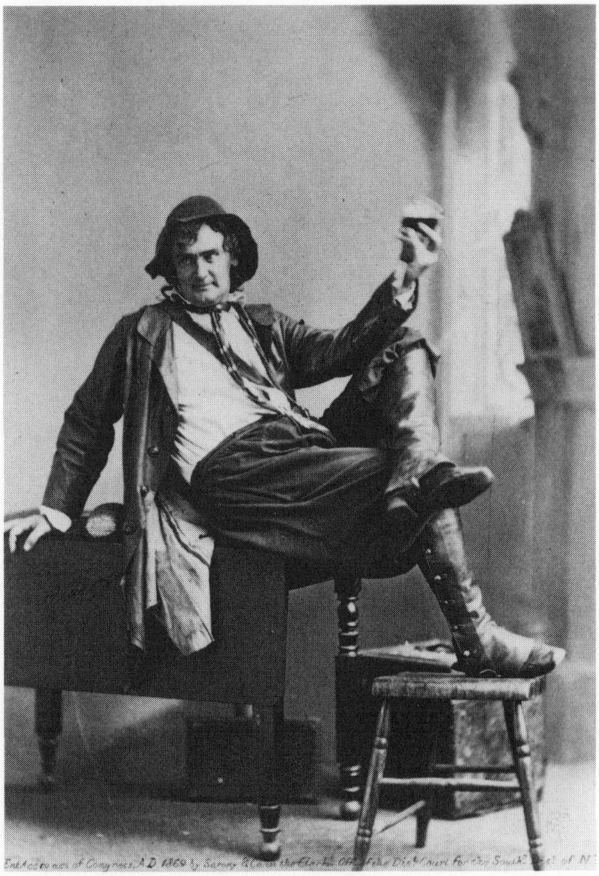

Joseph Jefferson III as young Rip Van Winkle. HTC.

Although originally Dutch, Rip seemed to audiences a typical American, as much a Yankee as Uncle Joshua. But Rip was a far cry from the sharp-tongued, rapier-witted Yankee country boy of the 1830s and 1840s. Jefferson softened the Yankee, substituting jocularity for acidic wit, sentimentality for social criticism. Perhaps even more importantly, where Brother Jonathan, the Yankee hero, had been an aggressive activist, successfully fighting evil and city-slickers, Rip was a passive, child-like victim, with little or no control over either his actions or his fate. This transformation symbolizes the change from the 1830s, when average Americans felt they were in control, democraticizing American political, economic, and cultural institutions—shaping the nation

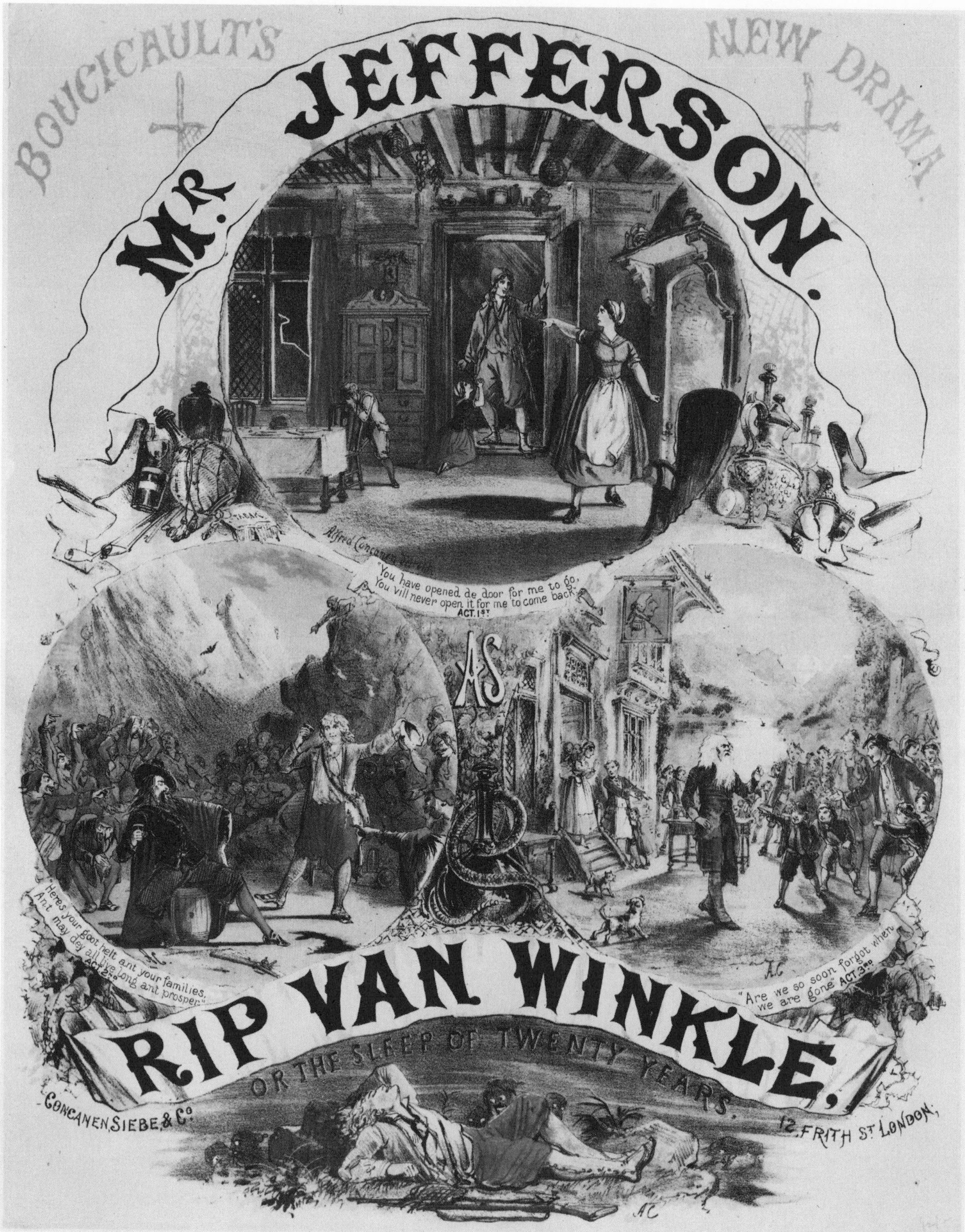
BOUCICAULT'S NEW DRAMA
MR. JEFFERSON.
"You have opened de door for me to go, You vill never open it for me to come back." ACT. 1ST
AS
"Heres your goot helt ant your families, Ant may dey all live long ant prosper." ACT 2ND
"Are we so soon forgot when we are gone" ACT 3RD
RIP VAN WINKLE,
OR THE SLEEP OF TWENTY YEARS.
CONCANEN, SIEBE & Co.
12, FRITH ST LONDON,

and its destiny in their own image—to the late nineteenth century, when unmanageable, incomprehensible forces seemed to be running their lives, when common people seemed more like puppets dancing on strings than free men determining their own fate. There seemed to be no solutions, no remedies for this predicament. The nostalgic shows at least offered reassurance that it had not always been that way and the slim hope that sometime in the future things might return to the good old days. But the way performers and audiences shaped their rural characters inevitably reflected the new realities, as hapless Rip did.

A similar softening took place in the frontier characters who were also central figures in the post-Civil War nostalgia craze. Between 1872 and 1896, Frank Mayo played Davy Crockett almost as many times as Joseph Jefferson played Rip. And, if possible, Mayo's Crockett was even farther removed from his pre-Civil War popular culture predecessors than Jefferson's Rip was from the Yankee. In contrast to the swaggering, crude, cocky, exploitative Crockett of the 1830s, Mayo's Davy more closely resembled James Fenimore Cooper's romanticized frontiersman. Mayo portrayed a rustic gentleman, one who is so soft that he has a sweetheart, a refined young woman whom he protects from wolves, blizzards, Indians, and the predictable mortgage-wielding villain. When she is injured, he even "tenderly" nurses her—woman's work unsuited for an earlier Davy Crockett. After a number of melodramatic close calls, they marry and live happily ever after.

Even Cooper did not domesticate the "free spirit" of the American woods, the glorification of the natural man spawned and perfected by the wilderness. Mayo's production was a different kind of morality play for a different age, a melodrama in which a frontiersman, subduing both natural and human enemies, heroically saved the helpless girl from evil and then settled down to a civilized

Joseph Jefferson III as the aged Rip. HTC.

Rip Van Winkle poster showing major scenes. HTC.

Frank Mayo carrying his beloved into the cabin in *Davy Crockett*. HTC.

life, much as the nation itself did in the late nineteenth century. In domesticating Davy Crockett, Mayo symbolically portrayed the taming of the West, the taming of the unfettered American spirit. Yet the play was not a tragedy but a triumph, a statement that American heroism need not be opposed to family life, the basic unit of civilized society. Mayo was not portraying the destruction of the mythic American, but suggesting that the strength of the American forest, the root of American greatness, could be channeled into building a great and loving civilization. Mayo's Crockett, tamed by a woman's beauty, seemed to late-nineteenth-century viewers an idealization of "true manhood," one with the tender emotions so often considered unmanly. No one could claim that Davy Crockett, even Mayo's Crockett, was unmanly.

Reviewers realized that Mayo's Davy was not a realistic portrayal of the frontiersman. "It must be admitted," a New York critic wrote in 1895, "that the backwoodsman of the stage bears very slight resemblance to the real pioneers of our *civilization in the wilderness* [a phrase that would formerly have seemed laughably contradictory]. But it is surely allowable," he continued "to idealize a character who is supposed to possess endurance and heroism." In other words, who wants a crude, bragging bully for a national hero? Another writer felt the play was a "poem of young Lochinvar dramatized and Americanized," a meaning not too subtly conveyed in the play when the heroine, after being rescued by Davy, read Sir Walter Scott's poem about Lochinvar aloud to the exhausted Crockett. As these reviewers realized, the playwright wanted to create much more than another action-packed frontier tale, much more than a spine-tingling melodrama. He wanted to create an idealized American hero combining strength and courage with tenderness, love, and a dedication to family life. The quarter-century of Mayo's stardom as Davy Crockett testifies to the play's success at what one critic described as the "assemblage of virtues" into "one ideal creation." That this "ideal creation" differed in almost every way except name from his show business predecessors of forty

Frank Mayo's Crockett getting married. HTC.

years earlier further underscored the great changes in American life between 1835 and 1875.

In the same years that Josh, Rip, and Davy brought lovable rural characters from the East to the Beaver Dams, William F. Cody rode out of the great plains and into the nation's theaters and arenas with a show that testified that hardy American pioneers still existed and that American greatness had grown out of the heroic conquest of the frontier, not out of cities or industrialism. These two images—the domesticated and the untamed frontier characters—beautifully complemented each other, providing between them reassurance of American heroes' humanity and of their manhood. Americans could not find a way to combine these two attributes in one figure. Cody, a sensation throughout America and Europe with his ritualized re-enactment of one of the central American myths, created a distinctively American entertainment form—the Wild West Show, the forerunner of the Western movie. Cody, a pony express rider, Union army scout, spy, and Indian fighter, first entered popular culture in the 1860s as a fictional character in dime novels, the inexpensive paperback books of the day. Then in 1872, Ned Buntline, author of the novels, persuaded Cody to leave Nebraska, where he was fighting Indians, acting as a guide for European buffalo hunters, and being elected to and resigning from the state legislature, to star in a play. When they first met in Chicago, Buntline planned to open in six days, even though he had a totally inexperienced star, no troupe, and no play. Relying on one of his novels, Buntline needed only four hours to write "The Scouts of the Plains." Cody and his fellow scout Texas Jack, who had never even seen a play let alone been in one, found the rigor of rehearsal eased by enormous quantities of

Mayo heroically defending his sweetheart by barring the door with his arms while wolves push through the walls. NYLC.

whisky, which made their lack of preparation seem less important. But the show went on in the six days anyway, with Buntline interviewing Cody and Texas Jack on stage about their exploits and then, whenever the reminiscences lagged, signalling for "spontaneous" Indian attacks. Both acts concluded with mock battles fought with loud war-whoops and barrages of gunshots that produced an ear-shattering din along with wild, flamboyant action. "We say nothing about acting," a critic sniped in 1873, "because none is apparent." But audiences loved the show.

Eastern newspapers and dime novels lavishly described the westward expansion and Indian wars of the 1870s and 1880s in all their gory detail, stimulating public curiosity about the wars and its heroes. Increasingly urbanized, physically inactive people found a source of escape, excitement, and vicarious identification with real heroes in the frontier shows. Combining the need for action heroes and for reassurance about the strength of American

BUFFALO BILL'S
WILD WEST
HISTORICAL SKETCHES
AND
DAILY REVIEW
COL. W. F. CODY
"BUFFALO BILL"
PRICE
10 CTS

manhood with the interest in the mythic West, the dime novels about him, and his own good looks, Cody became an instant celebrity. He was, after all, a real scout, hunter, and Indian fighter. People could believe his performance was more fact than fiction, more a real exhibition than a show.

Despite his instant popularity in the East and in show business, Cody, restless for a little real action, periodically returned to the West in the 1870s, as a $1000 a month guide for a wealthy English hunter and as a guide for cavalry units rounding up Arapahoes. In 1874-75, he organized his own troupe for "Scouts of the Plains, or Red Deviltry As It Is," touring with the crude melodrama featuring Indian war dances and attacks, lots of action, and, of course, Buffalo Bill's heroic rescues. In 1876 when his son died, Cody went back to war. Gold had been discovered in Indian land in the Black Hills of the Dakotas a few years earlier, and after miners flocked in despite government injunctions, war erupted, during which General George Custer and his men were annihilated. At the time of the "massacre," Cody was with a different unit fighting Cheyennes, when as Cody's press agent told it, a war chief personally challenged Cody to individual combat. The battle supposedly concluded with Cody scalping the Indian, thrusting his bloody trophy into the air, and bellowing: "The first scalp for Custer!" Right after the war, Cody capitalized on his well-publicized exploit with the "Red Right Hand, or Buffalo Bill's First Scalp for Custer," a title that doubtless did not hurt attendance. In subsequent years, he toured with similar action-studded shows based on the melodramatic rescue of helpless white settlers from blood-crazed savages who died three to five times a night, depending on the number of acts in the productions. Whether titled "The Knight of the Plains, or Buffalo Bill's Last Trail," "The Prairie Waif, a Story of the Far West," or "Twenty Days, or Buffalo Bill's Last Stand," the shows were interchangeable.

Cody's first scalp for Custer, detail from a Wild West Show program. NYLC.

A heroic portrayal of Buffalo Bill Cody on horseback. NYLC.

Indian attack on a stagecoach, detail from a Buffalo Bill Cody Wild West program. NYLC.

Then in 1883, Cody, with his money-belt bulging, planned a new show, one that would portray the saga of the West on a scale and with a freedom impossible within the confines of theaters. Cody envisioned an exhibition that would re-create the history of the American West, literally acting out a version of the national history, one including Indian villages, scouts and trappers, buffalo hunts, settlers moving west, the Deadwood stagecoach, the Pony Express, Indian attacks and rescues, and the Black Hills war. Cody's frontier circus toured the nation's arenas, drawing good crowds but losing money because of Cody's bad management. Like the huge traveling circuses, the Wild West Show was something new, something requiring sophisticated administration and organization, skills Cody lacked. When Nate Salisbury, the creator of profitable musical comedies, saw the Cody show, he realized its potential and took over its management. Like P. T. Barnum, J. H. Haverly, W. C. Coup and other producers, Salisbury expanded the size of the show to enhance its appeal, adding bears, elk, buffalo, famous plainsmen, and one hundred Indians including Sitting Bull. Shortly after that Annie Oakley—"Little Sure Shot" to Sitting Bull—already a crack shot and a veteran of vaudeville circuits and circuses at age nineteen, joined the show. But even though the show's great appeal drew large crowds, its huge traveling and production costs resulted in a $60,000 loss during the winter of 1884-85 alone.

When, in 1886, the show settled down in the East, it profited from small travel costs and huge audiences anxious to see the "educational exhibit in concrete form," the heroic greatness of America in what for Easterners was actually a fantasy or mythic setting. For sedentary Americans, Cody provided a living, breathing, shooting spectacle of manly combat, a direct link to the past. By keeping the trappings—even some of the participants—of the violent taming of the West and packaging them in a slick, harmless show, he filled a Staten Island arena throughout 1886-87, even in bad weather. To continue cashing in on the show's great appeal in New York, Salisbury moved it indoors into Madison Square Garden for the winter.

When the show was brought indoors and modestly renamed "The Drama of Civilization," it was tamed down. "Those who have seen the Wild West Show in an open field," a reviewer complained, "will not care for it at the Garden." Its principal appeals, "its wildness and savagery," had given way, he lamented, "to tame theatricality." Adding lavish scenery and new features to clearly delineate stages in the progression of "The Drama of Civilization," the pageant opens with the "Primeval forest," replete with wild animals and equally wild Indians. Next, emigrant trains move onto the prairie. After a roaring fire and a thundering stampede, the scene shifts to a cattle ranch, where an Indian attack interrupts a rollicking rodeo and brings the army galloping to the rescue. Finally, the pony express and stagecoach visit a mining camp which is robbed by outlaws and destroyed by a howling cyclone. (The Black Hills War was added later to complete the mythic conquest of the land and the Indians.) By adding these special effects and mounting the show on a proscenium stage, Salisbury further domesticated the production, but he retained enough action and violence while structuring the show into an epic of the taming of the West that it consistently filled the Garden's 15,000 seats, making both Salisbury and Cody wealthy.

Like Barnum and others, Cody, after establishing himself in America, took his show to Britain. It won the plaudits of the Prince of Wales and Queen Victoria, toured England with great success, returned briefly to the United States, and left again for a continental tour in 1889. The Wild West Show became an international sensation. In Paris, the show turned Western clothes, buffalo-robes, bearskins, Indian crafts, Mexican saddles, and buckskin clothes into sensations. In Rome, Pope Leon XII received the company and blessed Cody. In Berlin, Annie Oakley shot the ash off the Kaiser's cigar while he held it in his mouth. And everywhere they went, Cody freely sampled the local alcoholic beverages. Cody and the show were flying high. In 1893, Cody pitched the show outside the Chicago Columbia Exposition, reportedly attracting six million patrons.

Despite the show's great success and Cody's large income, he managed to get and keep himself in debt, by investing in every foolhardy scheme he heard of, by giving money to anyone with a hard-luck story, and by drinking up what was left. All his life he remained a hard-living, free-spending, action-seeking adventurer. In 1894, James A. Bailey, of Barnum and Bailey, bought half interest in the show, running it successfully with Salisbury as traveling manager for the next eight years. In the late 1890s, Bailey, doing what he knew best, made it an all-American production by adding a sideshow featuring snake-charmers, sword-swallowers, midgets, giants, magicians, jugglers, fire-eaters, a human ostrich, and a bearded Venus. Interest in the show remained high as did Cody's debts. By 1897, he owed Salisbury $100,000, and after Salisbury's death in 1902, the show and Cody

Romanticized sheetmusic cover of Buffalo Bill Cody, from 1892. HTC.

deteriorated rapidly. Never too drunk to fall off his horse, he continued to enjoy the high life and to stagger through tours in America and Europe until his death in 1917, spending his last four years with a second-rate circus after the Wild West Show went bankrupt.

Buffalo Bill was a poor businessman, a profligate, and not really much of an entertainer. Basically what he did was ride around the arena shooting Indians or glass balls thrown into the air and looking every inch the towering, handsome figure that a true hero should be. At least superficially, he represented something that late-nineteenth-century Americans and Europeans wanted to believe in—the mythic saga of genuine heroes taming the wilderness, paving the way for civilization, and producing a noble American national character, what one reviewer called "a manly race." Cody and much of his troupe had actually fought the battles, but the result was not great character or noble achievements. It was an egotistical drunk on horseback touring with a bing-bang-shoot-'em-up, the-only-good-Indian-is-a-dead-Indian show. Patrons, of course, did not see it that way; they did not want to. They saw an exciting, reassuring enactment of a basic American myth of manly combat resulting in the survival of the fittest. Cody's and his many show business successors' portrayals of the wilderness creating and rejuvenating American character made a much greater impact on popular thought than historian Frederick Jackson Turner's celebrated frontier thesis or William Graham Sumner's Social Darwinism. With minor modifications, Cody's saga—in the Western movie—remains a staple of American popular culture.

Ironically, the nation's greatest source of genuine heroism, the Civil War, did not become a part of popular drama, actually melodrama, until the 1880s when the passage of time had somewhat dulled the pain of the war. And even then the wounds were too tender, the scars too sensitive, to allow popular plays to focus on the brutal struggle or violent heroism of the bloody combat. To most Americans, the Wild West Show was a fantasy, but the Civil War remained a recurrent nightmare. Thus, popular plays about the war—William Gillette's *Held By the Enemy* and *Secret Service, Shenandoah,* and the many others—centered on healing the wounds, on pulling the American national family back together. Almost always set in the South, often focusing on a Union Army spy behind Confederate lines, the plays usually ignored the causes of

William Gillette captured by Confederates in *Secret Service.* HTC.

the war, the broad issues involved, and even the suffering. Instead, they concentrated on the harrowing situations the war imposed on individuals, which offered exciting opportunities for suspense, intrigue, and near-catastrophes. A love affair between a Union Army officer and a lovely Southern belle was the most common device personalizing the conflict, a device that created the classic melodramatic dilemma, the characters being torn between their duty and their feelings, their love for their countries and their love for each other. As in other melodramas, the heroines were most often called upon to make the greatest sacrifices. In one of the most popular of the Civil War plays, David Belasco's *Heart of Maryland,* for example, the Southern heroine climbed a forty-foot bell tower, where she swung on the bell's clapper so that the Confederate soldiers could not ring the alarm that would have prevented her beloved Union Army lover from escaping. These intersectional romances testified that common Americans, whether they happened to be born above or below the Mason-Dixon line, belonged together as one people. Together, the plays implied, they could survive the catastrophe of the Civil War or even the devastating onslaught of modernization.

Popular plays in their heyday might have helped the American people cope with modernization, but live drama in the concert halls of the heartland could not survive the forces of the new order forever. Modernization brought drama to the Beaver Dams; to a great extent, it shaped the plays' form, tone, and content; and it ultimately destroyed live theater as a major entertainment form for common Americans. In the early twentieth century, the mass-production technology of the machine age brought the centralized production and distribution systems that characterized the nation's industry and business to popular drama. A new industry, the motion picture industry, emerged, one that could record popular plays on film and offer the people fine shows featuring famous stars at inexpensive prices. Broadway had never gotten closer to Beaver Dam than Milwaukee, sixty miles away. But Hollywood reached right into the heartland, right into the Beaver Dams. Motion pictures changed the medium more than the message, from live actors on stages to inanimate, larger-than-life images on screens. Although films continued to exploit the formulas that traveling theater groups had discovered and although acting companies continued to tour with the "old chestnuts," never again was live drama the only show or even the best show in the Beaver Dams; never again could audiences of common Americans directly shape their dramatic entertainment; never again was live drama the people's theater.

CHAPTER SEVEN

THE EVOLUTION OF THE MUSICAL COMEDY

After the Civil War, when much of American show business was first developing into its familiar form, a great many common people found a temporary escape from the concerns, frustrations, and anxieties of modernization in the fantasy world of musical comedy, a world of dazzlingly beautiful productions, lovely women and handsome men, happy romances and even happier endings, and light-hearted humor, music, song, and dance. Early American musicals borrowed from European ballet, with its short-skirted women, from European extravaganzas, with their spectacular scenery, from European operettas, with their semiclassical scores, and from other American popular entertainment forms, with their folk-based songs, popular dances, earthy humor, burlesques of high culture, and their total disregard for dramatic continuity. Even though, or perhaps because, musicals were unlikely blends of elitist European culture and American popular entertainment, they proved extremely popular in the late nineteenth century.

The term "musicals" actually covered a wide-range of shows, from comic operas to variety revues. Some of the productions defied classification, but three basic types of musicals eventually evolved: the spectacular extravaganza; the show centered on everyday life, language, and lore of common Americans; and the European-based op-

BLACK CROOK

eretta. The lavish extravaganzas "educated" their audiences, just as Barnum's museum had "instructed" an earlier generation. But late-nineteenth-century Americans' curiosity focused not on the wonders or freaks of nature but rather on the nations and peoples of the world. The United States was becoming a world power, and show business brought the world to its audiences in its lavish productions set in exotic lands. These extravaganzas also appealed to and represented Americans' pride in the size of the nation's products, wealth, and power. Like the Centennial celebration that featured the largest buildings and machines ever seen, the opulent stage spectacles were truly breath-taking in scale and grandeur, making conspicuous consumption at least temporarily available to common people in the age of the "Robber Barons." The musicals that centered on common people reasserted the importance of average Americans, offered catchy songs and popular dances, and provided new themes, new characters, and new heroes for the new age. Coming well after the anti-aristocratic diatribes of pre-Civil War show business and at a time when common people's lives became extremely difficult and trying, the third form, the operetta or Comic Opera, offered democratic Americans a chance to experience vicariously the almost dreamlike upper-class world of elegance, grace, and order. These three strains remain part of the American musical stage to this day.

In the summer of 1866, Henry C. Jarrett, an aspiring young New York City theater manager, with the financial backing of Wall Street broker, Harry Palmer, brought a European ballet troupe to America and outfitted it with beautiful sets and the latest sexy French costumes. Since the late 1840s, European ballet dancers had proved great attractions in the United States (more for the women's short skirts than for the dancing), so Jarrett and Palmer looked forward to making a nice profit. But before the new troupe could open in New York, the theater it was booked into, The Academy of Music, burned down and the only other suitable theater, Niblo's Garden, had already booked an untried melodrama, *The Black Crook.* Jarrett and Palmer grew desperate as their high-priced company lay idle, not earning a cent. William Wheatley, the manager of Niblo's, felt uncertain about his shaky new production, so when Jarrett and Palmer suggested combining their two shows, Wheatley leapt at the chance to add a certain draw to his bill, even if it did produce an improbable combination of European ballet and spectacle with a melodrama loosely based on *Faust.* But since American audiences were accustomed to hodge-podge bills that mixed serious drama with variety acts and farces, few people at the time realized that Niblo's polyglot production of *The Black Crook* was a landmark production in the history of American show business, the first major step toward both the burlesque show and the musical comedy.

The show was an instant sensation, but certainly not because of the story: Hertzog, the black crook, contracts to deliver one soul a year to the devil in exchange for magical powers and an additional year of life. Meanwhile, evil count Wolfenstein kidnaps the heroine, Amina, and throws her lover, the hero, Rudolph, into a dungeon. As the end of the year approaches, Hertzog, who has singled out Rudolph as his annual victim, magically frees Rudolph from his cell and convinces him to

Dancing women from an 1874 version of *The Black Crook.* Author's collection.

Stalacta's grotto scene from *The Black Crook*. HTC.

set off in search of a fictional treasure supposedly buried deep in the forest. On his quest, Rudolph saves the life of a dove—white, of course—from a serpent. Lest the symbolism escape the audience, the dove immediately turns into Stalacta, the fairy queen, who exposes Hertzog's fiendish trickery. The tide has turned in favor of Virtue. In true melodramatic fashion, goodness is ultimately rewarded (Amina and Rudolph are married), and evil is punished (Wolfenstein is dead and Hertzog, the black crook, is carried off to hell by the agent of darkness).

The major value of the plot was not in its melodramatic machinations, although they were no more implausible than many others, but rather in the abundant opportunities it provided for spectacular special effects. "The scenery is magnificent," the *New York Tribune*'s critic observed, "the ballet is beautiful; the drama is—rubbish." To house what the producers agreed should be an elaborate extravaganza, they remade the Niblo's Garden stage. Every floor board moved in grooves, allowing crews to change the shape and structure of the stage during the production; trapdoors popped open and closed all over the floor; and the new machinery raised and lowered huge sets in seconds from the cellar, to the stage, to the rafters. The first act, devoted to plot development, dragged. But when the "Grand Ballet of Gems"—the gems portrayed by scantily clad women—opened the second act, the extravaganza, excitement, and sexual stimulation began. Besides the two hundred well-shaped female legs daringly displayed in flesh-colored tights, the production dazzled audiences with its special effects: scenes magically rising out of the floor, fairies soaring through the air, shimmering stalagmites and stalactites glistening in Stalacta's crystal grotto, a "hurricane of gauze" sweeping through a mountain pass, the dramatic appearances of satan, and a sensuous "pas de demons" dance in which four leotard-clad women wearing no skirts were possessed by the devil, demonstrating their possession with their devilish gyrations. On it went. For five and a half hours, the production's special effects and cavorting women stunned audiences, finally culminating in one last spectacular scene: "One by one, curtains of mist ascend and drift away," a critic gasped. "Silver couches, on which the fairies loll in negligent grace, ascend and descend amid silver rain. From the clouds drop gilded chariots and the white forms of angels. It is a very beautiful pageant." American audiences had never seen anything like it.

The "beautiful pageant" ran an unprecedented 474 performances in its initial New York engagement. To maintain interest in it during the sixteen-month run, the producers regularly added new attractions to the already sensational show: an opulent ballroom scene, two new ballets, a military music and drill production number, one hundred and fifty children in a "baby ballet," and an "original and wonderful mechanical donkey." The production was revived in New York City eight times between 1868 and 1892, while touring companies performed it throughout the nation, the original producers having franchised the exclusive territorial production rights. The most controversial facet of the production, its generous display of women's bodies, drew strong denunciations from ministers and newspaper editors. "The police should arrest all engaged in such a violation of public decency," bellowed James Gordon Bennett in the New York *Herald.* But by the mid-1860s, such condemnations of the show as "Sodom and Gomorra" and "ancient heathen orgies" seemed only to increase attendance. The times were changing.

Besides the leering old men that reviewers discovered in the front row seats and the large masses of common people in the gallery, high-society people went "slumming" to the production, some of the women in the audience reportedly rivalling the female performers in showing off their bodies. Society women attended *The Black Crook* in dresses with so much décolleté, one satirical journal sniped, that they were cut "V" shape in the back and "W" in the front. No one could stay away from the new sensation. Loving crowds as he did, P. T. Barnum could not resist the chance to make an appearance before the production's large audience. "Now watch the fuss they make over me," he boasted expectantly to a friend as he conspicuously swaggered into the theater. "In a moment you'll hear them say, 'there's Barnum—there in the box.'" But the patrons, focusing their attention on the stage and buzzing about the production, either did not notice or did not care about Barnum's presence—not even when he leaned far out of his box and loudly raised his voice.

As the first American musical show to achieve a long, prosperous run, *The Black Crook* demonstrated the huge potential audiences for lavishly mounted productions featuring music, dance, and pretty women in scanty costumes. But *The Black Crook,* based

The Kiralfy Brothers' 1887 revival of *The Black Crook*. HTC.

on European ballet and extravaganza, was far from an American show business form. The story of American musicals in the late nineteenth century is the story of the adaptation and naturalization of European productions to American tastes. American audiences loved grandeur, opulence, and colossal scale. And they loved looking at pretty women. But they preferred foot-tapping music, recognizable dances, understandable dialogue, and folksy humor. They liked European form and performance style, but they wanted American content. These two impulses—European sophistication and American vitality—continued to run throughout the history of American musicals. It was fifty years of experimentation and stupendous productions before producers found a satisfying, distinctively American blend.

In October 1868, a show opened in New York that was destined to break *The Black Crook*'s consecutive performance record. Although the new production offered a wide range of attractions, including its own "Baby Ballet," the first American roller-skating troupe, circus acts, bicyclists, subterranean grottoes, a lavish panorama of Naples, and stunning special effects like a steamboat explosion and fire, it featured a male star who substituted pantomime comedy for sex appeal. George L. Fox began his acting career in George C. Howard's first production of *Uncle Tom's Cabin* but later specialized in mime, becoming America's greatest pantomimist. The plot of *Humpty Dumpty,* even less important to the show than *The Black Crook*'s, bore scant resemblance to the Mother Goose stories from which it drew its title. The original fairy-tale characters appeared only briefly, a Fairy Queen transforming them into commedia dell'arte figures. Humpty Dumpty, for example, became the Clown—others became Harlequin and Pantaloon. The evening's entertainment mixed production numbers and pantomime comedy heavily laced with pathos. Fox a critic applauded, "was not content to please merely by being knocked down numerous times and jumping over tables and through windows. His muteness and passivity, were infinitely more ludicrous than the bustling antics of other clowns, as also was his affectation of ignorant simplicity and credulous innocence." Fox starred as The Clown over a thousand times before his death in 1877. His unique talent for evoking in his audiences a wide range of emotions accounts for his popularity when imitations of him failed. After Fox's death pantomime as a major American show business feature lay dormant for decades until motion pictures revived this comic art and Charlie Chaplin and Harold Lloyd perfected it. But if pantomime in musicals died with Fox, extravaganza and lavish production certainly did not.

In 1874, *Evangeline,* nominally a parody of Longfellow's poem, joined the growing number of lavish extravaganzas trying to cash in on *The Black Crook*'s and *Humpty Dumpty*'s great successes. But it was not just another spectacular production. It was a major step in the evolution of American musicals. Besides being the first show to be billed a "musical comedy," it was also the first to have an original score and to rely on common language, popular music and dance. Although supposedly a burlesque, a parody of Longfellow's poem, the play had little connection with it, using settings as far from the poem's Nova Scotia as Arizona and Africa, along with gimmicks as diverse as a spouting whale, a dancing "cow" played by two men in one costume, a woman in tights playing the male lead, and three-hundred-pound George Fortesque wearing a dress in a leading female role.

After seeing a touring English burlesque troupe and finding it "highly depressing" because of the peculiar density of the British humor," Edward E. Rice and a friend decided to see if they could do better. The result was *Evangeline,* a show that initially opened to fill a two-week summer-scheduling gap at Niblo's Garden with an economical production. But with its wide variety of features, the show became an unexpected and long-lived success, with versions of it touring the country for thirty years. Although Rice originally set out to win the "respectable family" audiences that were offended by the sexual excesses of *The Black Crook* and the early girlie shows, he managed to spice up his show by casting women in male roles and dressing them in tunics and tights. But this was not primarily a leg show. Besides the dancing cow, Rice's other unique creation, a mute observer wandering in and out of the production with a sometimes comical, sometimes philosophical attitude, intrigued audiences. Combining production numbers like a balloon trip to Arizona—a distant and exotic land at that time—with a varied series of songs, comedy routines, and dances, Rice created an appealing eve-

Geo. L. Fox's
ORIGINAL
H.D.
Broadway Theatre
728 & 730 Broadway N.Y.

ning's entertainment that continually drew large audiences, despite critics' condemnations. "What is there in *Evangeline*," one reviewer wondered in 1880, "that should ever have gained for it the amount of public favor it has enjoyed?" Few tried to answer the question directly, but Rice and many other producers unsuccessfully tried to reproduce *Evangeline*'s success. With its blend of sexuality and "cornpone," its contrasts between a huge man in a dress and a shapely woman in the hero's clothes, its earthy puns that one critic called "slanguage," its distinctively American content, its dancing cow, its silent observer-commentator who seemed in some uncertain way to raise the level of the production above that of the ordinary musical-comedy extravaganza, the original continued to outdraw and outlive its successors.

Since Europeans and European innovations regularly influenced the American musical comedy, it is fitting that three Hungarian emigrant brothers—Imre, Bollossy, and Arnold Kiralfy—raised extravaganza to its nineteenth-century heights in the United States, heights that left no room for embellishment until twentieth-century technology made new stage effects possible. Arriving in the United States in 1868, the performing brothers gained experience in the pioneering American extravaganzas, Arnold by dancing in an 1868 revival of *The Black Crook* and Imre and Bolossy by working as Harlequins in an 1871 revival of *Humpty Dumpty*. The brothers quickly realized that American audiences loved realistic large-scale spectacles, the kinds of productions they knew from Europe, and they resolved to create their own lavish shows. In 1875, the Kiralfy's truly dazzling production of Jules Verne's *Around the World in 80 Days* opened in the rebuilt Academy of Music. Focusing on the most exotic and romantic aspects of the story—Suez Canal, Hindustan, Calcutta, the Taj Mahal, a Brahmin cremation, elephants, an Indian raid in the American West, and "Fetish Dances, and Oriental Groupings by Lovely Maidens in Sumptuous Attire"—the show brought what seemed the entire world to American audiences with an unprecedented realism. "Nothing so splendid has ever been seen in this city," marveled a critic in New York, the city that had seen *The Black Crook, Humpty Dumpty, Evangeline,* and every other American extravaganza.

Like other successful businessmen in and out of show business, the Kiralfys meticulously planned every detail of their production. They discovered that using pastel colors for their backdrops, for example, created an atmosphere of spaciousness, beauty, and fantasy. It also threw the actors in the foreground into vivid relief, giving each scene a deepened sense of proportion, scale, and realism. The Kiralfys were the first American producers to make tree branches with irregular naturalistic patterns. Although audiences probably did not notice these little touches, they all added to the overall effect of the productions that seemed truly extraordinary even in the age of extravaganzas. But it was not attention to detail that attracted huge audiences for the shows; it was continual innovation. The Kiralfys boasted of their 1883, *Excelsior,* for example, that the "novel electric effects [were] by the Edison Electric Light Company, under the personal direction of Mr. Edison." The electric lighting was a special attraction; gas still provided the bulk of the illumination.

George L. Fox as the Clown in *Humpty Dumpty*. NYLC.

A scene from *Evangeline* featuring gigantic George Fortesque as a woman. HTC.

Lest Edison's new gadget not prove a great enough lure, *Excelsior*'s subject was no less than the entire story of the rise of modern civilization. Cast members took the parts of metaphorical figures like Light, Darkness, and Civilization as well as portraying peoples from all over the world—Indians, Arabs, Englishmen, Chinese, Turks, and Frenchmen—in a wide range of settings. Besides its many American performers, the huge cast of the gigantic production that had something for everybody also boasted the Parisian Eden Theatre Ballet Company, The Venetian Ballet Troupe, and "the most distinguished artists of the Scala Theatre of Milan." After three acts and twelve lavish productions, the show climaxed with "The Triumph of Light over Darkness and Peaceful Union of Nations." Such productions, that neatly capsulized the history of man, culminating with the United States, of course, provided frustrated late-nineteenth-century Americans with a reassuring sense of order and of national importance as well as with "information" about the world.

In 1888, after the brothers had split up, Imre staged *The Fall of Rome* as an outdoor spectacle on Staten Island using tons of armor, a huge ballet, elephants, chariot racing, and a cast of 2000! Three years later, he carried the extravaganzas to an absurd level, by combining with Barnum and Bailey's Greatest Show on Earth to stage *Imre Kiralfy's Sublime, Nautical, Martial and Poetical Spectacle: Columbus and The Discovery of Amer-*

ica. The spectacle began in Spain with the expulsion of the Moors, and then followed the career of Christopher Columbus: beseeching Isabella for funds, crossing the ocean (quelling a mutiny en route), discovering Indian-infested America, and returning to a triumphal reception in Barcelona. With the combined resources and talents of the nation's biggest circus and its greatest producer of extravaganzas, the *Columbus* show brought the originally European, ballet-based extravaganza to its nineteenth-century culmination, giving it American content, American form, and American grandeur, with the discovery of the nation as its theme and a circus as its cast.

In 1905, when the $2,000,000 Hippodrome Theatre, "the largest, safest, and costliest playhouse in the world," opened in New York City, extravaganza at last had a properly palatial home, the Radio City Music Hall of its day. Besides boasting the most modern theatrical machinery in the world, two huge stages capable of holding six hundred performers and one hundred and fifty animals at the same time, and seating for over 5000 patrons, it featured on its downstairs floor a restaurant, a cafe, a menagerie, and a sideshow. The shows drew huge crowds, but the management made a profit from its extremely expensive productions only by running each extravaganza for an entire year. The 1905 opening show set the pattern, offering a circus and a ballet in the first half and a full, two-act realistic war spectacle, *Andersonville,* in the second. From 1907 to 1915, the Shuberts, who rivalled Ziegfeld as the nation's most lavish producers, ran the Hippodrome, offering an incredible array of actually colossal spectacles: Wild West shows; full two-ring circuses; naval battles in huge water tanks; automobile races; airplane dogfights; huge fires; fierce tornados; howling hurricanes; and

Poster for the Kiralfy Brothers' lavish *Around the World in 80 Days.* NYLC.

the "Wars of the World," a kind of "Destruction's Greatest Hits," including the Crusades, the French Revolution, the Mexican-American War, and the Civil War. The 1913 show, *America,* dealt with the United States from the landing of Columbus to the evening rush hour at newly completed Grand Central Station in the *opening* scene! Subsequently, the audience visited the New Orleans levee, the Alamo, a New England farm, the East Side of New York, and the Panama Canal—each reproduced in lavish detail.

The productions and the theater itself were the stars at the Hippodrome, not the music, the performers, or the large numbers of shapely chorus girls. The shows continued in

Crusades scene from *Wars of the World* in the Hippodrome Theater. HTC.

their grand manner until 1925, when their appeal (perhaps undercut by motion pictures) decreased so much that the Hippodrome became a vaudeville theater, returning to its former glory only occasionally, as it did in 1935 as the home of Rodgers and Hart's grandly produced circus musical, *Jumbo*. During its heyday no other productions—not even Ziegfeld's—compared to the Hippodrome's for sheer grandeur and magnificance. But like a huge lumbering dinosaur, it could not survive a basic change in environment. The Hippodrome could not compete with motion picture technology's one-time-only production costs and frequent changes of bills. But it and the other extravaganzas that preceded it demonstrated that American audiences loved grandeur and huge spectacular pageants set in exotic lands, both of which motion pictures ultimately made into highly profitable box-office fare. The grand theaters, like the Hippodrome, the show business palaces, also made luxury and splendor available, at least temporarily, to anyone with twenty-five cents to spare, just as their stupendous shows "educated" the public about exotic lands and peoples, about the "magic" of new machinery and inventions, and about the glories of American history. Except for making spectacle a permanent feature of musicals, these huge shows, which more closely resembled circuses than normal theatrical productions, in the long run contributed little except glitter and glamour to the development of musical comedies.

While lavish spectacles dominated American musicals, small-scale, unpretentious musical productions that were focused on common people began to claim a place on the musical stage. In 1879, Nate Salisbury's Troubadours, a small group of traveling entertainers, returned to New York City from a Western tour through the Beaver Dam Concert Halls of the heartland. In New York, the troupe filled an open, off-season date at the San Francisco Minstrels' theater with a lighthearted, low-budgeted show, *The Brook*, which ran only two weeks but deserves an important place in the history of musicals.

The Brook was the first known production to employ what later became American musical comedy's distinctive characteristics. It told a story about average people and used vernacular music and dance to do it. *The Brook* featured no extravaganza, no machinery, no ballet, no elaborate choreography, no huge cast, and no women in tights. Its cast of five acted out the story of ordinary people going on an ordinary picnic, with somewhat embellished ordinary "hazards": salt spilling into the jam, fishbait "flavoring" the coffee, vinegar spicing up the sandwiches, and ants running all over everything and everyone. To these, Salisbury added a watermelon basket containing theatrical costumes instead of melons, which gave the picnickers a credible excuse to dress up, dance, and sing. After their frolic by the brook, they returned home and the play ended. It just ended—no great transformation scene, no huge production number, no extravaganza.

The object of the show, Salisbury explained, was "the natural reproduction of the jollity and funny mishaps that attend the usual pic-nic excursion." Unlike most musical productions of the day, it was not intended to be dazzling, awe-inspiring, or greater-than-life. As one critic observed, "it held nature up to the mirror." It made common people and everyday life subjects for musicals as well as for popular plays, while also perpetuating the prevalent stage image that the country, not the city, was the source of happiness and joy. *The Brook* and other similar productions provided a successful career for Salisbury until he took over management of the Buffalo Bill Cody shows, the sort of abrupt change that is "normal" for ambitious show business people. Because of Salisbury's success and because his type of show, then known as farce-comedy, was easy to finance, produce, and cast—not requiring ballet skills, trained voices, or large productions—Salisbury's Troubadours soon had many traveling competitors, troupes who carried the light musical comedies to the Beaver Dams of America, added a realistic, unpretentious quality to musical entertainment, and demonstrated that the American vernacular—the language, songs, dances, and humor of the common people—provided excellent material for musicals.

In 1879, the same year that Salisbury opened his rural, western-tested *The Brook* in New York City, Edward Harrigan and Tony Hart—a team that came to be known as the American Gilbert and Sullivan—opened their urban Bowery-tested *Mulligan Guards*. Harrigan established urban ethnic groups as major characters on the American stage. "It began," Harrigan recalled of his approach, "with the New York 'boy,' the Irish-American, and our African brother. As these grew in popularity," he explained, "I added the other prominent types which go to make up life in the metropolis and in every other large city of the Union and Canada. These are the Irishmen, Englishmen, German, Low German, Chinese, Italian, Russian, and Southern darky." As desperately

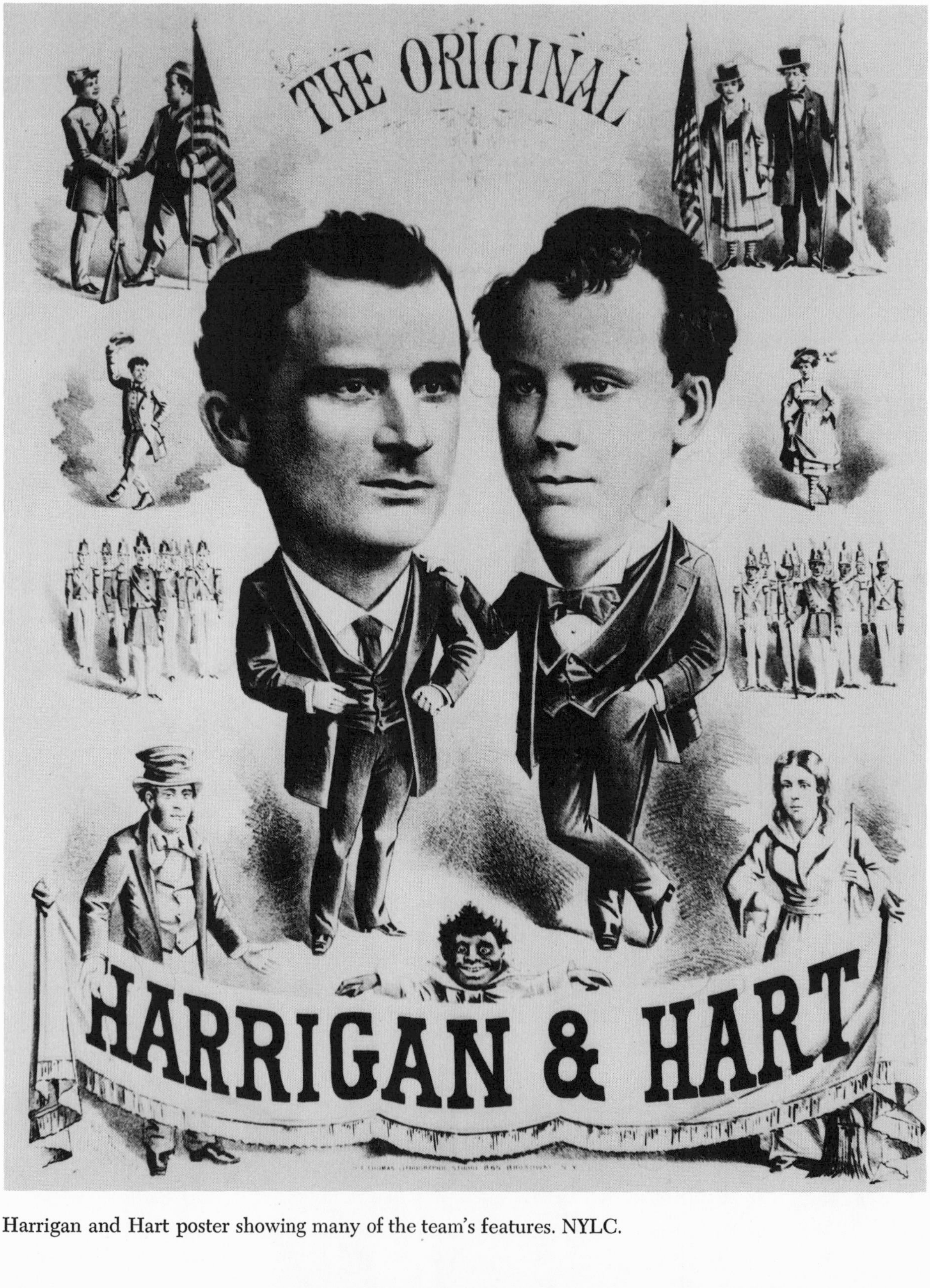

Harrigan and Hart poster showing many of the team's features. NYLC.

as late-nineteenth-century Americans wanted to seek refuge from their troubles in rural and frontier myths and to believe the population was homogeneous, the nation had to come to grips with the city and its increasingly diverse population. Beginning with Harrigan and Hart, continuing through the work of Charles H. Hoyt, and culminating in George M. Cohan's early-twentieth-century triumphs, the musical stage made urban life and people much more attractive and understandable.

As minstrels had first done thirty years before, Harrigan and Hart and their successors brought the vitality of the folk into show business. But they drew their characters from the ethnic neighborhoods of New York and other cities, not from the backlands. Unlike minstrelsy, Harrigan's comedy laughed *with* as well as at minority groups. Harrigan and Hart, like Gilbert and Sullivan, chronicled and satirized elements of their societies with a new realism, lively humor, and captivating music. But while the Englishmen focused on the upper classes, the democratic Americans concentrated on the lower classes. "Polite society, wealth, and culture possess little or no color and picturesqueness," Harrigan observed in terms that might have been lifted out of the 1830s and 1840s. "The chief use I make of them is as a foil to the poor, the workers, the great middle class."

As a boy, Harrigan, the librettist and dramatist of the team, got a good taste of New York city workingmen and of popular entertainment. Quitting school in 1859 at age fourteen, he knocked about as an errand boy, printer's devil, shipyard apprentice, and child actor, once giving a stump speech with Campbell's Minstrels at the Bowery Theatre. After he shipped out to New Orleans and San Francisco, he again found his way from the wharf to the stage, turning comic caricatures of Negroes and Irishmen into a successful show business career in the late 1860s. As part of a two-man act, he drifted back from the West to New York and back from vaudeville to minstrelsy. In Chicago with a minstrel troupe, he met Tony Hart, a fifteen-year-old minstrel female impersonator. They formed a partnership that endured and prospered for fifteen years. After several years of touring, they settled down in 1873 for a two-year contract at the Theatre Comique in New York City, where composer David Braham joined the team. Braham became the Sullivan to Harrigan's Gilbert. In the mid-1870s, the "Mulligan" material began to appear, first as skits and finally as full-length productions.

In his musical plays, Harrigan spun an intricate web of East Side New York's ethnic life, the Irish at the center and the others—especially blacks and Germans—intertwined with them. Set in his fictional "Mulligan Alley," the plays centered on Walsingham McSweeney's The Wee Drop Saloon. Across from the bar stood a two-story tenement, containing an Italian junk shop and Ah Wung's Chinese laundry and rooming house. Next door stood the headquarters of a Negro social club—whose elaborate ritual, including the Royal Burn-Alive Brotherly Grip, was the precursor of Amos 'n Andy's Mystic Knights of the Sea. Occupying the first floor of the club was a policy (numbers) shop run by Welcome Allup, the husband of the Mulligans' Negro maid, Rebecca (a role that Tony Hart starred in as one of his female impersonations). Dan Mulligan and his wife Cordelia were the focal points of the plays. But characters representing the other ethnic groups played critically important roles in the series. The Negro characters, all played by whites in blackface, provided the Irish's major competitors, and, though still stereotyped, they had a humanity

Design by Charles W. Whitman for a typical Harrigan and Hart scene. NYLC.

that was unusual for the nineteenth-century stage. Rebecca held her own in a running battle of words and wits with the Mulligans, and Palestine Puter proudly led the black Skidmore Guards, whose marching rivalled Dan Mulligan's Irish Guards. Gustave Lochmuller, a German butcher married to an Irish woman, provided Dan's political opponent and verbal sparring partner. These major characters, supplemented with other ethnic personalities, presented a dazzling array of big-city culture conflicts, ethnic humor, heavily laced with slapstick, catchy song and dances, and typical special effects like waterfalls, storms, and fires.

Although all his ethnic characters were important, Harrigan's most important achievement was presenting the Irish-American in a sympathetic way. Dan Mulligan, Harrigan's major character, which he himself played, came to America in 1848, fought in the Civil War, bought a grocery store, and became a successful local politician—a model American success story. Since the 1840s, Irish-Americans had had to endure strong prejudice in America including stereotypes of them as heavy-drinking brawlers, lazy fools who sold their votes, and agents sent by the Pope to subvert American democracy. Beginning in the 1850s when large numbers of Irishmen became minstrels, the minstrel show began to modify these negative images, but it was not until Harrigan traded his blackface make-up for his own face, his Negro dialect for his Irish brogue, that show business portrayed the Irish as real people. His Irishmen were laughed at, but they were also laughed with; they drank hard, but they also worked hard; they took graft, but only when they could not get jobs. Harrigan also praised their strong sense of group loyalty, applauded their heroism during the Civil War, lamented the human anthills they had to live in, and denounced the discrimination they had to endure. Although his and Braham's songs and skits did not endure, they pervaded the show business of the day with their humane portrayals of the Irish, portrayals that strongly influenced the great many people who knew nothing about ethnic groups except what they saw on stage.

The impact of Harrigan's messages was greatly enhanced because he was a superb entertainer, not a preacher. "I never dig up the mire in my plays," he explained. "It is only the lighter, better side of East Side life which I attempt to show." This did not mean that he portrayed only happy, carefree tenement dwellers. It meant that he knew the value of humor for communicating a serious message. "They may draw a tear—but only one," he explained of his instructions to his actors, "and a laugh must follow. The tear is necessary, or the character would not be well-drawn. There is pathos or tragedy in every life east of Elizabeth Street. The audiences must be aware of this, but only vaguely. My plan," he concluded in a 1903 interview, "is always to let the spectators do the thinking if they want to." He knew he had to keep his patrons laughing, if he wanted to keep them as patrons. When in 1882, for example, he got too serious about the plight of a Jewish pawnbroker in *Mordecai Lyons,* applause and attendance decreased. He quickly returned to his own ground with *McSorley's Inflation,* the story of an Irishman who runs for Congress courting the Negro vote and faces complications when his wife, played by Tony Hart, somehow finds herself in the middle of a "Colored Convention" and is rescued by a brigade of Irish market women in a rollicking romp of slapstick and ethnic slurs. "McSorley is Mulligan with a new name," a reviewer applauded, "and the Comique [Theatre] has regained its popularity," a popularity based heavily on working class people.

"I'd hate to play in a theatre without a gallery," Harrigan once confessed in a statement that epitomized his approach. His people were in the gallery, the common people he grew up with on the wharves. He not only played to them as many popular entertainers did, he played for them. They thought of him as one of them, as much their spokesman as their entertainer. He put them onstage, and they adored him for it. "It was the story of other seasons, all over again," the New York *Sun* observed of a typically rousing opening of an 1888 Harrigan and Hart show, "a lusty welcoming by voice and hand, a cheer from enthusiastic throats, an overflow of ready praise. . . . Nothing else in the city's theatrical history affords a similar spectacle; nothing else approaches it in its democratic eclat." Mulligan was Mose the B'howery B'hoy updated and expanded to include an entire community. Seeking to capture realistically the look, tone, and feel of his people, Harrigan bought costumes in second-hand clothing stores, drew material from the streets, and developed his plays onstage instead of on paper so he could be sure that his characters, sets, and dialects all seemed familiar to the b'hoys in the audience. With encores for nearly every number and speeches demanded from each of the resident company's old favorites on their first entrance, it often took the cast five hours to get through a three-hour show as the audiences wildly cheered their "old friends."

Edward Harrigan and Annie Yeomans as Dan and Cordelia Mulligan, the characters Harrigan used to humanize stage images of the Irish. Detail of illustration on page 184.

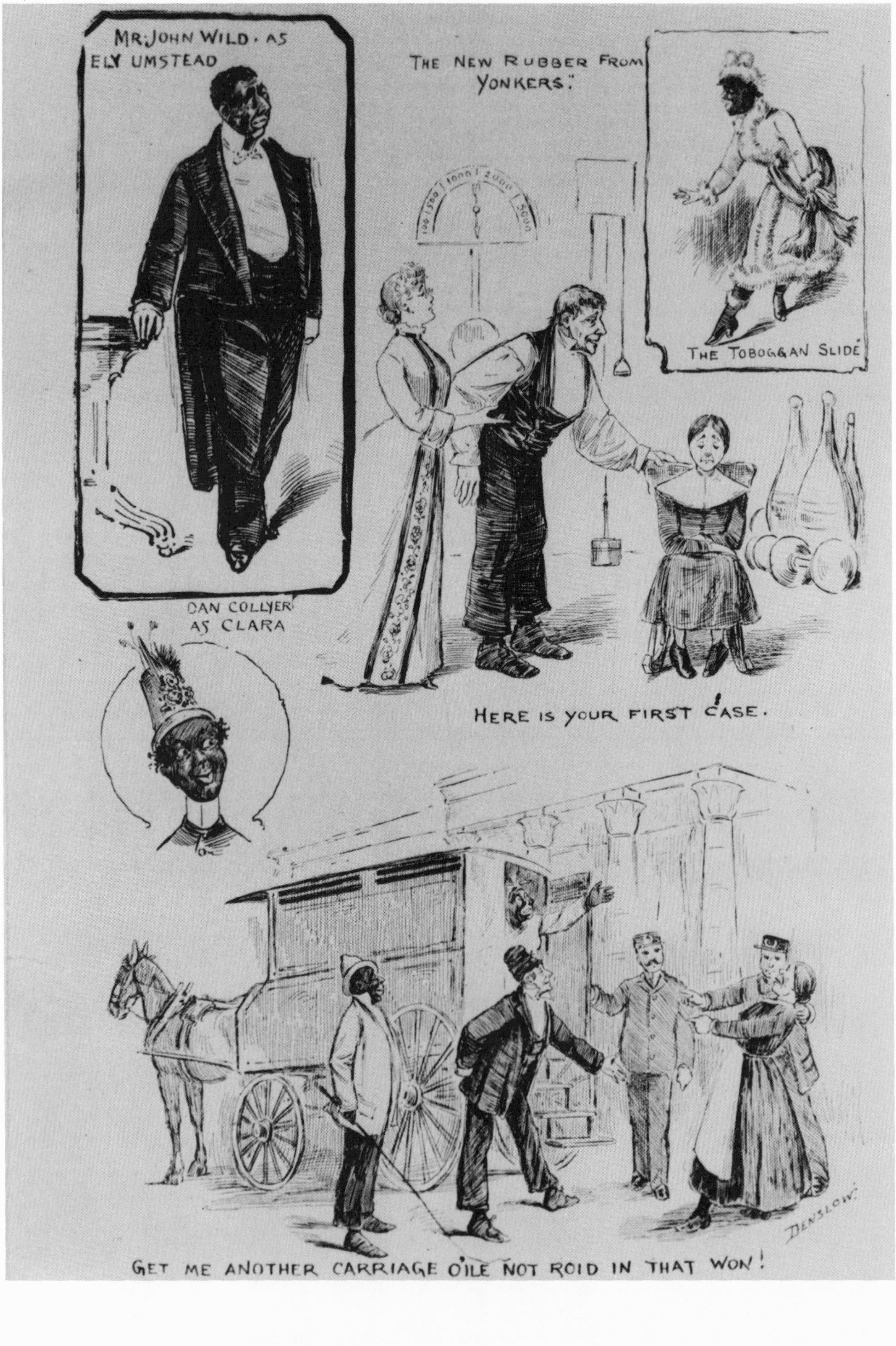
MR. JOHN WILD. AS
ELY UMSTEAD
"THE NEW RUBBER FROM
YONKERS."
THE TOBOGGAN SLIDE
DAN COLLYER
AS CLARA
HERE IS YOUR FIRST CASE.
DENSLOW.
GET ME ANOTHER CARRIAGE O'ILE NOT ROID IN THAT WON!

Although Harrigan and Braham's catchy songs did not endure, they were international sensations in the late nineteenth century. Besides being on the lips of minstrel troupes, vaudevillians, and New Yorkers of all sorts, the song "The Mulligan Guards" turned up in Rudyard Kipling's *Kim;* the British Coldstream Guards marched to it; Parisians sang it and the Viennese composer Karl Milloecker "borrowed" it for the first act finale of his *The Beggar Student.* Contemporary critics, including William Dean Howells, crowned Harrigan the American Dickens, Molière, Zola, Ibsen, and a theatrical Hogarth. The passage of time has proved that Harrigan did not belong in the same category with those classic writers and artists. At the time, he seemed as significant as he did because, when European naturalistic writing had not taken root in America, Harrigan drew on urban common people, even "low-life," for his material and realistically presented its vitality on stage.

Harrigan continued to work and rework his scenes of New York's vital street life and its serio-comic ethnic conflict. And Braham continued to turn out his songs until 1895 when Harrigan leased out his theater. After that, Harrigan sporadically produced new shows, centered as always on Irish-Negro conflicts, until his several farewell performances in 1908 and 1909. Ironically, the reasons for his shows' successes spelled their doom. They successfully captured the sights, sounds, and feelings of New York City ethnic life in the 1870s and 1880s. But times changed, and Harrigan did not. His plays became period pieces, as Mose the B'howery B'hoy had by Harrigan's day. Although his shows were as close to vaudeville and minstrelsy as to drama, they were an important step toward the American musical comedy that focused on common people, often on ethnic minorities or low-life. His shows brought a new reality and vitality, a new vogue for local and topical songs, and a new focus on city life and urban heroes to musical shows, making a deep impression on other producers and performers and opening the way for subsequent developments.

Scenes from Harrigan's *McNooney's Visit.* NYLC.

Following Harrigan and Hart's success, Charles Hoyt created a number of hit musical shows about city life. But, reflecting a characteristic that plagued musicals from their inception, Hoyt's shows made little if any effort to integrate the musical numbers into the plots. In one show, he even billed the songs and dances as "musical interruptions." Not limited to ethnic life or to New York City, Hoyt's series of successful urban shows had broader appeal outside New York than Harrigan and Hart's plays. His greatest hit, *A Trip to Chinatown,* for example, ran for 650 performances after opening in New York in 1890, the longest run of *any* nineteenth-century production in the nation's entertainment capital. Traveling companies also carried it throughout the nation, during this run and for years afterward. It was the disjointed, musical farce-comedy at its best—the final stage before George M. Cohan produced modern Broadway musical comedies in the early twentieth century.

Set in San Francisco, *A Trip to Chinatown,* had, at best, a flimsy plot: a young man and his uncle, both planning a rendezvous with the same young woman, wind up in different dining rooms of the same restaurant, the comedy resulting from the young couple's attempting to hide from the uncle, from the waiters confusing the orders, and from the young man's empty wallet. By the conclusion,

Scene from *A Trip to Chinatown* featuring Bessie Clayton in the butterfly dance. HTC.

the uncle pays the bill and everyone is reconciled, and they all live happily ever after. Needless to say, the plot was not the reason the show was such a hit. "To be sure," a Boston reviewer wrote in 1896, "Mr. Hoyt's humor smacks far more of the street and barroom than of the drawing room, this is undeniable. But," he had to admit, "it is excellent humor for all that." Loie Fuller's "Butterfly Dance," in which she swirled her skirts like butterfly wings, added another great attraction, as did the satires on current subjects like women's rights and the temperance crusade.

But the greatest reason for the show's success was the music that people hummed as they left the theater, songs that sold hundreds of thousands of copies of sheet music in the 1890s—the first time a musical show had so dominated popular music. When the show came in from its trial runs to open in New York, Hoyt realized it needed another strong musical number. With no time to write one for the production, he inserted a new song that he and his composer Percy Baunt, had just written, even though it had absolutely nothing to do with San Francisco, Chinatown, or a restaurant. The show's action simply stopped for this "musical interruption." Henry Conor, playing a country rube who had wandered into the Bowery, where he found himself surrounded by drunks and thieves, made his entrance and sang:

The Bowery! The Bowery!
They do such things, and they say such things
On the Bowery! The Bowery!
I'll never go there any more.

After he sang the six verses all the way through *twice* for the wildly cheering audience, the story in the San Francisco restaurant resumed. The production also featured another popular hit, "Reuben, Reuben, I've Been Thinking," and an early example of "payola," a bribe to plug or promote a song. Charles K. Harris' "After the Ball," which the show ultimately made a popular standard, had been a failure when introduced in vaudeville. But with an offer of $500 cash and a share of the royalties, Harris got his song into *A Trip to Chinatown,* even though it and its ballroom scene had nothing to do with the plot or setting. With the exposure the play gave it, the song, like many show tunes to follow, was a sensation, ultimately becoming the first American popular song to sell five million copies of sheet music.

Musical productions had come a long way by the 1890s. Lavish spectacles with large casts including chorus girls had become routine. Plots, characters, music, dance, and humor had all been Americanized. Popular music and hit songs now came from the musical stage as they earlier had come from minstrelsy. Shows took their pace and their content from city dwellers, reflecting the ever-spreading influence of urbanization on American life. The American musical comedy was emerging.

The first true master of the American vernacular musical comedy emerged in the early twentieth century. Although not born on the fourth of July as he frequently claimed, George M. Cohan was born on July 3, 1878, while his mother was touring in vaudeville. He grew up with show business in his blood and as his school, appearing on the variety stage as an infant with his song and dance team parents and remaining there for most of his life. The family act, the Four Cohans, including his sister Josie, became a leading vaudeville attraction by the end of the nineteenth century, with George writing all its material and acting as its business manager. With his eyes on the prestige that Broadway represented, he, in 1901, expanded one of his vaudeville sketches, *The Governor's Son,* into a musical comedy, secured the financing, and opened it on Broadway in a legitimate theater. But his dream was not yet to be realized.

The nervous cast, including the Four Cohans, was awed by Broadway, and the snappy vaudeville sketch had become an overblown, slow-moving full-length show. To make matters worse, George sprained his ankle in the first scene, hobbling through the rest of the production. After poor reviews and audiences to match, George took the show on a profitable road tour. The following year the Cohans again tried one of George's expanded skits on Broadway and again had to settle for a profitable road tour. But the ambitious, confident young Cohan, accustomed to stardom in the show business hinterlands, had eyes only for Broadway, which he called "the only Bell I wanted to ring."

His third effort at a Broadway musical, *Little Johnny Jones* in 1904, did not set off an immediate chorus of bells or of accolades. And after a lukewarm reception, the show quickly followed its predecessors, although it contained two songs destined to become classics of the American musical stage—"Give My Regards to Broadway," and "Yankee Doodle Boy." By then, the Four Cohans had dis-

Production number from George M. Cohan's *Little Johnny Jones*. HTC.

banded, and George worked hard on his new show, continually rewriting, honing, and quickening the pace. When he brought it back to Broadway, it enjoyed a good three-and-a-half-month run. In the play, an honest American jockey riding in England is unjustly accused of throwing a race after he refuses to co-operate with a gambler. But the jockey clears his good name in time to marry the girl of his dreams. The plot was much less important than Cohan's breezy, rapid-fire action and dialogue, his catchy songs, his exaltation of Broadway, and his gimmick of wrapping himself in an American flag and singing patriotic songs. By putting an urban American "Yankee Doodle Boy" in England, Cohan achieved an updated version of the traditional, naïve country boy in the wilds of civilization. In this case the Yankee Doodle from the city represented all-American goodness and honesty in a foreign land. Urbanism, traditional values, and patriotism were to be Cohan's major themes.

"Never was a plant more indigenous to a particular part of the earth than was George M. Cohan to the United States of his day,"

Oscar Hammerstein II later wrote of the artist who prospered during the flush years between the buoyantly victorious Spanish-American War and the disillusioning experience of World War I, years when the quality of life for common people began to improve, making even the rosiest predictions of further progress seem believable. "The whole nation was confident of its superiority, its moral virtue, its happy isolation from the intrigues of the 'old country,'" Hammerstein concluded. The modernization that so upset nineteenth-century Americans had concentrated on developing the basic industrial, transportation, and communication systems—factories, railroads, and telegraph lines—and brought few tangible improvements in common people's lives. But by the twentieth century, modernization bore fruit for average Americans—sewing machines, ready-made clothing, canned goods, and telephones. Cohan made the city the new symbol of American progress, wealth, and power—the fulfillment of the nation's democratic ideals. The twentieth-century Yankee Doodles emerged from the sidewalks of New York—not the New England woods—spoke in the rapid-fire pace of the city—not the slow drawl of the country—and had the brash, worldly knowledge of the metropolis—not the naïveté of the farm. Cohan embodied the new urban life styles and values, and he "sold" them to the nation. It was to be the American century, an unending parade of prosperity and progress. And Cohan was to lead the parade.

Cohan's second successful play, *Forty-Five Minutes from Broadway,* which opened in 1906, continued his praise of city life, mocking New Rochelle for its suburban provincialism, for its rubes and its lack of even one cafe. The title, which measured the travel time *from* New Rochelle *to* Broadway, underscored

George M. Cohan in *Little Johnny Jones.* HTC.

the message that the city, not the country, was the place to be. The jibes at New Rochelle prompted its city council to sponsor a boycott against the play, officially protesting that it libeled the city. But the councilmen soon realized that the innocuous show did little more than put the town on the map. In the play, a rich man dies on his country estate, promising to leave his money to his maid, Mary Jane. But when no will is found, his only living relative, with an entourage that includes an ex-showgirl, her nagging mother, and his secretary Kid Burns, a somewhat coarse, ex-horseplayer, appears to claim the estate. By making Kid Burns and Mary Jane the only decent, appealing people in the play, Cohan effectively substitutes a city-slicker for the traditional poor, but honest, country boy who shows up the pretentious as empty, dishonest people. After Burns and Mary Jane fall in love, the Kid finds the will leaving everything to Mary Jane. But when he refuses to marry an heiress, she tears up the will, preferring her love for Kid Burns to the love of money that obsesses the other characters. Besides the title song, the show's other hit was "Mary's a Grand Old Name."

As if he realized that he had left out an indispensable ingredient, Cohan produced another show that same year, his heavily patriotic *George Washington Jr.*, which he billed as "an American musical play." As in his other shows, part of the plot reworked the well-worn intricacies of melodramatic love affairs, but his other major theme represented a morality play for the new age. The play opens with a former United States senator turning his back on his country by taking his son to live in England, where the Senator plans to buy his way into British high society and to marry off his son, George, to a Lord's daughter. Disgusted by this scheme, George transforms himself into Superpatriot. Taking the name of the "Father of His Country," George Belgrave becomes "George Washington Jr.," literally cloaking himself in the flag as he sings: "It's the emblem of the land I love, the home of the free and the brave." But even Superpatriot can make an honest, patriotic error. Cohan originally titled the song: "You're A Grand Old Rag," a title inspired by, he claimed, a Union Army veteran who had carried the flag in Pickett's charge during the Civil War. The old soldier, as Cohan told it with his best sentimental patriotism, looked up at the flag with tears in his eyes as he choked out: "she's a grand old rag!" But whether the title was authentic or not, early twentieth-century Americans, who otherwise loved Cohan's use of slang, were incensed to hear their flag called a "rag"; and Cohan quickly changed the title to "You're a Grand Old Flag."

Cohan's simplistic, flamboyant patriotism echoed the same optimistic boosterism and belligerent rallying cries of the "manifest destiny" of the United States to rule the North American continent, if not the entire Western Hemisphere, that blackface minstrels, rustic Yankees, hardy frontiersmen, and bellicose Mose the B'howery B'hoy had trumpeted to the nation three-quarters of a century earlier. These optimistic sentiments, dampened by the Civil War and the shocks of early industrialism, again resounded around the nation at the turn of the twentieth century. In the 1840s, it was Kansas, California, the Southwest, and Oregon. In the early twentieth century, it was Cuba, the Philippines, the Caribbean, and the Panama Canal. Teddy Roosevelt might walk softly and carry his big stick, but not Cohan. Cohan strutted! His hat cocked down over his eyes, his nasal voice shouting out bursts of brash, confident boasts, his body exploding in cocky gestures and high-stepping dances, Cohan exuded confidence in his every move. Although certainly no country boys, and the farthest things from rubes, his heroes had many of the same basic qualities that their rustic predecessors had. Like Brother Jonathan, the Yankee, and the other anti-aristocratic heroes of the past, Cohan's heroes scorned European elitism and its American advocates—even, when necessary, their own fathers.

Also like his predecessors, Cohan's heroes were more popular with the common people in the galleries than with the critics in the boxes. Following Harrigan, Cohan boasted of bringing "actual living characters from the street to the stage." And critics did not always like what he brought. Cohan, a critic huffed, is "a vulgar, cheap, blatant, ill-mannered, flashily-dressed, insolent, smart Aleck who, for some reason unexplainable, . . . appeals to the imagination and apparent approval of large American audiences." He conveys "to the minds of ignorant boys," the critic protested, "a depraved ideal for their inspiration and imitation." Other less caustic critics were equally at a loss to explain why his "high-grade, second-grade productions" were so successful. The critics were using artistic criteria which were only partially able to account for his appeal. His shows, they realized, had an engaging new tempo and style, substituting the hectic, driving pace of the modern American city for the leisurely, refined elegance that characterized European-derived Comic Operas. "At times," a critic gasped about one of his shows, "it goes so fast that it almost bewilders and gives the impression of a great machine shooting out characters, choruses, songs, dances with rapid-fire quickness and precision." But his media was only part of his message. Critics failed to realize that the content of Cohan's shows—his unique combination of street-toughness and sentimentalism, of patriotism and optimism—was exactly what audiences wanted in the Progressive Era, the days of Teddy Roosevelt and William Howard Taft, when times were good and problems seemed solvable. In fact, "George Washington Jr.," converted his father from being a pretentious, aristocratic Anglophile to a patriotic American democrat. The new redeemed the old by reasserting traditional values as part of, not the opposite of, the modern, urban world.

Caricature of George M. Cohan in *Yankee Prince* (1908). NYLC.

Cohan's method of creating his shows added to their vitality. Like Harrigan, he did not write them. Once he had an inspiration, he assembled a cast and worked his idea out

THAT'S
MY
BOY!

on the stage, as the Four Cohans must have done with their song-and-dance act. All his life he had been learning how to appeal to audiences of average people. When he took what he had learned in vaudeville and brought it into musical comedy, it seemed a bold new development. "In the art of presenting musical comedy," a New York *Dramatic Mirror* critic admitted grudgingly, "Mr. Cohan is apparently without a peer." For a decade after the 1906 *George Washington Jr.*, Cohan produced a new musical almost every year, making himself "Mr. Broadway" by reworking and repeating the same themes, techniques, and styles. During World War I, he became an even greater celebrity with his song "Over There," virtually the nation's theme song during the "War To End All Wars."

But Cohan never again recaptured his pre-World War I popularity. The most immediate and common explanation for this was his unflinching, union-busting opposition to the Actor's Equity Association's ultimately successful strike to win union recognition. Arguing the individualist position in opposition to collective bargaining as Henry Ford did for so long, Cohan led the management forces in the bitter struggle against union recognition. When Equity won and other producers made their peace with it, Cohan stubbornly closed down his production company and swore he would never do another Broadway show. But when he eventually did mount new productions, they failed or had moderate success at best. Times had changed, and like Harrigan, Cohan had not. The naïve simplicity and buoyant optimism of the early twentieth century had been destroyed as Woodrow Wilson had been by the war and its disillusioning peace. Musicals too had changed, sparked in part by the new life Cohan himself had breathed into the tired old form. Everything had changed—everything but Cohan. Although he continued to win accolades for his past accomplishments and for starring in Rodgers and Hart's *I'd Rather Be Right*, show business was never again right for him because he was no longer singing his own songs in his own shows in his own way. When he went to Hollywood in 1932 to star in *The*

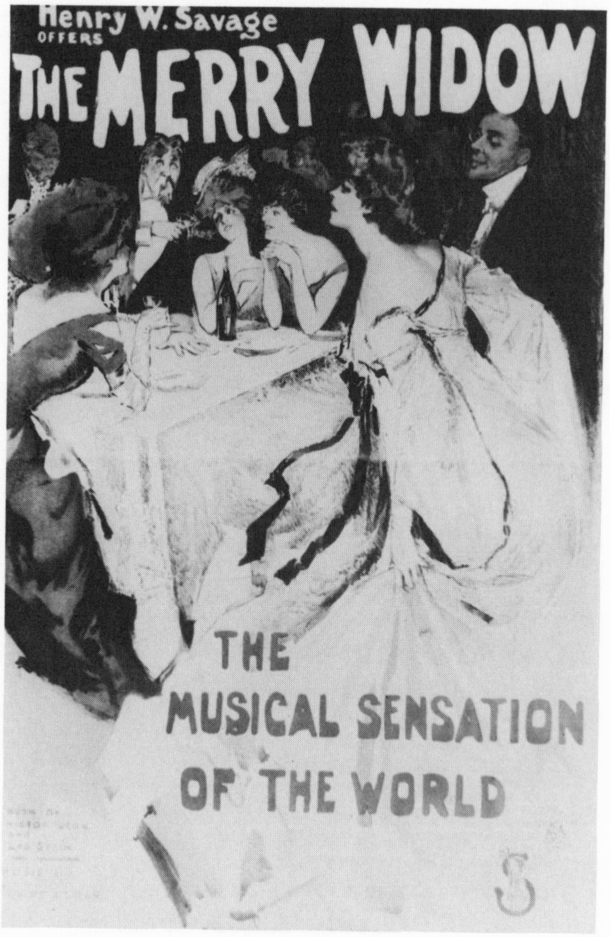

Poster for Franz Lehar's *Merry Widow*. NYLC.

Uncle Sam holding picture of Cohan framed with firecrackers. NYLC.

Scene from Victor Herbert's *Mlle. Modiste*. HTC.

Phantom President, producers and directors had the effrontery to teach him—George M. Cohan, Mr. Broadway—how to sing and dance. They even tried to tell him how to do his patented flag routine!

Cohan could not change himself, but he changed the musical stage. Depending on definitions, there are a number of productions that can be said to represent the emergence of the American Musical Comedy as a distinctive national form. Cohan's early shows are among the strongest candidates. Drawing on extravaganza for costuming and production numbers, on burlesque for satire and chorus girls, on operetta for romance and glamour, on vaudeville for stars, routines, and pacing, and on the public for American themes and images, Cohan's shows were not the end of musical comedy's development into cohesive, well-plotted, well-integrated shows. But they were an important landmark along the way. America came of age in the decades surrounding World War I, and so did the musical comedy, but not just in the Cohan mold.

The last major type of American musical, the Comic Opera or Light Opera, first took firm root in the United States in the late 1870s when Gilbert and Sullivan's *HMS Pinafore* dazzled Americans. Beginning in 1880, other romantic Comic Operas from London, Paris, and Vienna joined burlesques, extravaganzas, farce-comedies, and urban shows as major staples of the American musical stage. In 1880, ten comic operas were produced in New York; in 1883, the total rose to thirteen. The high quality of the music produced by first-rate European composers—Gilbert and Sullivan, Jacques Offenbach, and Johann Strauss—

partially accounts for this success, but if the shows had not met American tastes and needs, they would not have proved so popular. Focusing on upper-class life, often on romance between dashing young military officers and lovely young women, the operettas provided Americans with a sense of beauty, elegance, and social order, a welcome diversion from the problems of modern life, much as Busby Berkeley's lavish musical films served common people during the Great Depression of the 1930s. European comic operas remained a major component of the American musical stage well into the twentieth century, given new life by beautifully staged, waltz-dominated productions like Franz Lehar's *Merry Widow* of 1907.

American comic operas, little more than poor imitations of the originals, appeared frequently after the late 1880s, as composers and producers tried to cash in on this show business fad as they did with every other. Perhaps the only noteworthy product of these nineteenth-century American comic operas was the emergence of Lillian Russell as one of the most popular stars of the American stage. Like Jenny Lind, her popularity derived at least as much from her beauty and grace as from her voice and singing. "From early girlhood to the hour of her death," actor Francis Wilson observed in 1922, "she moved in a court of beauty of which she was the undisputed queen." In no other period of American show business history has one actress been so unanimously acclaimed the queen of the American stage, "The American Beauty." Having been raised by her mother to feel her beauty was a special gift that did not make her superior to other people and having had her voice trained by a leading New York musician, she was a composed, skilled young woman with a strong awareness of her own talent, beauty, and stature. Beautifully costumed and groomed, she regally promenaded through a series of otherwise undistinguished plays, later gracing American music halls and vaudeville houses with her presence and with selections from her operettas, adding dignity to every show she appeared in.

The young Lillian Russell in *HMS Pinafore*. HTC.

In the first decades of the twentieth century the American comic opera reached its peak of popularity and perfection because of men like Victor Herbert, who was born in

Lillian Russell in a beautiful poster for *The Butterfly*. NYLC.

Dublin, Ireland, in 1859, and educated in Germany as a classical cellist. At age twenty-seven, he came to the United States to play cello in the Metropolitan Opera Company's orchestra. While winning fame in upper-class circles as a cellist, composer, and conductor of classical music, he also learned to love popular music—bands, parades, operettas, and musical comedies—and to yearn for a broader audience. "Is it a crime to be popular?" he wondered out loud. "I believe that which is not popular is not of much benefit to the world." When the opportunity arose for him to become director of the 22nd New York National Guard Band, a post raised to national stature by his predecessor Patrick S. Gilmore, a man as responsible as John Philip Sousa for popularizing march music, Herbert leapt at the chance. Although he desired an even broader audience, wanting to write for the kind of folk theater that he associated with Harrigan and Hart, his training overpowered his instincts, and he soon found himself composing in the tradition of semi-classical Middle European operettas. In 1893, he wrote his first comic opera, designed especially for Lillian Russell, but it was never produced. The following year, his *Prince Ananias* opened in New York, and after that he produced a long series of shows featuring lyrical music and exotic settings—Venice, India, Afghanistan, Persia, and Egypt. After three years conducting the Pittsburgh symphony, he returned to Broadway in 1903, where he wrote a new show attempting to exploit the immense popularity of L. Frank Baum's musical comedy adaptation of his *Wizard of Oz*. Herbert's *Babes in Toyland* was set in "The Land of Mother Goose," which allowed for a wide range of fantasy. Although written as a take-off on another hit, Herbert's score was more enduring than its predecessor's. When the two shows are revived, *The Wizard of Oz* uses the familiar score written for the film version, but *Babes in Toyland* relies on Herbert's original music, including "Toyland" and "March Of The Toys."

Herbert's greatest musical, *Naughty Marietta,* set in Spanish-ruled New Orleans in 1780, is a typical comic opera centered on men in uniform, aristocratic ladies, flirtatious courting and courtly flirtation, highly involved but largely irrelevant intrigue and complications, and at least one grand ballroom scene—to say nothing of the inevitable happy ending: Captain Richard, on a mission to New Orleans to capture a pirate, meets and

A scene from Victor Herbert's *Naughty Marietta*. HTC.

falls in love with Marietta, an Italian noblewoman disguised as a commoner who had journeyed to Louisiana to marry a planter rather than submit to an arranged marriage with an Italian aristocrat whom she despises. And that is merely the background. Captain Richard refuses to admit to himself that he truly loves this flirtatious commoner, this "Naughty Marietta." Meanwhile, Adah, a beautiful light-skinned slave who loves her master Etienne, the Lieutenant Governor's son, realizes that he is beyond her reach and mourns in song. Then, the plot thickens. At a society ball, Etienne falls in love with Marietta, who has secretly fallen for Richard, who buys Adah from Etienne only in order to set her free, which infuriates the jealous Marietta, who agrees out of spite to marry Etienne, who is exposed as the pirate by Richard, who marries Marietta, who lives happily ever after. Somehow the plot allowed time for the cast to sing some of Herbert's loveliest songs, "I'm Falling In Love With Someone" and "Ah! Sweet Mystery Of Life."

In the next twenty years, Herbert poured out a number of lilting, carefully composed scores, replete with sentimental waltzes, charming melodies, and gay, quick tunes. Although no Strauss or Offenbach, Herbert was, up to that point, the greatest composer to write for the American comic opera, the first man to make it respectable as a unified, refined performing art. After that, Rudolph Friml, Sigmund Romberg, and others continued in this vein, as European comic opera with its fairyland settings and its heavy reliance on the waltz enjoyed great popularity in the United States in the decades surrounding World War I. But it never became distinctively American.

Like Herbert, American-born Jerome Kern, the man who ultimately brought American musical comedy to its full maturity, received his formal musical training in Europe. After studying on the Continent in his teens, he worked briefly in London as a songwriter for a popular musical theater before returning to the United States in 1904 at the age of nineteen. In the next decade, while he worked his way up in musical theater, as a song-plugger, music salesman, and rehearsal pianist, he saw the American musical stage dominated by European waltz-based operettas—the major exceptions to this trend being Cohan's shows and the lavish revues of Florenz Ziegfeld, the Shuberts, and others. Although these revues are discussed in depth in the last chapter, it is important to note that in the decades surrounding World War I the highly popular revues commanded the talents of a great many creative people. Many of America's most beloved composers—George Gershwin, Cole Porter, and Irving Berlin, for examples—wrote for revues in their heyday.

After working to make European musicals pleasing to American audiences as a "score doctor," Kern in 1912 began writing his own musicals. Joining with librettist Guy Bolton, he had his first success in 1915 with *Very Good Eddie,* an influential show that fourteen-year-old Richard Rodgers saw at least a dozen times, absorbing the sparkling and original music. In a much more sophisticated way than George M. Cohan, Kern was forging truly American music for the popular stage. "Kern was typical of what was, and still is, good in our general maturity in this country," Richard Rodgers later wrote, "in that he had his musical roots in the fertile European and English school of operetta writing, and amalgamated it with everything that was fresh in the American scene to give us something wonderfully new and clear in music writing."

Returning to the spirit of "everyday" farce-comedy, like Nate Salisbury's *The Brook,* Kern and Bolton (joined by P. G. Wodehouse after 1915) created a landmark series of musical comedies known as the "Princess Shows" for the intimate Princess Theatre where they were given. With modern characters speaking and singing in familiar language about familiar subjects in believable, often double-entendre situations, the shows established a close rapport with their audiences. In the small theater, the shows necessarily shunned the large casts, spectacular scenery, huge orchestras, and fairyland-like aura that then dominated the musical theater. Rather than the plots being little more than the space between the production numbers, Kern, Bolton, and Wodehouse integrated dialogue, humor, and action with the songs and lyrics and made them emerge from the characters and situations. "Every song and lyric contributed to the action," Bolton boasted of their hit *Oh, Boy!*. "The humor was based on situation, not interjected by the comedians."

Very Good Eddie centers on two honeymooning couples taking a trip on *The Catskill,* a Hudson river steamer. The couples become separated and find themselves with the wrong spouses. When Eddie and Elsie pretend to be married to avoid attracting attention, they undergo a long series of embarrassing and amusing incidents, until their spouses, Percy and Georgina, rejoin them at the Rip Van Winkle Inn. The mere mention of that beloved character's name would have evoked warm, nostalgic feelings for romantic bygone days, a fine ending for the light-hearted show.

This boy-gets-in-embarrassing-but-innocent-situation-with-girl formula furnished the team with its standard comic theme, as Kern, Bolton, and Wodehouse created their series of successful plays integrating natural sounding songs and humor into plausible everyday situations. "I like the way the action slides casually into the songs," cheered critic Dorothy Parker. "I like the deft rhyming of the song that is always sung in the last act by the two comedians and comedienne. And oh, how I do like Jerome Kern's music!" "It is my opinion," Kern observed in 1917 at the height of the Princess Shows' success, "that the musical numbers should carry the action of the play and should be representative of the personalities of the characters who sing them. Songs," he concluded in what can still stand as a challenge to composers and writers of musicals, "must be suited to the action and the mood of the play."

With great prestige but not great profits from his three years of Princess Shows, Kern was tempted into writing conventional, disjointed Broadway shows by the lucrative offers of major producers, especially Florenz Ziegfeld, the king of the musical stage in the years after World War I when the *Ziegfeld Follies* was synonymous with big-time show business. Ziegfeld and other producers cared little for Kern's theories of organic integration in musicals. They wanted love songs, specialty material, production numbers, and hit tunes in every show regardless of the story, situation, or characterizations. In 1920, for example, Kern and Bolton wrote *Sally,* which Ziegfeld commissioned to star his current paramour Marilyn Miller after her success in the *Follies. Sally* had formidable credits: sets by Joseph Urban, the genius of American stage design; the humor of Leon Errol, a leading comedian; a "Butterfly Ballet" finale composed by Victor Herbert; Bolton's book, which took Sally from obscurity to stardom in the *Follies;* Kern's music, which included "Look For The Silver Lining"; and Miller's radiant beauty, lovely legs, and considerable dancing talent. The dazzling show was a hit, running for 570 nights in New York before going on a long national tour. In the next six years, Kern turned out another fourteen of these financially successful but, for him, artistically unsatisfying musicals. In the 1920s, Vincent Youmans, George Gershwin, Cole Porter, and Richard Rodgers and Lorenz Hart also wrote a number of notable musical comedies, shows that produced some of the nation's most enduring songs, including "Tea For Two," "Someone To Watch Over Me," "I Got Rhythm," "What Is This Thing Called Love?" "Thou Swell," and "Blue Room." Jerome Kern was certainly not the only person creating exciting new musicals, but he did produce the show that set a new standard for the American musical stage.

When Kern and Oscar Hammerstein II combined to make a musical out of Edna Ferber's popular novel *Showboat,* many of their friends initially warned the two men that a story dealing with the harsh realities of Negro life in the South, with two unhappy marriages, and with miscegenation was totally unsuited for adaptation to the musical stage and would turn out to be a financial disaster even if it were an artistic success. But with the assurance of financial backing from Florenz Ziegfeld, Kern and Hammerstein ignored the warning. They could not help themselves. "We had fallen in love with it," Hammerstein later recalled of those exhilarating, creative days in which the two men compulsively labored on the new production. "We couldn't keep our hands off it. We acted out scenes together and planned the actual direction. We sang to each

Production scene from *Show Boat.* NYLC.

other. We had ourselves swooning." The result of their work also left the public swooning and left musical theater a distinctively American performing art. After opening in 1927, the show grossed about $50,000 a week for two straight years in New York, toured the nation for years, returned for another long New York run in 1932, played in London and Paris, and became one of the earliest part-sound motion pictures in 1929.

Centered on the Mississippi River showboat *Cotton Blossom,* the show tells several related stories involving both blacks and whites in the 1880s and 1890s. Instead of opening with a conventional upbeat chorus-girl production number, *Showboat* opened with Negro dockhands lamenting the back-breaking work of loading cotton, which at least implicitly protested the inequities blacks suffered. When a Southern sheriff discovers that Julie La Verne had a Negro ancestor somewhere in her past, he orders her and her white husband, Steve, off the showboat, but only after they melodramatically prick their fingers and mix their blood while swearing their eternal devotion to each other. The moving scene ends with Julie singing "Can't Help Lovin' Dat Man." In the most famous of the play's many famous songs, Kern evoked the mood and tone of Negro spirituals to protest movingly blacks' degraded and hopeless position and the society's indifference to it:

Dere's an ol' man called de Mississippi
Dat's de ol' man dat I'd like to be;
What does he care if de world's got
troubles?
What does he care if de land ain't free?

I get weary an' sick of tryin'
I'm tired of livin' an' skeered of dyin';
But ol' man river
He jes' keeps rollin' along!

Although *Showboat* was certainly not free of the caricatured low-comedy black characters that had amused whites since the beginning of American show business, the show did give a new dignity and depth to Negro characters on the musical stage, greatly expanding and even challenging the time-worn show-business clichés about happy, carefree Southern Negroes.

The major plot of *Showboat* details the rocky marriage of the *Cotton Blossom*'s Captain's daughter Magnolia. Magnolia's husband Gaylord Ravenal, a sometimes reformed gambler, deserts his family, forcing Magnolia to seek a job in a Chicago Music Hall, a job that Julie, who has been off stage for three acts since she was expelled from the showboat, just happens to have. Julie dutifully quits so

The show within the show in *Show Boat.* NYLC.

that her "better"—good ole Cap'n Andy's daughter—can take her place. But Julie's poignant rendition of "Bill," which she manages to squeeze in before quitting, is too difficult an act for Magnolia to follow, and she is a failure until Cap'n Andy, her father, convinces her to sing Charles K. Harris' old favorite "After The Ball." Finally, Magnolia leaves Chicago and returns to the showboat, a repentant and reformed Ravenal rejoins her, and their daughter Kim becomes the star of the showboat's own show.

Although the characters were rather simplistic, the plot rather predictable and corny, and the contrived "coincidences" almost laughable, the show deeply moved audiences in the 1920s and in its periodic revivals on stage and screen. Despite its weaknesses, it had the kind of emotional power that made *Uncle Tom's Cabin* a standard. Kern's marvelous score engaged its audiences at an unconscious emotional level, making the play seem much more credible, much less cliché-ridden than it actually was. With "Bill," "Can't Help Lovin' Dat Man," "Why Do I Love You?" "Make Believe," and "Ol' Man River," the music was, in the fullest sense of the word, the *heart* of the production. With *Showboat,* Kern demonstrated that an American musical could combine native themes, characters, and music into a cohesive, moving performing art.

Showboat was a turning point in the development of the American musical. "Some of of its best numbers are so successful in their combination of the theatrical elements, music, acting, scene," critic Stark Young prophetically observed in his review of *Showboat,* "as to suggest openings for the development not of mere musical comedy, but of popular opera." With Kern's achievements, the European operetta had been naturalized and democratized. Significantly, Kern completed the process by using a subject—the interaction of blacks and whites on the Mississippi river—that had spawned the first distinctively American show business form, the minstrel show. But Kern took this mythic American setting, drew on Afro-American music, on his European training, on his experience with the musical tastes of common, white Americans, and created a show that brought the major elements of the American musical stage together to form an *American* "popular opera."

CHAPTER EIGHT

THE GIRLIE SHOW

From STATUARY to STRIPTEASE

"I can advise no honorable, self-respecting woman to turn to the stage for support," Olive Logan, an ex-actress turned lecturer and writer, lamented in 1869. "Stripped as naked as she dare—and it seems there is little left when so much is done—she becomes a prize to her manager who knows that crowds will rush to see her, and who pays her a salary accordingly." Logan was not a prig nor a snob who disliked popular entertainment. (She loved minstrel shows when many people looked down on them.) But she was outraged at the deteriorating position of women on the American stage after the Civil War, when female sexuality and the "girlie show" first made a great impact on stage entertainment, when women's looks, not their talents, became the major requirements for their entering show business. Over a century ago, Logan had good reason to rail against "the nude woman" narrowing the roles and opportunities available to female entertainers. She and other observers were witnessing the first major exploitation of female sexuality in American show business, a development that ended with the burlesque show.

Like other forms of show business, the burlesque show developed in stages. At first, displays of women's bodies were featured only in disreputable variety houses, but they got broader public exposure in lavish musical extravaganzas and in troupes

Dancing girls in a Chicago variety show with a male audience. HTC.

of women doing parodies, "burlesques," while wearing revealing men's clothing. Gradually, the American burlesque show, a girlie show with female sexuality as its major feature, emerged. Then, in competition with other entertainment forms that continually became more sensual and daring, burlesque grew racier and racier over the years until it culminated in the striptease. Until the early twentieth century, women in burlesque wore tights, like body stockings, which revealed a great deal but nevertheless did cover the performers' bodies. In the mainstream of show business, "skin shows," in the literal sense, were a post-1920 phenomenon. Ultimately, burlesque shows outstripped most Americans' sense of propriety, leading to censorship and the disappearance of burlesque as a major branch of American show business. But even after the burlesque show receded to its sleazy origins, the girlie show remained a central feature of most show business forms. In fact, the principal reason that burlesque stripped itself to death was that other popular entertainment forms, forms with more respectable reputations and more diversified, more entertaining features, successfully absorbed burlesque's most sensual innovations.

During the 1847-48 theater season in New York City, women wearing only revealing tights began posing as "living statuary," portraying classical subjects and famous

Posing as classical statuary provided the earliest excuse for displaying women's bodies in theaters. NYLC.

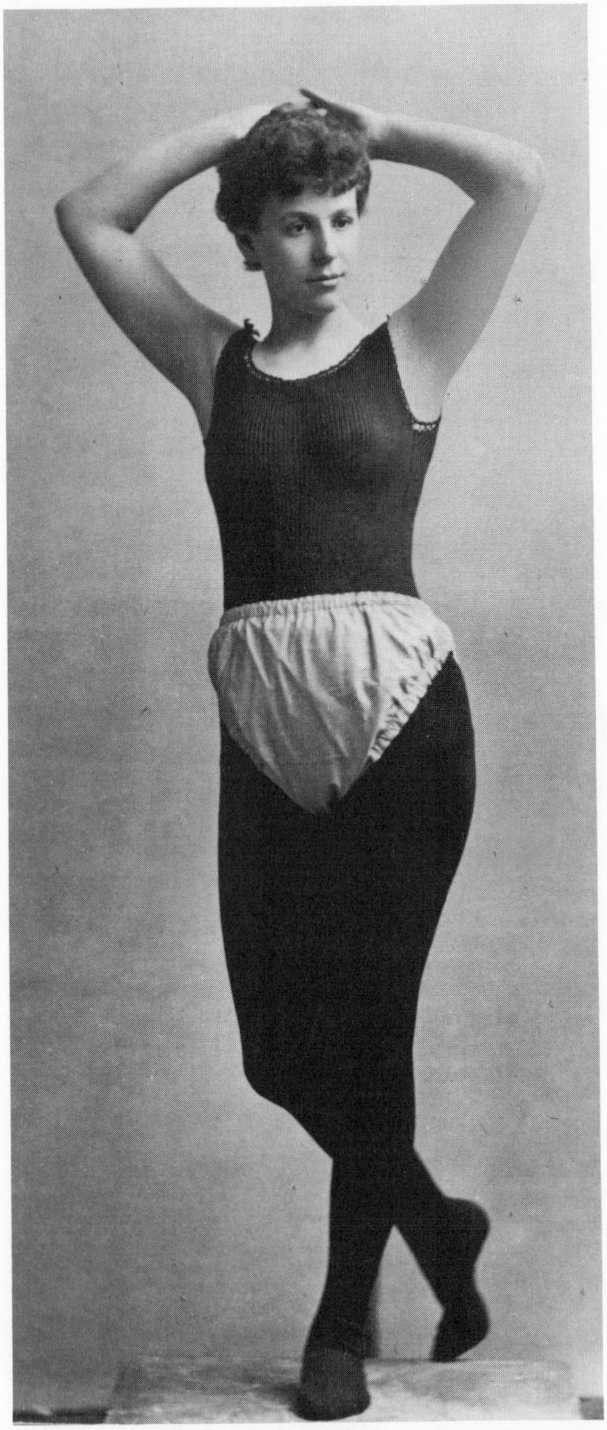

Clare Beckwith as a statue. HTC.

sculpture. This façade of culture provided both performers and patrons with rationalizations for what were actually nothing more than girlie shows. The Hall of Novelty, for example, advertised in 1848 "a young lady of faultless form" portraying Hiram Powers' famous and controversial nude sculpture, "The Greek Slave." Other living statuary represented subjects like "Psyche Going to the Bath" or "Venus Rising from the Sea" and drew huge audiences, as common people, especially men, suddenly discovered the beauty of classical art, at least when embodied by shapely young women. "The majority go," the *New York Tribune* complained, "because of depraved taste rather than pure love of art." Voicing what later became a stereotype of burlesque patrons, the New York *Herald* complained that statuary's heavily male audiences contained many "bald and greyheaded men armed with prodigious opera glasses and pocket telescopes," the better to see the fine points of the exhibits, no doubt. When police raided and closed down one of these "art centers," a disappointed patron poetically elegized:

Those nice tableaux vivants
Of beautiful young ladies, sans
Both petticoats and pants,
Who, scorning fashion's shifts and whims
Did nightly crowds delight
By showing up their handsome limbs
At fifty cents a sight.

From the 1840s on, women's bodies remained standard features of show business. But before the Civil War, women in revealing union-suit-like tights were on display only in disreputable variety halls and saloons or as alluring but minor decorations in semi-respectable theaters.

THE GIRLIE SHOW

Show business has produced some truly remarkable women who used their careers to establish liberated personal lives. One of the first of these emerged in the 1850s when an extraordinary woman burst out of the narrow restrictions traditionally imposed on her sex in the Victorian period. Known ultimately as "Cleopatra in a Crinoline," "The Royal Bengal Tiger," and "The Naked Lady," Adah Isaacs Menken won fame and notoriety starring in the stage version of Byron's poem *Mazeppa,* a role previously played only by young men. In the most celebrated scene, Menken, portraying the hounded hero, wore "fleshings"—skin-colored tights—which made her look naked under her brief costume. This then startling display of "skin" made her a highly controversial celebrity, frequently attacked for her immorality. But she performed the role in the best theaters in America and Europe, which helped establish female sexuality as part of the mainstream of show business and opened the way for the burlesque show.

What makes Menken so fascinating today, however, is not just that she might be considered "The Mother of the Girlie Show," but that she might also be considered "The First Isadora." Unlike many of the stage women who followed Menken in building their careers on their bodies, she was as much the exploiter as the exploited, using her stage career to fund her flamboyant, creative personal life. Dictating her own terms for her life, she was a highly controversial, fiercely independent Bohemian free spirit, an ardent defender of her adopted Jewish faith, the admitted mistress of A. C. Swinburne and Alexandre Dumas, a literary critic, a published poetess, and an intellectual with command of French, Spanish, English, German, Greek, and Latin. Women in the mid-nineteenth century simply did not do what Men-

Miss Chester in tights. HTC.

Adah Isaacs Menken as *Mazeppa*. HTC.

ken did. She not only defied conventions, she did so openly and proudly.

Menken captivated audiences with her fiery, magnetic, though undisciplined, performances. She "is like the gold in quartz veins—all in the rough," a New York critic observed, "and so must undergo the refining process of intelligent and critical audiences." She needed, the critic concluded, "taming down." But no one ever tamed her down. In 1861, she became the first woman to star in *Mazeppa.* In the most famous scene—the one that made Menken's career—the scantily dressed, tights-clad Mazeppa, strapped on a horse's back, rode up a spiral ramp, which gave audiences ample opportunities to see her body. She wore "baggy trunks . . . enough for three bathing suits" and a wide sash covering her breasts, but her arms, shoulders, and legs appeared naked to the audience which had never before seen "fleshings." Although modestly dressed by modern standards, she gained fame and notoriety as the Naked Lady. Besides her voluptuous beauty and her willingness to reveal it, she exuded excitement on stage, always seeming to be on the verge of an emotional explosion, like a smoldering volcano that drew as much attention for what it might do as for what it did.

Adah Issacs Menkin with her lover Alexandre Dumas. HTC.

More concerned with a full life than with a full purse, Menken spent her money as quickly as she earned it, which kept her broke even when her stage and literary careers developed. Traveling to London in 1863, she scored another great hit as Mazeppa, looking, in the opinion of the *London Review,* like "Lady Godiva in a shift." In the 1860s, she continued her intercontinental triumphs in San Francisco, New York, London, Paris, and Vienna. Everywhere she performed, she established and/or visited literary salons where she hobnobbed with the most famous intellectuals, writers, and artists on both continents. With typical bohemian abandon, she spent her first night with A. C. Swinburne to win a ten-pound bet with another friend. Their affair outlived the wager, but when she asked him to help get her poetry published, he chided: "My darling, a woman with such beautiful legs need not bother about poetry." She left him. Obsessed with proving her literary worth by publishing a book of her own poetry, she persuaded Charles Dickens formally to accept her dedication of the book to him and continually

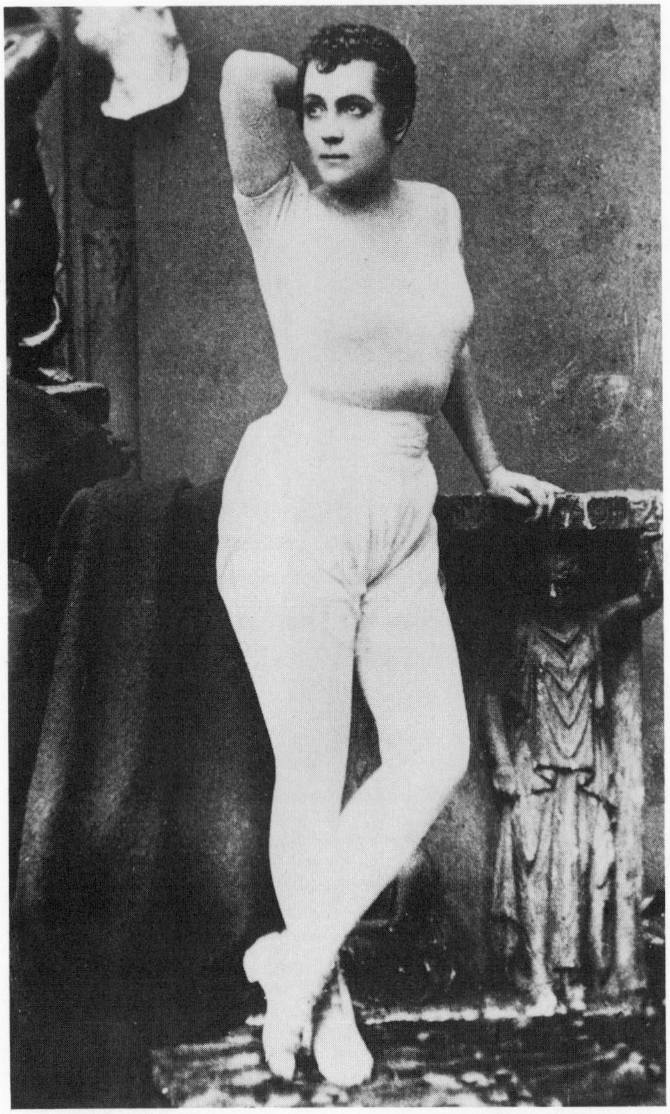

Menken shocked Victorians with her revealing costumes. HTC.

Adah Isaacs Menken in *French Spy*. HTC.

badgered her publisher to get the volume, *Infelicia,* released. But before the book appeared, she fell fatally ill. Although only thirty-three, she could serenely and accurately write to a friend: "Yet when all is said and done, have I not at my age tasted more of life than most women who live to be a hundred?" Without the exploitation of female sexuality in show business which she both profited from and helped create, she never could have tasted as much of life as she did.

Menken's great popular success with her "fleshings," of course, prompted many imitations. But few women in tights were accepted into the mainstream of American show business until *The Black Crook*. "Nothing fires the masculine bosom," a New York critic observed of a *Black Crook* audience, "like the anticipation of a ravishing prospect of calf." And *The Black Crook* offered glimpses of much more than calves. "The first thing that strikes the eye is the immodest dress of the girls with short skirts and undergarments of thin, gauze-like material, allowing the form of the figure to be discernible," minister Charles B. Smythe fumed. "The attitudes were exceedingly indelicate, *ladies* exposing the figures from the waist to the toe except for such coverings as we have described." And in the second act for the *pas de demons* dance, the four devilishly possessed, shapely dancers shed their skirts entirely, wearing only their tights.

The great successes and long runs of the many versions of *The Black Crook,* which included *White Crook, Red Crook, Golden Crook* and *Black Crook Jr.,* firmly established women in tights as a major feature of American show business, the first big step toward making the chorus girl a fixture on the American musical stage. But in *The Black Crook* and the other lavish musical extravaganzas, women's bodies were only one of many major

The Black Crook chorines. HTC.

Baba, one of the leg show successors to *The Black Crook.* NYLC.

attractions, and even then the women had to be trained ballet dancers. In this sense *The Black Crook,* like Adah Isaacs Menken, was more the background for than the first American girlie show.

When Lydia Thompson and Her British Blondes invaded New York in 1868, the girlie show began to take its familiar shape, making women's bodies its major feature and their figures, not their talents, the major requirements for the performers. Although the Blondes performed burlesque as parody in the classic sense of the word, their major attractions were their full figures and their large, shapely legs, which were amply revealed by the short tunics and tights they wore to play the male roles they burlesqued. This gimmick of dressing women in tunics and tights to play male roles, one Menken made famous in England as well as in America, served for decades as a thinly veiled guise for exposing women's bodies during the prudish Victorian period. The

Blondes' first American show, *Ixion,* featured Lydia Thompson in the title role. In the play, Ixion accompanied by Mercury (Lisa Weber) dines with Jupiter (Ada Harland, who, one critic punned, "could not have been more graceful, by Jove"). Ixion flirts with Juno (Alice Logan) and Venus (Pauline Markham, "as near a personal realization of the goddess of loveliness as one can expect in mortal woman"), and is then chastised by Jupiter. "This is not brilliant *per se,*" a New York critic admitted in a classic understatement. "The whole success of the piece depends upon dressing up all the above named good-looking young ladies as immortals lavish in display of person—and setting them to dance and sing in the most reckless burlesque manner." Olive Logan denounced a typical Blonde's lack of talent and artistry: "She trots down to the footlights, winks at the audiences, [and] rattles off from her tongue some stupid attempts at wit." At the height of the spectacularly produced *The Black Crook, Humpty Dumpty,* and other lavish extravaganzas, *Ixion* offered no special effects, no grand sets, no wondrous transformation scenes. It did not need to. The beauty of the Blondes' bodies, not the beauty of the production, was its major attraction.

"To represent Minerva with a fan and whisky flask, Jupiter as a jig dancer, Venus with a taste for the cancan, is all done we sup-

Romanticized poster of Lydia Thompson and troupe as Robin Hood and "men." HTC.

Lydia Thompson as Robin Hood. HTC.

pose, in a laudable spirit of burlesque," a New York critic sniped with tongue in cheek, "but we could almost hate Miss Thompson and her assistants for spoiling this pretty story." The story, of course, was irrelevant, as another reviewer noted: "It [*Ixion*] resembles an Irish stew as one minute they are dancing a cancan and the next singing a psalm tune. It is a bewilderment of limbs, belladonna and grease paint." The main features remained the women's lower limbs, the "nether extremities," and their shapely figures, as they mixed spicy songs and provocative dances with the classical references that supposedly justified their revealing costumes. Once established, the troupe dropped its lip-service to the classics and focused on its eye-catching assets. In 1873, for example, the Blondes concluded their show by lining up in what later became familiar chorus girl style and singing "a wild thrilling air, which says at the end of every verse, 'How's that for High!' And . . . they all give a very high kick indeed. It doesn't look pretty to see a lady kick," the female critic complained; "but the intelligent audience," she facetiously observed, "is in a frantic frenzy of delight, and hee-haws and howls with rapture."

The troupe's manager, Alexander Henderson, was not content to let the troupe's ample assets be the company's only source of publicity. He initially crowned them the "British Blondes," even though two of them were brunettes. But this did not seem to bother either reviewers or audiences whose eyes presumably were not focused on the women's hair. When critic E. F. House in 1869 denounced the troupe for driving legitimate drama off the stage (a view Olive Logan and a number of others shared) and implied that the women were immoral, Henderson publically branded House a liar. House's replacement at the newspaper responded to similar provocation by shoving Henderson, who then sued the critic and his newspaper, which created the desired sensation in New York newspapers. In Chicago, Wilbur S. Story, the editor of the Chicago *Times,* questioned the women's morality offstage as well as condemning their performances, provoking Lydia, Pauline Markham (Venus), and Henderson to waylay Story outside his office, whereupon Lydia literally horse-whipped him for impugning her honor. Story brought Lydia to court where she was fined $100, a cheap price for the national publicity that she and the troupe received from the incident. Henderson's Barnum-like flair for promotion through notoriety and the cast's well-turned, sturdy legs carried them on successful tours of the United States for twenty years.

Lydia Thompson and Her British Blondes, whom Olive Logan denounced as "brazen-faced, clog-dancing creatures, with dyed yellow-hair and padded limbs," had a great impact on American show business, making the stage, in Logan's somewhat overstated opinion, no place for an "honorable self-respecting" woman. In a letter to the *New York Times* Logan facetiously listed the series of questions she felt every female job applicant at a theater would have to answer in the late 1860s, a list that might have been just as appropriate a hundred years later:

1. *Is your hair dyed yellow?*
2. *Are your legs, arms, and bosom symmetrically formed, and are you willing to expose them?*
3. *Can you sing brassy songs, and dance the cancan, and wink at men, and give utterance to disgusting half-words, which mean whole actions?*
4. *Are you acquainted with any rich men who will throw flowers, and send you presents, and keep afloat dubious rumors concerning your chastity?*
5. *Are you willing to appear to-night, and every night, amid the glare of gas-lights, and before the gaze of thousands of men, in this pair of satin breeches, ten inches long, without a vestige of drapery upon your person?*

Pauline Markham smoking openly in public. HTC.

Although the British Blondes had a great influence in America, their classical burlesques with their rhymed couplets were as alien in the United States as *The Black Crook*'s European ballet. But the distinctively American girlie show, featuring women's bodies in an American format, quickly emerged in their wake. Because the girlie show, unlike the musical extravaganza or the comic opera, re-

Caricature of Lydia Thompson shedding "crocodile tears" over the criticism of her mortality. HTC.

quired no complex stage technology, no skilled composers, no highly trained performers, it became Americanized much more quickly than did musical comedy.

With the typical opportunism of the American show business producer, M. B. Leavitt, an admirer of P. T. Barnum, created the first American girlie show. Leavitt combined the most popular elements of other forms, taking the structure and features of the minstrel show, the name of the well-known Continental Rentz's Circus, the specialties of variety shows, and the shapes of lovely women from burlesque. The result, Mme. Rentz's Female Minstrels, opened to enthusiastic applause with its all female cast in 1870. The troupe proved so popular that within a year there were at least eleven female minstrel companies, one of which directly acknowledged its debt to Lydia Thompson by wearing blonde wigs. Besides offering conventional minstrel features, the female minstrels starred women impersonating men, including specialists like Mlle. De Granville who performed "FEATS OF STRENGTH, Assisted by Venus and Adonis." Although these troupes occasionally argued that women could be as effective as men at creating Negro characterizations (the basis of minstrelsy), most of the time they featured the special attributes that only women had:

TWELVE SYMMETRICAL
FEMALE FORMS
A bevy of beauty, The octroon
The blonde, The quadroon
The brunette, The mulatto
and the
BEAUTIFUL CREOLES

In revealing tights, female minstrels portrayed classic statuary; they dressed in tunics and tights to impersonate men; and they wore gowns slashed up the sides to reveal their tights-clad legs. "Every time my leg made its appearance outside of the cut skirt," one of these entertainers recalled, "it was greeted with great guffaws from some of the men present." The troupes provided their audiences with ample opportunities to see legs and to guffaw. Some troupes even had the women swing out over the audience to give patrons a closer look at the "merchandise."

Although some of these female minstrel troupes performed ordinary minstrel fare with the added appeal to Victorian audiences of women's bodies outlined and accentuated in tight-fitting men's clothing; others were little more than "skin shows," as an interview with a member of Duncan Clark's Female Minstrels revealed. "It's tough all around," one of the female minstrels explained of her life in the troupe. "Most of the girls are tough, we give a tough show, draw tough houses and have a tough time generally." She had started out from New York touring with a small acting company, but when it went bankrupt, leaving her stranded in Tennessee, she signed on with the female minstrels. Most of the other women in the minstrel troupe had not been professional entertainers, she explained. "The rest are women that had a crazy idea that they could sing or dance or had a fine shape. The manager picks them up here and there." As long as they looked good, they did not have to know much about show business. "The main thing, you see, is shape," she continued. "All they have to do is to put on their costumes and let the jays look at them. . . . All they need is a pair of tights."

She also had no illusions about the quality of the performance. "The show is a fake, and some pretty raw things are said on the stage," she admitted. But the rowdy male audiences loved it. "They go crazy over a woman when they see her in tights. One of our crowd is 45 if she is a day and as ugly as a carload of cross-eyed cats," she chuckled, "but she gets dozens of notes in every town we show in all because she wears a pair of black tights and kicks high." But even if the women got lucrative offers, they certainly did not get much respect. "Men go to that sort of a show to see something vulgar," she astutely observed in what could be taken as a general comment on burlesque audiences. "When they do see it they get mad and 'roast' the people on the stage, and if they don't see it they get mad and say that the whole thing is a fraud." But they kept paying to get in, and troupes like Duncan Clark's Female Minstrels, with what one reviewer labeled as its "vile" performance that "consisted chiefly in the exhibition of ten half naked women, who were with one exception, in various stages of age and ugliness," continued to tour and to prosper. The girlie show had arrived.

In the late nineteenth century, these troupes dropped both their pretense of being minstrels and their witty parodies, becoming simply what Leavitt called "Burlesque Troupes," companies clearly and openly selling female sexuality. "In San Francisco, we had advertised that we were going to put on the can-can," recalled John E. Henshaw, who began his acting career as a prop boy with Leavitt's Mme. Rentz-Santley Burlesque Troupe. "Mabel Santley did this number and when the music came to dum-de-dum, she raised her foot just about twelve inches, whereupon the entire audience hollered 'whoooo!' It set them crazy. . . . It became the talk of the town. The theatre was jammed, as a result, for three full weeks." On one of its trips West, however, the Rentz-Santley troupe did not prove as acceptable to authorities as it proved popular with audiences. In 1878, M. B. Leavitt and ten blondes from the Rentz-Santley company were arrested in San Francisco for what a policeman felt was "the most indecent [performance] he had ever witnessed." At the trial, Leavitt confidently provided the jury members with free tickets to the show; the jurors dutifully attended and then promptly handed down a guilty verdict. But despite such setbacks, burlesque troupes like Rentz-Santley's and Ada Richmond's Burlesquers, the Victoria Loftus Troupe of British Blondes, and Ada Kennedy's African Blonde Minstrels made the burlesque show part of the touring show business that honeycombed the nation in the late nineteenth century.

The first burlesque star to be crowned a "Queen," May Howard, began her career with a Rentz-Santley burlesque show. After starring in 1886-87 as one of the "birds" in *Bob Manchester's Night Owls,* she headed her own May Howard Company, "a leg show pure and simple," explained the chunky star, who boasted that she would employ no woman who weighed *less* than one hundred fifty pounds. The stocky woman with large thighs—some performers were even charged with wearing hip and thigh padding under their tights—continued to be the ideal until the turn of the century, when public tastes in feminine figures changed from the broad-hipped, big-busted woman to the slender, long-legged "chorus girl." Whereas May Howard in the 1880s featured short, hefty women, the six Floradora Girls, who created a public sensation in 1901 as ideal women, were each 5′4″ and 130 pounds. The public preference for the lithe woman had begun in the 1890s. Edna Wallace, one New York reviewer raved in 1898, "makes up in quality what she lacks in quantity. . . . She is a decided relief from the chunky young woman who is usually sup-

M. B. Leavitt burlesque *Spider and Fly*. NYLC.

The New Henry Burlesquers. NYLC.

posed to represent the ideal type of feminine beauty." But whatever the preferred shape, women's bodies never went out of style.

Although May Howard eventually graduated to "legitimate" stage shows, as did many of the most talented burlesque performers, troupes of women in tights toured the nation toward the end of the nineteenth century, continually spicing up the sexual content of their shows to keep ahead of the competition and to entice their prospective patrons. "Each year it gets harder and harder to get up something that will excite the public. The people have had so much shown to them that they don't pay any more attention to what used to be considered very *risqué* and naughty a dozen years ago," complained an anonymous performer who blamed liberalized women's clothing for the escalation of exposure on stage. "When a man can go out in Central Park and see a dozen pairs of well-shaped legs in tight-fitting knickerbockers for nothing," she griped in 1895, "he won't pay to go to the theatre unless he can see a great deal more."

The 1893 Chicago World's Fair provided the burlesque show that "great deal more"—Little Egypt's "Cootch dance," the American public's first exposure to the belly dance. "When she dances, every fiber and every tissue in her entire anatomy shakes like a jar of jelly from your grandmother's Thanksgiving dinner," the barker at the fair enticed. "Now, gentlemen, I don't say that she's that hot. But I do say that she is as hot as a red-hot stove on the fourth of July in the hottest county in the state." The "hootchy-cootchy" rippled throughout burlesque in the 1890s, reaching into vaudeville with tamer versions known as "oriental dances." But the "cootch" dance, with its combination of exposure, erotic movements, and teasing, provided a distinctive feature that helped establish the burlesque show as a separate form of American show business.

Rooted as it was in burlesque extravaganza, burlesque continued to be a loosely structured collection of songs, dances, humor, and skits that ranged from simple "skin-shows" like Duncan Clark's Female Minstrels to lavish, diversified revues and musical comedies. But all burlesque shows spiced up their product with lots of "hot" women and with heavy doses of salty comedy, often mixed together in racy sketches and off-color jokes. Some of America's greatest comedians, including Weber and Fields, Bert Lahr, Gallagher and Shean, W. C. Fields, Abbott and Costello, Red Skelton, Red Buttons, Phil Silvers, and many, many others, learned their trade while trying to make impatient audiences laugh while they waited to see the next display of female flesh. But the best of the comics, like the best of the other performers, including Fanny Brice and Sophie Tucker, rapidly graduated to vaudeville and other show business forms, draining burlesque of its best material, techniques, and performers.

At the turn of the century the prevalence of feminine sensuality in other forms of popular entertainment provided a serious challenge to burlesque. *Yankee Doodle Dandy,* an 1898 musical comedy featured Edna Wallace Hopper's long, slender legs and trim figure. "Realizing that she had not much to warble," a reviewer observed, she "is very generous in the display of her proportions, and by dispensing with the formality of trunks makes the best use of her resources." Praising another 1898 musical comedy, a critic identified its central appeals as "the scenery and the costumes, or more correctly the scenery and the lack of costumes." By the early twentieth century, the mainstream of show business had become much more *risqué.* Eva Tanguay, one of vaudeville's greatest stars, "The Queen of Perpetual Motion," brought sizzling sex appeal to the nation's most respectable variety houses

Little Egypt, whose cootch dance gained fame at the Chicago World's Fair in 1893. HTC.

with her uninhibited performance of her suggestive songs: "I Want Some One To Go Wild With Me," "It's All Been Done Before But Not The Way I Do It," "Go As Far As You Like," "Nothing Bothers Me," and her theme song "I Don't Care." She delighted in stunts like boasting to the press that she could carry her whole Salome dance costume in one closed fist. Tanguay's wild, untamed performance style, which exuded raw sexuality, made her one of the most famous, highly paid, and most imitated stars in the nation. Before World War I, Mae West (who never appeared in a burlesque show) brought her earthy undulation and her sexy voice to legitimate show business. Early in her vaudeville career she gained notoriety for her "enchanting, seductive, sin-promising wriggle" and her "wonderful champagne-laden voice." But vaudeville was tame competition compared to revues. The *Ziegfeld Follies* and the other big-time revues, besides their lavish production numbers and great comedy, "glorified the American Girl" by showing how glorious she looked without any clothes—first with bare legs, then bare breasts, and finally completely bare—in what Ziegfeld indignantly insisted were completely tasteful tableaux demonstrating inspirational sculpture and classical scenes. As musicals, vaudeville, and revues incorporated burlesque's tights, "leg shows," and "oriental" dances, burlesque had to uncover new attractions.

To survive, burlesque had to make a bold move. And when it moved, it *really* moved! "She began shaking her arms and the upper part of her body from side to side until the spangles covering her breasts blinked as though they numbered thousands," a Philadelphia reviewer wrote in 1915 about Millie De Leon, burlesque's first truly national sex symbol. "Slowly and in a manner hardly noticeable even through the transparent net which constituted the middle portion of her gown, the muscles of her body took on a wave-like motion. The undulation increased in rapidity. A purely muscular side to side movement . . . complicated the pattern and introduced a chaotic activity that probably lasted five minutes. Finally," the critic wrote, "Millie De Leon became unspeakably frank. From knee to neck she was convulsive. Every muscle became eloquent of primitive passion." De Leon worked her audiences masterfully. Driving the patrons to "groans, catcalls, and howls, of approval," she suddenly stopped, flipped back her skirt, and "revealed her nude right leg from knee almost to waist." The audience screamed, and De Leon resumed her seductive undulations, shimmying, bumping and grinding, rolling her eyes, and tossing her hair, while pretending to share in her audience's erotic fantasies. "Indescribable noises and loud suggestions mingled in the hot breath of the audience. Men in the orchestra rose with shouts. . . . And then, sensing her climax, Millie De Leon gave a little cry that was more a yelp and ceased."

Her explosive "cootch" dance, like a shocking earthquake, had ended, but its tremors were felt long afterward. Throwing tiny blue garters with her picture on them—her trademark—she snaked over to a box, leaned in, took a blushing boy's face in her hands, and kissed him. Then, she ran her fingers through another man's hair, kissing him with a loud smack, while turning to the audience and calling for men to join her onstage and to take off her garters. "Many a man took refuge behind the seat in front," the reviewer noted. De Leon was in effect challenging them to leave the safe anonymity of the audience where each man could freely fantasize that *he* was the cause of De Leon's erotic excitement and of her ultimate satisfaction, that *he* was a sexual superman the equal of this erotic bombshell. At least symbolically she gave each man in the audience a chance to act out his fantasy, to make love to her, to sweep her off her feet. Instead, he cringed down behind seat backs, fearful that she would single him out and publicly test his manhood. Only foolhardy young men ventured up on stage to be rewarded with her kisses, her hose, and her garters. But she made it clear at the conclusion of her act that she was mocking them, not submitting to them. After hugging and kissing the last boy who came forward, leaving her bright red lipstick on his forehead, she waved him away and called out with a "taunting laugh": "Put the light on him." The spotlight focused on the blushing boy as he stumbled up the aisle, while De Leon laughed heartily at the young man who had entered her exotic realm only minutes before expecting to be a confident conqueror and now left a humbled and ridiculed loser. De Leon never directly denounced her audiences, but she regularly laughed at them even as they panted at her. They strained to catch the garters she threw—souvenirs of the orgy of sensualism and passion she acted out. But they shrank from the prospect of personal contact with the woman they might later have said about: "I just wish I could have gotten my hands on her for a few minutes." Burlesque, even at its most erotic,

Revues continually forced burlesque to offer racier material. This scene was from the *Greenwich Village Follies of 1928*. HTC.

was a voyeuristic experience, a fantasy for its patrons. Like violent sports, it was a substitute or compensation for a lack of activity on the part of its patrons, a grasping for manhood, not an expression of it.

De Leon could enjoy her private laughs only because she put on such an exciting show and so cleverly got great amounts of free publicity by provoking censors, courting arrest and trial, and appealing to reporters. In 1903, while still an unknown performer who merited newspaper description only as "a member of 'The Girl in Blue' extravaganza company," De Leon learned the value of free publicity when a Brooklyn politician, out to make a name for himself, rushed "from the wings on to the stage, grasping her by the neck and dragging her off stage" before she could take her garters "from their resting place" and throw them to the audience. A large crowd, "hooting at the officer" who arrested her, followed her to the police station where she was officially charged with executing "a dance which was immoral and depraved." "Her dance," a newspaper dutifully reported, "is said to be Spanish in character. Those who have seen the dance say it resembles in many respects that executed several years ago by the celebrated Fatima." The notoriety of the arrest stimulated business and raised De Leon to a featured role.

A year later De Leon, now a star as "The Girl in Blue," made news by horse-whipping Chicago bank clerk Herman Haas, and making sure the press got the details of the story. "He was an awfully nice fellow," she explained, perhaps innocently batting her eyelashes at the reporter, "and they do say that I was to blame. But what could a girl do?" What indeed! It seems Haas caught one of her garters and sent it backstage with a $500 bill and an invitation to dinner pinned to it. "I did just as any girl would have done under the circumstances," she continued. "I kept the garter and the bill, and dined with him." Claiming to be a widower, he proposed marriage to her and "continued pressing money and jewelry on me, and sent me to Paris." But she was shocked to discover that the scoundrel was a married man with dishonorable intentions toward her. And "what could a girl do?" De Leon did "just as any girl would have done under the circumstances." She "hurried back to this country, went to the bank, and horsewhipped him." He was subsequently arrested in Panama for absconding with bank funds while Millie, flaunting the diamonds he had given her, recounted the sad story of how she—innocent young thing that she was—had been betrayed and ruined.

In the early twentieth century the Girl in Blue danced from city to city, from courtroom to courtroom, and from packed theater to packed theater. She occasionally "forgot" to put on her tights, which was an outrage to public decency but a guarantee of a full house. At other stops, she at times got caught up in the emotion of the moment and let venturesome young men actually take garters *off* her leg, sometimes even "enticing" them to reach *under* her skirt and up to her *knee!* Curiously, her memory failed and her excitement overwhelmed her judgment most often at the beginnings of her bookings, unfortunately "marring" the run with sensational publicity and "forcing" shocked citizens to see this outrageous spectacle for themselves. It happened in New York, Brooklyn, Indianapolis, Chicago, Detroit, New Orleans, and other stops on the

Millie De Leon, the "Girl in Blue," excited early-twentieth-century burlesque audiences with her writhing dances and garter throwing. NYLC.

tour. When she did not manage to get headlines with her "muscle dances," her garters, or leaving her lipstick brands on blushing boys, she boasted to reporters how she had "thrashed a masher"—a phrase that worked beautifully as a headline. Or she complained—again to reporters—about being exploited. "I am a poor hardworking girl who has wiggled twice daily all week for your amusement and edification," she reminded Chicago reporters in 1911, probably struggling to hold back crocodile tears, "and now when the management has all the wiggles I had, they refuse to pay me my salary."

There were a great many cootch dancers, but there was only one Millie De Leon. Combining Barnum's flair for publicity with a truly erotic dance, she made herself into a magnetic star, a true queen of burlesque. Although she removed her coat, parasol, bonnet, and gown during her act, she was not a stripper in the familiar sense of a performer whose act consisted primarily of a seductive removal of clothing. De Leon danced almost fully clothed, but as Mae West later explained: "It isn't what you do, it's how you do it." And Millie De Leon knew how to do it all. She had beauty, a good figure, sex appeal, and the ability to explode into a convincingly passionate, literally breath-taking eroticism. But so did a great many women who did not become stars. De Leon became the first real queen of American burlesque because she manipulated the sense of wickedness that many Americans associated with human sexuality, making herself a public sensation by using her alluring charms on the press as effectively as she used

Millie De Leon showing her garter. NYLC.

them on her audience. And she never lost the ability to laugh at them both.

Ironically, during the first two decades of the twentieth century, when De Leon became a national sex symbol with her uninhibited performances, burlesque shows in general became tamer and more routine as large national burlesque circuits emerged and sought respectability. These "wheels" as they were called (the shows revolved around the circuits like spokes) made burlesque into a big, centralized business, guaranteeing member theaters a regular supply of entertaining but uncontroversial shows and guaranteeing performers forty-five weeks a year of steady work if they complied with the "cleaned up" performance code. These touring shows contained comedians, production numbers, skits, chorus girls, and specialty acts, a mixture somewhere between musical comedies and vaudeville. Most of these "wheel" shows contained less suggestive material than burlesque had featured in the 1890s, less than vaudeville then offered, and far less than revues, like the *Ziegfeld Follies,* the *Passing Show,* and *George White's Scandals,* presented. Still losing its most talented entertainers to these other forms, "clean" burlesque had no way to compete with its racier competitors. Before long, it followed De Leon's lead to sensational eroticism.

Besides revitalizing its "dirty jokes" and sexy skits, burlesque found its ultimate weapon in its unique combination of skin, suggestion, and seduction—the striptease. Although there is no way to determine when women began to undress for a living on the American stage, by the 1890s Truly Shattuck advertised that she had "an entirely distinctive specialty in which is introduced an instantaneous change from full costume to tights." In the early twentieth century, cootch dancers took off more and more, as Salome's Dance of the Seven Veils swept show business from the Metropolitan Opera House to strip joints. Some of the small-time, rag-tag burlesque road companies had always been wild and licentious, getting away with and taking off as much as local law and bribery would allow. But these shows, like carnival peep shows, were at best on the fringes of show business. On the major, "legitimate" burlesque circuits, stripping was primarily a twentieth-century phenomenon, one taking decades to evolve into the striptease show of the 1930s.

Around World War I, the height of Tanguay's and the Ziegfeld Follies' popularity, many burlesque stars peeled down to their tights and hinted at much more. In *Yankee Doodle Girls,* a "wheel" burlesque show, Edna Victoria "with a slow undressing process interests the audience with a few contortions until she strips to tights when the interest wanes. . . . At one time it seemed," a critic noted, "as though Miss Victoria would make a sensational exposure and the excitement was high." Although Millie De Leon did occasionally forget her tights, the suggestion of bare skin sufficed to titillate audiences at most burlesque shows. Led by Sam Scribner, the Czar of the "clean" Columbia "wheel," burlesque officially resisted nudity, though no one was to blame, of course, if a shoulder strap occasionally broke or if tights occasionally split. Even in the most permissive areas of the country, the legal authorities tried to draw a rigid line between motionless statuary, which was acceptable as art, and nudity in motion, which was not. Beginning in 1925, burlesque shows followed revues by featuring bare-breasted women in artistic poses. But some of the women just could not seem to stand still, and others could not seem to keep on their clothes. As late as 1926, the police raided the *Band Box Revue*, for example, because its star Eve Bradford "took from her person her dress, garters, hose and chemise leaving parts of her body exposed to public view." And she no doubt moved while she did it! Presumably her act would have been acceptable if she had been nude when the curtain rose and if she had remained motionless while the audience studied her finer artistic points. But before long, the half-nude chorus girls in the high-class revues began to move—at first slowly walking while holding transparent chiffon over their breasts, then dancing and discarding the chiffon, and finally prancing out on runways wearing nothing but G-strings.

By the late 1920s, the lid was off, and so was everything else. "With the advent of short skirts on the street," *Billboard* observed, "leg shows lost their sex appeal, and, in self-defense, the operators of burlesque shows introduced the strutting strips . . . as far as the police permitted." Ann Corio, one of the most famous stripteasers of the 1930s, the girlie show's golden age, credits Carrie Finnell with creating the modern striptease. In 1928, Finnell, who started out as "The Girl with the Million Dollar Legs," had put on a lot of weight, so she needed an extra gimmick, which she found in talking to and teasing her audiences while only taking off a few items and promising to remove additional pieces of clothing at subsequent shows. Whether or not Finnell actually began the modern striptease, she did perfect and make famous another unique burlesque specialty, tassel-twirling—attaching a tassel to each breast and twirling them using nothing but pectoral muscles. "Carrie could do anything with those tassels," Corio recalled with awe. "She could make one go slow, the other fast. She could spin the left in one direction and the right in an opposite direction. . . . She could attach tassels to her derriere and have them spinning every which way while the bosom tassels revolved merrily on their own." With what was, to say the very least, an unusual novelty, Finnell billed herself as "The Remote Control Girl" and hypnotized viewers. "She has trained each generous bust to twitch on cue, jump to attention, and do just about everything," a reviewer quipped, "except sing 'April Showers' in Swahili."

Few could imitate Finnell's bizarre gyrations, but her other innovation—teasing the audience with slow, suggestive movements, building its expectations and playing to its sense of wickedness as she slowly, seductively undressed—was something any ambitious showgirl could try. And during the Great Depression many tried. The Depression and motion pictures seriously hurt most of show business, especially vaudeville, but not the girlie show. "Burlesque remains unique in that, among the various branches of show business," *Variety* observed in 1936, "it has the lowest rate of unemployment at the present time. No competent burlesque actors are out of jobs, and the demand for even 2nd rate talent is considerably in excess of supply." Movies, which hurt live vaudeville and revues and greatly narrowed the audiences for musicals and plays, did not offer the public, the male public, the titillation that burlesque provided. Burlesque stripteasers appeared in person, always offering the prospect, the hope that the patron might catch an intimate peek at forbidden "territory." Furthermore, burlesque was a special kind of escapism, one especially well suited to the 1930s. The strippers acted out basic male fantasies which could provide at least temporary boosts for the damaged egos of the many men who were thrown out of work and were unable to fulfill their normal roles as providers during the Great Depression. Whatever the reasons for burlesque's success, it boomed in the 1930s, reversing the normal talent drain, getting a fresh transfusion of bright young entertainers who raised burlesque to its pinnacle of popularity. The three greatest of these stars—Georgia Sothern, Gypsy Rose Lee, and Ann Corio—each rose quickly to stardom with publicity attracting specialties that embodied basic male fantasies about women.

Georgia Sothern, after years of touring vaudeville with her uncle in a song-and-dance act, found herself at age thirteen stranded in depression New York City, deserted by the performers her sick uncle had left her with, evicted from her apartment, and forced to sleep in a flophouse to keep from freezing. The desperate girl put on the black velvet dress that made her look eighteen, stuffed cotton in her bra to fill out the mature image, painted on extra-heavy make-up and went out to find work. But having absolutely no luck, she reluctantly entered a burlesque booking agent's office, even though she remembered vaudevillians contemptuously ridiculing poor acts by saying "they'd be lucky to get a job in burlesque . . . the Siberia, the salt mines, of show business." Before she knew what had happened, she had signed to open in Philadelphia as a stripper at forty dollars a week. Ashamed of her new job, she stammered out an ad-libbed stage name based on her home state, so that her relatives and friends would not know where she was working. After "a feast" on delicatessen food, she began fashioning her new costume, sewing rhinestones and ruffles onto black lace pajamas. Since she thought strippers bared their breasts (actually only the headliners were supposed to at most houses) and since she did not yet have any, she had a problem, a problem she ingeniously solved by using two bras—a black lace to wear under the pajamas and a flesh-colored, cotton-stuffed foundation to keep on when she took off the black lace bra. With her costume and her figure in her bag, she set out for Philadelphia.

As soon as she arrived, she went to a burlesque show for some clues about what she might do for an act. She had never even seen a strip show. When she saw rowdy men in the audience hooting and screaming at the coarse woman on stage to "take it off, baby!" while the stripper crudely peeled down to a G-string, thirteen-year-old Georgia ran out crying, swearing that no matter how hungry she got she would never do that kind of sleazy act. But before she could carry out her vow, she heard about and went to see Hindu Wassau, a classy, graceful striptease star who glided around the stage, casting a spell over the audience with the way she sensuously maneuvered her dress, giving the audience only tantalizing glimpses of her body. The audience did not whistle, stomp, shout, or scream at her. It sat spellbound until she finished, holding her gown hanging loosely behind her as a backdrop for her bare body, and then it rose in a standing ovation. Georgia left feeling encouraged that strippers even in the roughest joints could be artists with style and polish.

Planning to do an act like Wassau's, Sothern selected slow, sensuous music for the band and rehearsed her routine over and over again in her room. But on her opening night, when the terrified girl finally stepped onstage for her solo, she panicked, losing control of herself and racing ahead of the music. At the end of the first eight bars, "I was already completely without covering except for my panties and my lace bra and the cotton was streaming from me and falling all over the stage." Unconsciously, she tore at the curtain, whipped

Georgia Sothern, the "Hold That Tiger" Girl. HTC.

her black lace pajama top through the air, tore off her black lace bra, and wildly tossed her hair and the rest of her trembling body around the stage until the music finally stopped. The audience roared as the thirteen-year-old wandered off stage in a state of shock, not even realizing that she had stopped the show. Her instant success convinced her to retain this explosive, apparently uninhibited style and to adopt the frenzied staccato-tempos of "Hold That Tiger" as her trademark. Although her sense of abandon recalled Millie De Leon, Sothern took off a great deal more and was sexually much more explicit as she acted out the image of the sexy woman-child literally throwing off her inhibition in a fit of passion. "She was a cyclone of sex," Ann Corio recalled, "and she literally blew the walls down."

In contrast, Gypsy Rose Lee's style was to talk, to tease, to suggest, to wink, to talk, to take off something, to talk, to joke, to take off something else, to wink, to smile knowingly, to take off still something else, to wink, and finally to slither offstage, having taken off much less than most other burlesque stars. Yet, she could somewhat legitimately claim to be the "woman who made burlesque famous." Unlike Sothern, Lee was a teaser, not a stripper, letting her audience know that stripping was a game, a sexy, adult game. But like Sothern, Gypsy, too, knew her way around the popular stage before she entered burlesque. Pushed by their ambitious mother, Louise (her name before she became Gypsy) and her sister June Havoc began their long show business careers with a child act, "Madam Rose's Dancing Daughters," in vaudeville. While starting to work her way up, Louise played a bit part with Fanny Brice and starred in "Rose Louise and Her Hollywood Blondes." But when vaudeville bookings grew thin and burlesque boomed, her mother pushed the stage-wise, budding young woman almost literally into the G-string of a stripper who had been arrested. Louise took the name Gypsy Rose Lee and made herself a star with her blend of traditionally sexy apparel—black silk stockings, lace panties, red garters, and mesh netting—a witty, alluring patter, a slow teasing strip, and an intellectual wit that made her a publicity-producing hit with writers and reviewers. Although she loved the uninhibited response she got from her burlesque audiences, she resented being considered an untalented performer, "just a hootch dancer," and accepted an offer to play a major role in the Ziegfeld Follies of 1937. She later went on to star

Gypsy Rose Lee and Bobby Clark in a typical burlesque comedy routine. HTC.

Ann Corio as a young stripper. HTC.

on the legitimate stage and to write a best-selling novel and the memoir *Gypsy*, which became a hit musical play and film.

Ann Corio, the third of burlesque's most famous stars of the 1930s, was hooked on show business at the age of six when a neighbor took her to a vaudeville show. While growing up in Hartford, Connecticut, she stayed as close as possible to performing, acting in school and church plays, and spending all her free time backstage at the local theater, watching actresses put on their make-up, thrilling to the audience applause, and dreaming about being out in front of the footlights. During her freshman year of high school, she somehow got her strict mother's permission to join a girl friend working in the chorus of a touring Shubert musical comedy. But after only two weeks on the road, the homesick girl went back home to mama.

Yet, Ann soon rejoined her friend, this time in the chorus of a burlesque show, which she and her mother thought was just another form of vaudeville. Although initially shocked by what she saw and heard, Ann stayed and rose to soubrette (head chorus girl). When the manager offered her a chance to double her salary by becoming a stripper, she leapt at the chance but realized that she needed a gimmick to compete with her more widely known, more experienced colleagues. "I conceived an act based around the one virtue that drives men wild: innocence! I would be a pretty little girl with ruffled skirt," she recalled, "carrying a pail of candy kisses. I'd skip down the runway singing, 'Give Me A Little Kiss,' as I threw out the candy. . . . The more innocent I was, the more wicked they felt, and more often they paid their way through the turnstiles." As her fame and drawing power grew, Corio, like Gypsy Rose Lee, received an attractive offer from a big-time revue, *Earl Carroll's Vanities*. But since the deal included "extracurricular duties" with friends of the producer and paid only half her burlesque salary, she refused the job and went on to become one of the greatest burley drawing cards of the 1930s, later reviving the old form in 1963 with her show, This Was Burlesque. She made a long career out of "driving men wild" with her teasing, her feigned innocence, her beauty ("probably the prettiest girl in burlesque"), and "her slender symmetrical form à la natural as an optical feast of delight to her ever-increasing army of admirers."

Each of these three—Sothern, Lee, and Corio—entered burlesque as fresh-looking young women free of burley's clichés and determined to succeed in show business. Had there not been a Great Depression none of them probably would have gone into burlesque. But once in it, each of them realized that her job was to excite men, and each evolved a distinctive style that expressed her own personality. Unlike many strippers, who performed as mechanically and predictably as factory workers, these were not just women who took off their clothing in public; they were excellent performers who worked in show business' most blatant "girlie show."

But women's bodies and eroticism were not the sole province of burlesque, although a great many people—in and out of show business—wanted to believe otherwise. In fact, women as sexual objects pervaded American stage entertainment. With notable but infrequent exceptions, women in all forms of show business had to be shapely, pretty, or otherwise attractive to men. It was no accident that even serious actresses in America had to be "lookers." The "unpretty girl," critic Alan Dale observed while praising American stage beauties in 1910, "has even less of a chance in the United States than she has abroad. . . . She may have the voice of a nightingale and the equipment of a Bernhardt, but unless she has beauty of some sort she will have to fight, tooth and nail for her first chance. . . . They are not so particular over there. Perhaps," Dale suggested, "the [European] public is less sensual." Or, he might have conjectured, perhaps European men were less obsessed with having stage performers feed or even act out male sexual fantasies.

"Women as well as men frequent the theater," protested Mary Vida Clarke in 1918, and "they also have emotions which seek an outlet denied or limited by real life." To Clarke, show business' concentration on female sensuality was objectionable not because it offered exciting, provocative women for the men, but because it offered no comparable men for the women. And burlesque represented only the most extreme form of this. In the typical play, even the melodrama that was supposedly women's fare, Clarke noted, the heroine encounters a dashing European gentleman with a "glorious physique, a fascinating manner, a melodious voice, an engaging accent, and apparently all the physical, and intellectual, perfections that characterize these supermen . . . a figure in short to thrill the soul of any woman." But the heroine invariably turns her back on him for a "contemptible little whippersnapper." Even the lowliest chorus girl did not fall for him. This ridiculous situation, which left the woman in the audience no one onstage to identify or fantasize with, existed, Clarke astutely observed, to please the average male theater-goer. "Since he is himself probably possessed of insignificant personal charms, commonplace intellect, and indistinguished character, he finds it pleasing," she perceptively noted, "that the leading man in the comedy should be an individual of similar if not inferior type and should be preferred by the embodiment of all feminine fascination to a man who represented youth, beauty, and heroism." All of show business, she protested, served men's and neglected women's sexual fantasies. "Every ordinary masculine emotion is catered to by these girl and music shows, but," Clarke complained, "what sop is thrown to the starved feminine hangers-on? This feast of unreason is for her a famine. . . . The equal rights that women demand," Clarke argued in 1918 with words that retain a contemporary ring today, "should include equality of opportunity for emotional satisfaction in the musical comedy of the future, and in the public utility or futility of the theater." But the famine for women continued in male-dominated stage entertainment.

Feminine sex appeal was central to American show business. Burlesque simply stripped it of its façade of high culture or artistic respectability, openly admitting that it was a sex show that appealed to men's sexual fantasies. Strippers encouraged the man in the audience to project himself into the performance, to fantasize that the woman on stage was playing to him and him alone. The basic striptease act performed for the American male an age-old sexual ritual. The well-built, sensual woman began in full dress and in full control of her passions. To the throbbing beat of a primordial drum, she began to dance erotically for the men watching her, seeming to lose control of herself as the ritual, and her clothing, began to unfurl. Loosening her hair, she suggestively began to undress, building the excitement with gasps, pants, and sexual movements, until she writhed to the climax of her act. And then, the whole process began again as another woman appeared and began her version of the ritual.

During the 1930s, burlesque moved to the forefront of American show business, pushing its way onto Broadway and virtually monopolizing the Times Square area—the nation's entertainment center. Burlesque's great success bred competition, producing ever more daring and risqué shows and more brazen public advertising. And since all this took place uptown on Broadway where it could not be ignored, censorship was almost inevitable. A combination of local property owners, "legitimate" theater managers, politicians like Mayor Fiorello La Guardia, and clergy, branding burlesque insulting and outrageous, amassed public opinion against it, eventually forcing the major burlesque houses in New York City to close in 1937. Under probation and a strict code that banned the word "burlesque" and the striptease dance, the theaters were allowed to reopen with titles like "vaudesque" and features like Ann Corio in a sedate black dress with a large padlock on the zipper, singing "I Would If I Could, But I Can't." But burlesque could not survive without the key to that padlock. Similar restrictions in other major entertainment centers ended burlesque's brief rein as the queen of American entertainment and forced it back to the peripheries of show business.

Burlesque never became a respectable member in good standing of the mainstream of American show business because it was such a blatantly sexual form that it exposed the emphasis on female sexuality that pervaded show business, exposing American males' insecurity, fascination, and guilt about sexuality that in fact had made the girlie show popular in the first place. The masculine desire to look at and dream about beautiful women was so strong in the United States that it found expression in every form of show business, from melodrama and musical comedy to vaudeville and revues. Many men who might have wanted to go to the burley houses but felt uneasy about their indecent reputations could see much the same thing elsewhere. In a popular melodrama, men could see innocent young women threatened and seduced; at a lavish revue or musical comedy, they could ogle beautiful women naked or close to it; in vaudeville, they had Tanguay cutting loose or Mae West seducing them. And all of these were considered reputable, family shows, shows that continually forced burlesque to escalate its exploitation of female sexuality until the girlie show as a distinctive form was reduced to the trashy, indecent reputation and surroundings that had characterized it a century before.

CHAPTER · NINE

ONLY SKIN DEEP

THE · IMPERSONATORS

The glamorous singer swept across the stage, a vision of femininity in a black satin gown decorated with silver and turquoise, a black cape lined with light blue satin, and a black hat trailing long white plumes. Every sound of the soft, huskily seductive voice, every fluttering gesture of the butterfly-like hands, every slinking movement of the curvaceous body worked together with the song's words to convey that this was not just an ordinary Gibson Girl. This was *the* Gibson Girl. The members of the audience followed the graceful performer's every move with unusual concentration and fascination because they knew, if they stopped to remind themselves, that the alluring female figure before them was a man, Julian Eltinge—the greatest female impersonator in American show business. "I'll never forget the first time I saw him," recalled George Williams, a longtime prop man at B. F. Keith's Boston vaudeville theater. "I couldn't believe it was a man. He was the most beautiful 'woman' I ever saw on Keith's stage and that includes Lillian Russell and Ethel Barrymore and all the rest."

In the first thirty years of the twentieth century, some of the most dashing young gentlemen on the American stage were actually women creating male illusions. Performers impersonating the opposite sex—men portraying women and women portraying men—numbered among the most popular and most highly paid stars in American vaudeville. Never before or since have impersonators achieved such prominence or stature. For this reason and for what they reveal about the American people who made them stars, as well as for their intrinsic interest, the impersonators wrote an important, unique, and fascinating chapter in American show business.

In 1660, Mrs. Margaret Hughes played Desdemona in a new London production of Othello. Her very presence on stage created a public sensation, controversy, and scandal. Before then, Desdemona, Lady Macbeth, Kate, Viola, Juliet, Cleopatra, indeed all Shakespeare's and every other playwright's female characters had been played in England by boys who were specially trained to portray women. Before 1660, it was normal and perfectly respectable for males, even grown men, to play female roles. But after Charles II regained the English throne, ending Oliver Cromwell's stern Puritan rule, women, often mistresses of high-ranking men including the king, took to the public stage, in a reactionary period of licentious aristocratic indulgence. In a short time, actresses had taken serious roles away from all but the greatest female impersonators, men like Edward Kynastan, who successfully competed with actresses until his death in the early eighteenth century. After that time, English actors impersonating women played burlesque and comedy parts, but not serious refined roles. Ultimately, this comic impersonation produced the "dame tradition," a low-comedy caricature of a middle-aged, overweight nag, a role, usually relegated to music halls and cabarets, that survives in England to this day.

The English tradition of female impersonation was not transplanted to America at the turn of the nineteenth century, when serious drama took firm root in the new Republic. Yet, when the first new American show business form—the minstrel show—emerged, serious female impersonation, the realistic portrayal of women by men, became part of American show business. As the major purveyors of popular music, minstrels performed many romantic, emotional, and sentimental songs. But since American culture considered it unmanly to express tender emotions and feelings and since minstrel troupes were, with very few exceptions, all-male, minstrels felt obliged to create female characters to voice these sentiments. To make their blackface romances more appealing to whites, many of whom did not believe Negroes felt warm, human emotions, they created the "yaller gal," a beautiful, graceful woman combining the refined features of whites with black women's exoticism and availability. These roles were serious, not comic. When minstrels in the late 1840s dressed in women's clothing to portray these romantic characters in convincing, credible ways, female impersonation began in America.

Since minstrelsy was fundamentally a charade in which white men dressed, made-up, talked, and sang as if they were Negroes, and since minstrel blackface served as a liberating mask that enabled white men to do and say things they would not otherwise have done, it was not surprising that they occasionally portrayed women. In fact, the first female impersonation by minstrels seemed natural enough so that it passed virtually unnoticed. Whoever began the "prima donna" or "wench" role, as minstrels called female impersonation, George Christy, the star of the Christy Minstrels, first popularized it in the 1840s with his performance of "Lucy Long," a song of coquettish flirtation. By the late 1840s, the prima donna role was so well established that many play-

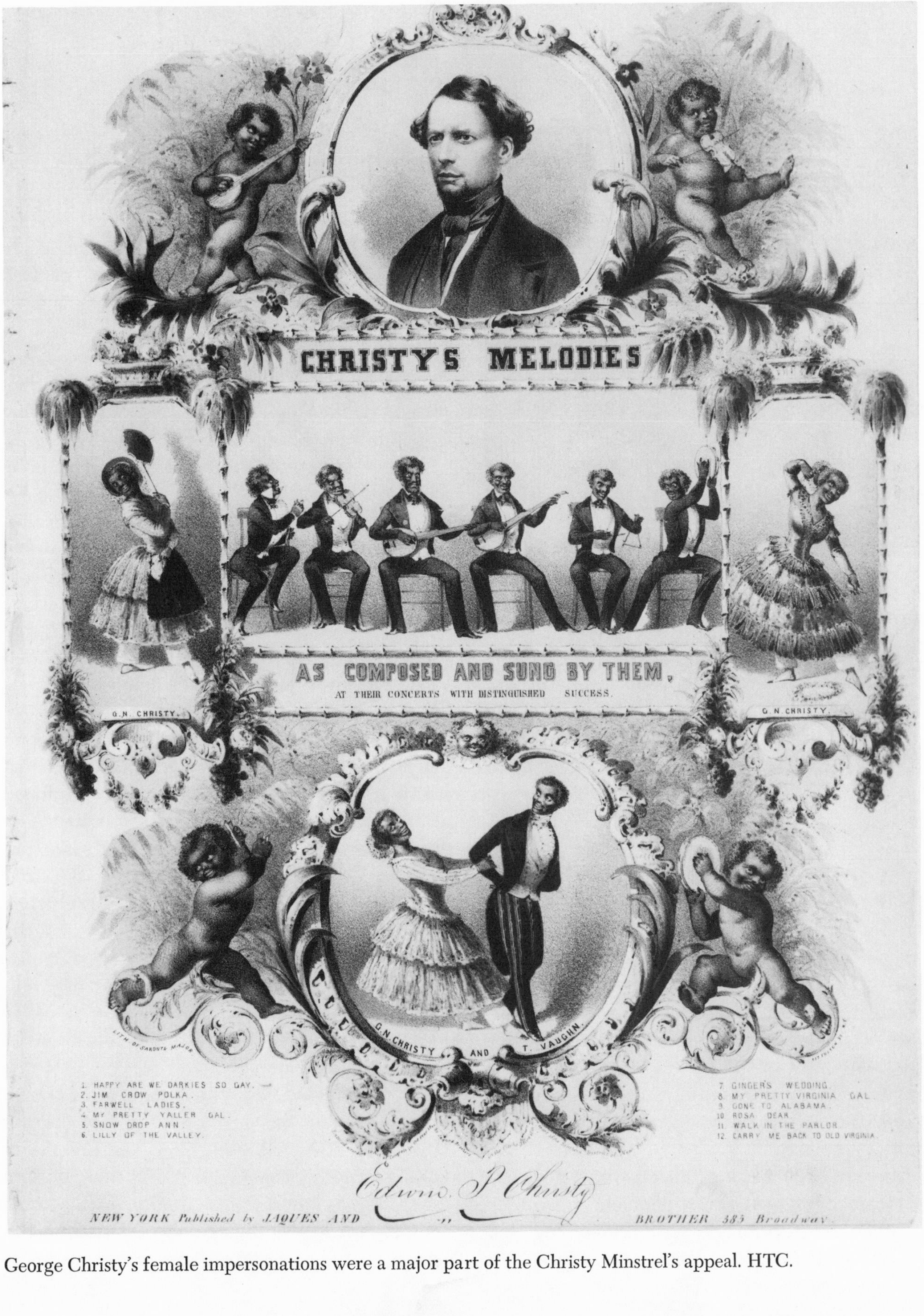

George Christy's female impersonations were a major part of the Christy Minstrel's appeal. HTC.

The Only Leon, the most acclaimed minstrel female impersonator. HTC.

bills and sheet-music covers pictured Christy and other male minstrels as elegantly dressed women dancing with formally attired male partners. But since performers in the small early troupes had to be extremely versatile, the prima donna was only one of their specialties. George Christy, for example, also starred as a comedian and became a romantic matinee idol. But in the 1860s when minstrel companies grew greatly in size and performers became much more specialized, troupes began to feature full-time prima donnas.

Unlike the low-comedy female role, the "Funny Old Gal," the American version of the "dame," which burly endmen played while dressed in mismatched clothing and huge "valise" shoes, the prima donna was played seriously in "a very delicate manner" by elegantly dressed performers. Some of these men, actress Olive Logan observed, were "marvelously well fitted by nature for it, having well-defined soprano voices, plump shoulders, beardless faces, and tiny hands and feet." With fluttering eyelashes and hearts, they flirted behind their fans, occasionally allowing their beaus to steal kisses. They also played sweet young things in their first love affairs and ingenues in burlesques of popular plays and operas, the latter perhaps having provided minstrelsy with the title "prima donna."

More than any other man, Francis Leon, who billed himself simply as "Leon," established the prima donna role as a major attraction. Leon began his minstrel career in 1858 at the age of fourteen, quickly rising to stardom as a beautifully costumed female illusionist. By 1864, he owned half of Kelly and Leon's minstrels, a troupe that created a sensation with its musically serious, lavishly produced burlesque operas featuring Leon as the heroine. The troupe did not survive, but it demonstrated Leon's great drawing power as a serious female impersonator. By 1873 the prima donna role was so firmly established, primarily because of Leon, that the New York *Clipper*, the *Variety* of its day, observed that "no well-organized troupe could be without one." By 1882 Leon was the highest paid minstrel and one of the most praised.

"Leon is the best male female actor known to the stage," the editor of the *Clipper* observed in 1870 while arguing that Leon's act was perfectly respectable. "He does it with such dignity, modesty, and refinement, that it is truly art." Like the sculptors, painters, and poets who created sensitive, artistic images of women, the editor argued, Leon did not burlesque women, he exalted them with his refinement, his voice, and his dancing. "He is more womanly in his by-play and mannerisms," another reviewer noted, "than the most charming female imaginable." "There is not, from the time of his entrance until he quits the stage, the slightest suggestiveness of a disguised member of the sterner sex," a Cleveland critic enthused. "From the tiny shoes, . . . the modishly cut skirt, the lines and contour of the face and neck, slope of the shoulders, the feminine expression of the face, the small ears, and finally the hair bound tightly round the well-shaped head in a modest Grecian knot—all combine to form one of the most perfect illusions possible." Many men dazzled with his feminine charms refused to believe he was a man. "Heaps of boys in my locality," a Rochester, New York, critic noted, "don't believe yet it's a man in spite of my saying it was." Leon was alluring enough, the writer continued, "to make a fool of a man if he wasn't sure."

Leon himself took great pride in successfully capturing the essence of femininity. A reporter who visited Leon's dressing room in 1881 found the closet full of women's clothing, the dressing table covered with "powder, paint, and perfume." "With real feminine pride," Leon explained that he wore no "costumes," only authentic women's clothing, from the $200 dress he had worn that night—only one of the 300 he owned—to his shoes, jewelry, lace petticoats, hose, garters, and "underclothing." He also prided himself on his dancing, singing, and good taste. His ballet dancing, he claimed, was "the real thing, not a burlesque. I took lessons of a good teacher and for seven years practiced my dancing for hours every day." He also claimed that in his youth he had studied voice with Errani, the maestro who taught Clara Louise Kellogg, a famous opera singer. Above all else, he boasted that he did absolutely nothing offensive or vulgar.

After Leon established the popularity of the prima donna role, many other males with high voices or falsettos, graceful movements, and opulent wardrobes joined the growing profession. Every minstrel troupe had a female illusionist, usually featuring him in lavishly produced, musically serious take-offs on light operas. "When a new opera came out in Paris," Leon recalled, "we took the best music, fitted it with burlesque lines with many topical hits and presented it in blackface. One of the big London critics," he bragged, "declared our opera was sung better than that of a high-grade white company in a swell theater of that city."

The nature of the prima donna role varied with the talents of the specific performer. William Henry Rice, for example, burlesqued actresses instead of operas, his greatest hit being Sara Hartburn in *Camille,* a role Sarah Bernhardt herself reportedly thoroughly enjoyed. Occasionally, minstrel impersonators performed sexually suggestive material that offended audiences. But even at the height of the Victorian period this rarely happened, probably because minstrels worked hard in those decades to sell their shows as wholesome family entertainment. In any case, Leon, Eugene, Bernardo, Ricardo, William Henry Rice, and many others who were less famous made female impersonation an accepted, popular, and lucrative part of American show business.

When the forces of modernization radically changed almost every facet of American life in almost every part of the nation, female impersonators appeared to change the most fundamental identity of all—their sex. Although it may appear that female impersonators conveyed the underlying unity of males

Leon wore a wide range of gowns, from the simple to the lavish. HTC.

and females and the superficiality of sexual roles, they, in fact, played to and underscored the nineteenth-century view that men and women differed in every way—emotionally, psychologically, temperamentally, and intellectually as well as physically. It was the scope and depth of these assumptions of difference that made impersonators' sexual transformations seem so incredible and so unique.

Changes in the roles of women and in the nature of family life deeply troubled a great many nineteenth-century Americans, a concern that found expression in newspaper articles, sermons, speeches, essays, serious novels, popular literature, and the popular stage. The women's rights movement, despite its publicity-oriented bloomers and its demands for long-overdue political, legal, and vocational equality, long remained a small, relatively powerless group. That it attracted as much attention as it did testifies to public anxiety about possible changes in women's roles and to the actual changes already taking place. Many women worked outside the home and away from their families; more women than ever attended college and learned vocations and professions; in a few states, women voted; a flood of literature reached into homes offering housewives exciting excursions into adventure, intrigue, and romance, suggesting that there could be much more to their lives than domestic chores and child-raising; and women starred in show business roles ranging from serious drama to girlie shows. All of these changes, but especially the highly visible "racy," liberated women in show business reinforced the fear that women—the traditional keepers of family, home, and morality—were forsaking these roles for lives that would accelerate the social and moral decay of the society.

By acting out, indeed epitomizing, the perfect lady-like woman in her traditional role, the serious female illusionist, whether consciously or not, addressed and capitalized on the public's concern about women's role in the society. Furthermore, for women in the audiences, especially for those first enjoying or envisioning middle-class respectability, the illusionists provided cheap lessons in etiquette, bearing, make-up, hair-styling, and dress. All serious impersonators prided themselves on wearing nothing but the latest coiffures and fashions, and reviewers invariably described these ensembles in elaborate detail. Besides, not being women, female impersonators were not challenging or threatening to female audience members. For the males in the audience the illusionist, on one level, offered the titillation of being sexually attracted to a character so beguiling and alluring that they momentarily forgot it was a male charade, while at the same time, they could feel superior to and much more manly than the performer. On a deeper, less conscious level, the illusionist offered men the comforting reassurance of soft, fluttery, helpless girls delighted to be in their places as men's inferiors. The female impersonators, neither men nor women on stage, threatened no one, but fascinated and delighted many.

Although Leon and other early female illusionists portrayed elegant ladies, in the late nineteenth century the matronly comedy role—a mixture of the "dame" and the "Funny Old Gal"—dominated female impersonation. In vaudeville, impersonators joked with comedy partners, burlesqued famous actresses, used double-entendre, sexually suggestive material, and devised the most incredible specialties. Charles Heywood, for example, appeared in "a mystifying costume, Half Gent's evening dress and Half Lady's costume, rendering an operatic Tenor and a Grand Prima Donna at the same time." Heywood actually performed with his left side done up as a woman and his right as a man and sang both parts alternately. As ludicrous and ridiculous as he must have looked and sounded, he reflected the general direction impersonation was taking in vaudeville. In musical extravaganzas virtually the only female impersonator was one of the biggest in the business—George Fortescue, who for twenty years cavorted in a comic role in the musical *Evangeline,* one of the staples of the late-nineteenth-century stage. But in 1884, when he starred as *Well Fed-Dora* in a burlesque of Fanny Davenport in her hit play *Fedora,* critics lambasted him. "The only idea which the author seems to have had," one reviewer sniped, "is that George Fortescue, being very large and very fat, would look absurd as the heroine of a French play. . . . He does look absurd—and there is an end of it. . . . he only looks very big and fat and absurd." Although Heywood and Fortescue admittedly represented the most ludicrous manifestations of impersonation, by the turn of the twen-

Three-hundred-pound George Fortesque with his comedy partner Ed Temple. HTC.

tieth century serious female impersonators creating the lovely illusions that represent the highest level of their craft were virtually nonexistent in American show business. Then Bill Dalton took Cakewalk lessons, and everything changed.

Bill arrived early one day in 1898 at Mrs. Wyman's dance studio while she was still working with eight chorus girls from a stage show. After they left, he could contain himself no longer and burst into laughter and into a parody of one large, awkward girl who had made a mess of even the simplest steps and movements. Mrs. Wyman could hardly believe her eyes. It was not just that Bill was funny, it was the way he moved, especially his arms and hands. They flowed and darted in soft, graceful curves and butterfly-like flutters that transformed what he intended to be a crude burlesque into a poetic dance. Since none of her female students was that graceful, she advised the fifteen-year-old boy to consider becoming a female impersonator, a career that would allow him to develop his special talents. After some misgivings, he decided to try the role in a local show, working with Mrs. Wyman three hours a day for a week, learning how to stand, walk, dance, and dress like a woman. A local newspaper gave him such a good review that he landed a female role in a Boston musical. Audiences and critics marveled at his illusionary skills. For the next five years, he lived in Boston, working as a bank clerk while perfecting his impersonation in amateur productions and in "fashionable entertainments, parlors, concerts, garden fetes and the like, at Bar Harbor [Maine], Newport [Rhode Island], and other resorts." Somewhere along the way, he became Julian Eltinge and decided to turn professional as a female illusionist. Whether or not his career actually began exactly this way, as Eltinge claimed it did, in 1905, he became a professional performer.

Quickly rising to featured, then star, status with his female illusions, he played vaudeville circuits and for two years toured with Cohan and Harris Minstrels, at least symbolically paying homage to Leon, the creator of his art. As with Leon and few others, critics raved about Eltinge's skill and argued the legitimacy of his illusions. "Just as a white man makes the best stage negro," enthused a critic confusing stage performances with everyday life, "so a man gives a more photographic interpretation of femininity than the average woman is able to give."

Eltinge's act, whether in minstrelsy or vaudeville, the United States or Europe, remained basically the same. Concentrating on even the most minute detail necessary to complete the illusion, he performed a series of perfectly costumed and choreographed female vignettes. In 1907, during which he created such a sensation in New York City that the New York *Daily Mirror* pictured him on its prestigious front page, he opened his performances with the Gibson Girl, outfitted in a "splendid black velvet princess gown, a marvelous wig, a becoming hat and pearl earrings and necklace, the whole making a stunning picture." He followed that with a "dainty young miss in a pink party dress," and closed his act by becoming a little girl, a tour-de-force that earned him five to six curtain calls every night.

Eltinge did convincing characterizations. Three years later when *Variety* reviewed "this artist in female drawings, who has no peer," he opened with "The Lady of Mystery," wearing a magnificent black gown draped from his

Julian Eltinge brought female impersonation to its height in America. HTC.

Julian Eltinge as a young girl. HTC.

A beautiful poster for one of the full-length musicals that starred Eltinge. NYLC.

right shoulder. "No woman," Sime Silverman, editor of *Variety,* thought, "could have worn the dress to more perfect advantage." Following the sophisticated opening, he appeared as a simple young woman in a light blue dress singing "Honeymoon In June Time." Next, he became a beautifully gowned colonial lady. He closed with a dazzling up-beat "That Spanish American Rag," in which he "wirled [sic] around the stage gracefully, swinging his arms in perfect rhythm and using his hands to make one forget they are there. There is no one, Sime observed, "man or woman, who can as skilfully [sic] and gracefully employ hands and arms as Mr. Eltinge." After praising Eltinge's great drawing power and his ability to fill both gallery and boxes, to pull the "class" into vaudeville as no other performer could, Sime concluded that "when vaudeville possesses an artist of this caliber, he is entitled to receive all the credit due him." In 1910, with vaudeville and musicals at the height of their popularity, featuring such great entertainers as Eva Tanguay, McIntyre and Heath, Nora Bayes, Harry Lauder, Fanny Brice, Weber and Fields, Fred Stone, and Ed Wynn, Sime Silverman, the leading critic of American show business, considered Julian Eltinge "as great a performer as there stands on the stage today."

In 1910, Eltinge had reached the pinnacle of vaudeville, getting top billing on the best circuits, lavish praise from the most important critics, and as much money as any other performer from the biggest promoters. So when he got a chance to star in a full-length Broadway musical comedy, generally considered a solid notch above vaudeville, he leapt at it. *Fascinating Widow* was an immediate hit, in which he played a man who had to disguise himself as a woman or women, a formula he then used in a series of successful musicals, including *The Crinoline Girl, His Night at the Club, Cousin Lucy, Countess Charming,* and *Her Grace the Vampire.* In 1910, he got the additional honor of having a New York City theater named after him. Although he starred in a war film, *The Adventuress,* the end of World War I caused the film to be withdrawn. Yet by 1919 he was reportedly worth over $250,000. He remained a star of the first order until he retired in 1928 to a Southern California ranch.

Since Eltinge was not just an ordinary vaudeville star but the most popular and celebrated female impersonator in American history, it is important to understand why he attained such financial and critical success. Despite all the praise he won, he also provoked bitter criticism, which indicated the sensitive nerves his act touched. "There is a considerable percentage of the younger male population [of Boston]," *Vanity Fair* complained in its 1908 criticism of Eltinge, "simply crazy to put on skirts and smirk and simper and act sissified for the public's entertainment." Boston, the center of the American Revolution, the article continued, was witnessing such a degeneration of its manhood that if the nation summoned Bostonians to arms "a goodly percentage of the young male defenders might want to run back because they had forgotten their powder puffs."

Few critics went to the extreme of *Vanity Fair,* but when Eltinge and Bothwell Browne, his principal competitor, simultaneously starred in "legitimate" musical comedies, the criticism mounted. "The sight of these men with pinched waists, high-heeled slippers, silk stockings, and fluffy lingerie," a critic understated, "is not calculated to inspire respect for either them or their profession." Eltinge and Browne, he continued, should play male roles instead of "pandering to the abnormal tastes of common-place theater-goers." The critic concluded by recalling the degeneracy he had seen in Cairo and in European capitals, where male prostitutes (though he, of course, did not use that word) with painted faces and revealing dresses circulated freely in public, testifying to the "pathetic decline" of social and moral values in the Old World. These critics feared that American manhood was going to hell in a wig, dress, and high-heeled shoes. More mundane critics, less concerned with the cosmic or at least national implications of two men starring as women in Broadway musicals, criticized the weakness of the shows and the questionable taste of parts of the performances. But the vast majority of the reviewers, while admitting that the shows lacked merit, applauded the quality, skill, and taste of the illusionists. Like beauty, taste and propriety are at least as much in the eyes of the beholder as in the actions of the performer.

A promotional photograph showing Eltinge in some of the roles he played in the musical, *Fascinating Widow.* NYLC.

Whether impersonators were homosexuals and/or transvestites and whether either should have disqualified them from being performers were the underlying questions in the controversy surrounding the impersonators. Perhaps the profession did provide an outlet for transvestites who had performing talents, and some impersonators, like a number of any other human category, may have been homosexuals. Although these considerations were irrelevant, the impersonators did have to cope with public inferences about their sexuality and masculinity. In many societies, female impersonators would be objects of curiosity. Many Americans, however, felt there was something wrong—not just unusual or strange, but *wrong*—about men successfully creating

Eltinge worked hard to create an offstage image of himself as a dashing "manly man." HTC.

beautiful illusions of femininity, actually seeming to become women. American culture was and is obsessed with masculinity and manhood. Since Davy Crockett, American popular culture has been studded with two-fisted, barrel-chested superman heroes. This tradition of greater-than-life, he-man fantasy figures perhaps originated in the days when the menacing wilderness and wild frontier intimidated ordinary human beings. Whatever the origins of this hard-shelled, tough guy model, American males are taught to avoid looking and acting like sissies. Serious female illusionists like Eltinge were professional "sissies." As such, they intrigued the public even as they seemed to symbolize social and moral decay.

As early as 1904, Eltinge realized that to become a full-fledged star and not just a passing curiosity he had to convince the public that his female illusions were merely stage roles. As meticulous as he was, it was no accident that he dressed off-stage to accentuate his masculinity, to call attention, for example, to the broad shoulders that he artfully disguised for his female roles. It was no accident that he cultivated a swagger and made sure that every interviewer or publicity agent knew about his interest and participation in athletics, ranging from outdoor sports like horse-back-riding to violent sports like boxing. Reviewer after reviewer stressed that off-stage Eltinge was a "manly man" who set women's hearts aflutter. "There is absolutely no trace of the effiminate [sic] about him," began a typical newspaper column about Eltinge. "He is athletic in built [sic] and well-proportioned, has an agreeable masculine voice, and good breeding stands out plainly in every action." To substantiate this image, Eltinge circulated stories about his exploits in one of the epitomes of American masculinity—the outnumbered hero defending his honor against toughs and bullies. In one version, burly stagehands at the Montauk Theatre insulted him as he came off-stage in costume and make-up. He said nothing, went directly back to his dressing room, quickly changed into his street clothes, walked quietly back to the wings, and "knocked the young men's heads together." Other versions had him taking on and beating up any number of rowdy, insulting drunks in barroom brawls. Whether or not such incidents actually took place, Eltinge made certain that anecdotes about them got extensive publicity as he carefully crafted a public image that sharply contrasted to his stage image.

Eltinge regularly invited newspaper and magazine writers backstage so that they could get to know him as he "really was." Besides recounting his athletic exploits and conveying a strong sense of masculinity, he also "confided" to them that he did not really like female impersonation but had to continue it because of public demand. Judging from the repetition in the articles about him, even in the phrasing, Eltinge must have put on as convincing and as well calculated a performance in his dressing room as he did on stage. As accessible as he *seemed* to be to the public and press, the real Eltinge appears to have been an intensely private man who jealously guarded his privacy by devoting considerable time and effort to building a personal image that satisfied his public's curiosity.

Julian Eltinge as Salome. NYLC.

Eltinge also never missed a chance to use his press contacts to build his reputation as a female impersonator. "I saw Julian Eltinge at the Palace Theatre the other evening," an excited New York City society woman reportedly told her dressmaker in 1918, "and he wore a gown I wish copied. It was simply perfect, and if you cannot get me one in which I will look just like Mr. Eltinge," she threatened, "I shall be obliged to find another modiste." Such Eltinge anecdotes pervaded the nation's press between 1905 and 1928, testifying to his publicity skills and to the public's interest in him. Many other entertainers tried to plant such stories, but the press published the Eltinge stories because it felt its readers wanted them and also because they were so unusual and eye-catching.

Around 1908, for example, Eltinge supposedly almost broke up a friend's marriage when he gave a picture of himself in the abbreviated costume he used for his Salome skit, a take-off on the dance of seven veils popularized by Eva Tanguay, to him—Joe Humphries, a Boston announcer sports authority and man-about-town. On the back of the picture, he wrote, "From your friend Jule." When Joe's wife found the sexy photo in his pocket, she exploded. And she got even madder when he tried to convince her that *this* Salome was a man, so he took her to see Eltinge perform. She fumed throughout Eltinge's series of alluring feminine illusions until he finally took off his wig and cut loose with his hearty baritone. With Joe out of the doghouse, the story concluded, he and Eltinge went to the boxing matches as they had planned. This story, so perfectly balancing the appeal of Eltinge's masterly feminine illusions with his off-stage

A cover of *Julian Eltinge Magazine,* which featured his makeup and beauty tips. NYLC.

masculinity, beautifully illustrates the dual images created by the man one critic aptly labeled "ambi-sextrous."

Eltinge would have had no need to mold his personal image of masculinity, no need for the stories about athletics or fighting, if it had not been for his totally convincing feminine images and the public's fascination with them. As an acknowledged beauty expert, one who knew tricks powerful enough to transform a "manly man" into what many thought was the most beautiful woman on the American stage, he freely shared his secrets with the public. In his *Julian Eltinge Magazine,* which was sold at his performances, and in his "candid" interviews he thoroughly described his preparation. Since early in his career he had studied every detail and nuance of femininity, working on carriage, the tilt of the head, movement of the hands, and positioning the feet. This "manly chap," one reporter revealed, did not use "false devices" to achieve his "beautiful neck and shoulders. Nature has given Mr. Eltinge a high full chest," the writer observed, "and his carriage is responsible in an important measure for the slender figure with its graceful feminine curves that thousands of women envy." His carriage, the writer might have added, got a big boost and strong support from his tightly laced corset, a model which he endorsed in advertisements along with lines of clothes, cosmetics, and "Willard White Co.'s Vaucaire Galega Tablets and Melrose Preparations, the Famous BUST DEVELOPER." These endorsements were *not* jokes, but a serious attempt to exploit commercially a star's popularity. Lillian Russell, Nora Bayes, and other beauties of the American stage did the same thing. But they were all women. Lillian Russell was always Lillian Russell and was always beautiful, so her tips might not have helped the average woman. But Eltinge knew how to work magic.

But to accomplish Eltinge's cosmetic magic it took much more than the blinking of an eye, the snapping of fingers, the utterance of a magic word, or even the lacing of a corset. It took him a full hour and a half to prepare for each performance. He shaved his beard, applied flesh-tone grease-paints to his face, and finished off his complexion with powders. He formed his eyes into almond

Corset advertisement featuring Julian Eltinge. Author's collection.

shapes, accenting the lids with blue and building up the lashes with black. "Lip rouge" completed his face. He rubbed his own white liquid preparation into his arms and shoulders, then powdered over the lotion to get the soft white effect he wanted. Trying to make his hands look smaller and more delicate, he powdered them white, rouged the fingers from the second knuckle to the tips and brightly painted his nails, which had the effect of tapering the fingers, and finally added blue pencil lines on the backs of his hands to make them look slender. He advised women never to hold the breadth of the hand toward the viewer. By presenting the narrow sides, the hands seemed longer and more delicate. Besides being two and half sizes too small, his shoes were always satin, which shone under bright lights making the feet look tinier. Finally, he styled his wigs to look soft and fluffy around the face and the back of the neck. The result of all this, he hoped, was the "ideal girl," what one writer called women the way "they ought to be."

In the wake of Eltinge's great success, a great many female impersonators entered show business. Many simply tried to imitate Eltinge but some added significant dimensions to the profession. Bothwell Browne, Eltinge's only real competitor, enjoyed a successful career that included vaudeville, musical comedy, and film. A native of Denmark, he taught dance in the San Francisco public schools for years before becoming a professional entertainer. By 1908, he toured the United Vaudeville circuit as the "creator of feminine illusions," including a plantation girl, a fencing maid, and a Gibson Girl. But he did not become a star until 1910 when he developed a sensational new act. "It was difficult to realize that the slender, lithe, and sinuous figure with its serpentine grace and wild abandon of dance was a man," a New York critic wrote of Browne's act, The Serpent of the Nile. In it, Browne, playing Cleopatra in a revealing costume, undulated with a live snake atop a raised throne. At the climax of the Dance of Death, he dramatically threw himself down the stairs to his stage death. In the "wiggling dance with nothing but gauze over the pit of his stomach," a Syracuse writer observed, "he makes his main impression which is not less suggestive by reason of the sex of the performer." By adding sensuality to Eltinge's realism, Browne made himself a star.

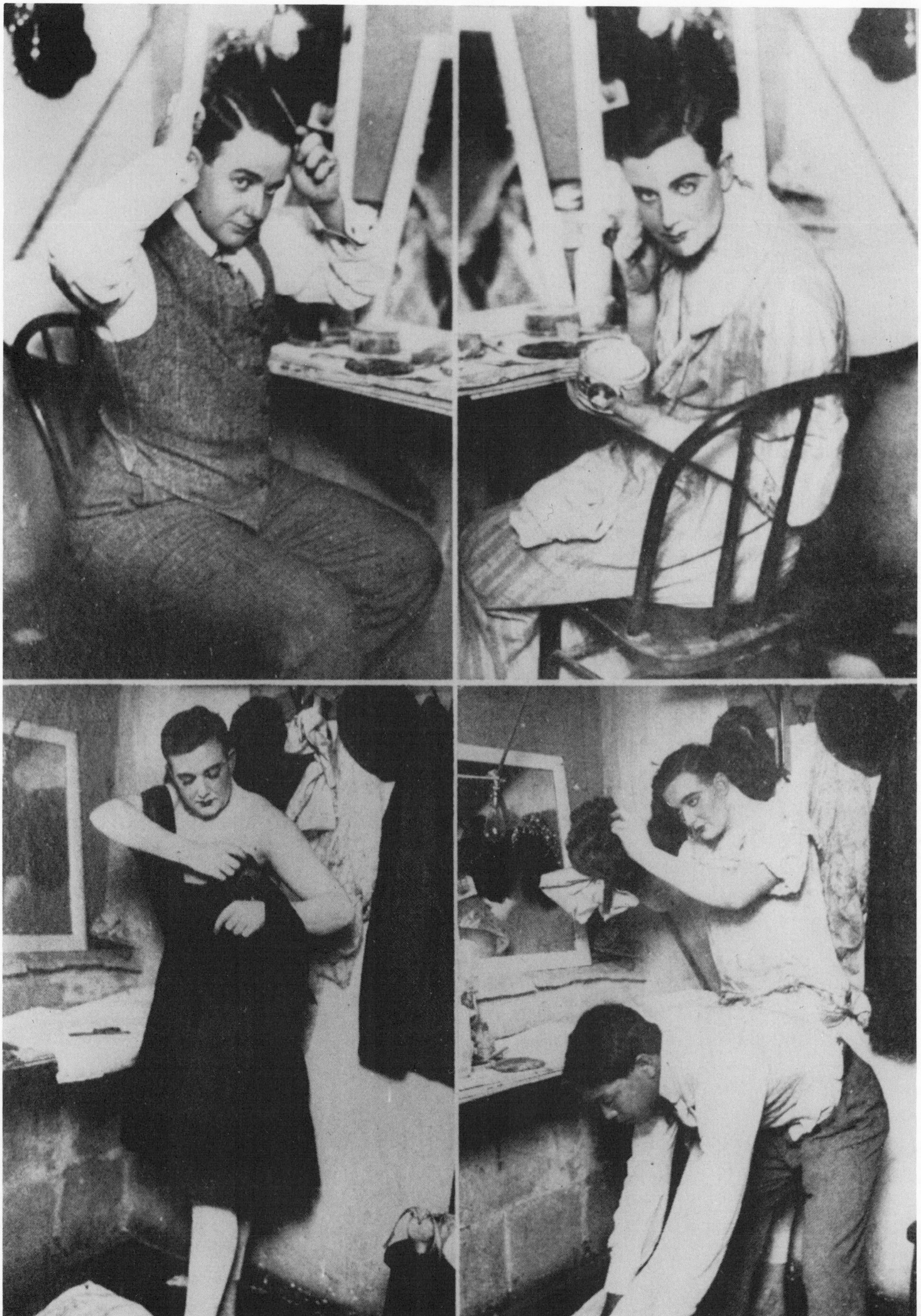

Although Eltinge did a Salome dance in 1908 at the time that dance swept show business, his version must have been very restrained. Critics never used the erotic adjectives for Eltinge that they used for Browne.

Browne's act, however, was far from a crass sex show. Some female impersonators did this type of act. The most famous of them, Bert Savoy, who played in the Ziegfeld Follies of 1918, created what critic Edmund Wilson called "a gigantic red-haired harlot, . . . reeking with the corrosive cocktails of the West Fifties" and given to vulgarity and double entendre. Browne worked a "great deal like Eltinge," *Variety* observed, "getting entirely away from the distasteful side and making the impersonation a thing of wonderment." His Cleopatra dance may have been sensual, even erotic, but to the *Variety* reviewer it was not distasteful. Like Eltinge, Browne had class and a versatile repertoire. His 1910 act, for example, included a glamorously gowned showgirl, a pantalooned parody of a suffragette, and a short-skirted, tight-sweatered fencing girl, as well as Cleopatra.

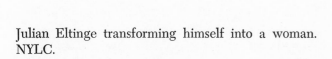

Bothwell Browne, Eltinge's only serious competitor, as a Gibson Girl. NYLC.

In beauty, grace, and attire, Browne rivalled Eltinge. Browne could outdance him but had a weak voice; so he made production numbers, especially erotic dances, the central features of his act. After he reached stardom, he even surrounded himself with beautiful chorus girls, a testament to his confidence in his own female illusions and to how heavily he relied on the appeal of women's bodies. In their production numbers, they frolicked as bathing beauties, cavorted "with joyful abandon about the stage" in a "bacchanalian revel," and did butterfly dances using special lighting to "represent the butterfly colorings in their filmy drapes." But Browne remained the major attraction, the loveliest of the lovelies. As the Green Venus, for example, he emerged in "transparent green draperies, with shimmering emeralds to light the blondness of his feminine representation" which climaxed with "a sensational bit of rhythmic pantomime." His starring role in *Miss Jack*, his 1911 musical comedy, unlike Eltinge's *Fascinating Widow*,

Julian Eltinge transforming himself into a woman. NYLC.

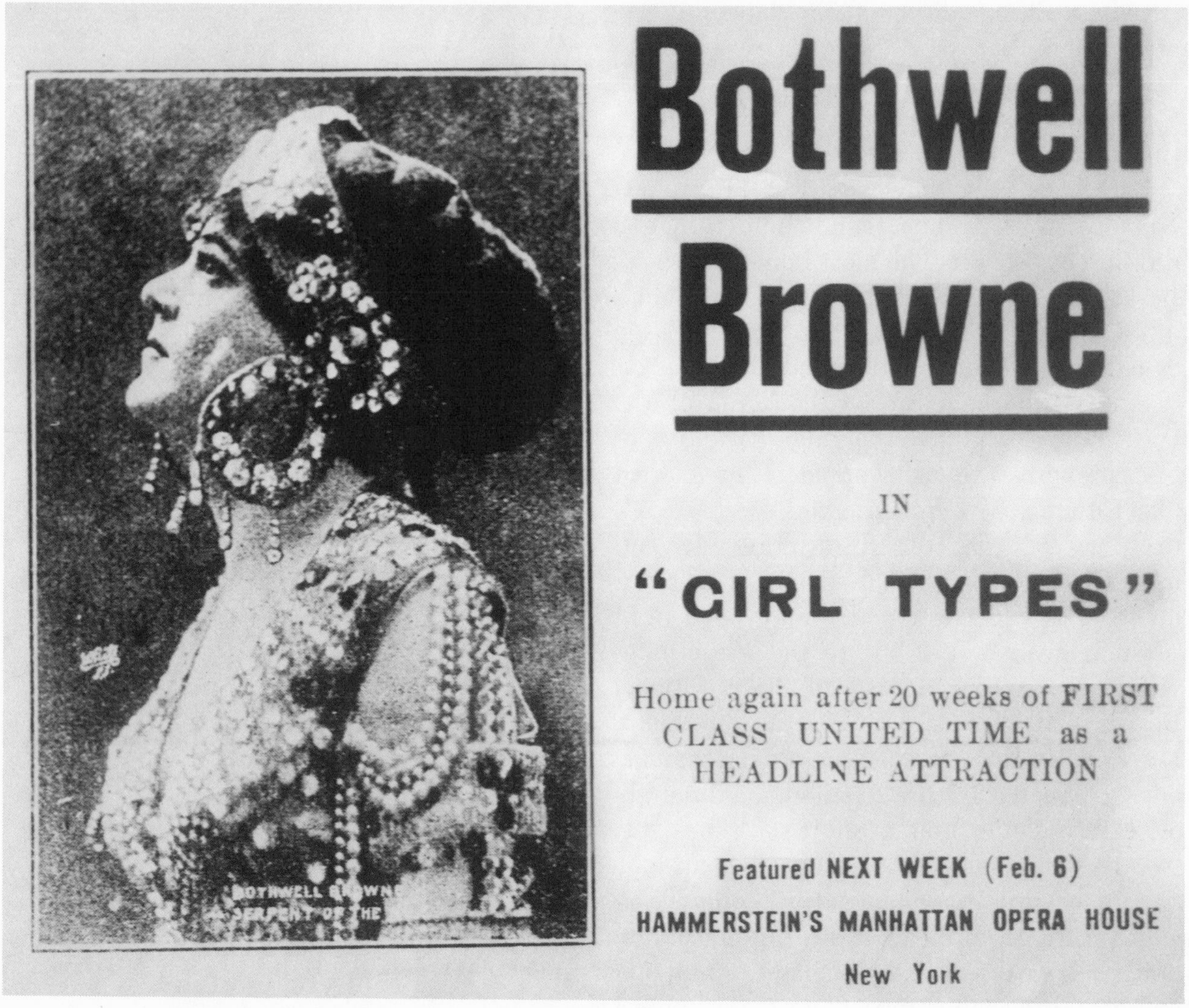
Bothwell
Browne
IN
"GIRL TYPES"
Home again after 20 weeks of FIRST CLASS UNITED TIME as a HEADLINE ATTRACTION
Featured NEXT WEEK (Feb. 6)
HAMMERSTEIN'S MANHATTAN OPERA HOUSE
New York

Advertisement for Bothwell Browne as "The Serpent of the Nile." NYLC.

proved short-lived. But he continued as a headliner in vaudeville and in 1919 starred in a Max Sennett feature film. Although he never reached Eltinge's stature as a celebrity, he remained a major show business attraction in the golden age of impersonation.

Eltinge and Browne were the most famous of the many female impersonators who performed their illusions in the nation's top, family oriented theaters in the thirty years before the Great Depression. But there were many others. "There are more female impersonators in vaudeville this season than ever before," *Variety* reported in 1923. "Three impersonators in one bill at a split week house recently is viewed as a record." The theater collection of the New York Public Library has material on at least fifty-five female impersonators, almost all of whom performed in the first thirty years of this century. There were

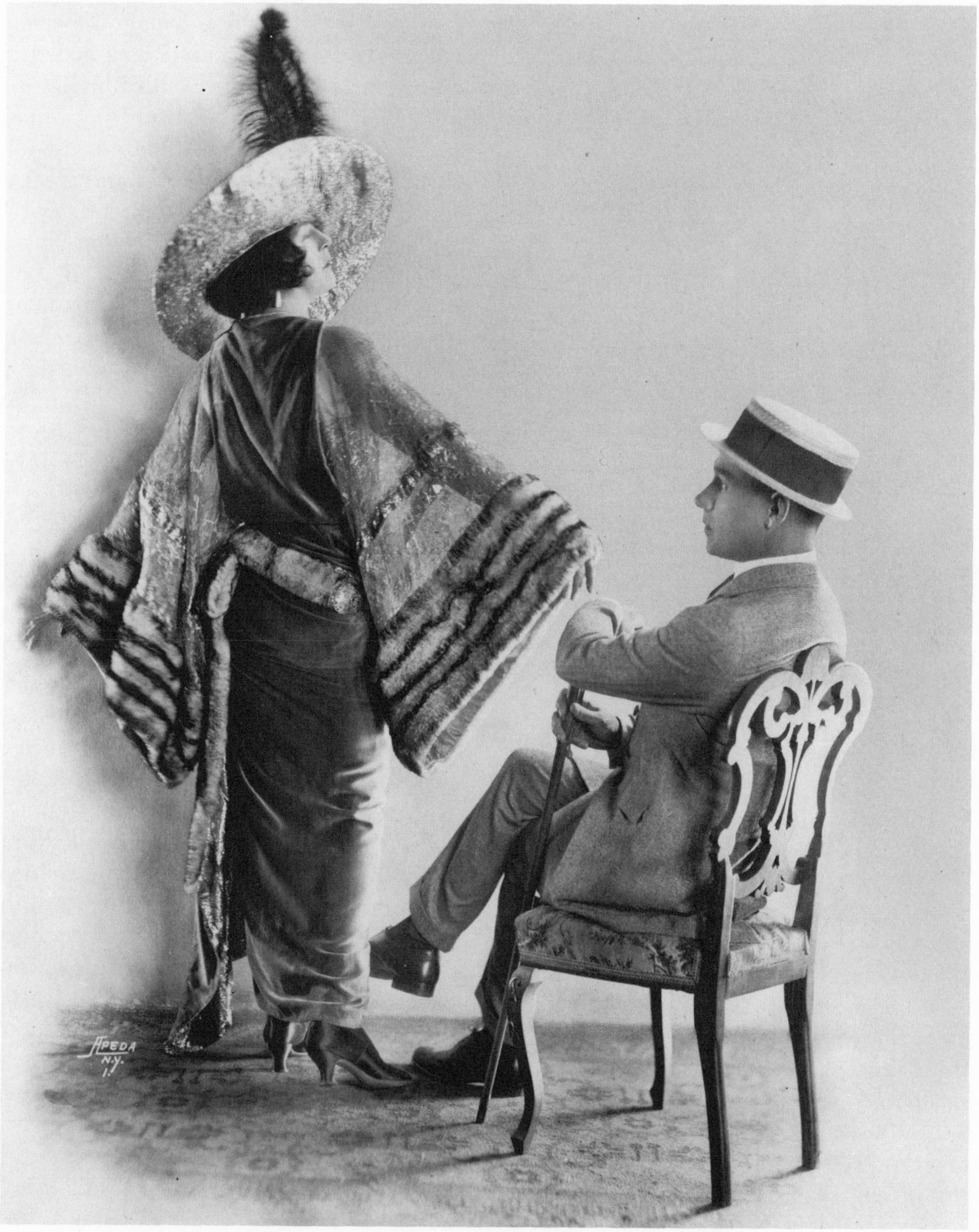

Bert Savoy (left) and Jay Brennan did a suggestive act. HTC.

Bothwell Browne as a fencing girl. NYLC.

basically three types: serious creators of models of femininity; the comic "dame"; and the sex or double-entendre act. A possible fourth, often combined with one of the last two, was the performer who reminded the audience during his act that he was a man. Whatever their style, most female impersonators had ordinary acts, but at least one other developed an ingenious gimmick.

Van der Clyde Broodway, a most improbable name for a Texan and an even more improbable name for a female impersonator, reportedly began his career as a male trapeze and tightrope performer with Ringling Brothers Circus and on the Orpheum vaudeville circuit. When a female trapeze artist—one of the angels in the Two Angels and the Devil—failed to appear for a show, Broodway put on her costume and became a flying angel. He subsequently became famous as Barbette, a female impersonator combining glamour, sex appeal, and a trapeze act. His act opened with a snow-white curtain parting to reveal a silver staircase covered with white carpeting. At the top, in a tight, shimmering dress with a long train of white feathers stood Barbette. After undulating slowly down the staircase to a couch, he teased the audience as he stripped off his headdress, gloves, and skirts. Then, he began his exciting, first-rate trapeze act.

Although Broodway captured the period's new standard of beauty with his fashionably trim figure, as a performing athlete he had special problems creating his striking female illusions. To soften the appearance of his muscular legs, for example, he had to wear woolen tights under his silk ones. But as with the other impersonators who excelled in these years, he had considerable talent as an entertainer as well as the facility for transforming himself into a vision of alluring womanhood.

Female impersonation had deep roots in American show business, dating at least back to the 1840s, but its counterpart, male impersonation, in which women created credible images of men, was imported from Britain at the turn of the twentieth century, an import that was never fully transplanted to the United States. Women had worn men's clothing and portrayed males on American stages since at least the late 1860s, when Lydia Thompson's British Blondes dazzled Americans with their burlesques of popular and classical plays. These performers took male roles primarily as an excuse to wear tights and to reveal their "nether extremities." But in 1894 Vesta Tilley brought refined male impersonation from England to the United States. To create her illusions of dashing young men-about-town, she always wore full-length men's trousers, whether smart formal wear or sailor suits. Impeccably dressed in finely tailored clothing, she used light music-hall songs of young dandies, songs like "Dear Boy, Ta Ta," "Only a Chappie," and "The Eton Boy" to quickly establish herself as a vaudeville star, what one 1903 writer called "probably the only woman who can boast of being a real matinee idol."

Although some reviewers felt that male impersonators did not set out to fool their audiences about their sex as female impersonators did, Tilley's male characterizations proved so convincing that some impressionable young women, taken with her "man-of-the-world," wrote her love letters, swearing their undying loyalty to her and begging her to stop claiming to be a woman and appearing in dresses to get publicity. She also received "the most peculiar and strange" love letters from men taken with her handsome young gentlemen. Like Eltinge, she argued that her performances did not reflect her character. "I rejoice in the realization that my tastes are decidedly womanly," she wrote in an article condemning the "mannish woman," "for I cannot stand the masculine woman."

Vesta Tilley as a formally dressed gentleman. HTC.

Like any other popular star, she had a number of competitors, most of whom also concentrated on characterizations of young blades. Hetty King, another Englishwoman, with "a wardrobe that would make the heart of the most Chesterfieldian beau palpitate with pleasure," won praise not only for singing boys' songs but singing them "as boys would sing them." In other words, she excelled at characterization. While describing her male attire in great detail, critics also emphasized that her act contained no "suggestion, innuendo, or double-entendre" and that she was a graceful, happily married "womanly woman" off-stage, neither suggestive, masculine, nor certainly not a "new woman."

Vesta Tilley as a jaunty young man. HTC.

While asserting their own offstage femininity, the male impersonators who concentrated on creating credible stage roles found that their stage behavior as men became instinctive. "When I don my masculine attire," American Kathleen Clifford explained, "I am a man—for the moment." On stage she found herself automatically reaching for a cigarette even though she did not smoke off-stage. In the same vein, she once found a misplaced brooch in the watch pocket of her stage vest where she had unconsciously put it as if it were a man's pocket watch. Like the other male impersonators, Clifford's wardrobe was critical to her success. The "smartest dressed man on the American stage," one critic observed, "is a woman." As with Eltinge, stories circulated about men having male impersonators' suits copied by their tailors. But Clifford found her special gimmick not in her clothing but in making quick costume changes onstage behind a shadow screen. Whether she intended this to be enticing or not, many men in her audiences probably kept a sharp eye on the screen imagining what was behind it and hoping to catch a glimpse of her between costumes.

Although several male impersonators, including Tilley, King, and Clifford, became top-notch stars, they created much less controversy and had far fewer competitors than men like Eltinge and Browne. The theater collection of the New York Public Library, for example, lists material on only fifteen male impersonators compared to fifty-five female impersonators. Why? Why were women less popular than men as impersonators? First of all, American audiences found women masquerading as men on stage much easier to accept than the reverse. Sarah Bernhardt, Henrietta Crossman, Charlotte Cushman, and a number of other actresses played Hamlet and

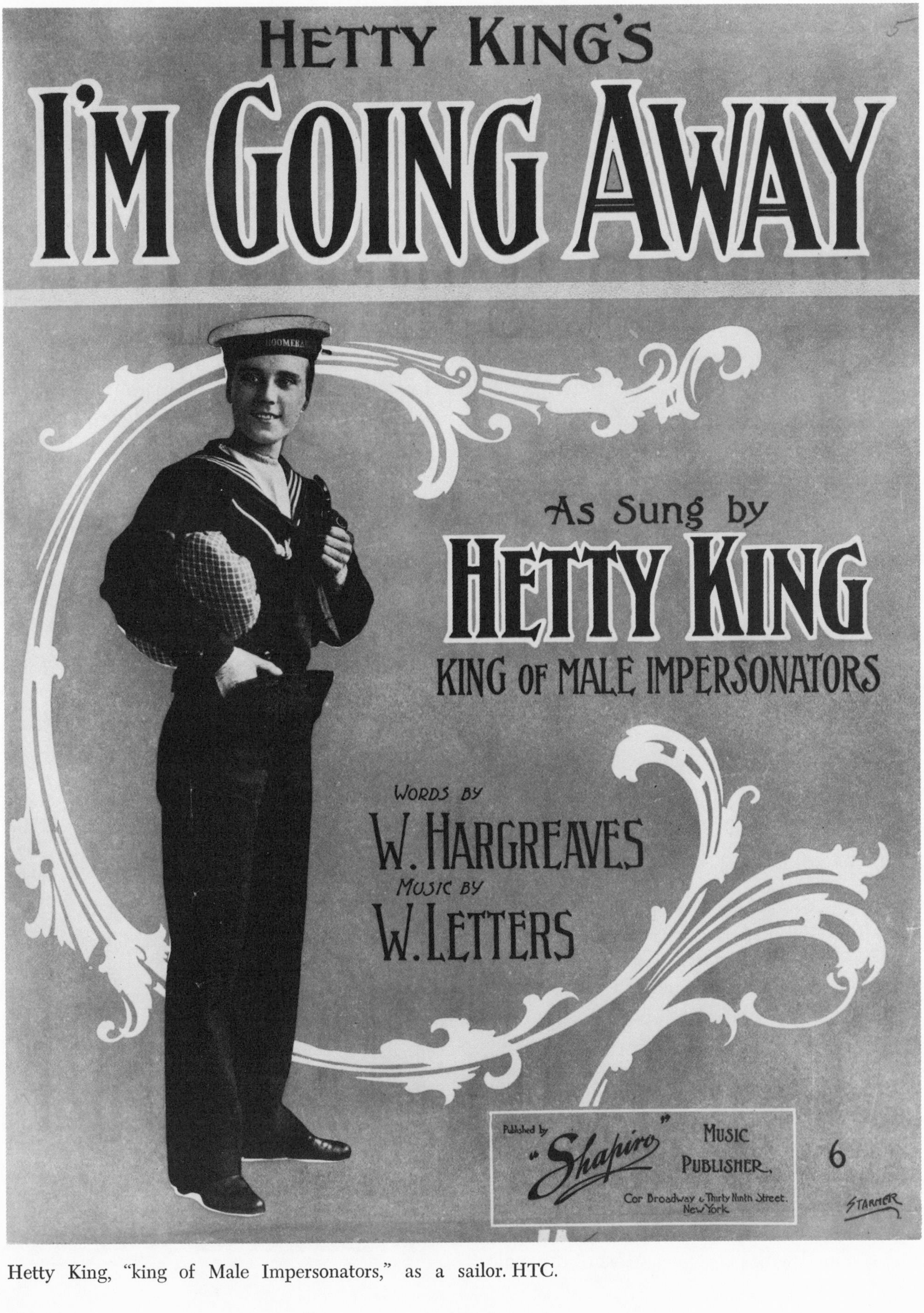

Hetty King, "king of Male Impersonators," as a sailor. HTC.

Sarah Bernhardt as Hamlet. HTC.

other serious male dramatic roles to critical acclaim and applause. Actors did not and could not do the same thing with comparable women's roles. Thus, male impersonators seemed less unusual and sensational than female to begin with. Secondly, despite the work of outstanding actresses, most women of the stage were there simply for men to look at, and this probably included male impersonators. Actresses initially donned men's clothing, especially tights, in the Victorian period to show off their bodies, and even trousers revealed much more than turn-of-the-century dresses lined with petticoats. Most of the male impersonators, observed vaudevillian-turned-writer Joe Laurie, Jr., "looked like women" on stage, perhaps because they wanted to remain proper "ladies," or perhaps because feminine sex appeal was one of their attractions. Unlike female impersonators, who portrayed sexually mature women, male impersonators portrayed only boyish young men. They never wore moustaches or beards, for example, masculine characteristics perhaps comparable to women's breasts as symbols of mature sexuality. Thus, male impersonators could easily be viewed as attractive young women in form-fitting men's clothing, attire that revealed their

Charlotte (left) and Susan Cushman as Romeo and Juliet. HTC.

bodies and allowed them to strike "provocative" poses. But for twentieth-century audiences who could go see Eva Tanguay take off all seven veils in her Salome dance or go to a girlie show, women in formal wear had only limited sex appeal. Finally, since Americans, especially men, were much more "hung up" on manhood than on womanhood, women dressed as men created much less taboo-violating sensationalism than did men dressed as women.

Despite their differences, both male and female impersonators had the same basic appeal. They seemed to do the impossible. "We vaudeville lovers are mostly very fond of it [impersonation]," observed a critic reviewing a bill containing both Kathleen Clifford and Bothwell Browne, "as we are of anything that looks impossible." Impersonation had the wonder of magic, where the viewer knows the illusion is an illusion but is still deceived by it—and loves every minute. Magicians and masters of deception like Harry Houdini were also major vaudeville attractions. In one sense, all of them—the female and male impersonators, the magicians, the escape artists—were updates of Barnum's humbugs, admitted deceptions that were entertaining and puzzling enough to persuade people to pay to be fooled. And as a Barnum's humbug, how it was done, how the magic worked, how the spell was cast fascinated the public. The magicians and escape artists who relied on sleight of hand, machinery, and deception for their appeal did not reveal their secrets. But the impersonators who depended on ends not means, on illusions not tricks, on images not gimmicks freely shared their techniques with their entranced public. Impersonators accomplished the most unbelievable transformation, the most impossible of all the impossible feats. They changed sexes, something many people might secretly have wanted to do but would never admit, let alone attempt. At least as importantly, impersonators reaffirmed traditional values and roles in a time of fundamental change, creating idealized images of males and females, of beautiful women, charming young girls, dashing gentlemen, handsome boys, and appealing but not vulgar seductresses. That female images were more diverse and sexier than the male was, in the last analysis, probably just further evidence that show business in its first century, like most other American institutions, was dominated by and shaped for men.

CHAPTER TEN

The Vaudeville Show

SOMETHING FOR EVERYONE

Like Topsy and like the United States itself, the vaudeville show "jes growed." It was not planned, nor was it a European import or adaptation. The word *vaudeville* is French, referring in the nineteenth century to light pastoral plays with musical interludes, but the shows were completely indigenous developments, the product of American saloon owners' attempts to attract free-spending drinkers by offering the added enticement of free shows to feed common people's insatiable appetite for fun as well as for food, fun that included early girlie shows that gave variety entertainment an initially bad reputation. When minstrel shows, wedded as they were to blackface, plantations, and Negroes, proved unable to adapt fully after the Civil War to changing public interests and concerns, show business promoters expanded variety shows, moved them into theaters, and cleaned up their reputation by purging them of objectionable material and advertising them as family entertainment.

By the 1890s variety shows, rechristened the more elegant sounding "vaudeville" in a final purge of the old disreputable image, replaced minstrel shows as the nation's most popular entertainment form. Paralleling the development of monopolies and trusts in other rapidly expanding businesses at the turn of the twentieth century, vaudeville grew into a highly organized, nationwide big business. Besides tracing

These images—boxing, women, and whiskey—gave early variety shows a bad reputation. HTC.

A raucous audience cavorting at a New York variety show. HTC.

vaudeville's evolution, this chapter concentrates on the qualities that distinguished vaudeville from all other entertainment forms: the underlying structure of its shows; the special demands it made on performers; the stars who seemed suited only for its format; the unprecedented popularity of its animal and magic acts; and the emphasis it placed on humor, and especially on ethnic humor. These distinctive qualities not only explain vaudeville's uniqueness, they also explain why the American people made vaudeville the most popular entertainment form in early twentieth-century America.

The career of Tony Pastor, the "father of American vaudeville," spanned the full range of pre-Civil War show business before he settled down and transformed saloon shows into family entertainment. As a six-year-old boy around 1843, he began to perform, singing about the evils of alcohol at temperance meetings, an ironic beginning for the man who later became perhaps the most famous saloon singer of his day in New York. In the mid-1840s, the

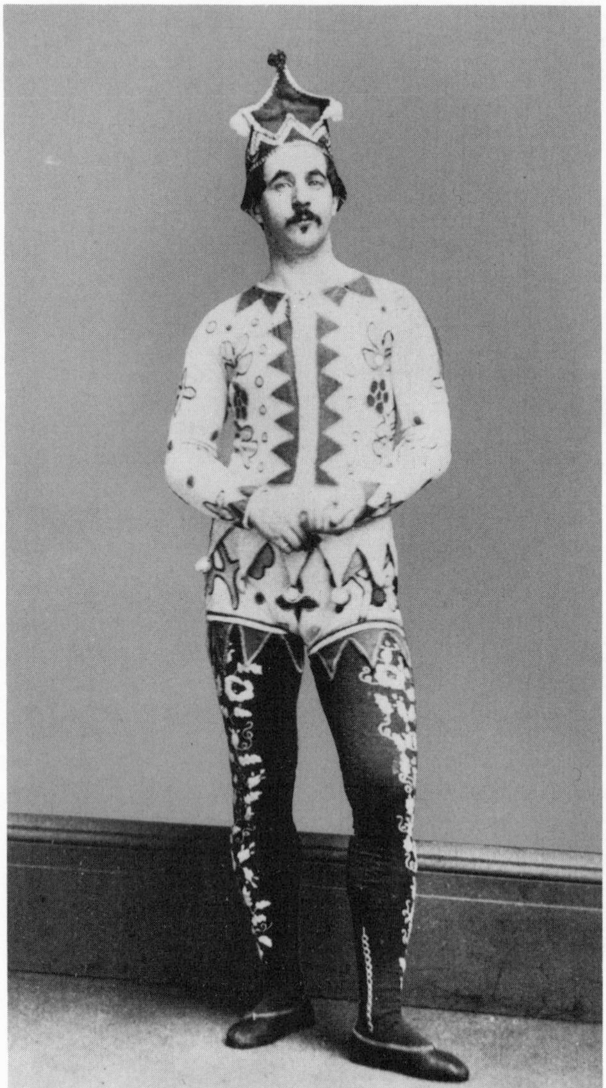

Tony Pastor, the Father of Vaudeville, began his career as a circus clown. HTC.

Boy Prodigy became a tambourine player and singer with the minstrel troupe at Barnum's Museum. After experience in minstrel shows, the talented young performer began a diversified circus career, working his way up from prop boy, to equestrian, acrobat, ringmaster, and finally to singing, dancing, joking clown. By the later 1850s, Pastor was a widely applauded clown. But in 1860, he began to perform in variety shows, in 1861 beginning a four-year run at 444 Broadway, a honky-tonk saloon. Probably embarrassed by 444's total lack of respectability, Pastor, in the frequent interviews he later gave, always glossed over that part of his career in favor of the ten years after 1865, which he spent staging and starring in variety shows in the Bowery, shows that he tried to clean up so they would appeal to more than the traditional masculine saloon crowds. During that decade, when minstrel shows began to travel widely, Pastor took his sanitized variety show on tour. This tour proved so successful that he made it an annual venture, one that was soon booked into high-class theaters—a major breakthrough for variety shows.

One of Pastor's typical traveling shows featured a blackface skit, The Colored Nurses; a male and female song and dance team; an Irish comedian; a woman playing the violin, guitar, xylophone, bells, concertina, and banjo; a gymnast and contortionist; a female dance team; a magic lantern exhibition; Pastor's comic songs, "which brought down not only the gallery but the parquette"; and a trapeze act that "resembled the gambols and eccentricities of monkeys." Besides being his own best attraction, Pastor was a striking character. Perhaps because of his background as circus ringmaster, he dressed flamboyantly, wearing a long frock coat, a vest with a prominent watch chain, high-laced patent-leather boots, and a shining opera top hat. Sporting a dashing handlebar moustache, the short, stocky Pastor swaggered through life, personally running his theater, booking his bills, and singing his songs. He was a master of the comic song, which, as he explained, poked fun at "some topic of the times which is capable of being looked at from a comical point of view." Before Will Rogers was born, Pastor considered the newspaper "the most valuable agent the vocalist has ever had for securing subjects for popular songs." Constantly creating new material, he sang about virtually everything, including the problems of the Civil War, the novelty of electricity, the plight of the workingman, the foibles of politicians, the Spanish-American War, and the frivolities of fashion plates. "I've introduced one or two new songs nearly every Monday night during the season," he boasted in 1895, "for the past thirty years." Whatever his topic, he played to the common people who made up his audiences, using the time-tested American popular formulas. "You can always depend on good songs with patriotism or freedom for their themes," he observed. "The average audience is almost invariably delighted by songs that laud the poor and toss the boots, so to speak, to the rich."

But in 1875, Pastor moved uptown from the Bowery to Broadway, leaving behind his established clientele and putting himself in direct competition with the Harrigan and Hart shows and with opulent musical extravaganzas, productions that taught him to appeal to a broader audience. Six years later, he moved into Tony Pastor's New Fourteenth Street Theatre, staged "high class" variety shows, and actively tried to build the family audience that variety had not yet consistently attracted. Besides cleaning up the show, Pastor enticed respectable women to his theater by offering major door prizes like sewing machines, new hats, and silk dresses; modest gifts like dress patterns; or sewing kits for every female patron. Pastor's gimmicks and his shows caught on, and other vaudeville theater managers quickly followed his example. Pastor remained primarily an early nineteenth-century trouper, an entertainer who thought in terms of running and performing in his own shows. But new promoters with the broader visions of the new age made vaudeville into a huge show business empire.

Tony Pastor made variety shows respectable and made himself into a celebrity with his topical songs and flamboyant dress. HTC.

The two men who built vaudeville into a national big business, Benjamin Franklin Keith and Edward Franklin Albee, came out of circus backgrounds like Pastor's. But unlike Pastor, they were businessmen, not performers. Keith, born in 1846 in New Hampshire, started by operating a circus candy concession

B. F. Keith's lavish New Theatre in Boston, an early vaudeville palace. HTC.

for a few years. Soon Keith was taking his own small shows on the road. He met with little success but was determined to make show business his career. Reverting to P. T. Barnum's pattern, Keith and a financial backer in 1883 transformed a small Boston store into the Gaiety Museum, whose only attraction at first was an infant midget "Baby Alice—The One Pound Baby." But even after Keith added a typical array of curiosities and exhibits, like Jo-jo the Dog-faced Boy, presented small variety shows on a stage constructed by laying planks over dry goods boxes, and expanded his attractions to a room upstairs, the ordinary dime museum did not draw well.

Then E. F. Albee, who also spent time with a traveling circus, went to work for Keith, and the two men began moving toward their eventual entertainment empire that would be crowned by opulent entertainment palaces—a long way from that one tiny dime museum. Keith made the first move. After observing that potential customers would leave the museum rather than wait for the variety show to begin, he staged continuous shows. But after an initial upturn in business, patronage fell off. "The trouble," Albee told his boss, "is that we are running the kind of a show where people, especially women, feel sort of sheepish to be seen. We've got to do something to raise the tone of the place." In 1885, Keith and Albee moved away from the rather sleazy "freak show" atmosphere. Redecorating the room into a Japanese garden complete with Kimono-clad Japanese waitresses serving tea, Keith and Albee staged an abridged one-hour version of Gilbert and Sullivan's *Mikado,* a current success in a major Boston theater. "Why pay $1.50 when you can see our show for 25 cents?" Albee advertised. Enough people found the advertisement and the abbreviated show appealing that Albee and Keith presented a season of "tabloid opera," which proved such a success that by mid-1886 they had enough money to lease a regular theater. After a year staging popularly priced plays, they presented their first continuous, completely reputable variety show, the type of show that led to their success.

Keith and Albee built their entertainment empire on three basic components. Aiming at family audiences, Keith absolutely insisted that every act had to eliminate any potentially offensive material, including "such words as Liar, Slob, Son-of-a-Gun, Devil, Sucker, Damn . . . also any reference to questionable streets, resorts, localities, and bar rooms."

Keith's theater managers enforced the restrictions rigidly by firing offenders on the spot. This strict censorship made performers mock Keith's theaters as "the Sunday school circuit." But patrons flocked to them. Again appealing to women and children, the continuous show began at about 9:30 A.M. and ran until about 10:30 P.M., the patrons being able to stay as long as they wanted just as they could in Barnum's Museum and would in motion picture theaters. But to keep crowds moving, especially on weekends and holidays, Keith and Albee opened the shows with "chasers"—acts so boring that, when they began to repeat their lifeless routines, they "chased" customers out—a more sophisticated version of Barnum's "egress."

Opulent interior of Keith's New Theatre set an enduring pattern. HTC.

The third major ingredient in the Keith-Albee formula—besides wholesome and continuous fun—was luxury. They built palaces for the people, where everyone with the price of admission was treated like an honored guest in an incredibly ornate mansion, one literally fit for royalty, where uniformed "servants" catered to the patrons' needs and whims—whether for refreshments, direction to seats, or assistance in powder rooms. It was as if exclusive millionaires' clubs or Barnum's fabulous Iranistan had been thrown open to the general public. For twenty-five cents anyone could feel like a king or queen for a day. More than twenty years before the construction of New York's Palace Theatre—the ultimate symbol of the lavish vaudeville house—Albee and Keith built the first vaudeville palace. When they opened their Colonial Theatre in Boston in 1894 only two American buildings rivalled it for opulence—the Imperial and Savoy hotels in New York. By that time, Keith and Albee already had expanded to a richly appointed theater in Philadelphia and one in New York that featured ushers in Turkish costumes and powder room attendants in lace caps and frilly aprons. But it was the Colonial Theatre in Boston that was the most sparkling gem in their show business crown.

Built during the depression of the 1890s at an unheard of cost of $670,000, the Colonial was truly palatial. The theater boasted a pillared, iron-worked, arched, gargoyle-bedecked exterior, marble ticket booths with gold domes, and a mirrored foyer with stunning painted panels. Velvet carpets led to the even more extravagant interior, with its brocade walls, plush seats, gorgeous paintings, and intricately decorated ceiling, or to its opulent restrooms with their shining brass fixtures and freshly cut flowers. But, ironically, at least as far as publicity was concerned, the theater's major attraction was in its basement. Albee often boasted that his greatest feat in showmanship was an inexpensive rug, the red carpet that covered the floor of the power plant. With the flair of a Barnum, Albee converted the theater's boiler room into a showplace. Its

Keith's and its successors made conspicuous consumption available to common people. HTC.

attendants, at least at tour time, wore spanking clean uniforms, kept the machinery immaculately clean, and used "solid silver" shovels to stoke the furnaces. Appealing to Americans' obsession with cleanliness, "the coal room with the carpet" generated tremendous publicity, publicity that further dignified the Albee-Keith style of vaudeville. If the coal bin of a theater were spic and span, its shows must certainly be above reproach. And people just had to see that incredible theater and the others that soon followed it.

At the turn of the twentieth century, vaudeville theaters proliferated at a dizzying rate, as minstrel houses had before the Civil War. In 1896, New York City contained seven vaudeville theaters; fourteen years later it had thirty-one. Chicago in 1896 had six variety or burlesque houses; in 1910, it boasted twenty-two vaudeville theaters. Philadelphia vaudeville houses expanded from twelve to thirty in the same years. As part of this great expansion, the truly stupendous Palace Theatre opened in 1913 at 47th and Broadway, the center of the nation's show business capital. The Palace immediately became the most prestigious house in the golden age of vaudeville, a period that symbolically began with the opening of Keith's Colonial Theatre in 1894 and ended when motion pictures took over the Palace in 1932. As vaudeville palaces popped up around the nation, chains of vaudeville theaters emerged throughout the country, as did burlesque and theatrical circuits in the same period. Most vaudeville chains numbered only a few theaters. But when B. F. Keith died in 1914, his vaudeville empire included six theaters in New York City, six in Brooklyn, two in Boston, two in Jersey City, two in Philadelphia, two in Cleveland, and one each in Atlantic City, Columbus, Lowell (Mass.), Indianapolis, Cincinnati, Louisville, Portland (Me.), Providence, and Pawtucket. As vaudeville boomed and demand for entertainers sharply increased, performers' salaries also exploded, from a few hundred dollars a week for a star to several thousand dollars a week for top headliners. Vaudeville was so popular that, even with the high costs of theaters and salaries, promoters made large profits. Vaudeville had become a nationwide big business.

Like the owners of other mushrooming businesses of the early twentieth century, vaudeville executives attempted to consolidate their empires and to limit competition. Joining with other theater owners, Keith and Albee formed the United Booking Office (UBO), which exclusively booked all performers for the members' theaters, as did similar theatrical and burlesque "monopolies." In effect, the UBO commission on the performers' salaries was a kickback to the theater-owners for the privilege of being booked on the circuit. UBO, led by the dictatorial Albee, whom Groucho Marx labeled "Ol Massa," took increasingly large cuts from performers' salaries, arbitrarily assigned them to undesirable, expensive-to-reach bookings, and could fire them after their third performance, leaving the performers stranded with no income and no booking. Facing such exploitation, some vaudeville performers attempted to organize a union, The White Rats, modeled on British music hall performers' Water Rats. In 1900, the White Rats tried to organize a strike, but, like many other turn-of-the-twentieth century fledgling unions that tried to oppose powerful big businesses, they were victimized by the power of the employers and by the disunity of the performers. Still, the White Rats grew stronger owing to the employers' insensitivity to legitimate grievances. Again paralleling industrial unionism, the entertainers' union found that, when it eventually gained strength, it faced a company union—The National Vaudeville Association (N.V.A.), an organization financed by Albee in 1916. To be booked into any of the Albee-dominated Vaudeville Managers Protection Association theaters, performers had to be N.V.A. members in good standing, which meant not being White Rats. The N.V.A. did remedy some of the worst management abuses and provided entertainers with a valuable new service. Performers could get protection for their material by filing their acts in sealed envelopes with the N.V.A. office, envelopes that would be opened if a performer charged that another entertainer had stolen his routine. With its strong power base, the N.V.A. won the battle with the White Rats, and the Keith Albee circuit spread, dominating big-time vaudeville in the East as the Orpheum circuit did in the West, setting up a far-flung circuit that performers, even the biggest stars, traveled.

"The vaudeville actor," recalled comedian Fred Allen, who began his long career as

The spotless boiler room, which was open to public tours, attracted a great deal of publicity for its cleanliness. HTC.

"Freddy St. James, The World's Worst Juggler," "was part gypsy and part suitcase!" Like nomadic herdsmen continually moving in search of greener pastures, vaudevillians traveled in search of better bookings, better reviews, and better contracts. Vaudeville consisted of much more than the Keith-Albee-Orpheum circuits, much more than the Palaces. There were literally thousands of small, second- and third-rate theaters scattered throughout the nation. And every one of them needed a continual supply of performers—the small-timers that made show business forms truly national institutions. The lives of the entertainers who played in the nation's Beaver Dams were important parts of the human story of vaudeville, a story that with only minor variations could apply to most other entertainment forms.

Since vaudeville theaters constantly needed fresh faces, performers continually had to travel. But troupes did not tour together, so small-timers lacked the moving

Professor Hermann, performing one of his magic tricks. HTC.

homes that circus performers had. Still, small-timers did live in a world apart, thinking, talking, and dreaming almost entirely about show business, as they literally lived out of their trunks. Many women troupers gave birth in dressing rooms, pullman railroad cars, or in the wings of theaters. Many babies slept comfortably in the tops of theatrical trunks or in bureau drawers. Many children got their baths in sinks, cut their teeth on sticks of greasepaint, and learned to read from programs, handbills, or scripts. Many troupers could not afford to buy their meals in restaurants so they cooked in tin plates on improvised sterno or gas jet "stoves." Small-timers even dated their lives by their engagements. A baby's birthday might be remembered by associating it with the time the act moved up to a better spot on a bill; an election might be dated as the week the act filled in for a star;

Herr Holtum, a cannon-ball juggler.

or a tornado might be recalled by the time a booking was canceled.

Gossip about theaters, hotels, managers, agents, audiences, and other performers pulled traveling entertainers together into a tightly-knit group with its own lore and traditions. The uncertainties and instabilities of life on the road, for example, frequently made the hotel desk clerk, who often had to collect rent from penniless entertainers, into an adversary. Performers delighted in swapping stories about hoodwinking the clerk, stories that freely blended fact, fiction, and fantasy, stories that told about clever small-timers packing suitcases with bricks or with telephone books so the clerk would think the performers had bags full of valuable clothing and would give them credit with their luggage as collateral. Others laughed about sneaking out without paying their bills by dropping suitcases out windows or by putting on as many layers of clothing as possible and casually sauntering out as if they were just stepping out for a few minutes. Small-timers also stayed together even in the off-season, which in pre-air-conditioning days was the summer. Communities of performers sprang up about New York and Chicago, the centers of the eastern and western vaudeville circuits. So many performers spent the off-season on Long Island that they formed their own social club, The Long Island Good Hearted Thespians Society (LIGHTS). One of LIGHTS' major functions was its huge Christmas party complete with a gigantic tree, beautiful decorations, a traditional feast, and, of course, an unusually dramatic visit from Santa Claus. It was a typical American Christmas celebration—except that it took place on the Fourth of July.

As the entertainment circuits grew and the numbers of traveling performers greatly increased, show-business-oriented inns emerged throughout the nation, providing small-timers with homes away from home, sanctuaries where they could rent inexpensive, clean rooms and get three filling meals a day, where they were not gawked at, and where they could relax and trade boasts and gossip with other performers. Word quickly spread among small-timers about these places, often by means of notes written on theater dressing-room walls, notes that warned about clip-joints as often as they recommended good buys, like Abuza's Home Restaurant, a typical small-timers' hangout in Hartford. Mama Abuza provided huge five-course dinners of her home-cooking for twenty-five cents with

E. D. Davies, a ventriloquist with his dummies. HTC.

The Lillis Sisters, bicyclists. HTC.

the songs of the Abuza's daughter thrown in for free. Abuza's Home Restaurant never made it out of the small time, but after getting a taste for show business from the constant buzzing of the diners, Sophie Abuza did—after she changed her name to Tucker.

For small-timers as well as for big-timers show business was virtually their entire lives. When they got good bookings, good billings, or good audiences, *everything* seemed great, and all the long, uncomfortable travel, all the small, dingy rooms, all the discomfort, and all the disappointments seemed worthwhile. When the act went poorly, nothing seemed good. But, even then, many small-timers found solace in their hopes and dreams. After years and years playing in the same sorts of theaters and in the same place on bills, many acts knew they would never make it out of the small time. But few experienced entertainers left show business by choice. Performing got in their blood, and for them there was no other business. Whatever the town they played in, whatever the quality of the theater, whatever their place on the bill, whatever the size of the crowd, performers had their moment on stage with the audience. In the magic glow of the footlights, in the warmth of an enthusiastic audience an ordinary performer could be lifted, at least for that moment, to exhilarating heights. More than anything else, that feeling kept professional small-timers going. "Vaudeville old-timers may not be wallowing in affluence in later life," concluded Fred Allen, "but each small-timer has his store of memories that will help him to escape from the unhappy present into the happy past."

For its patrons, the show, not the lives of the performers, was the important thing. Vaudeville presented its audiences with an incredible variety of performers and material, ranging from slapstick comedy to dramatic readings, from trained animals to opera singers, from sexual impersonators to ballet dancers, from ethnic humor to production numbers. Ironically, the show business form that seemed the most unstructured, that seemed little more than an entertainment hodgepodge, was in fact meticulously planned and highly structured to offer a balanced variety, to build excitement and expectation, to pulsate with its own rhythm, and to convey a sense of order and unity. The form of the vaudeville show was a new ritual for the new age. Like the nation itself in the age of immigration and modernization, the vaudeville show combined an odd assortment of distinctive pieces. In this sense, it *was* a hodgepodge! But unlike the nation, the vaudeville show managed to arrange the pieces into a cohesive, unified whole.

Vaudeville had the rapid-fire pace of the modern city as well as its diversity. The entire show whizzed before the audience like the view from an elevated railroad. But its carefully crafted structure focused the potentially blurred vision into a pleasing, balanced composition. While the audience was still entering and being seated, an action-oriented "dumb act" opened the show, an act that did not depend on being heard for its appeal. Whether animals, dancers, or acrobats, the first act was set on the full stage area, which conveyed a feeling of spaciousness as well as of action and vitality, suggesting that a full exciting show was to come. To settle down the audience, the second spot featured "a typical vaudeville act," often a male and female singing duo or a comedy team that could perform in the narrow space in front of a drop curtain while the stagehands set up the scenery for the production to come, so there could be rather elaborate scenes without slowing up the rapidly paced show. "With number three position," observed George A. Gottlieb who booked the Palace Theatre, "we count on waking up the audience. . . . from now on it [the show] must build right up to the finish." A comedy sketch usually filled this slot, but it had to be very different from the first two acts so that the audience would already feel the rich variety of the show and anticipate what was still to come. The fourth spot went to the "first big punch of the show." The next act, which climaxed the first half of the show, was "as big a 'hit' as any number of the bill" to leave the audience buzzing at intermission.

The show was constructed to set up the stars. If a production number closed the first half, for example, a top comedy act might precede it, and the third spot would not be a comedy sketch but some other upbeat number. The second half opened in front of a drop curtain with an act, often a comedian, that would maintain the gaiety and pace but not be so good that it would prevent the rest of the bill from building. Next, the stage blossomed into a well-mounted production, often a playlet featuring a comic or dramatic headliner. In the eighth spot on the nine-act bill, the booker offered his biggest star, usually a comedian or comedy team. A "showy act" completed the program, leaving the audience with a feeling of abundance, while also allowing early leavers to exit without disrupting the show. "A command of the art of balancing a show," a vaudeville writer observed, "is a part of the genius of a great showman." The structure produced a pace, rhythm, and unity that greatly enhanced the appeal of each act and of the show, providing still another example that there was much more to show business than met the eye.

The vaudeville show drew material and performers from all other show-business forms—musical comedy, burlesque, drama, the minstrel show, and even the circus. In this sense, vaudeville was a smorgasbord of the richest American entertainment fare. But it was, at the same time, something unique, something with its own distinctive format, pace, and performance techniques, something that made demands on performers that no other show business forms made. Vaudevillians appeared only once in each show, regardless of how famous, how well paid, or how popular they were. And they appeared for only a very limited time, normally about ten minutes for lesser acts and twenty to thirty minutes for stars. That one brief appearance was a make-or-break opportunity. In their one shot, performers had to win the audience immediately, to hold its attention, to entertain it, and then quickly to get off stage. They had no time to unfold stories, to develop characters, to make mistakes, or to experiment with ad libs. Like sprinters at track meets, vaudevillians had to start at full speed and then maintain the pace for their entire, short stints. "The vaudeville stage makes such demands upon its artists that they are compelled to perfect everything," critic Gilbert Seldes perceptively observed. "They have to establish an immediate contact, set a current in motion, and exploit it to the last possible degree in the shortest space of time." The refinement vaudeville demanded was not, Seldes noted, in substance, but in technique. "The materials, they are trivial, yes; but the treatment must be accurate to a hair's breadth."

In front of live audiences, the performers continually worked on their acts, studying, adding, honing, and modifying their every movement, word, gesture, and expression. If they improved, they moved up; if not, they remained small-timers. To paraphrase Mae West, it was not so much what they did, but how they did it that determined vaudevillians' success. With the extensive vaudeville circuits that ensured constantly changing audiences, performers could make entire careers out of one perfectly executed routine. And many did. "You know, all you needed in vaudeville was seventeen good minutes," George Burns once reminisced. "If you had seventeen good minutes, you could work for seventeen years. There were so many theaters, you wouldn't come back to the same one for four years and who would remember what you did the last time you were there?" But while they were there, performers had to be good, or they would not get a chance either to move up or to return.

"The great acts in vaudeville are those which could not be perfectly appreciated elsewhere," observed Gilbert Seldes. "It is an independent act, wholly self-contained, not nearly so appropriate in any other framework, except possibly a one-ring circus." The vaudeville act stood alone, out of context, with no other part of the show to carry it. It did not need diversity or depth, but it had to have strong initial impact and great short-run appeal. Trained seals would not have made a satisfying evening's entertainment, but they made a fine, short vaudeville act. For half an hour Houdini absolutely captivated his audiences; Eva Tanguay may have lacked the diversity to hold her audiences for a whole show, but few could match the appeal of twenty minutes of her frenzy. Many vaudevillians easily made the transition to other forms of show business, but some of vaudeville's most popular performers, some of its superstars, seemed able to reach their full potential as performers only in vaudeville.

Perhaps the most sensational of the unique vaudeville stars was Eva Tanguay, often called "the female Jolson." "The history of Eva Tanguay," as one reviewer observed, "is practically a capsule history of vaudeville." Born in 1878, Tanguay grew up in the years when vaudeville matured into the most popular form of show business. She began performing as a child, and then, like most other entertainers, she spent years playing in small-time shows. Even early in her career when she was still an unknown, she had that indefinable, special quality that emanates from great entertainers. When she earned only $30 a week (she later earned $3500 a week) and played only a supporting role in a second-rate musical, she caught a critic's eye as someone "sure to make a name for herself," someone with truly unusual but mystifying appeal. "Miss Tanguay's voice contains no more music than a buzz saw," the Buffalo, New York, reviewer observed, "she has no more repose than a mad dog fleeing before a mob of small boys, and she still has the rudiments of acting to learn." But audiences loved her. "Miss Tanguay has little to recommend her," the critic prophetically concluded, "and yet she has the very things that go to make theatrical stars." But like other performers who were able to hold the public's affection for a long time, who were not just "shooting stars," Tanguay had to spend years learning how to entertain in the best possible schools—the nation's theaters—and with the best possible critics—the public. In the late 1890s, she toured in a number of undistinguished musical and vaudeville shows. As late as 1898, she was still unknown enough so that one burlesque theater spelled her name "Tanqueray." But her reputation grew as she improved her performance techniques. Soon, no one misspelled her name.

Eva Tanguay, one of vaudeville's most exciting performers. HTC.

When at the turn of the century Oscar Hammerstein booked her into his Victoria Theatre in New York, she knew she faced a make-or-break point in her career. She confided to a friend that she was so frightened by her important New York opening that she felt like canceling the booking and remaining on the road, fears her first appearance did nothing to dispel. Her opening matinee performance drew little audience applause as the nervous Tanguay could not fully cut loose with her usual uninhibited power. But that night was different. "She gave an exhibition of abandon I never have seen equaled," a reviewer gasped. "Back and forth across the stage she pranced and hopped . . . displaying a physical strength and endurance which were abnormal." The audience's emotional outburst equalled Tanguay's, and she was on her way.

Tanguay's performance style did not change once she broke into the big time. Once she found something that worked, she stayed with it. In this sense, she was a vaudevillian through and through. Her style had three closely related elements: an emotional intensity that stunned audiences with its raw power, a devil-may-care attitude and uninhibited actions and gestures that mocked all the conventions of proper demeanor for a woman, and suggestive material that titillated audiences. Tanguay created an aura of untamed, liberated female sexuality. Facing an

Explosive Eva Tanguay created an image of total abandon, including bare feet and tousled hair. HTC.

audience, she shook her already tousled hair, kicked out her legs, threw back her head, laughed provocatively, and then exploded in songs and movements that fed her image of sexual freedom and abandon. "She is a tornado, a whirlwind, a bouncing bundle of perpetual motion," one writer recorded. "She screams, she shouts, she twists and turns, she is a mad woman, a whirling dervish of grotesquerie. She is unlike any other woman on the stage."

Grasping for ways to describe her performance, critics called her "The Little Cyclone on Legs," "The Queen of Perpetual Motion," a magnet, a dynamo, or "like a bunch of firecrackers in an overheated stove"—images of boundless energy and explosive power. But her appeal went beyond that. When women's rights advocates fought for women's political emancipation, Tanguay proclaimed their sexual freedom. She was no coy seductress, no "giddy girl" playing the old "lady-like" roles in more revealing clothing, as were so many early twentieth-century stage women, including the Ziegfeld Girls. Tanguay was a mature woman who scoffed at convention and openly proclaimed her lusty sexuality. At the end of each wild performance, she always sang her theme song to testify that "I Don't Care, I Don't Care, What They May Think of Me." Her liberated image appealed to women as well as men. "At the stage door wherever she appears," a surprised writer observed, "crowds of women swarm in order to catch a fleeting glimpse of her as she enters her carriage."

When the Salome dance—an updated version of the seductive biblical dance that cost John the Baptist his head—became a rage, Tanguay became the most famous Salome dancer. She threw her veils, like her inhibitions, to the winds, and she promoted herself with a great flair for public relations. She once called a press conference to show reporters her new Salome costume, an enticement that drew a full house. But Tanguay walked in fully clothed, smiled, looked down at her clenched fist, and slowly opened her hand to reveal a few beads and a small piece of gauze as she asked reporters what they thought of the costume. The "media event" yielded her the publicity she wanted as did each of her Salome dances. "What there was of her costume fitted splendidly," one reviewer observed, "but there wasn't much. A few beads sprinkled here and there and a splash of green gauze . . . didn't hamper her in the gyrations which followed." Another critic quipped that her "costume can hardly be described at length." But even after her writhing Salome dance, in which she "danced like one possessed," her audiences would not let her leave the stage until she sang "I Don't Care."

Tanguay fully realized the value of publicity, especially notoriety, and she got it, using calculated stunts like holding her Salome costume in the palm of her hand, claiming that she had lost tens of thousands of dollars worth of jewelry which she somehow always "found," soaring 5000 feet in the air on a balloon ride, hunting big game, springing into a den of tigers to pose for photographers, and announcing that she was writing a semi-autobiography entitled *A Hundred Loves,* in which "some people will recognize instances and situations." To reporters, she insisted with mock righteousness that she was not at all "naughty." "I never drink," she teased, and "I never smoke." She also got unplanned publicity from her frequent temperamental outbursts. She hollered at unresponsive audiences, threw a stagehand down a flight of stairs because he was in her way when she went to take a curtain call, walked out on shows when her billing was too small, and grabbed a chorus girl by the hair and threw her up against a wall for making wisecracks about Tanguay's love life. With her attention-getting antics and her crowd-pleasing performances, Tanguay was such a great draw that even the Keith-Albee circuit featured her, the managers making a rare exception to their restrictive censorship when Tanguay cut loose and audiences screamed their approval.

But even when she stood at the very pinnacle of American show business, Tanguay suffered deep personal doubts and anguish. She confided to a friend that she felt that her success was "just luck. People speak of my personality," she observed. "I don't know what that personality is. I don't even know what they are talking about." Like many other performers who carried on highly emotional love affairs with their audiences—like Al Jolson, Bert Williams, Judy Garland, and Janis Joplin—Eva Tanguay was plagued by insecurity and the insatiable need for love, affection, and acceptance. Finally she was left with nothing. Tanguay lost her fortune in the stockmarket crash of 1929. By that time, she was fifty years old, past the age when she could excite audiences with her raw, vital sexuality, and past the golden age of vaudeville.

Tanguay was certainly not the only woman to star in vaudeville. But many other female headliners, including Lillian Russell, Elsie Janis, Gertrude Hoffman, Nora Bayes, Marilyn Miller, and Irene Franklin, tended to be rather conventional female singers or dancers, carrying on the traditional, fragile, ladylike images. Yet, Sophie Tucker belted out her earthy songs; Mae West camped and vamped her way through her numbers; and Fanny Brice clowned her way into audiences' favor. There were all sorts of women in vaudeville, as there were all sorts of acts of every kind. Innumerable song-and-dance teams crooned, soft-shoed, and pattered their ways through their parts of the bills with catchy popular songs and light jokes. Comic farces, many dating back to minstrel shows, convulsed audiences with laughter. These and other music and comedy features were show-business staples, rather than uniquely vaudeville phenomena. But two show-business specialties—trained animals and magic acts—enjoyed far greater popularity during vaudeville's golden age than at any other time, an unusual popularity that demands explanation. Both were particularly well suited to vaudeville's structure and format, but so were other "dumb acts" like acrobats and trapeze artists which

Tanguay was one of the most imitated stars, a fact she turned into a hit song. HTC.

Madame Nelson and her trained doves, one of many small, trained animal acts in vaudeville. NYLC.

never achieved the vaudeville prominence that animal acts, magicians, and escape artists attained. They had something that was right for the time as well as for the vaudeville show.

Animal acts were, of course, nothing new, and neither was their popularity, as the long history of menageries and circuses clearly demonstrated. But there was something new, something different, about the vaudeville animal act. Circuses featured exhibitions of animals as exotic, natural curiosities and of the ritual of the courageous lion-tamer heroically subduing nature's most ferocious, savage beasts. But vaudeville presented far different rituals. Its animals, for the most part, were small and friendly—dogs, birds, seals, and monkeys—and they played at being human. They skated, rode bicycles, talked, danced, ate with forks, lit and smoked cigarettes, drank beer, and staggered like drunks. Vaudeville's primarily urban audiences had no need to see the repeated re-enactment of the ritual of man dominating nature. They were far from the frontier in every way. Instead, they seemed to want to see man as a model of what all living things aspired to be—not man as king of the beasts. They wanted to see animals raised to the level of man, not man reduced to the level of animals. They also wanted light, frivolous entertainment, images of happiness and fun—not of fear and danger. The twentieth-century threats to people and civilization came not from animals and nature, but from machines and science. Taming nature no longer reassured common people that they could control their lives. For modern city dwellers, animals were playthings—not challenges. The challenges came from the twentieth-century sorcery—science and technology.

Magicians of all sorts proved greater drawing cards in the golden age of vaudeville than at any other time in American history. There were, of course, many reasons magicians were so popular. Their acts had an inherent fascination. People knew that they were being fooled, but they could not see how it was being done. But that attraction in magic is universal. The unusual early-twentieth-century popularity of magicians in vaudeville had more to it than that. Making live animals appear and disappear, reading people's minds, suspending bodies in the air, hypnotizing customers, and sawing people in half, magicians seemed to defy natural laws, just as science seemed to do in the age of horseless carriages, telephones, radios, and flying machines. Both magicians and scientists mystified the public with their "tricks," and both informed the public that there were reasonable explanations for everything they did. Scientists would reveal their secrets, but they did it in terms few laymen could understand, highly technical terms that left many people puzzled, bewildered, and intimidated. Magicians would not reveal their secrets, but they in effect made their magic, and by connection the new magic of science, less threatening. At the end of their tricks, magicians showed the audience that everything was all right, that no harm had been done. The hypnotized regained control of their minds; the floating bodies got their feet back on the ground and walked away; and the two halves of the woman were rejoined as beautifully as ever. Stage magic reassured the public that people could control the mysterious powers over mind and matter and could use them for harmless fun.

The most famous of the vaudeville magicians (using the word in the broad sense), Harry Houdini, underscored these points about magic acts providing a comforting new ritual for the scientific-technological age that tended to dwarf and threatened to engulf average citizens. Originally named Erich Weiss, Houdini took his name from Robert-Houdin, one of the European magicians who stopped claiming special spiritual powers for his profession. Harry Houdini not only told his audiences that he had no special powers, but he also exposed spiritualists and mediums that he considered frauds and charlatans. "There is nothing mysterious about me or my work," he typically lectured a New York audience during a 1906 performance. "I'm a New Yorker, was born in Harlem, where I still live. I began my stage career as a magician some fifteen years ago, and gradually worked into this branch of work [escape artistry]. I have made a study of locks for years, and I can usually tell at a glance at a lock just what mechanism it is. Of course I have a secret method of picking locks. That's my business." Houdini claimed only to be a knowledgeable businessman with his own professional method. His business was entertaining people by doing what seemed to be the impossible.

Houdini was an excellent performer with a great flair for the dramatic, so even as he argued for rational scientific explanations for everything he played up the theatrical aspects of his act. Houdini began as a dime-museum magician doing card tricks, and he remained a collector of magic stunts and books throughout his career, but he gained fame as an escape artist. To make his escape acts credible, Houdini had to establish that he was really trapped; to succeed in show business, he had to attract attention.

Early in his career, Houdini, with the flair of a P. T. Barnum, brilliantly arranged a stunt that met both of these requirements. He had himself locked into a New York prison cell. He even stripped himself naked so jailers could search him thoroughly before "throwing away the key." Almost as soon as the door clanked shut behind him, he triumphantly emerged. Such dramatic escapes earned Houdini the credibility and recognition he needed to make himself a top drawing card. Over the years, he had himself handcuffed and manacled by members of police departments; he was tied, bound, and locked up by experts of all sorts, including being straitjacketed by attendants from mental asylums. These stunts caught the public's imagination, and crowds flocked to see Houdini's miraculous escapes. Whenever interest in his act waned, he carried off a new publicity stunt, like being bound, locked up, nailed into a coffin, and thrown into the East River. In 1912 he immersed himself in a milk can filled with water. The can and the case it was in were then padlocked, and Houdini had to escape or drown. Fighting to breathe, Houdini was out of the can and the case in about a minute. Part of Houdini's appeal was that he risked death in some of these famous stunts. But there was much more to his appeal than defying death. For his dangerous tricks, he always had assistants standing by to rescue him in case he was not out in time, and he made no secret of this.

Harry Houdini in chains, manacles, and handcuffs. HTC.

Houdini's basic appeal was that he got out of the most restricted, most confining human predicaments. Like Pearl White, who in *The Perils of Pauline* escaped from buzz saws, railroad trains, and other mechanical "demons," Houdini demonstrated that the individual could master the gadgets that had been designed to imprison him—the locks, handcuffs, manacles, strait-jackets, and jail cells. Nothing could restrain or intimidate Houdini. And he continually reminded his audiences that he had no special talents or "gifts." He preached that people had to be informed to control technology, but the image he conveyed was one of the untamable, indomitable individual. As the mythic frontiersmen conquered the frontier and the lion-tamer controlled beasts, the magicians and escape artists manipulated mysterious forces and restrictive gadgets in the age of intimidating science and menacing technology.

Vaudeville's greatest attraction was an old, not a new ritual—laughter. The average

The Rogers Brothers in typical comedy costumes. HTC.

show was about half-comedy, a far larger proportion of the bill than was devoted to any other type of entertainment. Comedy dominated vaudeville because its audiences needed to laugh in an age of great tension. But American comedy flowered in vaudeville because the format and structure of the show proved virtually a perfect school for comedians, especially comedians who relied on jokes, slapstick, or easily recognized caricatures. On the other hand comic actors and many other entertainers, who needed time to develop their characterizations or who needed the continuity, supporting cast, or the repeated appearances of full-length productions, made their reputations and perfected their talents in other forms of show business and then appeared in vaudeville doing "bits" of their normal material. Vaudeville's short time slots and single appearance gave comics enough time to be effective but not enough time to go stale, teaching them to concentrate their best material in one short act that had perfect timing and delivery. With the audience's undivided attention focused on them, which did not happen in most plays or musicals, comedians could capitalize fully on the infectious quality of laughter, quickly getting audiences laughing, keeping them laughing, and leaving them laughing. Vaudeville, in short, forced comics to perfect the skills that brought them success in other entertainment forms. It is no surprise that many of America's most beloved comedians emerged out of vaudeville, stars like W. C. Fields, Will Rogers, Fred Allen, Milton Berle, Jack Benny, and George Burns and Gracie Allen.

Burlesque shows also proved excellent training grounds for comedians. But when burlesque comedians got a chance to move up to vaudeville, most of them seized it. Burlesque lacked vaudeville's respectability and status. But even more importantly, burlesque, with its focus on sexuality, limited the range of comedians' repertoires as well as the attention they got from the audiences. Many great comedians began their careers in burlesque, including Bud Abbott and Lou Costello, Fanny Brice, Red Buttons, Phil Silvers, and Bert Lahr. But most of them matured in vaudeville or other entertainment forms. Bert Lahr, for example, learned many of his physical, mugging comic techniques during the five years from 1916 to 1921 that he spent on the burlesque circuits competing with sexy women for attention and with experienced comedians for laughs. But once established, he moved on to vaudeville, musical comedies, and film.

Vaudeville audiences wanted to have fun and to laugh, so the flexible show provided

Bert Lahr in a burlesque comedy routine. NYLC.

them with comedy of every conceivable sort, from slapstick to animal acts, from song-and-dance teams to jugglers, from monologues to skits. Many of the comedy trends that began in minstrel shows continued and matured in vaudeville. In 1920 as in 1850, Americans loved word play. One comedian claimed to be an oculist because he took eyes out of potatoes. Another said he bought two fish, but when he unwrapped the package he found three—two fish and one smelt. A deaf character rejoiced in being arrested because he was going to get his hearing. A crook told a judge he was a blacksmith because he forged names. Heat traveled faster than cold because people could catch cold. Men were like dough because women needed them. A tennis player

was arrested for "raising a racket" but looked forward to a private invitation to the court.

Audiences also continued to laugh at the funny interplay between knowledgeable straight men and ignorant comedians, just as they had at jibing between minstrel interlocutors and endmen. When a comedian claiming to know geography said that the world was oblong in shape, the straight man told him that the world was the same shape as his father's cufflinks. "They're square," the comic beamed with a simpleton's delight. His tutor patiently explained that he meant the ones he wore on Sunday, not on the weekdays. "Oh," the comic shouted, "The Sunday ones, they're round." All right then, the straight man asked expectantly, what is the shape of the world? "Square on weekdays and round on Sundays."

The urban influence that had begun in minstrel shows increased in vaudeville, as stage humor, like the vaudeville show itself, took on the pace and tone of the city. Some comedians still used long-winded, slowly developing, richly textured anecdotes and stump speeches, but vaudeville comedy generally tended more toward short, punchy jokes. When, for example, a boss chastised his employee for going to a baseball game when he said he wanted to go to his mother-in-law's funeral, the worker did not respond with a long, involved excuse. He simply shot back: "I did want to, but she isn't dead yet."

Another reflection of the growing urban influence on vaudeville comedy was the broadening of the range and the importance of ethnic characters. Minstrels had added Irish and Germans to their cast of caricatures, but minstrelsy was so wedded to blackface that it could not carry the change to its logical conclusion when immigrants swarmed into America in unprecedented numbers. By the early twentieth century, vaudeville reflected the ethnic diversity of the nation, which included minstrelsy's black caricatures but featured the new immigrant groups. To differentiate their Irish, German, Italian, and Jewish characters (blackface clearly set off the Negro characters), comics emphasized each group's unusual traits and exaggerated their dialects, which made the immigrants seem more alien, more "foreign" than they actually were. Like many people in the audiences, vaudeville's ethnic characters had to cope with the complexities of urban life, with the bewildering variety of different peoples, and with trying to communicate effectively. "Waita one minoots," a typical Italian character called out to his companion. "I no can walka fast. My uncle isa sick." His friend could not understand why a sick uncle would slow anyone down, until the frustrated character finally screamed "my uncle! my uncle!" and pointed to his ankle. The same confused Italian character thought that the mayor was a horse (a mare), that a diploma was the plumber, and that a pallbearer was a polar bear. Another prominent facet of this ethnic humor, as of urban life, was intergroup conflict. When Mike, a typical Irish character, learned that a frightful explosion had killed forty "Eyetileians" and one Irishman, Mike simply said: "the poor man."

Vaudeville's simplified, ethnic stage characters were at their best only partially accurate distortions of reality. But they made immigrants seem understandable to the general public and to each other. They also gave people—immigrants and non-immigrants—an ego-boasting chance to feel superior to the

Bert Lahr, one of many great comedians who apprenticed in burlesque. NYLC.

"dummies" they laughed at on stage. But vaudeville's ethnic humor was often shaped and performed by members of the group portrayed, as Edward Harrigan had crafted his Irish characters from his own experience. This meant that despite the exaggerated dialects, the twisted language, the strange costumes, and the odd behavior, vaudeville's ethnic humor often contained strong doses of humanity that reminded audiences that immigrants were people. Vaudeville's dialect comedy also in effect taught immigrants and especially children of immigrants, who were caught between strange Old World customs and strange New World customs, about how to get along in America.

The masters of the two-man dialect-comedy act, Joe Weber and Lew Fields, like a great many other twentieth-century show business greats, emerged out of the Jewish ghetto in the Lower East Side of New York. As boyhood friends, Weber and Fields, like many other children, escaped from their dismal lives into the glamorous world of show business, first as customers and then as performers. The two boys visited the Bowery Theatre whenever they could, while also trying to help out their impoverished families by earning money selling cakes, soda water, and cigarettes. But the boys dreamed of show-business careers. At age nine, they got a chance to entertain at an Elks Club social, and they flopped. Soon after that, the persistent boys got a booking in a cheap dime-museum variety show, the type of museum that B. F. Keith later ran in Boston. "We were blackface comedians then," Weber recalled of their start in the 1870s, the heyday of the minstrel show when most comedians did wear blackface. Like many other comedians, they were "determined all the time that we would both become great tragedians. Whenever we could save a few pennies we went to see [Edwin] Booth," Weber reminisced, "and the other great actors of those days." But they quickly realized that they had to make their livings as comedians—and as ethnic comedians. If they were to remain in show business, they had to entertain and to portray common people.

"We used to hang around a saloon in our neighborhood, not to drink," Weber explained, "but to hear the talk of the Germans who frequented it and in that way we got a good many new lines." From their observations, they, like Edward Harrigan, George M. Cohan, and Bert Williams, gathered their material, and, like so many other popular entertainers, they hammered it into solid routines by shaping it to please their audiences. "We never wrote out our parts," Fields recalled; "we used to work the acts up as we went along. Lines that got a laugh we kept, others we dropped." While still in their teens in the early 1880s they toured as typical small-timers, continually collecting material and honing their ethnic-comedy act. By 1895, they were successful enough to open their own Music Hall, where for nine years they combined burlesques of stage hits with variety acts and their own distinctive comedy, which strongly influenced vaudeville's developing ethnic comedy. Out of one of their visits to a saloon grew perhaps their greatest routine. "Suddenly we heard a fight going on at one of the pool tables in the rear of the room. . . . Cues and balls began flying, so did a stream of broken English," Fields recollected. "Then and there 'Web' and I decided we had a scheme for a new act."

Weber and Fields' Pool Room Sketch, which became a vaudeville classic, typified the two-man ethnic-comedy act at its best. To begin with, the pair looked funny. The tall, skinny Fields sharply contrasted to the short,

Joe Weber, Lew Fields, and company parodying the popular musical *Florodora*. HTC.

portly Weber, with his bulging, padded belly. Fields played Meyer, an aggressive hustler who bullied the mild, trusting Weber, Mike. And they sounded funny. Both men used their own German-Jewish-English dialect. "I don't know dis pool business," Mike begins. "Vatever I don't know, I teach you," Meyer assures him. That exchange opens the long hilarious series of verbal misunderstandings, some unintentional, some part of Meyer's plan to victimize Mike. Since Mike is new at the game, Meyer generously announces that he will give Mike "otts," which means Meyer puts up five dollars to Mike's ten and puts the wagers up on a high shelf that only he can reach, announcing "der one dot gets de money vins the game." Mike has a little trouble understanding that he has to "bust dem [the balls] before I break dem," but the game gets going anyway, Meyer making up the rules as he needs them. When Meyer "scratches" by driving the cue ball into a corner pocket, for example, he triumphantly claims four balls credit because "only best players can dodge all der other balls und get in der hole." When Meyer insists that Mike name the ball he is shooting at, even though Meyer calls out only "der round one" or "der colored one," Mike names his target "Rudolph." When Mike fires the cue ball into a side pocket, he whoops excitedly about the four balls that feat entitles him to. But the quick-thinking Meyer immediately explains that while hitting the cue ball into a *corner* pocket is a "scratch," hitting it into a *side*

Lew Fields and Joe Weber in one of their classic comedy bits.

pocket "dots an itch," which means Mike has to forfeit four balls to Meyer. Finally realizing he will lose the game no matter what he does, Mike jumps up on the pool table, takes the fifteen dollars, and starts for the door. When Meyer grabs him, Mike fires one of Meyer's "rules" back at him: "Der one dot gets de money vins the game." For all his cheating, conniving, and smooth talking, Meyer's misuse of English loses the bet for him.

Besides giving everyone a good laugh, the skit conveyed the immigrant's difficulties communicating in English, his seeking friends and companions in social centers like pool halls, and his problems dealing with America's highly competitive, often exploitive games. But it also showed the humanity of characters like Mike and Meyer. Despite the combative relationship between them, Mike would periodically blurt out: "I luff you, Meyer," crudely expressing the affection that underlay their continual sparring, the affection that many American "hard-guys" found so difficult to express. For fifty years, Weber and Fields worked their comedy magic, humanizing the old caricatures as they delighted audiences.

Vaudeville taught its lesson about immigrants with laughter, but it taught the lessons nonetheless. For a great many Americans, vaudeville was a major, if not the only, source of information about ethnic groups. Few if any patrons or performers consciously realized that vaudeville played such an important role in shaping public images of ethnic minorities, of course. But that is precisely why humor could work in this way. No one had to take it seriously, not even acknowledge that it said anything important. On the surface, audiences were just having fun, and comedians were just making careers for themselves by making people laugh. But it was no accident that the subjects of comedy changed as public issues and problems changed, no accident that at the height of immigration, the decades between 1890 and 1920, ethnic comedians enjoyed their greatest popularity.

By the time vaudeville died, a death that can be symbolically dated in 1932 when movies took over the Palace Theatre, America had already sharply restricted immigration and had at least superficially "Americanized" immigrants. There was no longer a great need for caricatures of European immigrants in American humor. The new comedians who served only their apprenticeships in vaudeville—in contrast to performers who spent most of their careers there—did little ethnic humor, though many of them were members of minority groups. It was these second-generation vaudeville comedians, people like Burns and Allen, W. C. Fields, Will Rogers, Jack Benny, Milton Berle, Fred Allen, and the Marx Brothers, who successfully made the transition to the new mass media. Some, like Chico Marx, with his "Italian" dialect, continued the old immigrant caricatures, but they were exceptions. These new comics carried vaudeville's techniques, though not its ethnic stereotypes, to the center of America's mass culture. Stereotypes of Negroes persisted, reaching incredible popularity in radio's and television's *Amos 'n Andy*. But such material had been a central feature of American popular culture since its inception.

The Golden Age of Vaudeville and The Golden Age of Comedy coincided. But they were certainly not synonymous. The Golden Age of Comedy referred to motion picture, not stage, comedy, indicating that the new mass medium was capturing the public's fancy, which should have served as serious warning to producers of live show business. But vaudeville managers consistently underestimated the threat of motion pictures, a threat that by the 1930s had severely crippled live entertainment, especially vaudeville, which relied on the common people's patronage. Some vaudeville bookers, in fact, even used early biograph films as chasers to empty out their theaters. As movies got better, vaudeville simply incorporated them as it did other appealing novelties. In 1917, four vaudeville theaters, for example, featured "Mr. Thomas A. Edison's latest invention . . . the Kinetophone, which promises to be familiarly known throughout the country in a short time as the 'talkies.' " A typical reviewer did not see a great future for the new feature, though he admitted that "as a novelty the talkies were a success to judge by the enthusiasm of the various audiences." In the short run, the critic was right. The Kinetophone, which tried to synchronize motion pictures with phonograph records, was so ineffective that it got more unplanned laughs than planned ones.

Until the late 1920s, the new mass media—movies and radio—though growing in popularity, had not seriously challenged show business. Movies brought the sight of great stars; radio brought their sounds to every corner of the nation. Only show business brought both. But then, in 1927, Al Jolson, "Mr. Show Business," "The World's Greatest Entertainer," starred in a show that changed the course of popular entertainment. In *The Jazz Singer,* Jolson did nothing that he had not been doing for years. But he did it in a motion picture. When Jolson looked out at the nation's movie audiences with a twinkle in his eyes and a smile on his face and delivered his famous line: "You ain't heard nuthin' yet," his voice boomed from the screen, testifying to the final arrival of talking motion pictures and sounding the death knell of vaudeville and other live show business as the most popular entertainment forms in the country.

Chapter Eleven

Florenz Ziegfeld and his Follies

In 1917, a dazzling new show that included Fanny Brice, Bert Williams, W. C. Fields, Will Rogers, and Eddie Cantor opened in New York City and then triumphantly toured the nation. But, surprisingly, those five great comics were not the show's major features. The show was the *Ziegfeld Follies,* and its leading attractions were the beautiful, alluring Ziegfeld Girls, the breath-taking, sensational production numbers, and Ann Pennington's dimpled knees. Florenz Ziegfeld typically offered the public laughs—and lots of laughs—but he relied on an aura of feminine glamour and grace to distinguish his shows. But Ziegfeld was far more than just the "glorifier of the American girl." The *Ziegfeld Follies* was in many ways the culmination of the first century of American show business.

Ziegfeld took the most appealing features of other popular entertainment forms and shaped them into a sophisticated new entertainment package. His fast-paced, diversified, stylish show glittered with the opulent, conspicuous consumption that mass audiences loved, while it offered the magnificent staging and grand scale of extravaganzas, the romantic melodies, lively songs, and captivating dances of musical comedies, the greatest Negro star of the period, the blackface performers who perpetuated the spirit if not the form of the minstrel show, the sharp comedy and rapid-fire pace of vaudeville, and the beautiful, seductive women of burlesque merged with the female impersonator's lovely models of femininity to produce the sensual, elegant Ziegfeld Girl.

Florenz Ziegfeld's career is a fitting conclusion to this book. After the development of show business from a small-scale venture to a perfectly respectable, national big business, Ziegfeld brought it to the heights of its perfection, popularity, and status as a truly democratic institution that was not only accepted but admired. Common people once had to fight with the upper classes to establish entertainment that the masses of people could enjoy and afford. By Ziegfeld's day the two groups had to fight only for seats. The *Follies* symbolized the golden age of show business, the decades preceding the Great Depression, the last period before radio and motion pictures replaced live stage shows as the most popular entertainment forms in the country. Besides that, Ziegfeld himself was a truly extraordinary showman cut from the P. T. Barnum mold. The two showmen both had the same great promotional instincts, the same flair for staging and grandeur, the same sense of the public's tastes and desires. But a half-century separated them, a half-century that saw revolutions in the nature and quality of American life and of show business. Barnum began "the show business" with humbugs and freaks. Ziegfeld brought it to its climax with glamour and elegance.

Symbolizing the changes that had taken place in the half-century between Barnum's and Ziegfeld's births, Ziegfeld was born in the middle of the country, in Chicago—not on the East Coast—and to relatively well-to-do immigrant parents—not to a poor, Yankee tinkerer. Also unlike Barnum, Florenz Ziegfeld, Jr., grew up in an aura of comfort, beauty, and culture. His father's elegant College of Music, which served as the family residence and business, was more a place to take lessons and to buy instruments than a conservatory for serious study. Around the house buzzed what passed in mid-century Chicago for the cultural and social elites. When Florenz was at the impressionable age of four, the Chicago fire destroyed the college, teaching the boy lessons that he never forgot—that beautiful things represent status and that they can disappear quickly in a puff of smoke. When his father later tried to push Florenz into his revived music business, the boy, perhaps partially out of rebelliousness, instead turned to the captivating vitality and excitement of popular entertainment, which his father detested as unrefined and uncivilized.

When Buffalo Bill Cody's *Wild West Show* rode into Chicago in 1883, Ziegfeld, Jr., was one of the hundreds of thousands of people who flocked to see the legendary figure and his re-enactments of heroic myths of the taming of the West. In fact, the sixteen year old played hooky from school and spent all his savings revisiting the spectacle. Finally, he summoned the nerve to accept Cody's nightly challenge for an audience member to take on Annie Oakley in a shooting contest, a challenge that proved so popular that Cody offered the boy a job. When the *Wild West Show* packed up and left Chicago, so did Ziegfeld. But his first show business adventure ended quickly a few weeks later when his outraged father overtook the show and forced him to return home. In one sense, his later career, which was obsessed with presenting beautiful shows and elegant women and with living the good life regardless of cost, can be interpreted as an attempt to prove to his father that show business could be refined and cultured.

The brief stint with Buffalo Bill left young Ziegfeld infected with the show business bug. But after graduating from high school, he obediently took the job that his father arranged for him as secretary-treasurer of the musical college, although the young man did stage vaudeville shows on the side for Chicago society organizations—blending popular entertainment, social acceptance, and glamour, the combination he later used in his show business career. When he was twenty-two, he began to exhibit his P. T. Barnum-like propensity for humbug and promotions, briefly staging "The Dancing Ducks of Denmark" in a tent in a Chicago park. The featured performers in what Ziegfeld claimed was an imported act were ducks imported from a local farm. Training them to dance proved very easy. Ziegfeld simply built them an iron stage to perform on, put gas jets under it, and hired an assistant to turn up the heat when the show began. The ducks never failed to "dance and sing" when thrust onto the hot plate. Before Ziegfeld could collect many fifteen-cent admissions, the Society for the Prevention of Cruelty to Animals closed his show. His next animal act, The Invisible Brazilian Fish, drew no S.P.C.A. protests but neither did it draw many people willing to pay to look at an illuminated aquarium filled with nothing but water. By 1890, few urban residents fell for or enjoyed the humbug and pranks that had made Barnum famous fifty years before. They wanted something new and exciting. The Chicago World's Fair in 1893 gave it to them.

Ziegfeld, Sr., found himself in charge of musical events for the fair and foolishly sent his son to Europe to engage classical musicians. Instead, the young Ziegfeld brought back military bands and run-of-the-mill music hall acts—acrobats, magicians, trapeze artists, and jugglers. Ziegfeld, Sr., fumed, refusing to use these entertainers at first. But when his classical concerts failed to draw and he found himself deeply in debt, he decided to let his son put on the vaudeville show. The ordinary variety bill did not do well either. Meanwhile, Little Egypt was playing to standing-room-only crowds with her publicity-producing "cootch" dance. Young Ziegfeld realized he needed a sensational attraction for his variety show. He found it in New York in the body of a German-born entertainer, not a "cootch" dancer, but a vaudeville strong man, Eugene Sandow, who claimed to be the most powerful man on earth after he had won a London competition of strength with Samson, the man who previously claimed the title. An American promoter, thinking Sandow would prove a great attraction, brought him to New York to headline the variety show in the Casino Roof Garden (where the Negro musical sketch *Clorindy* was soon to create a sensation). But Sandow, without adequate promotion, drew poorly, so Ziegfeld easily bought his contract.

With his promotional skills, Ziegfeld made Sandow into a crowd-attracting, crowd-pleasing celebrity, much as Barnum learned his trade with Signor Vivalla. To begin with, Ziegfeld plastered Chicago with posters of the muscular Sandow. On opening night the program concluded with Sandow's rather ordinary act—holding a man in the palm of his hand, bending a poker, and lifting 300-pound weights. The major event came after the performance when Ziegfeld announced that all women willing to contribute $300 to charity could go backstage and feel Sandow's muscles. By making this self-indulgent act seem a civic-minded, therefore totally respectable gesture, he persuaded tittering Chicago society matrons to gasp and giggle over Sandow—for the benefit of charity, of course, but also for the benefit of the newspaper people whom Ziegfeld made sure got the full story and a good angle for pictures. And Ziegfeld had only begun. He had Sandow walk through formal gardens with a female reporter to show

Eugene Sandow, Ziegfeld's first successful promotion. HTC.

that he was a gentle, flower-loving man; he had Sandow tell of having been a 98-pound weakling until he saw a statue of Hercules and decided to build himself into a living likeness, which cast Sandow as a self-made man, a model for young boys; he challenged doctors to find a single flaw in Sandow's body to disprove the claim that he was the "perfect man"; and he made certain that audiences got a good look at Sandow's major attraction—his body. Playing up the "beefcake" appeal, Ziegfeld replaced the traditional strong man's white tights and leopard skins, which covered most of the body, with a pair of skimpy, skin-tight silk shorts, and a garland of bay leaves for his head. Sandow wore nothing else except the bronze body make-up he occasionally used to catch the stage lights. With such stunts, Ziegfeld made Sandow into a celebrity.

Ziegfeld also refashioned Sandow's ordinary act to make it more theatrical. The new Sandow exhibition opened with the beefy, scantily clad muscle man flexing his way through classical poses; then, his accompanist was wheeled in at the piano. Sandow lifted the pianist high in the air with one hand, put him down to applause, and then nonchalantly lifted the piano! As a finale, the strutting strong man hefted a huge dumbbell. When he put it down, a man crawled out of each ball, which made the stunt seem an incredible feat, even though it probably involved no more than the 300 pounds he normally lifted. Finally, three horses walked over a plank that rested on his glistening body. By using these live, everyday "props," he demonstrated his strength in terms and with objects that were real and familiar to audiences. In six weeks, Ziegfeld netted $30,000 from Sandow. Like Barnum, Ziegfeld knew how to stage and to promote an otherwise ordinary act as a sensational attraction.

In winter of 1893, Sandow and Ziegfeld set out on a national tour with new publicity stunts or at least retellings of old ones at every stop. In San Francisco, Sandow fought a lion that turned out to be so docile that it was laughable, but only, Ziegfeld and Sandow claimed, because Sandow had wrestled him into total submission at a rehearsal. In a later act, Sandow picked up two women in satin bloomers riding bicycles and carried them around at arms length. His strength was real, and so was his showmanship. The tour reportedly earned Ziegfeld a quarter of a million dollars, most of which he quickly spent on the high-stakes gambling that he loved but never mastered and on his expensive life style. Differences soon developed between the two men, and they went their separate ways. Ziegfeld's aptitude for show business promotion and his career as a showman were well launched. Sandow continued to tour as a vaudeville star for years before retiring to England, where he died of a stroke at age fifty-six after trying to lift an automobile out of a muddy ditch.

After parting with Sandow, Ziegfeld lived regally in New York City. What he did not squander gambling he spent on tailored clothes and expensive night spots, where he made friends with "Diamond Jim" Brady and other wealthy men who became his financial backers. Eager to mount another money-making show business venture, Ziegfeld convinced the popular comedy team of Evans and Hooey to reunite and to headline a revival of the hit comedy *A Parlor Match,* with which they had toured successfully for years. Ziegfeld wanted to add new topical music, like the bicycle song "Daisy Bell" (with its refrain of "Daisy, Daisy, Give Me Your Answer Do") and to find an exciting new female star to renew interest in the comedy. Traveling to Europe to find the woman, Ziegfeld and Evans learned that the best music hall performers had already been booked by other American producers. But when they saw Anna Held, a pretty young woman who had enjoyed some success in Paris singing "Come And Play With Me" with her French accent and her provocative, saucy sexuality, they felt sure they had their star. As he was to do many times in his career, Ziegfeld fell in love with the new attractive woman in his life and used all the charms he had seen his father use to captivate his female customers—to say nothing of baskets of flowers and a diamond bracelet—to win her affections and to secure her signature on a contract.

Then, as Barnum had done fifty years earlier with Jenny Lind, Ziegfeld planned a promotional campaign to make his unknown European import into a crowd-drawing celebrity in America. Nothing better reveals the great changes that the half-century had made in American public values than the striking differences between Ziegfeld's promotion of Held and Barnum's of Lind. Ziegfeld made Held's eccentricity, glamour, and sexuality his major themes, while Barnum had stressed humility, patriotism, and charity. Ziegfeld sailed out to greet Held's arrival with a yacht filled with a thirty-piece band, New York reporters, and celebrities like Diamond Jim Brady and his famous paramour Lillian Russell. Ziegfeld felt no need for Barnum's parade of b'hoys to make Held seem a woman of the people. Show business was now so well established as a popular institution that its stars served as the embodiments of common people's dreams and aspirations, as a sort of "democratic royalty." To meet the rest of the press in her hotel suite—a replica of Marie Antoinette's boudoir—Held, at Ziegfeld's instructions, dressed in a semi-transparent negligee and began the conference by frivolously asking: "What exactly eez a cocktail?" By treating the reporters to a feast of pâté, truffles, and champagne as well as to her "cute" misunderstandings, her misuse of English, and, of course, her hour-glass figure, Held provoked the desired press coverage as a beautiful, seductive woman.

By the time Held finally opened in *Parlour Match,* Ziegfeld's press agents had already made her a famous celebrity. Her premiere, like Lind's, was a major event that attracted a great deal of publicity because

Anna Held, Ziegfeld's first wife and first female star. HTC.

she had already attracted a great deal of publicity. With changes in content, the Barnum style still worked. Her publicity stunts, her figure, her grace, her beautiful gowns, and her lusty rendition of "Come And Play With Me" made her a popular sensation, despite critics pointing out that she was not an exceptional performer. "Her abilities are of the most ordinary kind. Her voice is not sweet or very strong, and she uses it with no remarkable skill," a *New York Times* reviewer sniped. "She would not be a 'sensation' at all if the idea had not been ingeniously forced upon the public mind that she is . . . naughty."

Like Barnum, Ziegfeld realized that to maintain the public's interest in his features, he had to maintain his promotions of them. His next promotion of Held ingeniously focused on both her femininity and her exoticism. After disclosing to the press that Held took daily milk baths to keep her skin soft and beautiful, Ziegfeld sanctimoniously announced to reporters that the milk they had been receiving had not been fresh enough, so they would not pay for it. At the same time, he secretly ordered the milkman to say he was suing for $64 in unpaid milk bills. To add to the sensation, Held gave a press conference while soaking in a tub of milk. The press lapped it up. In a kissing contest, Held passed out after the 115th kiss, far short of the record of 1000 but enough to get extensive newspaper coverage. When a judge's carriage accidentally knocked Held off her bicycle, Ziegfeld got the press to report that Held had heroically seized the reins of the judge's horse and saved his life. When automobiles were still exciting new curiosities, she challenged American women to a car race from Philadelphia to New York City. Besides these stunts, Ziegfeld made her wardrobe part of the publicity campaign to make Anna Held into a national celebrity. She boasted of wearing $20,000 dresses, sable coats, priceless pearls, shoes studded with diamonds and rubies, jeweled garters, and lace corsets that fastened with ruby buttons. A line of clothes bearing Anna Held's name appeared on the market to cash in on her image as a racy, exciting young woman.

In the late 1890s, as the beautifully costumed Held paraded through a series of inconsequential roles, Ziegfeld began to develop the spectacular staging that later made him so famous. Each fall he opened a new Held show that played a limited New York run before Ziegfeld and Held took it on a limited tour, leaving time for the couple to take a long vacation and to plan next year's show, a pattern Ziegfeld continued with his *Follies.* Each show had to be more elaborate and more lavish than the last because its principal appeals were Held's and the show's beauty—not the quality of the music, plot, or performances. The pattern of escalation of opulence and relative neglect of content also became a permanent part of Ziegfeld's life—personal and professional. Ziegfeld and Held lived their glamorous lives in the grand manner, ostensibly as man and wife. But she had been married and never divorced, so, even though she and Ziegfeld announced that they had been secretly married, the couple never actually wed. For their "normal" expenses, which included annual European trips and a thirteen-room suite in a New York hotel, they spent a fortune. On top of that, Florenz continued to lose prodigious amounts on gambling. In 1906, he had to sign over title to his property to a casino owner and to sign a large promissory note.

Perhaps jolted out of complacency by his financial difficulties, Ziegfeld made the 1906 Held show, *The Parisian Model,* the first production that bore clear signs of what later became Ziegfeld's trademarks. The plot—Anna is a model who falls in love with, battles for, and eventually wins a painter while a comedian appears in a number of silly disguises, including as an old woman—was unimportant. What were important were the beautiful, sexy women in revealing outfits. Anna changed stunning costumes in every scene and suggestively sang: "I Can't Make My Eyes Behave." Gertrude Hoffman, the co-star, and sixteen other women did a daring feature in which they lay down and kicked their legs in the air, bells on their ankles ringing in time with the orchestra while the turntable they lay on revolved, giving all of the audience a good view. In another shocker, Hoffman, dressed as a boy, danced closely with Held. But the greatest sensation of the production, the one that impelled men to return night after night, came when six statuesque women wearing floor-length cloaks entered the artist's studio, positioned themselves behind six easels that hid them from thigh to shoulder, and threw off their cloaks, leaving their bare shoulders and legs exposed to the audience, suggesting that they were completely nude, when they were not. Anna, too, offered erotic glimpses of herself in her corset and flesh-colored stockings when during one number she changed costumes six times on-stage, concealed only partially by a group of chorus girls. The lavish production climaxed with 150 people gathered in the artist's salon, the chorus girls arranged in the shape of a silver fan. Then, the golden curtains at the back of the stage parted to reveal Held in a picture frame. The living painting stepped out of the frame to sing a reprise of "I Can't Make My Eyes Behave." The show, needless to say, was a great hit, the protests against its immorality, some of which Ziegfeld paid for, only swelling the crowds. After thirty-three weeks on Broadway it toured successfully, returning in late 1906 for another 179 performances.

At Anna's suggestion, Ziegfeld decided to branch out into a new area, adapting the spicy Parisian revue to American tastes. To house his new show, he decided on the informality of the rooftop garden of the New York Theatre, which he had converted into a replica of a Parisian cafe and renamed the more exotic-

Anna Held just could not seem to make her eyes behave, especially in front of the press or an audience. HTC.

sounding Jardin de Paris. In 1907, he presented the first of the *Follies*, then simply called *The Follies* (he inserted his own name in 1911)—a fast-paced collage of raucous, broad comedy, snappy production numbers, parodies of celebrities and fads, and lots of pretty women. Rapid-fire pace and dazzling color characterized the *Follies* from the beginning as did the women, who daringly appeared in bathing suits, who parodied the Salome craze, and who marched through the audience beating snare drums as "drummer-boys." Although it used rich costumes and gently lampooned prominent people like President Theodore Roosevelt, Andrew Carnegie, and John D. Rockefeller, the *Follies of 1907* offered more titillation than opulence, more legs than laughs.

Amy Leslie, the same Chicago critic who had sauntered through the gardens with Sandow fourteen years earlier, praised the show's "flaming excitement" but felt Grace LaRue's dance as Miss Ginger of Jamaica was "a shocking exhibition by reason of a costly and altogether indecent costume with which the young dancer took such prohibited liberties as to pass all bounds of proper behavior." She found the Salome dance coarse and regrettable.
A male [illegible]
pellent, [illegible]
critics e[illegible]
which c[illegible]
rolled in[illegible]
frolickin[illegible]
sang: "C[illegible]
Then, o[illegible]
bathing [illegible]
rel. "The[illegible]
the audi[illegible]
"that he [illegible]
lice put [illegible]
but it w[illegible]
top thea[illegible]
years, Ziegfeld made the *Follies* less overtly sexual and more subtly sensual, wisely shunning competition with burlesque shows and appealing to a much broader audience, including many women who could identify with these lovely fantasy figures.

Despite critics' objections to the show's lack of continuity, its sexuality, and its vulgarity, they had to admit that audiences loved it, "laughter being incessant and applause generous." Following the pattern he had established with the Held shows, Ziegfeld opened the *Follies* in New York and then took it on tour, closing in time to begin work on the following year's productions.

Even though the first *Follies* netted Ziegfeld about $100,000 for his original investment of $13,000, he also continued to produce full-length musicals. In 1908, he produced *Moulin Rouge,* a musical starring a Danish ballerina and featuring an innovative production number in which hunters on horseback galloped across the stage after their pack of hounds, a stunning special effect. Although much less spectacular, the *Follies of 1908* had enough appealing attractions to draw well. After Gertrude Vanderbilt sang "Take Me Around In A Taxi Cab," the Ziegfeld Girls cruised around the stage wearing flimsy costumes, headlights, red tin flags, and for hire signs. The show also featured Nora Bayes and her husband Jack Norworth singing their composition, "Shine On, Harvest Moon." Otherwise, the *Follies of 1908* was not particularly distinguished or sensational.

The *Follies* was still primarily a sideline for Ziegfeld. His biggest production that year was *Miss Innocence,* his most lavish vehicle yet for Held. But during preparation of the show, Ziegfeld learned that she was pregnant. He insisted that she have an abortion rather than abandon the show. When she refused, the ambitious Ziegfeld forced her to undergo the surgery against her will. Even though she went on with the play, which proved another great success, Ziegfeld's selfish act destroyed the relationship between them. At the end of the run, she left for Europe by herself, leaving Ziegfeld, in her own words "to heaven and Lillian Lorraine," the woman Ziegfeld picked out of the chorus to understudy Held in *Miss Innocence* and to replace her in his bedroom. Throughout his life Ziegfeld had an insatiable drive not only to display beauty, but to possess it—in his clothing, housing, and women. For close to twenty-five years, he had a series of affairs with Ziegfeld Girls. Like Barnum, he seemed to need continual reaffirmation of his worth, his manhood. Barnum got it from the public adulation he cultivated and thrived on. Ziegfeld got it from his private affairs with beautiful, young women as well as from producing beautiful, new shows.

In 1909, Ziegfeld devoted all his professional efforts to the *Follies,* and the results were striking. This show's features typified what became standard Ziegfeld fare—fast-paced, lavish productions that focused on beauty, spectacle, and topical humor, including in 1909, the opera, classical sculpture, African big-game hunting, patriotism, and airplanes. The wide-ranging revue opened in the court of Venus, giving the audience a glimpse of the feminine attractions that it would see much more of as the evening wore on and the women wore less. Typifying Ziegfeld's pace, the scene quickly shifted to the Metropolitan Opera House, where the performers satirized temperamental opera stars and Oscar Hammerstein. Next, Lillian Lorraine, bathing beautifully in soap bubbles, sang "Nothing But A Bubble." Then, the stage was transformed into an African jungle for a parody of Theodore Roosevelt's recent hunting trip. Big, ungainly Sophie Tucker in a leopard costume sang about the animals' fear of T.R. and a lion obligingly held a large bull's-eye in front of himself. T.R. decided instead to shoot an apple off its head, a scene that reportedly convulsed Roosevelt with laughter. The first act concluded with forty-eight women, each dressed as a state of the Union and wearing a hat in the shape of a battleship, promenading around the stage and then ducking behind a

The battleship production number from the *Follies of 1909*. HTC.

screen. The stage lights dimmed, and the battleship hats lit up, giving the effect of the ships bobbing in a harbor with the New York skyline in the background.

After intermission, the show reopened with beautiful women portraying popular drawings of women. Then chorus girls, dressed as airplanes, sang "Up, Up In My Aeroplane" as Lillian Lorraine emerged from the ceiling in a "flying machine" modeled on the Wright brothers' plane that had been patented only three years earlier. Circling the theater, she threw American Beauty roses to the cheering audience below. This was "easily the most novel and ingenious effect seen in any production similar to the *Follies,*" the New York *Dramatic Mirror* critic applauded, probably qualifying his praise because of the Hippodrome Theatre's stupendous extravaganzas. The finale of the *Follies of 1909,* set in the Polo Grounds, featured the chorus girls as "the prettiest and shapeliest" baseball players ever seen. As an encore, the cast played catch with the audience. The dazzling show drew large crowds as well as lavish critical praise. "Mr. Ziegfeld's entertainment makes it clear," the *Dramatic Mirror*'s reviewer concluded, that the greatest folly of 1909 would be to miss the *Follies of 1909*.

If the *Follies* lacked anything at that point, it was comedy, a deficiency Ziegfeld soon remedied. He never permitted comedians to slow up the pace of the show or to divert the focus from the women and the production numbers, but he assembled a dazzling array of comics. In 1910, he added Fanny

Brice, whom he discovered in a burlesque house, and Bert Williams, the most famous Negro comedian of the time. In 1911, he brought in Australian comedian Leon Errol, whose rubbery-legged stunts convulsed *Follies* audiences for years. *Follies* audiences were introduced in 1914 to Ed Wynn, "the perfect fool." In 1915, W. C. Fields joined the cast and stopped the show. By 1917, Eddie Cantor and Will Rogers also added laughs to the shows. But while each year brought stunning new *Follies* productions, it also brought ambitious revue competitors.

Leon Errol and Bert Williams, two of Ziegfeld's greatest comedians, in a skit from the *Follies of 1911*. HTC.

The Shubert brothers, Sam S., Lee, and Jake J., had emerged as major producers in the early twentieth century by opposing the massive theatrical syndicate of the Frohmans, Klaw, and Erlanger. Jake Shubert, who disliked and envied Ziegfeld, produced in 1908 *The Mimic World,* an imitation of the *Follies.* Shubert originally subtitled it *Follies of 1908,* until Ziegfeld forced him to drop the word "follies," which remained Ziegfeld's unofficial property for more than a decade. The Shuberts dropped out of the revue business, concentrating their efforts on the expansion of their own theatrical empire, including the opening of their Winter Garden Theatre in 1911 with an explosive performance by their greatest single attraction, Al Jolson. By 1912, Jake Shubert was again ready to challenge Ziegfeld for revues' big profits. Reaching back into American show business history, Shubert named his new revue after the *Passing Show of 1894*—the first lavish American revue. Shubert's *The Passing Show of 1912* featured a chorus of eighty beautiful women who strutted right out into the audience on the Winter Garden's innovative runway. Otherwise, like the *Ziegfeld Follies, The Passing Show* offered lavish production numbers (staged by Ned Wayburn until Ziegfeld hired him away), parodies of current events and popular shows, and revealing visions of beautiful women. Both revues drew well, but *The Passing Show* never became as famous as the *Follies,* partially because it was an imitation but also because the Shuberts could imitate but not equal Ziegfeld at the type of show he did best. *The Passing Show* passed from the stage in 1924, but Ziegfeld still had to fend off other popular revues—*George White's Scandals* (1919-39), the *Greenwich Village Follies* (1919-28), and *Earl Carroll's Vanities* (1923-32). These revues were racier than the *Follies,* but none of them surpassed the *Follies* in popularity, though they did provide Ziegfeld with competition that reinforced his compulsion to escalate the lavishness and expense of the *Follies.*

Despite the attractions of the other revues, a single man—Al Jolson—provided the only New York opposition that seriously challenged the *Follies* as the most popular revue-type entertainment form. Jolson actually performed in musicals. But regardless of the vehicle he starred in, regardless of how large his supporting cast was, Jolson gave what amounted to one-man shows, shows that earned him the title Mr. Show Business. He defied categorization, just as he towered over all other performers. Few challenged the claim that he was the World's Greatest Entertainer. If the *Follies* were the productions that climaxed the first century of American show business, Al Jolson was the performer that represented the quintessence of the popular entertainer.

The son of deeply religious Jewish parents who fled from Russia to find a better life in America, Al Jolson grew up as Asa Yoelson in Washington, D.C. Like many other children of immigrants, Asa rebelled against his family's Old World ways to prove himself as good as any native-born American. He and his brother Hirsch joined street gangs, ran away from home, changed their names to Al and Harry Joelson, and fell in love with show business. When about fourteen, Al ran away with Walter L. Main's Traveling Circus, which folded shortly after he joined it, souring the

Competitors, like *Earl Carroll's Vanities,* forced Ziegfeld to keep expanding his shows. HTC.

A stunning production from *Irving Berlin's Music Box Revue*. HTC.

boy on the circus, but not on show business. At the turn of the century, he and his brother performed in burlesque shows: *The Mayflowers, The Little Egypt Burlesque Show,* and *Dixon and Bernstein's Turkey Burlesque Show.* In 1903, they joined old-timer Joe Palmer in a vaudeville musical-comedy act, shortening "Joelson" to "Jolson" so the act's name would fit the billing better. On this tour, Al first donned blackface make-up. He later claimed that a Negro dresser had told him: "You'd be much, much funnier, boss, if you blacked your face like mine. People always laugh at the black man." As it had for Bert Williams, the blackface seemed to liberate Jolson as a performer, allowing him to cast off all of his inhibitions when he put on his stage mask.

In 1905, after gaining experience with the trio, Al Jolson went out on his own, boastfully advertising in *Variety:* "Watch me—I'm a wow." To begin his new career with a fresh start, Jolson traveled to California, getting his first major recognition while performing in 1906 in makeshift theaters after the San Francisco earthquake and fire. He loved the enthusiastic, responsive crowds, answering their ap-

Al Jolson blacking up to go on stage. NYLC.

plause and shouts with encore after encore and with his soon to be famous line: "You ain't heard nothin' yet." Thriving on audience acceptance, Jolson blossomed as an entertainer with his own highly emotional, personal style, and he began to rise in the profession. By 1907, he earned $250 a week touring in western vaudeville. Again he advertised in *Variety,* billing himself "The Blackface with the Grand Opera Voice" and prophetically promising: "Perhaps you've never heard of me—but you will."

In 1907, Lew Dockstader, a great blackface comedian, heard about Jolson and signed him for Lew Dockstader's Minstrels, the most famous minstrel show of its day, one that guaranteed Jolson exposure in the big-time and an education from Dockstader, an experienced, crowd-pleasing comedian who knew all the tricks of the trade. In a short time, Jolson had won a featured spot in the show. With time off for a stint in high-class vaudeville, Jolson remained with Dockstader until 1911, when he appeared in the Shuberts' first production in their glittering new Winter Garden Theatre. Jolson started with only a small part in the last scene of his first show, but he quickly moved up to a larger part and to stardom. After that, Jolson rapidly rose to his dominant position in show business, a position so unusual that it demands explanation. What made Jolson so popular?

Like P. T. Barnum, Jolson applied business terminology to his craft. "I am a salesman of songs and jokes," he observed in 1919. "Just as any other man sells merchandise, I have to sell my goods to the audience. . . . I got selling experience in small stores," he continued; "these stores were called vaudeville." And, he should have added, the minstrel show. Jolson credited Lew Dockstader with teaching him what he felt was the most valuable lesson he had ever learned as a performer. "In an audience of fifteen hundred," Dockstader once lectured him after Jolson had ridiculed an audience as "dopes" because they had not laughed at a skit, "there may be a few blockheads; but the great majority can appreciate good, simple comedy, anyway. If we had been working right to-night, if our stuff had had snap and swing to it, we'd have got the laughs." Jolson never forgot that incident and in later years he passed Dockstader's advice along to other performers. "If I don't get laughs and don't get applause," Jolson capsulized the philosophy of the popular entertainer, "the mirror will show me who is to blame." Jolson also followed Dockstader's advice that performers had to have high quality "good, simple" material with "snap and swing to it" if they expected to make their sales. "Every joke I tell," he explained, "has to be simple and short. . . . Also, to be really funny, jokes have got to be personal. They have got to be about something people have experienced themselves, or at least know all about." Every part of Jolson's act was calculated to establish and build his rapport and involvement with the audience. "Any song I sing has got to have a swing to it, so that I can get the people tapping their feet, swaying their heads, or humming the tune along with me."

One of the keys to Jolson's unparalleled success was his ability to establish a special, intimate relationship with his audience. He treated his patrons like friends, shaking hands, chatting, and gossiping with them as well as entertaining them. "In vaudeville, I had learned that the average human being loves to have people get confidential with him and tell him inside stuff that he thinks no one else knows about," Jolson revealed. When he first saw the Winter Garden Theatre, which he quickly made his personal domain, he immediately focused on the narrow runway out into the audience. Runways had previously been used only by chorus girls. "But the moment I saw it, I knew it gave me a big chance," Jolson recalled. "I used it to get confidential with the audience by running up and down on this platform, stopping for a chat with people, and by kidding the audience and the performers in general. And the effect of this method of entertaining or of selling my goods was, and is to-day, truly remarkable." Jolson even wished there had been a runway over every aisle "because that would make it possible for me to get the intimate appeal with just that many more people." Jolson loved the feeling he got from this personal relationship with the audience. "When you have a crowded house you can feel the electric what-do-you-call-em surging across the footlights between your audience and yourself, and then you know you've got 'em." And they had him.

No matter how successful he became, Al Jolson in some ways always remained little Asa Yoelson, trying to prove he was as good as everyone else, trying to prove that he belonged, trying to prove that he was somebody. He needed audiences' continual, undivided acclaim, acceptance, and affection. He had to have their total adoration. He could not have played in the *Follies* because he could not share the spotlight with anyone. He could not bring himself to share his audiences' love. Typically, he would stop in the middle of one of his musicals, walk down to the footlights, look out at "his friends," the audience, and ask: "Do you want me—or do you want the show?" The answer was always a roaring demand for him and him alone. Then he dismissed the rest of the cast, undid his collar, and threw himself fully and totally into a one-man show, joking, chatting, laughing, gossiping, and singing until he was about to drop.

Besides his carefully selected material, besides his intimate interaction with his patrons, Jolson had an explosive performance style that would have made him a top-flight entertainer, even if he had not so fully understood and developed the other facets of his craft. As with the other truly great live entertainers, no one could identify or describe what made Jolson so special, but everyone who ever saw him perform in his prime felt it. As they did with Eva Tanguay, reviewers and critics tried to convey Jolson's style by calling him an "electrical personality," a "human dynamo" who generated "explosive power," "electrical energy," "galvanic animation," and "violent

energy." They used the most powerful metaphors they could think of, metaphors drawn from the early twentieth century's mysterious, almost mystical, new sources of electrical and industrial power and energy. Jolson himself thought of his act in terms of movement, rather than power. "The surest way to kill me off," he reflected, "would be to make the stage about ten feet wide where I would have to stand in one place." In 1919, he revealingly admitted that the only facet of show business that he disliked was making phonograph records because he had to sing right into the horn. "That means that I have to stand quietly in one spot while I sing," he complained, "which is a practical impossibility for me." The first time he made records, he continued, he insisted that he "be allowed to run around the room, snap my fingers, throw back my head and make any movement I wished to make." The results were poor quality records. But no matter how hard he tried, he could not stand still and sing into the megaphone. "The result," he reported, "is that now, when I make a record, two men have to hold me to keep my mouth in the horn. And when I get through a song they are as exhausted as I am." Nothing indicates better than this story the way Jolson performed and the way he found himself inescapably caught up in his performance, a quality that critic Gilbert Seldes could describe only as "daemonic possession."

On stage, in his heyday, Jolson proved as uncontrollable, as possessed, as he had in that recording studio, and the effect was breathtaking. "He does more than make 'em laugh," Seldes wrote of Jolson's stunning performances; "he gives them what I am convinced is a genuine emotional effect ranging from the thrill to the shock. I remember coming home after eighteen months in Europe, during the war, and stepping from the boat to one of the first nights of *Sinbad*," a Jolson show that featured "Rockabye Your Rockabye Baby With A Dixie Melody," "Swanee," and "Mammy." "The spectacle of Jolson's vitality had the same quality as the impression I got from the New York skyline—one had forgotten that there still existed in the world a force so boundless, an exaltation so high, and that anyone could still storm Heaven with laughter and cheers." Jolson even had the same effect on other top performers. Curious about how Jolson could draw at least as many customers as the lavishly produced, entertainment-rich *Follies*, Eddie Cantor, one of the *Follies*' and the nation's greatest entertainers, went to a Winter Garden matinee to see Jolson. "Something happened that afternoon," Cantor admitted to some friends. "For five weeks I just couldn't work properly again. I couldn't compete with Jolson." No one could. But the *Follies* could.

In 1912, just as competition mounted, Ziegfeld's attention was diverted from the *Follies*. After the long run of *Miss Innocence* ended, Held divorced him after a legal ruling that theirs had been a common-law marriage. Lillian Lorraine, now married to someone else but still actively pursued by Ziegfeld, totally rejected him, while she herself sank deeper into the compulsive drinking that was to plague her throughout her life. In this period of despair over beautiful, temperamental women, Ziegfeld in 1913 met Billie Burke, a bright, witty, and stable actress with money, social status, and a beautiful mansion on the Hudson—the attributes Ziegfeld so respected and desired. He resolved to marry her, and turning on his charm and depleting florists, he finally succeeded in 1914.

Al Jolson singing to his "mammy." NYLC.

A beautiful Joseph Urban production for the *Ziegfeld Follies of 1923.* NYLC.

In 1915, perhaps in response to the Shuberts' success with *The Passing Show,* perhaps because he was settled with Billie, and perhaps because he sensed that the onset of World War I meant the public wanted dazzling escapist shows to get its mind off world problems, Ziegfeld returned to the *Follies* with new zeal and a new production team. The *Follies* had outgrown even Ziegfeld's talents and energies. It had become a big, elaborate business requiring top-notch, specialized organizers and planners. Ziegfeld kept his hand in at every stage, but he acted as much as editor as creator. Joseph Urban, the brilliant set-designer, was the most important new staff member. The Viennese-born architect had won fame for his building designing in Europe and had won the grand prize for designing the Austrian building at the St. Louis fair of 1904. But despite his ability to achieve breath-takingly beautiful effects, Urban initially had difficulty designing for stage shows because his creations took too long to set up, which destroyed the continuity and pace of the shows. When Ziegfeld hired him to design for the *Follies,* he explained that speed was essential to the revue's success and that they had to alternate scenes in front of drop curtains with the lavish sets. Urban made the adjustments and produced the most stupendous *Follies'* sets. He meticulously constructed painted scale models of each set, co-ordinating colors and lighting effects. Urban's bold use of color, his flair for the exotic, and his sense of massive scale made him ideally suited to work with Ziegfeld. Ned Wayburn, hired away from the Shuberts, generally supervised the Ziegfeld Girls' selection, training, and rehearsal. As opposed to the casual, inconsistent methods Ziegfeld had used in the past, Wayburn standardized audition procedures for the chorus girls, though Ziegfeld continued to exercise his prerogative in selecting chorines for the show and for himself.

In 1915, Ziegfeld expanded his revue offerings, adding a rooftop show, the *Midnight Frolics,* to the *Follies,* now a major theatre production. He envisioned the *Frolics* as an intimate, lavish, and risqué show for the wealthy. Ziegfeld had Urban redesign the rooftop room of the New Amsterdam Theatre, where the *Follies* played downstairs; hired Lady Duff-Gordon, the British society woman whose fashion salon was a New York society rage (Billie Burke bought her clothes there), to design the costumes; and hired fashionable painter Ben Ali Haggen to paint tableaux, which Ziegfeld decorated with live nude women, but only when the classics demanded it, of course. Since Ziegfeld wanted the *Frolics* to be the sophisticated, sexy show that the *Follies* was not, he objected to hiring a new western comedian, but Will Rogers got a trial booking anyway and delighted audiences with his pungent understatements about current events in a style that recalled the caustic comments of the rustic Yankee characters who played an important part in the emergence of American show business. No one escaped Rogers, not even his employer. "This is a great show," Rogers observed in the 1917 *Follies.* "Remember the first scene, where all the girls sit around on big pillows and a table in the center? Well, it cost Mr. Ziegfeld $10,000 for the costumes in that one scene alone. But why he doesn't let 'em wear 'em I don't know."

In 1916, Ziegfeld branched out still further, producing Irving Berlin and Victor Herbert's *The Century Girl,* essentially a more co-ordinated extension of the *Follies,* with Urban's typically beautiful and varied sets: a gigantic Grand Central Station scene, a lush glade of exotic flowers and plants, a reproduction of a famous illustration from *Alice in Wonderland,* and a realistic underwater scene replete with seductive mermaids. Urban crowned the show with his much copied, ceiling-high, curved staircase down which beautiful women grandly promenaded.

Ziegfeld resurrected the Barnum tradition of overwhelming his patrons by packing more into each show than they could fully absorb. The rapid-fire pace of the *Follies* was one of his important techniques. Ziegfeld typically unveiled a stunning scene with a wide range of features, including women, and then seemingly almost as soon as it appeared, it disappeared, replaced by another short-lived set and routine. Ziegfeld relied on suggestion. He gave his audiences appetizing tidbits of a huge, varied banquet that left them satisfied but still craving more, rather than gorging them on gigantic servings of rich fare that left them stuffed and satiated. When others presented beautiful women and turned *up* the lights, critic George Nathan perceptively observed, Ziegfeld turned *down* the lights; when others featured great dancers for fifteen minutes, Ziegfeld put on good dancers and limited them to a few minutes, making them seem

Fanny Brice and Will Rogers in the *Ziegfeld Follies of 1924.* NYLC.

Fanny Brice and W. C. Fields in the *Ziegfeld Follies of 1924.* NYLC.

[illegible] eft his [illegible] to see [illegible] is au- [illegible] they [illegible] more [illegible] seem- [illegible] orous [illegible], this [illegible] s ac- [illegible] 1917, [illegible] supplemented Urban's sets and Wayburn's chorines with the routines of Fanny Brice, Bert Williams, W. C. Fields, Eddie Cantor, and Will Rogers—all in one show! Except for special events, like benefits, there has probably never been another such line-up of first-rate comedians in one show. And Ziegfeld personally did not especially like comedy. (He never thought Fields was funny, even when audiences howled at him!) He included as much comedy as he did because audiences liked it. But comedy never dominated the *Follies.* In fact, Ziegfeld tended to think of and use the comics as fill-ins between production numbers. At one rehearsal, for example, Ziegfeld stoically watched a long W. C. Fields routine that convulsed the crew. "How long did it take?" Ziegfeld coldly inquired. "Twenty-eight minutes," came the reply. "How long does it take the girls to dress for the next scene?" he continued. When he learned that it took seven minutes, he turned to Fields and ordered: "Cut the sketch to seven minutes."

Although he always insisted that his shows should meet his high and expensive standards of excellence—using only the best materials, the best designs, and the best performers—Ziegfeld never lost sight of the popular promoter's basic commitment to pleasing the public. He produced the types of shows he did, he explained in 1912, "because the public

A production from the *Ziegfeld Follies of 1923.*

wants them and is willing to pay exceedingly large prices to get the style of entertainment it most desires. I am not in business for my health. I desire to make money." He acknowledged that many reviewers originally criticized the *Follies* for having no plot, but he felt that this lack was "the secret of my success with *The Follies,*" because audiences had grown tired of the empty plots that characterized most musical comedies—a strange comment for a man who regularly produced musical comedies, but then he undoubtedly felt his shows were exceptions. Ziegfeld realized audiences loved the lavish production numbers and the upbeat song, dance, and humor. In essence, he took the scale, grandeur, and glamour of musical-comedy productions and combined them with the variety and pace of vaudeville shows. From sophistication to slapstick, from eroticism to innocence, he offered something for everybody. Like Barnum, he made what people wanted to see seem respectable. People who would never have gone to a burlesque house could not only go see the *Follies* and feast their eyes on the Ziegfeld Girls, but they could also boast of the visit as if they had attended a major cultural event. He played to popular tastes and desires, as well as to his own. "I do not produce the 'Follies' to please the critics," he emphasized. "I produce these shows for the public."

Although Prohibition killed the *Frolics,* Ziegfeld kept on producing his *Follies* for the public and committing his own follies throughout the 1920s. Both at great cost. His long series of affairs with showgirls, which had earlier been at least nominally love affairs, grew almost compulsive and strictly sexual as he grew older, as if he were trying to regain his youth by possessing the virtually unending caravan of youthful beauties who dutifully filed in and out of his office. Billie Burke threatened to divorce him, and, although she did not go through with it, she spent most of her time on tour or in Hollywood, while Ziegfeld remained in New York living like a self-indulgent, rich playboy. All his life had been concerned, indeed consumed, by superficiality in both his personal and his professional affairs. He had nothing else. Appearances were his only reality.

Ziegfeld presented models of alluring, elegant femininity on his stage, images that appealed to women as well as men. He prided himself on "glorifying the American girl," on making the showgirls *actually* glamorous, not just apparently glamorous. He outfitted them in beautiful clothing made only of top-quality fabrics. When a Ziegfeld Girl wore a silk dress, it was actually made of *silk*—and *good* silk—not of material that would look like silk under the stage lights. Ziegfeld was obsessed with presenting actual beauty—not the appearance of beauty. His superficial materialism was his major weakness. But it was also a strength as a producer of spectacles. He demanded elegance, and he made sure he got it. He dressed the Ziegfeld Girls beautifully so they would feel as well dressed and sophisticated as any woman in the audience. He bought them only the best, treated them like the best, and expected them to act like the best, to radiate pride and confidence. This self-assurance distinguished Ziegfeld Girls from chorines. He expected them to maintain their lady-like behavior off-stage as well as on, but this did not, of course, mean they should not be courted, wined, and dined by wealthy gentlemen—that was one of the fringe benefits that made the job so exciting. It meant that they should do whatever they did with grace, class, and style.

Although Irving Berlin did not write "A Pretty Girl Is Like A Melody" for the *Follies* until 1919, it, in a sense, had been Ziegfeld's theme song ever since the end of his tour with Sandow. In the *Follies,* Ziegfeld offered more than the simple melody of a pretty girl; he offered a rich and varied symphony of beautiful women. Ziegfeld intentionally selected all sorts of women for the *Follies*—tall and short, light and dark, slender and robust—redheads, blondes, brownettes, and brunettes. He wanted to have at least one woman in the cast for each customer's taste. His women had to have two basic traits. He never said it, but they had to be Caucasians. Of the some three thousand women he chose to be Ziegfeld Girls, there were no orientals and no Negroes. Josephine Baker, an elegant, sexy black singer who emerged out of *Shuffle Along* and gained fame in France, appeared in the *Follies of 1936* that was produced after Ziegfeld's death by Billie Burke and the Shuberts, but she was a featured performer, not a Ziegfeld Girl. Besides being white, the only other requirement was that the women "must attract men. You cannot define the quality," Ziegfeld explained in one of his many discourses on beauty. "In one word, I would say it was promise; a promise of romance and excitement—the things a

Golub Studio N.Y.
6951-113.

man dreams about when he thinks of the word *girl* . . . that haunting quality. Some plain women have it, only when they have it they're not plain any more."

Ziegfeld looked only for the promise, the haunting quality. He and his staff taught them the rest in what amounted to a finishing school. The showgirls learned how to smile, to speak, to move, and to walk in the straight-backed, aloof Ziegfeld strut that showed off their costumes and their bodies. They learned that a few well-tailored, simple dresses were better than many cheap, ill-fitting ones, that legs looked more alluring in silk stockings than bare, that make-up was to be used scarcely if at all. In short, he taught them tasteful understatement that emphasized their natural beauty. After the first *Follies,* with its Salome dance, there were no more "cootch" routines. Ziegfeld offered the public alluring elegance. When he used stationary nudes on stage, it was only in Ali Ben Haggin's "artistic" tableaux, and then he surrounded them with lace, flowers, and beauty. Even then he and they relied on suggestion not exposure, on sensuality not sexuality.

Becoming a Ziegfeld Girl was the dream of innumerable attractive young women around the country. Thousands of them made the trip to New York, hoping to be seen by Ziegfeld and given a chance to join the show. Since the average Ziegfeld Girl did little except promenade, it was reasonable for thousands of young women to envision themselves in that role, and in the role of being wined and dined by wealthy men, a role almost as well publicized as the *Follies* themselves. At least some of the women in the

Ziegfeld Girl, 1924.

Ziegfeld Girl, 1925.

shows did rise to stardom and did receive expensive jewelry as well as flowers, proposals as well as propositions.

Vera Maxwell, for example, had run away from her poverty-stricken family at age fourteen, beginning a career of dancing in show business. Years later, when Ziegfeld first laid eyes on her, he decided to put her in the *Follies.* In her first year, 1911, she did little except walk around with the poise, grace, and beauty her job required. But the next year, she got a chance to introduce a new, whirling dance, The Seasick Dip, a dance that despite its name became a rage, as did the lovely Maxwell. She had the well-publicized love affairs that fed the image of the high-living Ziegfeld Girl, including a long, serious one with a married

Ziegfeld Girl, 1925.

man. Rising in the profession, she earned as much as $1000 a week at the Palace. Determined to avoid the poverty that burdened her youth, she saved and invested her money wisely, even riding out the stockmarket crash and the Great Depression. She also did charity work for the many *Follies'* performers who unwisely squandered their money and health in their flush and giddy days of glory, people like Lillian Lorraine and Jessica Reed, both of whom drank to excess and died in poverty, or like Anna Daly, who committed suicide after being discarded by Ziegfeld.

No one knows how many other tragedies developed after the success of becoming a Ziegfeld Girl; no one knows how many of the chosen few realized even part of their dreams and how many lived lives no different from other relatively well paid chorus girls. Ziegfeld's promotion and the large number of notable personal and professional successes obscure the realities of life for the Ziegfeld Girl. After all, Ziegfeld and the *Follies* sold dreams, not nightmares. Thousands of girls and women wanted to believe that they might become Ziegfeld Girls and lead a life off-stage that was even more beautiful and glamorous than the lovely, graceful visions conveyed in the shows. Ziegfeld "glorified the American girl" for women as well as for men.

Marilyn Miller, the greatest star to emerge out of the *Follies,* epitomized the dream. But, like most other performers who became stars, Miller had had a long show business background before she got her big chance. She began performing in 1903 at the age of four with her parents' typical vaudeville song and dance act, The Columbia Trio, which later expanded to The Five Columbians when two other sisters joined. Marilyn, billed as Miss Sugarplum, became a kind of pre-Shirley Temple, wowing audiences with her blonde curls, her satin outfits, silk top hats, oversized white gloves, and flashy dance steps. After being a great hit in England, the tall, almost skinny teenager in 1914 got her first New York booking, moving the next year into the Shuberts' *Passing Show* and later into some of their musicals, as she blossomed into a beautiful young woman with, what a jealous Billie Burke had to admit were, legs that "have never been matched for slim, provocative beauty." She danced and charmed her way into the *Ziegfeld Follies of 1918.*

With Ziegfeld's showmanship, staging and promotion, the rather weak-voiced young woman with fifteen years of performing experience became an "instant" sensation. She may well have spent some nights with Ziegfeld initially, but, after she was established, she repeatedly fended him off, even going so far as to insult him in public. He continued to feature her in his shows and to court her. In 1920, Ziegfeld enshrined her as his greatest star and the symbol of the *Follies* dream when he had Jerome Kern and Guy Bolton write a full-length musical to star her, the first *Follies* star to be so honored. *Sally* opened with Miller as a dirty-faced, orphaned waif and recounted her Cinderella, rags-to-riches rise to fame in the *Ziegfeld Follies* and to acceptance in high society. The optimistic message, epitomized in Miller's hit song "Look For The Silver Lining" and *Sally*'s many other attractive upbeat features, made it perfect for the onset of the "Roaring Twenties." The show ran for three years, completing Miller's personal rise to the top, with the very real pay-off of a $5000-a-week salary as well as the status that went with stardom. She was the dream come true. She *was Sally*. And the *Ziegfeld Follies* went on offering every woman at least the fantasy of glamour, fame, and wealth.

Marilyn Miller, the epitome of the Ziegfeld Girl, as Sally. HTC.

Ironically, the woman who proved the *Follies*' most enduring and popular star was not a glamorous beauty queen, but an ordinary-looking clown—Fanny Brice. After a stint on the amateur night "circuit" in her mid-teens, Brice talked her way into a job with Seamon's Transatlantic Burlesque Troupe, one of the "cleaned up" shows. Her first break came when she sang "Sadie Salome," a Yiddish parody of Salome acts written by up-and-coming songwriter Irving Berlin. Berlin not only provided her with the sort of comic material that brought her into the *Follies*, but he also convinced her to use the Jewish dialect that later became such an important part of her act. "I had never had any idea of doing a song with a Jewish accent. I didn't even understand Jewish," the young performer recalled. "But, I thought, if that's the way Irving sings it, that's the way I'll sing it." The first time she sang "Sadie Salome," she wore a heavily starched sailor suit that made her squirm as she sang. The audience roared with laughter as the gawky young woman twisted, contorted, and grimaced her way through the dialect parody. Like any good popular performer, the seventeen-year-old Brice retained the crowd-pleasing gyrations as she built a

The caricature of Fanny Brice captures her comic movement and dynamism. HTC.

repertoire centered on her acquired dialect, her awkward gestures, and her facial mugging, a repertoire that ultimately made her America's greatest comedienne.

When Ziegfeld saw her in *College Girls*, a typical "wheel" burlesque show and immediately wanted her for the *Follies*, the excited young woman could not believe it. For days after he signed her up, she roamed the theater district, showing her contract to anyone she thought was connected with show business. "In about four or five days, the contract was torn to pieces," she recalled of folding and unfolding it repeatedly. "With that stiff paper, it cracked and nobody could make it out. . . . I think I wore out eight before the *Follies* even went into rehearsal." That was what it meant, even in 1910, to get a part in the *Follies*. Her first *Follies* number, "Lovey Joe," a dialect "coon song," earned her twelve encores and an expanded part in the show, as she quickly rose to stardom. Her comedy, based on her infectious, personal style, allowed her to laugh at herself as well as to make her audiences laugh with her and at her characters.

Like other great show business performers, she had an intimate feeling for and rapport with her patrons. "I never worked out any business ahead of time," she recalled. "It would only happen when I hit that audience, because they speak so much louder than my mind . . . they would tell me what they wanted. . . . There is no director who can direct you like an audience." Also like other great entertainers, she was totally caught up in her performances. "You get your first laugh—boom! You're going. You lose yourself." During the rest of her career, Brice convulsed audiences with her sometimes wacky, sometimes earthy, always funny humor.

But like the proverbial clown, Brice often cried behind her mask, especially during her marriage to Nick Arnstein, a profligate, unfaithful ladies' man and a compulsive gambler whose shady deals ultimately resulted in his imprisonment. Through it all, Fanny remained devoted to him, suffering intense personal pain while she made her audiences laugh. Out of her anguish, came her heartrending version of "My Man," which many consider to be her finest performance. In a real sense, she fulfilled the comedian's perennial ambition of playing a tragic role. In 1921, on a darkened stage, she stood in a simple black dress, looked out at her audience and began to sing in an untypically soft, quiet voice:

It cost me a lot,
But there's one thing that I've got—
It's my man.

Because of detailed newspaper accounts of her marital problems, the audience knew that this was not just another song. She did not write it, or even select it, but it was unquestionably *her* song:

Oh, my man I love him so . . .
I don't know why I should
He isn't good
He beats me too
What can I do?

What's the difference if I say
I'll go away.
When I know I'll come back on
My knees some day?
For whatever my man is
I am his forever more!

If anything ever truly stopped a show, Brice's "My Man" stopped the *Follies of 1921*. The audience, *her* audience, sobbed, and then it cheered and cheered.

With "My Man," Brice proved that she could make audiences cry, but it was her ability to make them laugh that made her a star, a star whose career spanned forty years and carried through burlesque, the *Follies*, vaudeville, plays, motion pictures, and radio stardom as "Baby Snooks." In her career, she lampooned Theda Bara, Camille, evangelists, cockneys, Indians, ballet dancers, royalty, and hula dancers. Even in her satires and parodies, she was an eminently humane comedienne, sensitive to the feelings of the people and the characters she laughed at. She regularly used Jewish dialect, for example, but was determined to avoid offending or belittling her people. "In any thing Jewish I ever did," she pointed out, "I wasn't standing apart, making fun of the race. I *was* the race, and what happened to me on stage is what could happen to them." She laughed with people—not at them, often using pathos to broaden her

Fanny Brice burlesquing a hulu dancer in the *Ziegfeld Follies of 1923*. NYLC.

Eddie Cantor in *Whoopee*. HTC.

Besides a number of marginal or unsuccessful musicals, Ziegfeld in the 1920s also produced the hit shows *Kid Boots* and *Whoopee* for another of his great *Follies* stars, Eddie Cantor. Cantor, born Edward Israel Iskowitz in New York's Lower East Side Jewish ghetto, was raised by his grandmother after both his parents died in his youth. He grew up in poverty, learning that he could earn small change by performing in the streets and finding show business as a way out of the ghetto and out of poverty. At age sixteen, he won five dollars in an amateur contest. He later became a singing waiter in a Coney Island saloon where Jimmy Durante played the piano, and in 1912 he toured in Gus Edwards' "Kid Kaberet" show that also included a youthful George Jessel. After touring for a few years in vaudeville, Cantor got his big break when Ziegfeld hired him for the *Frolics*. He quickly moved on to

humor's emotional impact and to add a deeper human dimension to her material. "Second Hand Rose," one of Brice's greatest hits, demonstrated this blend of comedy and pathos. Portraying the daughter of a dealer in second-hand goods, Brice complained that "I never get a t'ing that ain't been used." Everything Rose owned—her clothes, shoes, hose, "poils," and pajamas—had belonged to someone else. "Even Jakie Cohen, he's the man I adore," she lamented with bitter-sweet humor, "had the nerve to tell me he's been married before. Everyone knows that I'm just second-hand Rose from Second Avenue." There was nothing second-rate about Fanny Brice, whose talents carried her to success after success in the *Follies* and to a long show-business career.

Eddie Cantor with an aggressive "friend" in a rumble seat, the *Ziegfeld Follies of 1927*. NYLC.

Florenz Ziegfeld. NYLC.

a featured role in the *Follies* and to fame. After a stint with the Shuberts in the early twenties, Ziegfeld lured him back into the fold in 1923 with the chance to star in *Kid Boots.* As Boots, Cantor played a crafty caddie at a Florida golf resort who sold golf lessons to people who did not need them and bootleg whiskey to people who did. The show's success proved beyond all doubt that Cantor's banjo-eyed, hand-clapping, jumping-jack antics could carry a full-length show. *Whoopee* (1928) cast Cantor as a hypochondriac journeying to a dude ranch and featured what became one of his all-time favorite songs, "Makin' Whoopee." The show led Cantor directly into motion picture stardom. Ziegfeld also produced *Showboat,* the show that brought the American musical to its maturity. But for all his notable successes with musical comedy, Ziegfeld's greatest innovation was the *Follies.*

Ziegfeld's compulsion to be the "king of the beautiful" drove him to keep producing the *Follies* and other musicals and to keep insisting on absolutely first-rate material for every part of the shows even after he lost money on them. For a 1924 musical flop, *Louis the XIV,* for example, he insisted on using for a banquet scene a real gold cloth and a real gold service that cost $50,000. The cast ate gourmet food prepared by a genuine chef who never even appeared in the show. For the 1927 *Follies* he paid $23,000 for a shipment of Parisian tights alone. The production costs of the show before it opened totaled $289,000—over twenty-two *times* what the first *Follies* had cost two decades earlier. Besides the high costs of his shows, of his lavish life style, and of his losses at gambling, he lost over a million dollars in the stockmarket crash. Perhaps still trying to prove himself to his father, he continued to live in the grand style he had learned in his youth and to produce the same costly shows. But in the early Depression the time-tested styles seemed time-worn, over-worked formulas. Yet, like Barnum, Ziegfeld never retired. Show business was his life. When he died in 1932, he left Billie Burke a million dollars in debt but left American show business a glowing legacy. His name is still synonymous with glamour and elegant beauty. The *Follies* still stands as a glittering symbol of the Golden Age of American Show Business.

BIBLIOGRAPHICAL ESSAY

My primary concern in this bibliographical essay is to give credit to the many writers whom I have drawn upon for information, insights, and ideas. I also want to direct readers to some of the other books and articles on the history of American show business, but I have not attempted to be comprehensive in a field as vast and far-reaching as this. The variation in coverage from subject to subject reflects my interests and knowledge as well as the work that has been done on the topics. For the inevitable omission of outstanding books and articles, I apologize in advance. This bibliography, like this book, is in many ways as much a beginning as an end.

There is no single volume covering the first century of American show business. The best general introduction is Foster Rhea Dulles' *A History of Recreation: America Learns To Play,* 2nd ed. (New York, 1965), an informative, entertaining story of Americans' use of their leisure time, which includes much more than show business. Russel Nye, *The Unembarrassed Muse: The Popular Arts in America* (New York, 1970), includes a brief sketch of stage entertainment as part of his survey of popular culture. Abel Green and Joe Laurie, Jr., begin their *Show Biz: From Vaude to Video* (New York, 1951) with 1905. The published materials on which the book is based are cited in the chapter essays, but the book also relies heavily on research in unpublished primary sources from the period. The Harvard Theatre Collection and the Theatre Collection, The New York Public Library at Lincoln Center, Astor, Lenox, and Tilden foundations, contain vast, rich resources of programs, playbills, posters, photographs, engravings, sheet music, scrapbooks, and newspaper- and magazine-clipping collections which have provided a great deal of the material for this book. In the chapter essays, I have not attempted to specifically identify the individual items I have used from these collections. To have done so would have burdened readers with a huge number of references that few people would be interested in pursuing. I would be pleased to identify the sources for my statements and quotations to anyone who inquires.

CHAPTER ONE

There is no survey of American popular theater, but the histories of American drama offer considerable information, though not always great interpretative insights. Among the best are John Anderson, *The American Theatre* (New York, 1938); Oral Sumner Coad and Edward Mims, *The American Stage* (New Haven, 1924); Mary C. Crawford, *The Romance of the American Theatre,* 2nd ed. (Boston, 1925); Bernard H. Hewitt, *Theatre U.S.A., 1668-1957* (New York, 1959); Arthur Hornblow, *A History of the Theatre in America,* 2 vols. (Philadelphia, 1919); Glenn Hughes, *A History of the American Theatre* (New York, 1951); Richard Moody, *America Takes the Stage* (Bloomington, Ind., 1955); Lloyd Morris, *Curtain Time* (New York, 1953); Arthur H. Quinn, *A History of the American Drama from the Beginning to the Civil War* (New York, 1943); and Howard Taubman, *The Making of the American Theatre* (New York, 1965). T. Allston Brown's encyclopedic *History of the American Stage* (New York, 1870) is useful for information on pre-1870 performers.

Regional studies reveal the breadth of drama before the Civil War: Henry Welch Adams, *The Montgomery Theatre, 1822-1835* (Birmingham, 1955); William G. B. Carson, *The Theatre on the Frontier: The Early Years on the St. Louis Stage* (Chicago, 1932); James H. Dorman, *Theater in the Antebellum South, 1815-1861* (Chapel Hill, 1967); Edmond Gagey, *The San Francisco Stage* (New York, 1950); Philip Graham, *Showboats: The History of an American Institution* (Austin, Texas, 1961); Stanley W. Hoole, *The Antebellum Charleston Theatre* (Tuscaloosa, Ala., 1946); John S. Kendall, *The Golden Age of the New Orleans Theater* (Baton Rouge, 1952); George R. MacMinn, *The Theater of the Golden Era in California* (Caldwell, Idaho, 1941); Claire McGlinchee, *The First Decade of the Boston Museum* (Boston, 1940); Edward Mammen, *The Old Stock Company School of Acting, A Study of the Boston Museum* (Boston, 1945); George C. D. Odell, *Annals of the New York Stage,* 15 vols. (New York, 1927-49); James D. Reese, *Old Drury of Philadelphia: History of the Philadelphia Stage, 1800-1835* (Philadelphia, 1932); Constance Rourke, *Troupers of the Gold Coast* (New York, 1928); Arthur H. Wilson, *A History of the Philadelphia Theatre, 1835-55* (Philadelphia, 1935).

For the development of the new, mass audience, I have drawn heavily on David Grimsted's excellent *Melodrama Unveiled: American Theater and Culture* (Chicago, 1968), Chapter 3; Foster Rhea Dulles' insightful *A History of Recreation: America Learns To Play,* Chapter 6; and Francis Hodge's fine *Yankee Theatre: The Image of America on the Stage, 1825-1850* (Austin, Texas, 1964), Chapter 2. The emergence of a common man's culture is discussed in these books and in Robert C. Toll, *Blacking Up: The Minstrel Show in Nineteenth-Century America* (New York, 1974), Chapter 1, and in Carl Bode, *The Anatomy of American Popular Culture, 1840-61* (Berkeley, 1959). The close relationship between folklore and antebellum popular culture is documented in Richard M. Dorson, *American Folklore* (Chicago, 1959), Chapter 2. The development of public entertainment in the colonial period is well surveyed by Foster Rhea Dulles, *A History of Recreation,* Chapters 1 to 3. Hugh F. Rankin studies *The Theater in Colonial America* (Chapel Hill, 1965) as do the general histories of drama. Specialized studies of types of plays and roles provide great insights into early American dramatic tastes: Esther Dunn, *Shakespeare in America* (New York, 1939); Daniel F. Havens, *The Columbian Muse of Comedy: The Development of a Native Tradition in Early American Social Comedy, 1787-1845* (Carbondale, Ill., 1973). The stage Yankee is discussed and analyzed in depth in three works that I have used extensively: Richard M. Dorson, "The Yankee on the Stage," *New England Quarterly,* XIII (1940), 467-93; Francis Hodge, *Yankee Theatre;* and Constance Rourke, *American Humor* (New York, 1931); Rourke perceptively notes the merging of the Yankee and the frontiersman. Mose the B'howery B'hoy is examined fully in Richard M. Dorson, "Mose the Far-Famed and World Renowned," *American Literature* XV (1943), 288-300. Carl Bode, in *Anatomy of American Popular Culture,* discusses the democratic appeal of *Lady of Lyons* and the *Fashion.* Actress Anna Cora Mowatt, who wrote the *Fashion,* left a rich record of her career in her *Autobiography of an Actress, or Eight Years on the Stage* (Boston, 1854); Eric Wollencott Barnes' *The Lady of Fashion* (New York, 1954) is a broadly based biography of Mowatt.

Edwin Forrest's life and career are thoroughly discussed and examined in Richard Moody, *Edwin Forrest: First Star of the American Stage* (New York, 1960), and in James Rees, *The Life of Edwin Forrest with Reminiscences and Personal Recollections* (Philadelphia, 1874). White American attitudes toward Indians and Negroes are discussed in Winthrop D. Jordan's brilliant *White Over Black: American Attitudes Toward the Negro, 1550-1812* (Chapel Hill, 1968); in Leslie A. Fiedler's *Waiting for the End* (New York, 1964); and in Roy Harvey Pearce's *The Savages of America: A Study of the Indian and the Idea of Civilization,* rev. ed. (Baltimore, 1965). Portrayals of Indians in American drama are surveyed in Richard Moody's *America Takes the Stage,* pp. 78-110. The Astor Place Riot is analyzed in Richard Moody, *The Astor Place Riot* (Bloomington, 1958). Other antebellum urban riots are discussed in Richard M. Brown, "Historical Patterns of Violence in America," in Hugh

Davis Graham and Ted Robert Garr (eds.), *Violence in America* (New York, 1969, Signet ed.), pp. 43-80. Acting styles are discussed in Garff B. Wilson, *A History of American Acting* (Bloomington, 1966).

CHAPTER TWO

The Barnum Museum in Bridgeport, Connecticut, displays a wide range of Barnum memorabilia, but the major repository of the showman's papers is the Bridgeport Public Library. The best way to understand Barnum remains reading his own writing, especially *Struggles and Triumphs: or, Forty Years Recollections of P. T. Barnum Written by Himself* (Buffalo, 1873), the other versions of his autobiography, and his *Humbugs of the World* (New York, 1866). Of the Barnum biographies, Neil Harris' *Humbug: The Art of P. T. Barnum* (Boston, 1973) is the best, being especially strong on analyzing Barnum's career in its social, economic, entertainment, and intellectual contexts. I have relied on Harris for, among other things, the development of museums. John R. Betts studies "P. T. Barnum and the Popularization of Natural History," *Journal of the History of Ideas* XX (1959), 353-68. M. R. Werner's *Barnum* (New York, 1923) provides a solid narrative that branches beyond the autobiography and develops a critical perspective. Constance Rourke's chapter on Barnum in *Trumpets of Jubilee* (New York, 1927) is excellent, as is most of her work. Irving Wallace's *The Fabulous Showman: The Life and Times of P. T. Barnum* (New York, 1959) is the least valuable of the recent biographies. The astute observation that Barnum had common American traits only in "vastly heightened" form was made by Heywood Broun, one of the early twentieth century's most perceptive and sensitive critics of popular culture, in the New York *World,* April 3, 1923. The glorification of George Washington is perceptively explained by Daniel Boorstin in *The Americans: The National Experience* (New York, 1965), Chapter 39. For more information on Tom Thumb, see Alice Curtis Desmond, *Barnum Presents General Tom Thumb* (New York, 1954); on Jenny Lind, see Joan Bulman, *Jenny Lind* (London, 1956), and Gladys Denny Shultz, *Jenny Lind: The Swedish Nightingale* (Philadelphia and New York, 1962). Barnum sparked a tremendous amount of periodical writing. Among the best are Joel Benton, "P. T. Barnum, Showman and Humorist," *The Century Magazine* (August 1902), 580-92; and Gamaliel Bradford, "Phineas Taylor Barnum," *Atlantic Monthly* (July 1922), 82-92.

CHAPTER THREE

A handy guide to the vast resources in circus collections is Richard W. Flint, "A Selected Guide to Source Material on the American Circus," *Journal of Popular Culture,* VI (Winter 1972), 615-19. The comprehensive bibliography for circus books and articles is Raymond Toole-Stott, *Circus and Allied Arts, A World Bibliography,* 4 vols. (Derby, England, 1958-71). The standard circus histories that I have relied most heavily upon are: Earl Chapin May, *The Circus from Rome to Ringling* (New York, 1936) and George Chindahl, *History of the Circus in America* (Caldwell, Idaho, 1959), which includes information on Mexico and Canada as well as on the United States. Other general works on the circus that contain useful information are Wilson Disher, *The Greatest Show on Earth* (London, 1937); John Durant, *The Pictorial History of the American Circus* (New York, 1957); Dexter W. Fellows and Andres A. Freeman, *This Way to the Big Show: The Life of Dexter Fellows* (New York, 1936); C. P. Fox and Tom Parkinson, *Circus in America* (Waukesha, Wisconsin, 1969); Charles Philip Fox, *Circus Parades: A Pictorial History of America's Pageant* (Watkins Glen, New York, 1953); Marian Murphy, *Circus* (New York, 1956); Dave Robeson, *Al G. Barnes, Master Showman, As Told by Al G. Barnes* (Caldwell, Idaho, 1935); Gil Robinson, *Old Wagon Show Days* (Cincinnati, 1925).

Earl Chaplin May, in *The Circus from Rome to Ringling,* describes Astley's and John Bill Ricketts' equestrian shows. Frank Melville's recollections about equestrian acts are in "The Circus of the Old Days," *New York Sun,* April 3, 1904. Besides the circus histories, Foster R. Dulles, *A History of Recreation,* provides useful information on early animal exhibitions and menageries. Maria Ward Brown's *The Life of Dan Rice* (Long Beach, New Jersey, 1901) contains Rice's valuable reminiscences as well as other material on his life. Most histories give W. C. Coup the credit he deserves for conceiving and organizing the massive Barnum circus. He tells his own story in W. C. Coup, *Sawdust and Spangles: Stories and Secrets of the Circus* (Chicago, 1901). The leapers are discussed in Earl Chapin May, *The Circus from Rome to Ringling,* Chapter 26. Charles R. Sherlock surveys the wide range of death-defying acts that have fascinated the public in his "Risking Life for Entertainment," *Cosmopolitan,* 35 (October 1903), 613-26.

The best articles on moving the tent cities are: Hartley Davis, "The Business Side of the Circus," *Everybody's,* 23 (June 1910), 118-28; Albert Lee, "The Moving of a Modern Caravan," *Harper's Weekly,* 39 (May 25, 1895), 493-95; Cleveland Moffett, "How the Circus Is Put Up and Taken Down," *McClure's,* 5 (June 1895), 49-61; Charles T. Murray, "On the Road With the Big Show," *Cosmopolitan,* 29 (June 1900), 115-28. Charles T. Murray, "In Advance of the Circus," *McClure's,* 3 (August 1894), 252-60, describes the routines of advance men. One of the best expressions of the hypnotic impact the circus had on children all over the country is in Fred Stone's *Rolling Stone* (New York, 1945), the enjoyable autobiography of a would-be boy acrobat who ultimately becomes one of Broadway's biggest stars as the scarecrow in the original production of *Wizard of Oz.*

Circus people's separate world is revealed in a great many sources; among them are: George Conklin, *The Ways of the Circus, Being the Memories and Adventures of George Conklin, Tamer of Lions* (New York, 1921), one of the best accounts of all aspects of circus life in the forty years after the Civil War; Charles P. Cushing, "Behind the Scenes at the Circus," *Independent,* 99 (August 2, 1919), 156-58, 164-65; Karl E. Harriman, "Social Side of the Circus," *Cosmopolitan,* 41 (July 1906), 309-18; Cleveland Moffett, "Behind the Scenes in the Circus," *McClure's,* 5 (August 1895), 277-86, which includes the observation that nothing changed for the performers even when the circus moved daily; L. B. Yates, "Hittin' The Grit," *Saturday Evening Post,* 194 (August 13, 1921), 8-9, 92-94. For the Ringling Brothers, see John Ringling North and Alden Hatch, *The Circus Kings* (New York, 1960) and Gene Plowden, *The Amazing Ringlings* (Caldwell, Idaho, 1969).

CHAPTER FOUR

An in-depth analysis and explanation of the form, content, appeal, and history of the minstrel show, along with extensive documentation, is in Robert C. Toll, *Blacking Up: The Minstrel Show in Nineteenth-Century America.* Hans Nathan's *Dan Emmett and the Rise of Early Negro Minstrelsy* (Norman, Okla., 1962) is especially good on early minstrel music and dance, on the evolution of blackface entertainment, on the first minstrel troupe, and on Dan Emmett and the history of his most famous song, "Dixie." Carl Wittke's *Tambo and Bones* (Durham, No. Car., 1930) is a reliable narrative of minstrel history. Dailey Paskman and Sigmund Spaeth, *Gentlemen Be Seated! A Parade of the Old Time Minstrels* (New York, 1928), is more entertaining than perceptive. Edward LeRoy Rice, *Monarchs of Minstrelsy* (New York, 1911), is a mine of information. Stephen Foster's life and career is traced in R. P. Nevin, "Stephen C. Foster and Negro Minstrelsy," *Atlantic Monthly,* XX (November 1967), 608-16, and John Trasker Howard, *Stephen Foster: America's Troubadour* (New York, 1934). Carl Bode, in *Anatomy of American Popular Culture, 1840-61,* points out the prevalence of the escape theme in Foster's lyrics.

Minstrel reminiscences are available in Al G. Field, *Watch Yourself Go By* (Columbus, 1912); J. J. Jennings, *Theatrical and Circus Life* (St. Louis, 1882); Ralph Keeler, *Vagabond Adventures* (Boston, 1872); M. B. Leavitt, *Fifty Years of Theatrical Management* (New York, 1912). Marion S. Revett, *A Minstrel Town* (New York, 1955), recounts entertainment in Toledo, Ohio, through biographies of important minstrels, including J. H. Haverly, the greatest minstrel promoter. The best articles on minstrel shows are: Ray B. Browne, "Shakespeare in American Vaudeville and Negro Minstrelsy," *American Quarterly,* 12 (1960), 347-91; Harry R. Edwall, "The Golden Era of Minstrelsy in Memphis: A Reconstruction," *West Tennessee Historical Society Papers,* 9 (1955), 29-48; Alan W. C. Greene, "'Jim Crow,' 'Zip Coon': The Northern Origins of Negro Minstrelsy," *Massachusetts Review* (1970), 385-97; Charles Haywood, "Negro Minstrelsy and Shakespearean Burlesque," in Bruce Jackson (ed.), *Folklore and Society* (Hatboro, Penn., 1966), pp. 77-92; Olive Logan, "The Ancestry of Brudder Bones," *Harper's,* LVIII (1879), 687-98; and Cecil L. Patterson, "A Different Drum: The Image of the Negro in Nineteenth Century Songsters," *California Language Association,* 8 (September 1964), 44-50. For the long history of the minstrel show in England, see Harry Reynolds, *Minstrel Memories; The Story of Burnt Cork Minstrelsy in Great Britain from 1836-1927* (London, 1928).

CHAPTER FIVE

William Henry "Juba" Lane's career is perceptively discussed in Marian Hannah Winter's fine article

"Juba and American Minstrelsy," *Dance Index,* VI (1947), 28-47. Winter also demonstrates the great impact of Afro-American dance on the minstrel show. Marshall and Jean Stearns in their excellent *Jazz Dance* (New York, 1968) analyze the importance of black dance and dancers on American show business. They also include material on a wide range of black performers, making their book one of the best sources for the general history of Negroes in show business. The other major survey is Langston Hughes and Milton Meltzer's *Black Magic, A Pictorial History of the Negro in American Entertainment* (Englewood Cliffs, N.J., 1967).

The careers and repertoires of black minstrels are examined in Chapters 7 and 8 of Robert C. Toll's *Blacking Up: The Minstrel Show in Nineteenth-Century America.* Tom Fletcher's *100 Years of the Negro in Show Business* (New York, 1954) blends reminiscences and history in an uneven but very useful narrative focused on individuals. Recollections of black minstrels are in W. C. Handy, *Father of the Blues* (New York, 1941); Dewey "Pigmeat" Markham, *Here Come The Judge!* (New York, 1969); and Ike Simond, *Old Slacks's Reminiscences and Pocket History of the Colored Profession from 1865 to 1891,* edited by Robert C. Toll and Francis Lee Utley (Bowling Green, Ohio, 1974). Black minstrels have received little attention from biographers. The exception is James Bland, though the writing about his life and career is marred with errors: John Jay Daly, *With a Song in His Heart* (Philadelphia, 1951); Kelly Miller, "Negro Stephen Foster," *Etude* (July 1939), 431-32, 472; and Charles Haywood, ed., *The James A. Bland Album of Outstanding Songs* (New York, 1946). Sam Lucas is discussed in Toll, Fletcher, and James Weldon Johnson, *Black Manhattan* (New York, 1930). The careers of Anna and Emma Hyers and other early Negro musicians are traced in Maude Cuney-Hare, *Negro Musicians and Their Music* (Washington, D.C., 1936); Alain Locke, *The Negro and His Music* (Washington, D.C., 1936); Eileen Sothern, *The Music of Black Americans* (New York, 1971); and James Monroe Trotter, *Music and Some Highly Musical People* (Boston, 1882). Ragtime music and musicians are expertly examined by Rudi Blesh and Harriet Janis in *They All Played Ragtime* (New York, 1966, rev. paperback ed.). James Weldon Johnson's *Black Manhattan* offers an invaluable first-hand account of the development of Negro musicals, which is also discussed in Cecil Smith's *Musical Comedy in America* (New York, 1950). Lindsay Patterson, ed., *The Negro in Music and Art* (New York, 1968), brings together a useful collection of articles.

The portrayals and participation of Negroes in plays including musicals, are discussed in Doris E. Abramson, *Negro Playwrights in the American Theatre, 1925-1959* (New York, 1969); Frederick W. Bond, *The Negro and the Drama* (Washington, D.C., 1940); Sterling Brown, *Nego Poetry and Drama* (Washington, D.C., 1937); Edith Isaacs, *The Negro in the American Theatre* (New York, 1947; Loften Mitchell, *Black Drama* (New York, 1967). Lindsay Patterson, ed., *Anthology of the American Negro in the Theater* (New York, 1967), is a useful anthology. James V. Hatch, *Black Image on the American Stage, 1770-1970* (New York, 1970), is an unannotated bibliography of plays by or about Negroes. Herbert Marshall and Mildred Stock have written a biography of *Ira Aldridge: The Negro Tragedian* (Carbondale, Ill., 1968).

There is no outstanding biography of Bert Williams, but his life and career are traced in Ann Charters, *Nobody: The Story of Bert Williams* (New York, 1970). Mabel Rowland, ed., *Bert Williams, Son of Laughter* (New York, 1969, reprint ed.), is a collection of tributes to Williams written shortly after his death. Williams astutely discusses his views of comedy and racial discrimination in "The Comic Side of Trouble," *American Magazine,* 85 (January 1918), 33-35, 58-61. The range of praise that Williams won is indicated by Booker T. Washington, "Bert Williams," *American Magazine,* 70 (1910), 600-604, and Eddie Cantor, *As I Remember Them* (New York, 1963), pp. 48-51.

Excellent accounts of *Shuffle Along* and other Negro shows of the 1920s are in Robert Kimball and William Bolcom's *Reminiscing with Sissle and Blake* (New York, 1973). Ethel Waters with Charles Samuels, *His Eye Is on the Sparrow* (New York, 1951), contains the frank story of Ethel Waters' rising from ghetto poverty through the black entertainment circuits to the center of big-time show business. There is no biography of Bill Robinson, but his career is well discussed in the Stearns' *Jazz Dance.* The history of blacks in American films is analyzed by Donald Bogle in *Toms, Coons, Mulattoes, Mammies, and Bucks* (New York, 1973).

CHAPTER SIX

Late-nineteenth-century plays have received little attention from dramatic historians, but there is material in the general histories of drama and theater cited in the references for the first chapter and in Arthur H. Quinn, *A History of the American Drama Since the Civil War* (New York, 1943). The Beaver Dam Concert Hall and many of the shows that played there are enjoyably and thoroughly described in *Town Hall Tonight* (Englewood Cliffs, 1955) by Harlowe Hoyt, whose grandfather ran the Concert Hall in Beaver Dam, Wisconsin. This book is one of the best ways to understand what show business was like in the late-nineteenth-century American heartland. Philip C. Lewis, *Trouping* (New York, 1973), is a fine account of the major traveling shows. James J. Geller's *Grandfather's Follies* (New York, 1934) provides brief descriptions of nineteenth-century popular plays. William Lawrence Slout, *Theatre in a Tent: The Development of a Provincial Entertainment* (Bowling Green, Ohio, 1972), discusses the tent shows that carried late-nineteenth-century theatrical tradition into the twentieth century.

David Grimsted's *Melodrama Unveiled,* though stopping in 1850, is the best way to understand the public's fascination with melodrama. Many writers have commented on melodrama. With a pejorative tone, Porter E. Browne discusses the audiences and plays in "Mellowdrammer," *Everybody's,* 21 (September 1909), 347-54; Clayton Hamilton compares melodrama to other types of plays in "Melodramas and Farces," *Forum* (January 1909), 23-32; H. J. Smith perceptively explains melodrama's appeals in "Melodrama," *Atlantic,* 99 (March 1907), 320-28. The various forms and features of *Uncle Tom's Cabin* are described in rich detail by Harry Birdoff in *America's Greatest Hit* (New York, 1947). Robert C. Toll's *Blacking Up,* pp. 93-96, examines minstrels' ridicule of *Uncle Tom's Cabin.* Additional information and perspectives on the play are in: J. C. Furnas, *Goodbye to Uncle Tom* (New York, 1956), pp. 257-84; Frank J. Davis, "Tom Shows," *Scribner's Magazine* (April 1925), 350-60; and Ralph Eugene Lund, "Trouping with Uncle Tom," *The Century* (January 1928), 331-37.

James Jay Brady's *Life of Denman Thompson* (New York, 1888) chronicles Thompson's career. *The Autobiography of Joseph Jefferson* (New York, 1890) fully details Jefferson's career as Rip Van Winkle. Richard Moody discusses the frontier plays in his *America Takes the Stage.* "Buffalo Bill" Cody's stage career is covered in Rupert Croft-Cooke and W. S. Meadmore, *Buffalo Bill, The Legend, The Man of Action, The Showman* (London, 1952), Chapters 11-18, and Jay Monaghan, "The Stage Career of Buffalo Bill," *Journal of the Illinois Historical Society,* XXXI (December 1938), 411-23. The career of David Belasco, the pathbreaking director who raised American drama to new artistic heights while still delighting popular audiences with productions like *Heart of Maryland,* is told in David Belasco, *The Theatre Through Its Stage Door* (New York, 1919), and Craig Timberlake, *Life and Work of David Belasco* (New York, 1954).

CHAPTER SEVEN

The best, most comprehensive history of the American musical remains Cecil Smith's excellent *Musical Comedy in America* (New York, 1950). David Ewen's encyclopedic *New Complete Book of the American Musical Theater* (New York, 1970) is a fine reference work for histories of shows, including primary sources. Stanley Green's *The World of Musical Comedy* (New York, 1960) richly tells the story of the musical stage through the careers of its major composers and lyricists. Other useful surveys are Lehman Engel, *The American Musical Theatre* (New York, 1967), which concentrates on post-1940 shows; David Ewen, *The Story of America's Musical Theater* (Philadelphia, 1961); and Abe Laufe, *Broadway's Greatest Musicals* (New York, 1969). Edward Marks, *They All Had Glamour* (New York, 1944), offers rich detail on early musical extravaganzas as well as on glamorous stars. The early sections of the chapter are drawn from these sources. The careers of the Shubert brothers are recounted in Jerry Stagg's *The Brothers Shubert* (New York, 1968).

E. J. Kahn, *The Merry Partners: The Age and Stage of Harrigan and Hart* (New York, 1955), recounts the careers of Harrigan and Hart. Isaac Goldberg perceptively discusses Harrigan and Hart as he does the minstrel show in *Tin Pan Alley* (New York, 1930), which is much broader in scope than the title indicates. George M. Cohan's life and career are covered in John McCabe, *George M. Cohan: The Man Who Owned Broadway* (New York, 1973), and Ward Morehouse, *George M. Cohan, Prince of the American Theatre* (Philadelphia, 1943). In his own *Twenty*

Years on Broadway (New York, 1924), Cohan chronicles his rise to fame but offers few real insights. He demonstrates how fully he analyzed and understood how to manipulate audiences' feelings in "The Mechanics of Emotion," which he published with George Jean Nathan in *McClure's*, XLII (November 1913), 69-77.

On Lillian Russell, see Parker Morell, *Lillian Russell: The Era of Plush* (New York, 1940) and Richard O'Conner, *Duet in Diamonds, The Flamboyant Saga of Lillian Russell and Diamond Jim Brady in America's Gilded Age, by John Burke* (New York, 1972). My discussions of Victor Herbert and Jerome Kern rely heavily on the general histories of musicals cited above, especially Stanley Green's *The World of Musical Comedy.* America's great musical comedy songwriters have received considerable attention from biographers, including George Eells, *The Life that Late He Led: A Biography of Cole Porter* (New York, 1967); David Ewen, *Richard Rodgers* (New York, 1957); Michael Freedland, *Irving Berlin* (New York, 1974); Edward Jablonski and Lawrence Stewart, *The Gershwin Years* (New York, 1958); Joseph Kaye, *Victor Herbert* (New York, 1931); Robert Kimball and Alfred Simon, *The Gershwins* (New York, 1973); Deems Taylor, *Some Enchanted Evenings; The Story of Rodgers and Hammerstein* (New York, 1953); Edward N. Waters, *Victor Herbert, A Life In Music* (New York, 1955) and Alexander Woolcott, *The Story of Irving Berlin* (New York, 1925).

CHAPTER EIGHT

Olive Logan's protests against the girlie show are forcefully expressed in her *Apropos of Women and the Theatre* (New York, 1869) and in her *Before the Footlights and Behind the Scenes* (Philadelphia, 1869), an autobiography rich in details on drama, popular entertainment, and audiences, which was reprinted in Philadelphia in 1871 as *The Mimic World and Public Exhibitions.* The appearance of woman as statuary is discussed in Foster Rhea Dulles, *The History of Recreation,* Chapter 6, and in the standard histories of the burlesque show: Ann Corio with Joe DiMona, *This Was Burlesque* (New York, 1968); Bernard Sobel, *Burleycue* (New York, 1931), which is rich in anecdotes; Bernard Sobel, *A Pictorial History of Burlesque* (New York, 1956), which includes quotable, informative text along with the photographs; and Irving Zeidman, *The American Burlesque Show* (New York, 1967), the fullest discussion of the history of burlesque.

Adah Isaacs Menken is discussed in detail in Bernard Falk, *The Naked Lady, A Biography of Adah Isaacs Menken,* rev. ed. (London, 1952); Edward Marks, *They All Had Glamour,* pp. 241-58; and Constance Rourke, *Troupers of the Gold Coast, or the Rise of Lotta Crabtree* (New York, 1928), pp. 174-85. For *The Black Crook,* see Edward Marks, *They All Had Glamour;* Cecil Smith, *The Musical Comedy in America;* and Joseph Whitton, *The Naked Truth! An Inside History of the Black Crook* (Philadelphia, 1897), as well as the histories of burlesque. Lydia Thompson's career is also traced in these histories; the quotes are drawn from Sobel's *Pictorial History.* Female minstrels are discussed in Robert C. Toll's *Blacking Up: The Minstrel Show in Nineteenth-Century America,* pp. 138-39, and in the standard histories of burlesque.

Mae West, *Goodness Had Nothing To Do with It* (Englewood Cliffs, 1959), is an enjoyable though poorly written narrative indicating how important sexuality was in show business, even for non-burlesque female performers. The barker's pitch for Little Egypt is from Sobel *Pictorial History.* Irving Zeidman discusses Millie De Leon and early strip-teasing in his *American Burlesque Show.* Georgia Sothern's *Georgia: My Life in Burlesque* (New York, 1972) frankly and fully discusses her life and career. Gypsy Rose Lee's *Gypsy* (New York, 1957) tells the story of her long show business career. Ann Corio's story and her observations about Carrie Finnell and other burlesque stars are in her *This Was Burlesque.* Alan Dale's observations about the great importance of beauty for female American performers are in his "Stage Beauty and Brains," *Cosmopolitan,* 50 (March 1911), 517-22. Mary Vida Clarke's witty and perceptive observations about show business expressing men's but not women's fantasies are in "Sauce for the Gander and Sawdust for the Goose," *Dial,* 65 (December 14, 1918), 541-43. The censorship of burlesque is treated most fully in Zeidman's *American Burlesque Show.*

CHAPTER NINE

Little serious writing has been done about sexual impersonators in America. Roger Baker's *Drag: A History of Female Impersonation on the Stage* (London,

1968) provides the European background for this chapter, but Baker devotes only one chapter to Julian Eltinge and American impersonators. Esther Newton's *Mother Camp: Female Impersonators in America* (Englewood Cliffs, 1972) is an ahistorical, anthropological study of female impersonation in the mid-1960s. The careers of Francis Leon and minstrel female impersonators are examined and explained in Robert C. Toll's *Blacking Up,* pp. 139-45. Joe Laurie, Jr., discusses and partially explains the sexual impersonators in his *Vaudeville: from Honky-tonks to the Palace* (New York, 1953), pp. 87-95. Newspaper and magazine coverage of Julian Eltinge was extensive, but he still awaits the recognition and study he deserves. Frances Steegmuller interviewed "Barbette" and published the results in "Onward and Upward with the Arts," *New Yorker,* 45 (September 27, 1969), 130-43. Critic Ashton Stevens' interview with Bert Savoy is in Stevens' *Actorviews* (Chicago, 1923), pp. 113-18. Male impersonators are recognized in "Actresses in Men's Roles," *Current Literature,* 30 (May 1901), 620, as well as in many newspaper articles.

CHAPTER TEN

The history of vaudeville is best approached through Albert McLean's stimulating, if not always satisfying, *American Vaudeville as a Ritual* (Louisville, Ky., 1965), which analyzes vaudeville's central symbols and rituals as expressions of the values, needs, and desires of its massive, urban audiences; Douglas Gilbert's *American Vaudeville: Its Life and Times* (New York, 1940), which abounds with information in a rather inconvenient format; performer Joe Laurie, Jr., combines solid history, information on performers and specialties, with personal anecdotes in his very valuable *Vaudeville: From the Honky-tonks to the Palace;* Bernard Sobel, critic and publicist, includes informative narrative with the many photographs in his *A Pictorial History of Vaudeville* (New York, 1961). I have drawn on all of these for the development of vaudeville into the most popular form of American show business. For more on Tony Pastor: Parker Zellers, *Tony Pastor, Dean of the Vaudeville Stage* (Ypsilanti, Michigan, 1971). Vaudeville palaces are discussed in Laurie, *Vaudeville,* pp. 481-99; McLean, *American Vaudeville as a Ritual,* Chapter 9; Edward Renton, *The Vaudeville Theater: Building, Operation, Management* (New York, 1918); and Marian Spitzer, *The Palace* (New York, 1969). The efforts to form a vaudeville union are detailed by one of its central organizers, George Fuller Gordon, *My Lady Vaudeville and Her White Rats* (New York, 1909). The standard vaudeville histories recount the story of the White Rats, the United Booking Office, and the National Vaudeville Artists.

The lives of small-timers are movingly described in: Fred Allen's perceptive and entertaining autobiography, *Much Ado About Me* (Boston, 1956), especially Chapter 14; Antoinette Berton, "In the Chorus," *Harper's Weekly,* 54 (June 18, 1910), 9-10; Wallace Irwin, "Country Clubs of Broadway," *Colliers,* 50 (October 26, 1912), 10-12, 30; Joe Laurie, Jr., *Vaudeville,* pp. 237-49; Bennett Musson, "Week of One Night Stands," *American Magazine* (June 1910), 203-13; Mary Shaw, "The Actress on the Road," *McClure's,* 37 (June 1911), 263-72; and Virginia Tracy, "The Home Life of Actors," *Colliers,* 48 (October 21, 1911), 19-20, 26-27. The structure of the vaudeville show is analyzed by George A. Gotlieb, booker for the Palace Theatre, in "Psychology of the American Vaudeville Show," *Current Literature,* 60 (April 1916), 257-58; in McLean, Chapter 5; and in Hartley Davis, "The Business Side of Vaudeville," *Everybody's* 17 (October 1907), 527-37. The special qualities of vaudeville acts are explained by Gilbert Seldes in his book of perceptive essays on popular culture, *The Seven Lively Arts,* rev. ed. (New York, 1962, paperback), pp. 223-28.

Eva Tanguay's career is briefly sketched in Douglas Gilbert, *American Vaudeville,* pp. 327-31; and Joe Laurie, Jr., *Vaudeville,* pp. 58-59. Sophie Tucker's *Some of These Days* (New York, 1945) and Mae West's *Goodness Had Nothing To Do with It* (Englewood Cliffs, 1959) reveal what life was like for strong women in vaudeville. The change in the animal ritual from circuses to vaudeville and the scientific basis of magicians' appeal, including Houdini's, are based on Chapter 7 of Albert McLean's *American Vaudeville as a Ritual.* Harry Houdini's views are expressed in his *A Magician Among the Spirits* (New York, 1924) and *Miracle Mongers* (New York, 1920); also see Harold Kellock, *Houdini* (New York, 1928). I also drew on McLean's Chapter 6 for some of my views on vaudeville comedy. Joe Laurie, Jr., provides considerable information on comedy in *Vaudeville,* as do the other works on vaudeville. The careers and repertoires of Weber and Fields are discussed by Felix Isman in *Weber and Fields* (New York, 1924). Among the useful autobiographies of vaudeville comedians are Fred Allen, *Much Ado About Me;* George Burns, *I Love Her That's Why!* (New York, 1955); W. C. Fields, *W. C. Fields by Himself; His Intended Autobiography* (Englewood Cliffs, 1973); and Donald Day, ed., *The Autobiography of Will Rogers* (Boston, 1949). Bert Lahr's life and career are sensitively told by his son, John Lahr, in *Notes of A Cowardly Lion* (New York, 1969).

Among the best articles on a wide range of vaudeville subjects are Cyrus T. Brady, "A Vaudeville Turn," *Scribner's Monthly,* 30 (September 1901), 351-55, which exposes the use of "plants" in audiences; Frank B. Copley, "The Story of a Great Vaudeville Manager, E. F. Albee," *American Magazine,* 94 (December 1922), 46-47; Hartley Davis, "In Vaudeville," *Everybody's,* 13 (August 1905), 231-40, which traces the development from variety to vaudeville including the most popular types of acts; Robert Grau, "The Amazing Prosperity of the Vaudeville Entertainer," *Overland,* 57 (June 1911), 608-9; Robert Grau, "The Origin of Amateur Night," *Independent,* 69 (October 20, 1910), 851-52; Norman Hapgood, "The Life of a Vaudeville Artiste," *Cosmopolitan,* 30 (February 1901), 393-400; Edwin Muir Royle, "The Vaudeville Theatre," *Scribner's Monthly,* 26 (October 1899), 485-95, describing the respectable vaudeville houses with their strict censorship rules; Charles R. Sherlock, "Where Vaudeville Holds the Boards," *Cosmopolitan,* 32 (February 1902), 411-20; and Vadim Uraneff, "Commedia dell'arte and American Vaudeville," *Theatre Arts Monthly,* 7 (October 1923), 318-28.

CHAPTER ELEVEN

Ziegfeld's life and career are most fully traced in Charles Higham, *Ziegfeld* (Chicago, 1972). The other major sources about Ziegfeld and his *Follies* are: Billie Burke with Cameron Shipp, *With a Feather on My Nose* (New York, 1949), the autobiography of Ziegfeld's second wife; Eddie Cantor, *Ziegfeld the Great Glorifier* (New York, 1934), a tribute to Ziegfeld from one of his greatest stars; Randolph Carter, *The World of Flo Ziegfeld* (New York, 1974), a beautifully illustrated, solid book; Lady Lucile Duff-Gordon, *Discretions and Indiscretions* (London, 1932), the memoirs of the woman who designed the clothes for the *Follies* at its height; Marjorie Farnsworth, *The Ziegfeld Follies* (New York, 1956), occasionally unreliable on details; and Patricia Ziegfeld, *The Ziegfelds' Girl* (Boston, 1964).

The general histories of American musicals include the *Follies* and its revue competitors, as does Robert Baral, *Revue* (New York, 1962). Jerry Stagg's *The Brothers Shubert* details the careers of the Shuberts. Al Jolson's life and career are traced in: Michael Freedland, *Jolson* (New York, 1972), and Pearl Sieben, *Immortal Jolson: His Life and Times* (New York, 1962). Jolson made one of the clearest statements of the audience orientation of the popular entertainer in his "If I Don't Get Laughs and Don't Get Applause–The Mirror Will Show Me Who Is To Blame," *American Magazine,* 87 (April 1919), 18-19, 154-58. Gilbert Seldes' reflections on Jolson's appeal are included in his excellent book *Seven Lively Arts,* pp. 175-85.

The observation that one of the keys to Ziegfeld's success was his subtlety and suggestion, in contrast to his blatant rivals, is drawn from George Nathan's *The World in Falseface* (New York, 1923), pp. 102-12. The careers of Ziegfeld's stars are covered in Eddie Cantor as told to David Freedman, *My Life Is in Your Hands* (New York, 1928); Eddie Cantor, *Take My Life* (New York, 1930); W. C. Fields, *W. C. Fields by Himself; His Intended Autobiography* (Englewood Cliffs, 1973); Donald Day, ed., *The Autobiography of Will Rogers* (Boston, 1949); Norman Katkov, *The Fabulous Fanny: The Story of Fanny Brice* (New York, 1953); Robert Lewis Taylor, *W. C. Fields, His Follies and Fortunes* (New York, 1949). Marjorie Farnsworth's *Ziegfeld Follies* provides good information on the Ziegfeld Girls, as does the contemporary press.

COMPARATIVE CHRONOLOGIES

THE DEVELOPMENT OF AMERICAN SOCIETY*

1607 An English colony is established in Jamestown, Virginia.

1613 The Dutch establish a trading post in what later becomes New York City.

1619 The first slaves arrive in Jamestown.

1620 Pilgrims reach Plymouth, Massachusetts.

1629 Puritans establish Massachusetts Bay Colony. In the next century English colonies are established from Maine to Georgia.

1688 Quakers make the first important American protest against slavery.

1692 Witch trials rock Salem, Massachusetts.

1720 With 12,000 people, Boston is the largest English colonial city. Philadelphia has 10,000 and New York has 7000.

1721 The first smallpox inoculations are given in America.

1739 Slave revolts rock South Carolina, leaving scores of blacks and whites dead.

1742 Benjamin Franklin invents his room-heating stoves.

1755 "Yankee Doodle" is composed as a British satire of rustic colonials.

CHRONOLOGICAL OUTLINE OF AMERICAN SHOW BUSINESS

1716 A theater opens in Williamsburg, Virginia.

1728 The first lion is exhibited in the colonies.

1732 A play, *The Recruiting Officer,* is performed in New York.

1749-50 A troupe of English actors tours the colonies.

1752 A company of British actors led by Mr. and Mrs. Lewis Hallam takes up residence in the colonies.

* Based on: Gorton Carruth and Associates (eds.), *The Encyclopedia of American Facts and Dates* (New York, 1956); Joseph Nathan Kane, *Famous First Facts* (New York, 1933); and Richard B. Morris (ed.), *Encyclopedia of American History* (New York, 1953).

COMPARATIVE CHRONOLOGIES, 1750-1794

AMERICAN SOCIETY

1750s A stagecoach ride from Philadelphia to New York takes three days, driving eighteen hours each day.

ca. 1760 Benjamin Franklin devises bifocal lenses.

1765 Colonists protest against the British Stamp Act, the first major political step toward the Revolution.

1773 Outraged colonists throw British tea into the Boston harbor.

1775 Colonists and British troops fight battles.

1776 Colonists declare their independence of the British crown.

1780 Pennsylvania is the first state to abolish slavery.

1782 General Cornwallis surrenders 8000 British troops at Yorktown.

1783 The American colonies become independent states and unite under the Articles of Confederation.

1788 The Constitution is ratified and goes into effect.

1789 George Washington becomes first president of the United States of America.

1793 Eli Whitney invents the cotton gin, making cotton production on a large scale feasible.

A federal fugitive slave law requires returning runaway slaves to their owners.

AMERICAN SHOW BUSINESS

1767 John Street Theatre is the first permanent theater built in New York.

1771-72 George Washington visits the theater at least nineteen times.

1774 The Continental Congress bans plays and other public amusements.

1787 *The Contrast,* the first successful play featuring an American character, premieres.

1792 John Bill Ricketts brings his equestrian circus to America, touring with it for years.

1794 Chestnut Street Theatre opens in Philadelphia.

Boston repeals its 1750 law prohibiting plays.

Federal Street Theatre opens in Boston, as drama takes root in the new nation.

COMPARATIVE CHRONOLOGIES, 1795-1826

AMERICAN SOCIETY

1800 Washington, D.C., becomes the American capital.

1801 Thomas Jefferson is inaugurated as the third president, succeeding John Adams.

1806 The first successful gas lights are installed on an American street, in Newport, Rhode Island.

1807 The first steamboat sails.

1812 The United States goes to war with England.

1814 The British capture and burn Washington, D.C.

Francis Scott Key writes "The Defence of Fort Mc Henry," soon retitled "The Star-Spangled Banner."

1817 A steamboat sails from Louisville to New Orleans, opening the way for steamboat navigation of the Mississippi River.

1820 New York is the nation's largest city with its 125,000 residents; Philadelphia has 113,000. By **1860**, the population of New York surpasses 1,000,000 and Philadelphia exceeds 500,000, as urbanization sharply increases.

1825 The Erie Canal opens, linking New York City to Lake Erie and the West.

Standardized sets of cheap pressed glassware are first marketed.

AMERICAN SHOW BUSINESS

1795 John Bill Ricketts builds his own circus building in Philadelphia, entertaining Presidents Washington and Adams.

1796 The first elephant is exhibited in America.

1816 Elephant "Old Bet" is shot by a Maine farmer after leading a successful menagerie on tour. Many increasingly large menageries follow.

1820 Nathan A. Howes is the first American to own a circus.

1821 Nathan A. Howes and Aaron Turner's circus is the first to perform under a canvas tent.

1821 The 2500 seat Park Theatre replaces its 300 seat predecessor as demand for popular plays mushrooms.

1825 A Boston audience drives British actor Edmund Kean from the stage for insulting Americans.

1826 James Hackett begins his rise to fame playing Yankee characters.

COMPARATIVE CHRONOLOGIES, 1826-1836

AMERICAN SOCIETY

1828 Andrew Jackson is elected president and political parties are democraticized in the next decade.

The first passenger railroad is chartered.

1830 The first American railroad locomotive is built.

1831 Nat Turner's slave revolt kills fifty-seven whites before being suppressed.

1832 The first American horse trolley begins running in New York City to serve the growing urban population.

1833 The American Antislavery Society is formed to work for the abolition of slavery in America.

The first penny daily newspaper appears, a major step toward mass-oriented journals.

Nathaniel Currier and James Merritt Ives become "Publishers of Cheap and Popular Pictures."

AMERICAN SHOW BUSINESS

The 4000 seat Bowery Theatre opens in New York.

Edwin Forrest, America's first prominent tragedian and first star, achieves stardom in *Othello.*

1828 T. D. Rice learns the "Jim Crow" song and dance from an aged Negro and makes it into a blackface sensation, greatly increasing the demand for Ethiopian Delineators.

Edwin Forrest offers a cash prize for the best new American tragedy about an Indian. The winner, *Metamora,* proves one of Forrest's greatest hits.

1820s Ethiopian Delineators, blackface white song and dance men, become popular performers.

Circuses perform throughout the country, merging equestrians, clowns, and menageries.

Isaac Van Amburgh makes the lion-tamer a major circus act.

1831 *The Gladiator,* another of Forrest's prize winners, is a popular favorite with its democratic themes.

1835 The Zoological Institute is formed to limit competition in the growing circus business.

P. T. Barnum enters show business exhibiting Joice Heth, allegedly the 161-year-old black woman who had nursed George Washington in his youth.

1836 Barnum tours as secretary, treasurer, and ticket seller with Aaron Turner's Circus.

COMPARATIVE CHRONOLOGIES, 1839-1846

AMERICAN SOCIETY

1839 Abner Doubleday formulates rules for baseball.

1840 The United States has 3328 miles of railroad tracks, compared to 1818 in all of Europe.

1844 Samuel F. B. Morse puts the telegraph into practice.

1845 Texas is annexed by the United States.

1846 War erupts between Mexico and the United States, ending with Mexico giving the Southwest and California to the United States.

The Smithsonian Institution is established.

Elias Howe invents the sewing machine.

AMERICAN SHOW BUSINESS

1839 A typical St. Louis theater offers 157 different plays in one season, indicating the stress on variety in early drama.

1841 P. T. Barnum, previously a failure in show business, buys the American Museum and promotes it into a famous attraction.

1843 Barnum transforms midget Charles S. Stratton into General Tom Thumb.

The Virginia Minstrels perform the first minstrel show, making it a popular sensation.

1844 Barnum and Tom Thumb score great hits with Queen Victoria and European audiences on a three-year tour.

British tragedian William Macready and Edwin Forrest develop a vitriolic rivalry.

The Drunkard, a sentimental, temperance drama opens in Boston.

A minstrel troupe performs in the White House, symbolizing minstrelsy's broad acceptance.

1845 The *Fashion,* lampooning aristocrats, opens in New York, the work of American actress Anna Cora Mowatt.

Dan Rice becomes a star as a "wise-cracking" circus clown.

Negro William Henry "Juba" Lane is acclaimed as the best minstrel dancer while performing with white minstrels. In 1848, Lane emigrates to England.

1846 Christy Minstrels open in New York, setting the form of the minstrel show with the troupe in a semicircle, the comedians on the ends, and the interlocutor in the middle.

COMPARATIVE CHRONOLOGIES, 1846-1851

AMERICAN SOCIETY	AMERICAN SHOW BUSINESS
The first baseball team, the New York Knickerbockers, is formed.	
	1847-48 Women in revealing tights pose as statuary in variety halls.
	late 1840s George Christy and other male minstrels seriously portray women, establishing female impersonation in America.
1848 Gold is discovered in California, triggering the gold rush.	**1848** P. T. Barnum builds his palatial Iranistan, the San Simeon of its day.
Amelia Bloomer introduces "Bloomers," trousers for women.	Stephen Foster's "Oh! Susanna," and "Old Uncle Ned" are published and popularized by minstrels. "Camptown Races," "My Old Kentucky Home," "Old Folks at Home," and others follow.
The first women's rights convention is held.	
The antislavery Liberty Party nominates a candidate for president, as the conflict over slavery intensifies.	**1848** Mose the B'howery B'hoy, a New York City common man character, delights urban mass audiences.
	William Macready tours the United States to boos from Edwin Forrest fans, as the Macready-Forrest conflict escalates into a class as well as nationalistic struggle.
1849 Amelia Bloomer publishes *Lily,* a woman's rights and temperance journal.	**1849** Dan Rice fields his own circus.
	A riot against William Macready and his upperclass American supporters explodes in the Astor Place Opera House in New York, leaving 31 dead and 150 injured. After this, stage entertainment fragments into popular and elitist forms.
1850 Henry Clay's political Compromise of 1850 avoids a break between slave and free states.	**1850s** Minstrel shows dominate popular entertainment.
	1850-51 P. T. Barnum promotes a national tour for Swedish Opera singer, Jenny Lind.
1851 Gail Borden makes the first evaporated milk.	**1851** Barnum's Great Asiatic Caravan Museum and Menagerie, featuring Tom Thumb and ten elephants, begins a four year tour.
I. M. Singer is the first successful sewing machine manufacturer.	

COMPARATIVE CHRONOLOGIES, 1852-1860

AMERICAN SOCIETY

1852 Harriet Beecher Stowe's *Uncle Tom's Cabin* is published and becomes an issue in the slavery controversy.

The Free Soil Party, denouncing slavery as a sin, is formed.

1854 The Republican Party is established by Whigs, Free Soilers, and antislavery Democrats. It is virtually a Northern sectional party in its positions and base.

A virtual civil war begins in the Kansas-Nebraska territory over whether slavery should be legal there.

The Life of P. T. Barnum, Written By Himself is first published.

1858 The washing machine with rotary action is patented.

1859 Spectators at baseball games are first charged admission.

John Brown and a band of supporters seize an armory in Virginia hoping to spark violent slave revolts throughout the South. Brown and his men are captured and executed.

1860 The Democratic Party splits into pro-slavery and compromise factions, each with its own presidential candidate.

The Pony Express is established.

Republicans nominate and elect Abraham Lincoln president.

South Carolina secedes, followed within a year by ten other slave states.

AMERICAN SHOW BUSINESS

1853 Serious dramatic adaptations of *Uncle Tom's Cabin* prove a great attraction in northeastern cities.

P. T. Barnum produces a "pro-Southern" version of and minstrel troupes parody *Uncle Tom's Cabin.* These versions outlive the serious adaptation.

1858 Francis Leon begins his long career as a female impersonator, quickly rising to stardom, a position he retains into the 1880s despite heavy competition.

1859 "Dixie" is premiered by Bryant's Minstrels in New York.

late 1850s Black minstrel troupes, with Negro performers, sporadically appear in the North.

COMPARATIVE CHRONOLOGIES, 1861-1865

AMERICAN SOCIETY

1861 The Confederate States of America is formed.

The Civil War begins.

1862 Julia Ward Howe writes "Battle Hymn of the Republic."

John D. Rockefeller invests $4000 in an oil refinery, which ultimately becomes the Standard Oil Company.

1863 The Emancipation Proclamation frees slaves in Confederate States still in revolt.

The first paper dress patterns are sold.

President Lincoln proclaims Thanksgiving Day as a national holiday celebrated on the last Thursday in November.

1864 George Pullman builds his first railroad sleeping car.

1865 Robert E. Lee surrenders the last major Confederate Army, virtually ending the war.

Abraham Lincoln is assassinated.

The Thirteenth Amendment abolishes slavery.

AMERICAN SHOW BUSINESS

1861 *East Lynne,* one of the most popular late-nineteenth-century melodramas, opens its long career.

Adah Isaacs Menken first appears in flesh-colored tights as Mazeppa, bringing the display of women's bodies into respectable show business.

Major minstrel troupes, previously resident, urban companies, begin to travel widely; within a decade most minstrel troupes are road shows as competition mounts, people move west, and transportation improves.

Tony Pastor, the Father of Vaudeville, begins a four-year run in a New York variety house with an off-color reputation.

1865 Barnum's American Museum burns down.

Adam Forepaugh fields his first circus; for decades he heads one of America's leading circuses.

San Francisco Minstrels begin a nineteen-year run in New York, the last resident minstrel troupe in the nation's entertainment capital.

COMPARATIVE CHRONOLOGIES, 1865-1869

AMERICAN SOCIETY

1867 Congressional reconstruction of the Confederate states is begun, using Negro voters as a political base for the Southern Republican Party and new state constitutions.

The first practical typewriter is built.

1868 The Ku Klux Klan mobilizes Southern whites to violently intimidate Negroes and supporters of Reconstruction.

Ulysses S. Grant is elected president.

1869 Susan B. Anthony becomes president of the National Woman Suffrage Association.

The transcontinental railroad is completed.

The Cincinnati Red Stockings becomes the first professional baseball team.

Chewing gum is patented.

The first intercollegiate football game is held.

Henry J. Heinz opens the first processed food factory.

AMERICAN SHOW BUSINESS

Black performers get a toehold in show business as minstrels.

Joseph Jefferson, III, plays Dion Boucicault's *Rip Van Winkle,* a part he performs for nearly forty years.

Tony Pastor begins cleaning up variety shows, transforming them from saloon to family entertainment.

1866 *The Black Crook,* the lavish forerunner of both musical comedies and girlie shows, opens as a great hit that tours widely and is revived frequently throughout the century.

1868 *Humpty Dumpty,* a musical featuring pantomimist George L. Fox, premieres; Fox plays the role of the Clown until his death in **1877**.

Lydia Thompson and the tights-clad British Blondes dazzle Americans with their voluptuous figures.

Barnum's New American Museum burns down.

Dan Costello's Circus is the first to make a transcontinental tour.

1869 Sam Lucas begins his long, distinguished career as a black performer.

COMPARATIVE CHRONOLOGIES, 1870-1877

AMERICAN SOCIETY	AMERICAN SHOW BUSINESS
1870 The first Negroes are elected to Congress.	**1870** Mme. Rentz's Female Minstrels and their many imitators combine the appeals of minstrelsy and of women's figures in the first mainstream American girlie shows.
1871 Oleomargarine is first manufactured.	**1871** P. T. Barnum heads a large circus, actually organized by W. C. Coup who created the modern traveling circus.
1872 Montgomery Ward opens the first mail-order store.	**1872** Frank Mayo opens in *Davy Crockett,* a role he plays for almost a quarter-century.
William Marcy "Boss" Tweed is convicted of corruption in New York City politics.	William F. "Buffalo Bill" Cody first appears in a play.
1873 The first cable car is put into use in San Francisco.	**1873** W. C. Coup adds a second ring to the Barnum circus.
1874 Philadelphia opens the first American public zoo.	**1874** *Evangeline,* the first show billed as a "musical comedy," is also the first to feature an original score with popular music, dance, and language.
	1875 The Kiralfy brothers produce *Around the World in 80 Days* on a truly lavish scale.
	Tony Pastor moves his variety show from the Bowery uptown to the central show business area on Broadway.
	James Bland, "The Negro Stephen Foster," enters black minstrelsy and publishes his first songs—"Carry Me Back to Old Virginny," and "Morning by the Bright Light."
1876 The telephone is patented and put into operation.	**1876** Denman Thompson begins his twenty-four year career as Uncle Joshua in *The Old Homestead,* a play glorifying rural life.
National baseball league is formed.	"Buffalo Bill" Cody fights in the Black Hills Indian Wars and then returns to the stage as an even greater attraction.
The first intercollegiate football association is established.	
1877 The first inter-city telephone lines begin to operate.	**1877** J. H. Haverly's United Mastodon Minstrels greatly expand the size and splendor of minstrel shows to compete with other entertainment.
Violent strikes rock the nation's railroads.	

COMPARATIVE CHRONOLOGIES, 1877-1883

AMERICAN SOCIETY

The first bicycle factory opens.

1878 Thomas A. Edison patents the phonograph.

The Edison Electric Light Company opens.

1879 The first floating Ivory Soap is marketed.

1881 President James A. Garfield is assassinated.

1882 The first restrictions are imposed on immigration into the United States.

John L. Sullivan becomes American heavyweight boxing champion.

AMERICAN SHOW BUSINESS

Anna and Emma Hyers, Negro opera singers, tour with their serious musical production, *The Underground Railroad,* which includes Sam Lucas.

1878 Sam Lucas is the first Negro to star in the title role in *Uncle Tom's Cabin.*

James A. Bailey's circus emerges as a major rival to Barnum.

Gilbert and Sullivan's *H. M. S. Pinafore* creates a rage in America for light opera.

1879 Mlle. Zazel is shot sixty feet out of a circus cannon as the Human Cannon Ball.

1879 Nate Salisbury's Troubadours pioneer in musicals centered on common people's lives.

Edward Harrigan and Tony Hart open their ethnic *Mulligan Guards,* a musical play, in New York, the first of many that they create in the next decades.

1870s Live bloodhounds, Jubilee singers, and novelty acts are added to minstrelized versions of *Uncle Tom's Cabin.*

1880 Ten comic operas open in New York, offering the public high society, romance, and beautiful music.

Barnum and Bailey merge their circuses.

Hazel Kirke, a popular melodrama, premieres.

1881 Tony Pastor attracts women to his "high-class" variety shows by giving away dress patterns and sewing kits.

1882 Barnum and Bailey's Circus buys Jumbo, the world's largest elephant, from the London Zoo, creating great controversy and publicity.

The Ringling Brothers field their Classic and Comic Concert Company, a small Wisconsin variety show.

1883 Buffalo Bill Cody begins touring with a Wild West Show, a career he continued until his death in 1917.

COMPARATIVE CHRONOLOGIES, 1883-1893

AMERICAN SOCIETY

1884 The first baseball World Series is held.

1886 The Statue of Liberty is unveiled.

The American Federation of Labor is formed.

Electric street trolleys begin to run on city streets.

1889 I. M. Singer manufactures electric sewing machines.

Walter Camp names the first All-American football team.

1890 Wyoming is the first state to include women as voters.

1891 Thomas A. Edison patents the radio.

The zipper is patented.

1892 Ellis Island becomes the receiving station for immigrants.

The first ferris wheel is built for the Chicago World's Fair.

Basketball is invented.

1893 Edison's kinetoscope shows motion pictures.

Henry Ford road tests his first automobile.

AMERICAN SHOW BUSINESS

B. F. Keith, later the greatest vaudeville producer, opens a small dime museum in Boston.

1880s Female Burlesque Troupes tour broadly, making little pretense that their bodies are the major attractions.

Primrose and West Minstrels make minstrel shows almost indistinguishable from musicals and vaudeville.

1887 B. F. Keith and E. F. Albee present their first continuous, respectable variety shows.

1888 Imre Kiralfy stages *The Fall of Rome* outdoors on Staten Island with a cast of 2000.

1889 The Ringling Brothers run a successful two-ring Mid-western circus.

1890 Charles Hoyt's urban musical *A Trip to Chinatown* begins its run of 650 performances, setting the record for all nineteenth-century productions.

1891 Imre Kiralfy combines with Barnum and Bailey's Circus to stage their colossal *Columbus and the Discovery of America.*

1893 Little Egypt excites visitors to the Chicago World's Fair with her "cootch" dance.

COMPARATIVE CHRONOLOGIES, 1893-1898

AMERICAN SOCIETY

One of the worst economic depressions in American history begins.

1894 Widespread labor strikes are often met with violent repression.

1895 King C. Gillette develops the safety razor.

1896 Motion pictures are first commercially exhibited.

1897 The first American subway is completed in Boston.

1898 The United States fights a war with Spain in Cuba and the Philippines.

AMERICAN SHOW BUSINESS

Florenz Ziegfeld enters show business by promoting strongman Eugene Sandow into a show business attraction at the Chicago World's Fair.

Bert Williams and George Walker form their black vaudeville act.

1894 Victor Herbert's first Comic Opera, *Prince Ananias,* opens.

Vesta Tilley, the foremost male impersonator, makes her first trip to America from England.

B. F. Keith opens his palatial Colonial Theatre in Boston, leading the way for many other vaudeville palaces.

1895 Nate Salisbury stages *Black America,* the epitome of the black minstrel show, by building a stereotyped plantation peopled with Southern Negro performers in Staten Island.

David Belasco's *Heart of Maryland,* a Civil War melodrama, premieres; Belasco soon becomes a pioneering director who raises the American stage to new heights of perfection.

1896 William Gillette stars in his Civil War melodrama, *Secret Service.*

New York has seven vaudeville theaters; in **1910** it has thirty-one. Other cities experience similar booms.

James A. Bailey takes the Greatest Show on Earth on a six-year European tour.

Ziegfeld signs Anna Held, a sexy European singer, promoting her into a great drawing card in America.

1898 *A Trip to Coontown,* the first musical written, produced, and performed by Negroes, begins the break from the minstrel show.

Clorindy, a black revue written by Will Marion Cook, opens in a roof garden on Broadway.

COMPARATIVE CHRONOLOGIES, 1899-1905

AMERICAN SOCIETY

1899 Joseph Campbell Preserve Company introduces canned, condensed soup.

1900 The population of New York City is nearly 3.5 million; Chicago and Philadelphia also exceed a million residents.

There are almost 1.5 million telephones in America.

The first American automobile show is held in Madison Square Garden.

1901 Theodore Roosevelt becomes president after William McKinley's assassination.

1903 The Wright brothers first successfully fly an airplane.

Henry Ford forms Ford Motor Company.

1904 Edison develops cameraphone, the first sound motion pictures.

Progressive politicians and reformers expose corruption and injustice, ushering in a period of legal reforms.

The ice cream cone is invented at the St. Louis Exposition.

1905 The first theater devoted exclusively to motion pictures opens.

AMERICAN SHOW BUSINESS

1901 After success in vaudeville with The Four Cohans, George M. Cohan writes and stars in his first Broadway musical.

1902 Bert Williams and George Walker's Negro musical comedy, *In Dahomey,* establishes them as major stars.

The Ringling Brothers circus provides major competition for Barnum and Bailey's.

1903 Victor Herbert's *Babes in Toyland* proves a great success.

Al and Harry Jolson join Joe Palmer to form a vaudeville trio.

Millie De Leon begins her rise to burlesque stardom throwing her garters to the audience.

1904 George M. Cohan scores his first Broadway success with *Little Johnny Jones,* bringing the pace and vitality of vaudeville to musicals.

1905 The Hippodrome Theatre, the largest, costliest American theater, opens and for years houses stupendous extravaganzas.

Julian Eltinge begins to tour vaudeville and minstrel shows as a female impersonator.

COMPARATIVE CHRONOLOGIES, 1905-1909

AMERICAN SOCIETY

1907 The first electric washing machine is marketed.

1908 Mother's Day becomes a holiday.

8000-10,000 nickelodeons show motion pictures.

Jack Johnson, a Negro stevedore, becomes heavyweight boxing champion.

Henry Ford introduces the Model T, a common people's automobile.

1909 The National Association for the Advancement of Colored People is formed to work for civil rights for blacks.

AMERICAN SHOW BUSINESS

Two competing burlesque circuits emerge as show business booms.

Sam Scribner tries to clean up his Columbia burlesque circuit but faces continually racier competition from vaudeville and revues.

Al Jolson begins his vaudeville career as a single.

1906 George M. Cohan's *George Washington Jr.* ushers in a decade of annual Cohan shows that make him "Mr. Broadway."

Ziegfeld produces one of Anna Held's most sensational yearly musicals, *The Parisian Model.*

1907 At Held's suggestion, Ziegfeld stages a spicy revue, the *Follies of 1907*, a blend of topical humor and sexuality that proves so popular that Ziegfeld makes it a yearly show that epitomizes show business.

Al Jolson begins a tour with Lew Dockstader's Minstrels.

Franz Lehar's *Merry Widow* scores a success with its waltzes.

Ringling Brothers purchases Barnum and Bailey's Greatest Show on Earth after Bailey's death.

Julian Eltinge attains star status as a vaudeville female impersonator.

1908 Ziegfeld produces his second *Follies* and Held's greatest success, *Miss Innocence.*

Jake Shubert creates *The Mimic World* revue to compete with the *Follies.*

COMPARATIVE CHRONOLOGIES, 1910-1915

AMERICAN SOCIETY

1910 Boy Scouts of America is incorporated.

1910 Father's Day becomes a holiday.

1912 Woodrow Wilson is elected president.

Campfire Girls and Girl Scouts are organized.

1913 Henry Ford sets up the first assembly line for producing automobiles.

Federal income tax is implemented.

1915 Long-distance telephone lines open between New York and San Francisco.

AMERICAN SHOW BUSINESS

1910 Bert Williams, on his own after George Walker fell ill, becomes the only Negro in the *Follies.*

Black performers are largely excluded from Broadway until 1921.

Victor Herbert's *Naughty Marietta* is a great hit.

Ziegfeld discovers Fanny Brice in a burlesque show.

Julian Eltinge stars in *Fascinating Widow,* the first of a series of full-length Broadway musicals, playing four female and two male roles.

A New York theater is named for Julian Eltinge.

Bothwell Browne emerges as a major competitor to Eltinge as a female impersonator.

1911 Bothwell Browne stars in a major musical, *Miss Jack.*

The Shuberts open the Winter Garden.

Al Jolson takes Broadway by storm.

1912 The Shuberts' *Passing Show of 1912* begins its twelve-year rivalry with the *Ziegfeld Follies.*

Eddie Cantor tours with Gus Edwards' *Kid Kaberet,* which also includes a youthful Georgie Jessel.

To meet revue competitors, burlesque performers begin to "strip" on stage, suggesting more than they reveal.

1913 The Palace Theatre, the epitome of the big-time vaudeville house, opens in New York.

1915 Joseph Urban, a brilliant set designer, joins the *Ziegfeld Follies* and creates some of its greatest productions.

Eddie Cantor becomes a Ziegfeld star.

COMPARATIVE CHRONOLOGIES, 1915-1924

AMERICAN SOCIETY

1916 The United States fights an undeclared war in Mexico.

1917 The United States declares war on Germany.

1919 Constitutional amendments outlaw alcoholic beverages and extend the vote to women.

President Wilson futilely campaigns for American participation in the League of Nations.

Jack Dempsey becomes heavyweight boxing champion.

Radio Corporation of America is formed.

1920 The first commercial radio station offers regular programming.

Warren G. Harding is elected president promising a return to "normalcy" after decades of reform and crusading.

1921 New laws sharply restrict immigration, imposing quotas based on the existing ethnic composition of the population.

1924 There are 2.5 million radios in America.

AMERICAN SHOW BUSINESS

Jerome Kern with Guy Bolton creates his first successful musical, *Very Good Eddie,* a show that integrates lyrics with the plot.

Sam Lucas is the first Negro to play a lead in a motion picture, *Uncle Tom's Cabin.*

1917 *Ziegfeld Follies* features Fanny Brice, Eddie Cantor, W. C. Fields, Will Rogers, and Bert Williams as well as beautiful women and productions.

Vaudeville theaters show sound motion pictures as a curiosity.

1919 George Gershwin writes his first musical, *La, La Lucille.*

1920 Jerome Kern, with Guy Bolton, creates the musical *Sally* for Ziegfeld's star Marilyn Miller.

Richard Rodgers and Lorenz Hart combine on their first musical, *The Poor Little Ritz Girl.*

1921 Eubie Blake, Noble Sissle, Flourney E. Miller, and Aubrey Lyles open their musical *Shuffle Along,* the show that returns blacks to the center of show business.

1921-24 At least eight major Negro musicals open on Broadway.

1923 Eddie Cantor stars in his first musical *Kid Boots.*

1924 George and Ira Gershwin combine on their first musical, *Lady Be Good.*

COMPARATIVE CHRONOLOGIES, 1925-1956

AMERICAN SOCIETY	AMERICAN SHOW BUSINESS
1925 Mrs. William B. Rose is inaugurated governor of Wyoming, the first female governor.	**1925** Vincent Youmans scores a great success with *No, No Nanette.*
John T. Scopes is tried in Tennessee for teaching Darwin's theory of evolution.	mid-**20s** Slow striptease dances replace shimmies and "cootch" dances in burlesque to compete with ever more revealing revues.
1927 Charles A. Lindbergh completes the first solo flight over the Atlantic.	**1927** George and Ira Gershwin combine on *Funny Face.*
Babe Ruth hits a record sixty home runs.	Rodgers and Hart create *A Connecticut Yankee.*
	Jerome Kern and Oscar Hammerstein, II, write *Show Boat,* which culminates the development of the American musical.
	Al Jolson films *The Jazz Singer,* bringing the voice of Mr. Show Business to movies, sounding the death knell of live show business.
	1928 At age fifty, Bill "Bojangles" Robinson is "discovered" by white audiences.
1929 The stockmarket crash signals the onset of the Great Depression.	
	1930s Led by the striptease and bare breasts, burlesque takes off during the Depression while other shows suffer.
1932 Franklin Delano Roosevelt is elected president.	**1932** Motion pictures displace vaudeville in the Palace Theatre.
	1937 Burlesque houses in Times Square and other major theater districts are closed and allowed to reopen only without the striptease.
	1956 Ringling Brothers, Barnum and Bailey give the last circus performance under canvas big tops.

ACKNOWLEDGMENTS

I owe debts of gratitude to many people. My friends Richard and Merren Carlson gave me absolutely invaluable assistance and suggestions by reading and editing several versions of each chapter. Besides this editing, Richard worked wonders with many of the illustrations, transforming my often faulty negatives into excellent prints. Sheldon Meyer, vice president of Oxford University Press, provided perceptive criticism and suggestions from the conception to the completion of the book. Vivian Hausch, assistant managing editor of O.U.P., helped greatly with the editing and rewriting of the first two chapters as part of her thorough editing of the manuscript. Evan Konecky, Ellen Greene, and David Laufer of O.U.P. did a beautiful job with the design, layout, composition, and artwork that so greatly enhance the visual appeal of the book. Most of the excellent illustrations in the book are from the Harvard Theatre Collection. Jeanne T. Newlin, curator of the H.T.C., provided invaluable assistance and suggestions at several stages of the research, including graciously opening the collection to me while it was officially closed for moving to its new quarters. Without the illustrations my wife and I were able to find on that visit, with the help of Martha Mahard and Ellen Carlin, the book would be much less effective visually. Curator Paul Myers' excellent staff at the Theatre Collection of the New York Public Library at Lincoln Center was always very helpful despite being extremely busy serving the public as well as researchers. Everyone there assisted in the research, but Monty Arnold, Dr. Rod Bladel, and Maxwell Silverman were especially helpful. My wife, Judy, worked beside me throughout most of the research. With her good taste and judgment, she is indispensable in helping me talk out my ideas and interpretations as well as in selecting material and illustrations. In every way, we are partners.

INDEX

Show titles and references to illustrations are italicized; song titles are in quotation marks.

INDEX

INDEX

INDEX

INDEX